International Tax Evasion in the Global Information Age

David S. Kerzner • David W. Chodikoff

International Tax Evasion in the Global Information Age

palgrave
macmillan

David S. Kerzner
Toronto, Canada

David W. Chodikoff
Toronto, Canada

ISBN 978-3-319-82096-5 ISBN 978-3-319-40421-9 (eBook)
DOI 10.1007/978-3-319-40421-9

Softcover reprint of the hardcover 1st edition 2016

Printed on acid-free paper

This Palgrave Macmillan imprint is published by Springer Nature
The registered company is Springer International Publishing AG
The registered company address is: Gewerbestrasse 11, 6330 Cham, Switzerland

Endorsement

"It is difficult to conceive of better timing for a volume on international tax evasion in the global information age. The volume provides the most comprehensive study of the topic to date and appears just as the OECD and G20 leaders have identified this subject as a central issue in international taxation for the next decade. This book should be on the desks of all practitioners and policy-makers."

— **Richard Krever**, Director, Taxation Law and Policy Research Group, Monash University, Melbourne

"Tax evasion is one of the most important topics in the current international tax environment. This book thoughtfully considers the rapid growth of measures to combat tax evasion and addresses the delicate balance between the rights of states and those of taxpayers – a very accessible and worthwhile read."

— **Liesl Fichardt**, Partner, Head of Tax Disputes, Clifford Chance LLP, London

Foreword

In recent decades, the topic of cross-border tax information exchange has attracted considerable academic and policy attention. Beginning with the OECD's *Harmful Tax Competition* report of 1998, OECD countries (and later many non-OECD countries) began to emphasize the need for effective cross-border exchange mechanisms, mainly to inhibit offshore tax evasion. The main mechanism derived from these reform efforts is the tax information exchange agreement (TIEA), which is typically negotiated between an OECD country and countries that are sometimes labelled tax havens. Ongoing globalization, technology change, reduced tax revenues, and concerns about international money laundering and terrorist financing via tax havens have propelled cross-border tax information exchange to even greater policy prominence.

Indeed, there are now over 800 TIEAs worldwide, a stunning development in the international tax regime, where change is normally glacially paced. But do TIEAs work? Will these agreements effectively inhibit offshore tax evasion and other global financial crimes? David Kerzner has written the first book to critically examine these questions and concludes the answer is no.

According to David, TIEAs do not and will not work effectively for a number of reasons, including the lack of an automatic exchange mechanism (as TIEAs emphasize the "information on request" approach). He also worries that tax havens may not meaningfully cooperate to enforce their TIEAs, as these countries do not have the political and economic incentives to do so. He notes that OECD countries further complicate the problem by often maintaining financial secrecy laws to encourage inward investments from non-residents.

A challenge for David, as alluded to above, is the fast-changing nature of the political environment that surrounds cross-border tax information exchanges, to be contrasted, again, with the traditional stability of a regime whose main legal elements remain wedded to policies developed by the League of Nations roughly a century ago. As explored in this book, however, a sea change provoked by a series of developments has occurred with respect to global tax information exchanges.

First, a series of tax leaks and scandals — UBS in Switzerland, HSBC in France, the financial data leak obtained by the International Consortium of Investigative Journalists, and so on — has suggested that the problems of offshore tax evasion, international money laundering, and terrorist financing are much greater than previously suspected. Second, in the wake of the 2008 global financial collapse, many governments find themselves in a precarious fiscal situation and are less tolerant of revenue losses associated with (criminal) offshore tax evasion and (legal) aggressive international tax planning (as evidenced by the ongoing OECD base erosion and profit shifting (BEPS) reforms). Third, beginning in 2010 the United States embarked upon its own aggressive (overly so according to the analysis in this book) and largely unilateral efforts to track down "US persons" (US citizens, green card holders, and others) living abroad to inhibit offshore tax evasion, through a regime commonly known as the *Foreign Account Tax Compliance Act* or *FATCA*.

These and other developments are pushing governments to consider other cross-border exchange mechanisms in addition to TIEAs, leaving in their wake a complex regulatory environment involving enhanced automatic exchanges via traditional tax treaties, US sponsored intergovernmental agreements to implement *FATCA*, the development of "sons of *FATCA*" by some European governments, and a multilateral agreement to encourage more automatic sharing of bulk taxpayer information. These developments, according to David, have eclipsed, at least to a certain extent, the earlier policy debate surrounding TIEAs. Enhanced tax information exchanges have led to corresponding worries about taxpayer privacy and the potential misuse or abuse of this information by governments that may not have sufficient legal protections in place.

Beyond policy concerns, the current regulatory environment is promoting increasingly complex tax laws as well as supporting administrative pronouncements from tax authorities. For instance, the *Treasury Regulations* surrounding the *Internal Revenue Code*'s *FATCA* provisions (*Code* sections 1471 to 1474) already exceed 600 pages. For US taxpayers living abroad and seeking to comply with *FATCA* and other tax laws, the IRS produces over 7,000 pages of additional guidance, including instructions and forms! Both Davids have done an admirable job of boiling down many of these technical tax laws and policies for the reader, with a focus on the rules that govern tax information exchange between Canada and the United States.

Accordingly, this study contributes in a significant way both to the ongoing policy and academic debate surrounding cross-border tax information exchanges and to a tax practitioner's ability to effectively advise clients that have been swept up in the new regulatory environment.

Kingston, Ontario — Arthur J Cockfield

Preface

Illegal tax practices such as tax evasion cost governments billions of dollars in lost revenues. Countries like Canada, the United States, and the United Kingdom rely on the ability to exchange information with tax havens and other countries to administer their tax system and combat tax evasion. A country that allows the rich and elite to hire professionals to hide their assets offshore so they can escape paying their share of taxes risks that its people will question the fairness of the government's revenue authority. More than that, allowing offshore tax evasion to go unchecked may call into question the very legitimacy of the government's taxing function and send a signal to all taxpayers that it's okay to cheat.

As explained in this book, where there is bank secrecy, there is often a convergence of evil: international tax evasion, global financial crime, and international terrorism. As Professor Arthur Cockfield observes in his study of the 2013 "big data" leak by the International Consortium of Investigative Journalists (ICIJ), offshore service providers such as trust and finance companies take advantage of tax haven secrecy to help individuals engage in global financial crime. Commenting on the guilty plea of BNP Paribas in 2014, US District Attorney Cyrus R Vance, Jr recognized that such shared values in the international community as human rights, peaceful coexistence, and a world free of terror are dependent on the enforcement of our laws and, in particular, on a banking system that is not permitted to be a conduit for criminal activity. The string of global banking scandals from 2008 to 2015 and from UBS to HSBC connotes a code of conduct observed by executive leaders that runs counter to such values, and is neither moral nor right. The 2016 announcement by the ICIJ of the Panama Papers, an additional leak of more than 11.5 million financial and legal records revealing more than 214,000 offshore entities, occurred just before the publication of this book. The Panama Papers solidify the conclusions of this book that from 1998 to 2015 the OECD has been papering over the challenges posed by exchange of information. The Panama Papers are evidence of flaws in the strategies to combat tax evasion of the OECD and the Global Forum on Transparency and Exchange of Information for Tax Purposes (Global Forum), strategies that are explained in this book, and strategies that governments like Canada's and those of many other countries have come to rely upon.

During the past eight years, countries have signed hundreds of single-purpose treaties to exchange information known as tax information exchange agreements (TIEAs). Canada has signed twenty-two TIEAs. In 2013, at the direction of the G20, the OECD was urged to introduce automatic exchange of information throughout the ranks of its 120 member states that at that time composed the Global Forum as a global economic priority to combat tax evasion. The OECD has since introduced its Common Reporting Standard for automatic exchange of tax information. This book presents the most comprehensive study of the use of TIEAs by both the OECD and Canada in the war against tax evasion. The conclusions reveal why automatic exchange of information is not the magic bullet that the OECD claims it to be and why countries like Canada and other members of the Global Forum need to be resilient, innovative, and aggressive in adopting new homegrown strategies to defeat tax cheats (see Chapter 11, Section B).

As part of the veritable tsunami of new laws on global exchange of information, the United States has implemented an unprecedented information exchange program known as the *Foreign Account Tax Compliance Act* (*FATCA*) in over eighty nations, including the United Kingdom. *FATCA* is designed to force foreign financial institutions to give up the names of US account holders or face substantial penalties. *FATCA* and the new IRS offshore disclosure programs now have approximately 8 million US citizens living outside the United States in their gunsights.

The extraterritorial enforcement by the United States of its tax and reporting laws (which is dealt with in detail in the book) combined with the new Common Reporting Standard poses inescapable challenges for estate planning and private wealth advisers globally.

As lawyers and authors who practice and write in the area of international tax controversy, we saw the need for a book on international tax evasion and global exchange of information. The research for this book has been greatly informed by David Kerzner's PhD dissertation, completed at Queen's University in Kingston, Ontario. We wrote this book to provide an essential tool that can be readily accessed not only to assist professionals in the banking, financial, legal, tax, and accounting sectors to grasp a technical understanding of these new legal regimes but importantly to explain the policy drivers and problems surrounding these changes. We also believe that an understanding of the themes in this book will allow leaders in the financial services sector to create new strategies and policies throughout their organizations to manage these new global challenges and to avoid the steep downsides that we are witnessing today with the unprecedented extraterritorial application of US administrative powers.

Toronto
May 2016

David S. Kerzner
David W. Chodikoff

Acknowledgements

The legal research that constitutes the foundation of this book began in 2009 as part of my doctoral degree at the Faculty of Law, Queen's University, in Kingston, Ontario, which was successfully completed in 2014. I am grateful for the support of Associate Dean Sharry Aiken and Associate Dean Mark Walters, of the Faculty of Law and the School of Graduate Studies at Queen's University, throughout this enormous undertaking. As a student, I deeply valued the tremendous support of and encouragement from Sharry Aiken, Phyllis Reid, and Rose M Silva at Queen's University. I would also like to express my gratitude to the family of the late Eric W Cross for their support of the memorial fellowship in his name. I was especially fortunate for the commitment and involvement during my PhD studies of two extraordinary teachers and scholars at Queen's University: the late Associate Dean Stan Corbett (of the Faculty of Law) and Professor Daniel Thornton (of the Business School). The right words fail me in expressing my gratitude to my supervisor, Professor Arthur Cockfield, for sharing his brilliance as a tax scholar with me on this project and his qualities of humility, grace, and kindness as a mentor and guide on this long journey.

I would also like to say thank you to these individuals, who during the course of this project generously offered their guidance: Brian Arnold, Nathan Boidman, Thomas Tung-Pi Chen, David Chodikoff, Tim Edgar, William Flanagan, Neil Harris, Bobbe Hirsh, Jinyan Li, Alan

Macnaughton, Philip Wright, and Bruce Zagaris. I am especially in debt to the following individuals for their comments on earlier drafts of this research: Allison Christians, Arthur Cockfield, John Freeman, Wanjiru Njoya, Jean Thomas, and Daniel Thornton. They are not responsible, however, for any possible errors, or the opinions or positions advocated, for which the authors are alone accountable.

A volume such as this, which involves statutes and cases concerning the laws of Canada and the United States, combined with the legal regimes derived from international organizations, presents many editorial challenges and complexities. My co-author and I wish to acknowledge the outstanding work of our editors on this manuscript, Alisa Posesorski, Victor Selby, and John Sawicki. We are most grateful for their dedication and camaraderie during the writing of this book. We are both profoundly indebted to our Canadian publisher, Jeff Miller. Jeff was ever patient, always good-humoured, and focused on producing a work of excellence. I wish to also express my thanks to Michelle Wood for her assistance with formatting earlier drafts of this manuscript. To my co-author, thank you for your steadfast friendship.

Lastly, the greatest of thanks to my parents, Albert and Anita Kerzner, my sisters, Roanne Kerzner and Marla Wasser, and my brothers-in-law, Stephen Caffrey and Larry Wasser, who provided much love and inner strength throughout these past years.

David S. Kerzner

I am grateful to my long-serving "Chief of Staff," Filomena Mendonca. Without Fil's steady hand on the demands of my private practice, I would not have had the time to work on this important project. I am also thankful for the wonderful family support I received from my wife, Tanya, son, Daniel, brothers, Mark and Richard, and my mother, Beverley.

David W. Chodikoff

Contents

Abbreviations

Act	*Income Tax Act* (Canada)
Automatic Exchange	automatic exchange of information
BSA	*Bank Secrecy Act* (US)
Canada–US Tax Treaty	*Convention between Canada and the United States of America with respect to Taxes on Income and on Capital*
CEN	capital export neutrality
Charter	*Canadian Charter of Rights and Freedoms*
CIN	capital import neutrality
Code	*Internal Revenue Code* (US)
CRA	Canada Revenue Agency
CRS	Common Reporting Standard for automatic exchange of tax information (OECD)
DTC	double tax convention
EOI	exchange of information
FATCA	*Foreign Account Tax Compliance Act* (US)
FBAR	Report of Foreign Bank and Financial Accounts (US)
FDAP income	fixed or determinable annual or periodic income
FFI	foreign financial institution
FinCEN	Financial Crimes Enforcement Network (US)
FINTRAC	Financial Transactions and Reports Analysis Centre of Canada
FIU	financial intelligence unit
GDP	gross domestic product

Global Forum	Global Forum on Transparency and Exchange of Information for Tax Purposes
IDR	IRS Form 4564 (Information Document Request)
IGA	intergovernmental agreement
Implementation Act	*Canada–United States Enhanced Tax Information Exchange Agreement Implementation Act*; *Economic Action Plan 2014 Act, No 1*
IRS	Internal Revenue Service (US)
KYC rules	know-your-customer rules
MCA	*Model Competent Authority Agreement* (OECD)
Model Tax Treaty	*Model Tax Convention on Income and on Capital* (OECD)
Model TIEA	*Agreement on Exchange of Information on Tax Matters* (OECD)
NAFTA	North American Free Trade Agreement
OECD	Organisation for Economic Co-operation and Development
QI	qualified intermediary
RRSP	Registered Retirement Savings Plan (Canada)
TIEA	tax information exchange agreement
TIN	taxpayer identification number
TRACE program	treaty relief and compliance enhancement program (OECD)
VDP	Voluntary Disclosures Program (CRA)

List of Tables

Table of cases

1

Introduction and the Problem of Offshore Tax Evasion

1 Introduction

1.1 Picture of the Problem

It is estimated that the offshore banking industry shelters over $7.5 trillion, which costs governments lost revenues of at least $200 billion a year.[1] Another estimate puts the amount of money in offshore tax haven accounts in 2010 at $21 trillion (such a figure is comparable to the size of the economies of the United States and Japan combined).[2]

[1] See Gerard Ryle et al, "Banking Giant HSBC Sheltered Murky Cash Linked to Dictators and Arms Dealers" (8 February 2015), online: International Consortium of Investigative Journalists www.icij.org/project/swiss-leaks/banking-giant-hsbc-sheltered-murky-cash-linked-dictators-and-arms-dealers.

[2] See Janet McFarland & Bill Curry, "Document Leak Reveals Widespread Use of Tax Havens" *Globe and Mail* (5 April 2013), online: www.theglobeandmail.com/report-on-business/economy/document-leak-reveals-widespread-use-of-tax-havens/article10797329/. The estimate is from a report by James S Henry, a former chief economist with the global consulting firm McKinsey & Company. According to the article in the *Globe*, *ibid*, the top five tax haven destinations for Canadian dollars in 2011 were Barbados ($53.3 billion), Cayman Islands ($25.8 billion), Ireland ($23.5 billion), Luxembourg ($13.8 billion), and Bermuda ($13.2 billion). Not all of these amounts are attributable to tax evasion. These figures do not specifically break down which amounts may be attributable to funds held offshore by multinational enterprises, or directly or indirectly

D.S. Kerzner, D.W. Chodikoff, *International Tax Evasion in the Global Information Age*, DOI 10.1007/978-3-319-40421-9_1

A recently announced "big data" leak containing over 2.5 million tax haven documents revealed dealings of over 70,000 taxpayers and also of over 120,000 offshore corporations and trusts.[3] The big data (which was followed by an even bigger data leak in 2016) was uncovered by over eighty-six journalists in forty-two countries.[4] Commenting on the leak as

---

(e.g., through nominee entities) to undeclared accounts of individuals. In 2005, one estimate of individual tax evasion was $50 billion, based on an estimate of holdings by high net worth individuals invested outside the United States at $1.5 trillion (using a rate of return of 10 percent and a tax rate of approximately one-third to arrive at the estimate of $50 billion): see Joseph Guttenberg & Reuven Avi-Yonah, "Closing the International Tax Gap" in Max B Sawicky, ed, *Bridging the Tax Gap: Addressing the Crisis in Federal Tax Administration* (Washington, DC: Economic Policy Institute, 2005), cited in Jane G Gravelle, *Tax Havens: International Tax Avoidance and Evasion* (Washington, DC: Congressional Research Service, 2013) at 23. Another estimate by the Tax Justice Network puts the worldwide revenue loss from individual tax evasion for all countries at $255 billion (using a 7.5 percent return and a 30 percent tax rate): see Richard Murphy, John Christensen, & Jenny Kimmis, *Tax Us If You Can* (September 2005), online: Tax Justice Network www.taxjustice.net/cms/upload/pdf/tuiyc_-_eng_-_web_file.pdf, cited in Gravelle, *ibid.* The Tax Justice Network estimated offshore wealth at $21 trillion to $32 trillion: see James S Henry, *The Price of Offshore Revisited* (July 2012), online: Tax Justice Network www.taxjustice.net/cms/upload/pdf/Price_of_Offshore_Revisited_120722.pdf, cited in Gravelle, *ibid.* Ms Gravelle, *ibid* at 24, observes that the US cost on these estimates could approach $100 billion. Estimates of unpaid tax since 2006 uncovered by CRA audits are over $4.5 billion: see David Simms, "Offshore Tax Dodgers Coming under Greater Pressure" *CBC News* (21 February 2013, updated 9 March 2013), online: www.cbc.ca/news/business/taxes/offshore-tax-dodgers-coming-under-greater-pressure-1.1353349. Estimates of Canadian funds in tax havens in 2013 were $170 billion: see Janet McFarland, "Canadians' Offshore Tax-Haven Holdings Rise 10 Per Cent, to $170-Billion" *Globe and Mail* (2 May 2014), online: www.theglobeandmail.com/report-on-business/international-business/canadians-tax-haven-holdings-rise-10-per-cent-to-170-billion/article18400026/.

[3] In 2013, the International Consortium for Investigative Journalists announced a leak containing over 2.5 million tax haven documents: see Arthur J Cockfield, "Big Data and Tax Haven Secrecy" (2016) 18 *Florida Tax Review* 1 at 2. Professor Cockfield, *ibid* at 47, offers a taxonomy of offshore tax evasion behaviour around tax haven service providers and their clients. He calls for a more integrated policy response among the separate government agencies and across separate but related legal regimes (tax, criminal, banking, antiterrorism) to more effectively fight global financial crime.

[4] See *ibid.* In 2016, an additional leak of more than 11.5 million financial and legal records revealing more than 214,000 offshore entities was announced by the International Consortium for Investigative Journalists: see the Panama Papers, online: https://panamapapers.icij.org/20160403-panama-papers-global-overview.html. The files that compose the Panama Papers are from the database of the offshore law firm Mossack Fonseca and were originally obtained from an anonymous source by the German newspaper *Süddeutsche Zeitung*: see Luke Harding, "What Are the Panama Papers? A Guide to History's Biggest Data Leak" *Guardian* (5 April 2016), online: http://gu.com/p/4tvyz/stw. The Panama Papers have prompted investigations into and crackdowns on tax evasion by tax authorities and governments around the world as well as new global collaboration on reducing tax evasion and aggressive tax avoidance: see Holly Watt, "Panama Papers: Global Tax Officials to Launch Unprecedented Inquiry" *Guardian* (12 April 2016), online: http://gu.com/p/4ta47/stw. The Panama Papers solidify the conclusions of this book that the OECD has been papering over

part of his ground-breaking research on big data and tax haven secrecy, Professor Arthur Cockfield observed, "For the first time, the secret world of tax havens was revealed in great detail."[5] He notes that offshore service providers — such as trust and finance companies — take advantage of tax haven secrecy to help individuals engage in global financial crime through various tactics including assisting clients to launder or "normalize" illegal income so that funds can be repatriated to their home.[6]

As discussed in Chapter 2, such practices interfere with tax policy objectives that many nations have adopted to promote equity in the administration of their tax system. Countries like Canada and the United States, which tax their residents (and citizens in the United States) on income that they earn throughout the world, rely on the ability to exchange information with tax havens and other countries to administer their tax system, and combat tax evasion.[7] During the past eight years, countries have signed hundreds of single-purpose treaties to exchange information, known as tax information exchange agreements (TIEAs). Canada has signed twenty-two of these TIEAs. In 2013, the G20 and the OECD decided to move to adopt a standard to combat offshore tax evasion: automatic exchange of information (Automatic Exchange).[8] International crime, international terrorism, and money laundering also benefit from bank secrecy and the ability to hide billions of dollars in offshore accounts. TIEAs were created by the OECD in 2002 to bolster information exchange as a means to fight tax evasion.[9] Since 2002

the challenges posed by exchange of information and call upon individual countries more than ever to pursue aggressive and innovative homegrown strategies.

[5] Cockfield, above note 3 at 47.

[6] *Ibid.*

[7] See Diane Francis, "Lip Service to Money Laundering: Failure to Apply Controls a Serious Threat to Global Economy" *Financial Post* (26 September 2015) FP2, online: http://business.financialpost.com/diane-francis/lip-service-to-money-laundering-failure-to-apply-controls-a-serious-threat-to-global-economy, noting that the Toronto and Vancouver condominium markets are driven by hot money flows that have increased housing prices to excessive levels and that in Canada, banks operating in Hong Kong, London, and tax havens facilitate flows out of China and elsewhere. Ms Francis, *ibid*, also observes that Canadian governments, like those in Europe and the United States, compound the problem by resembling giant secrecy havens in that they do not require disclosure of beneficial ownership.

[8] For a discussion of Automatic Exchange, see Chapter 8.

[9] For a discussion of the policy objectives behind TIEAs, see Chapter 6.

more than 1,500 exchange of information (EOI) relationships (including TIEAs) have been entered into by governments.[10] Very little has been published about these special treaties, including about Canada's own growing TIEA network. Moreover, how Canada and the United States exchange taxpayer information with other jurisdictions and with each other is poorly understood, especially at a time of arguably the most significant developments in the field such as Automatic Exchange and the *Foreign Account Tax Compliance Act*.[11] The global effort toward Automatic Exchange, described in Chapter 8, is likely to result in increased use of TIEAs as fiscal agencies ramp up their offshore tax examinations.

1.2 Objectives of This Research

The primary objective of this book is to evaluate the capacity of TIEAs specifically and EOI more generally to be an effective tool against offshore tax evasion. This book does so, first, by reviewing the policy objectives of TIEAs to later determine their performance against these stated objectives. Second, it reviews domestic and international alternative legal mechanisms to obtain foreign-based taxpayer information to later evaluate the effectiveness of TIEAs in combatting offshore tax evasion as compared with these alternative legal mechanisms, particularly those used by the United States. The central argument of this research is that in their current form TIEAs offer fiscal authorities like CRA and other fiscal agencies around the world a very limited capability to uncover existing tax evasion by residents of Canada and other OECD member and developing countries. This research reviews the TIEA network in Canada, the development and implementation of TIEAs by the OECD and the Global Forum on Transparency and Exchange of Information

---

[10] See OECD, Global Forum on Transparency and Exchange of Information for Tax Purposes, *Information Brief* (Paris: OECD, 2013) at 4. See also OECD, Global Forum on Transparency and Exchange of Information for Tax Purposes, *Progress Report to the G20 Leaders: Global Forum Update on Effectiveness and On-going Monitoring* (Paris: OECD, 2013) at Executive Summary, online: www.oecd.org/tax/transparency/progress_report__G20.pdf.

[11] For a discussion of the *Foreign Account Tax Compliance Act*, Subtitle A of Title V of the *Hiring Incentives to Restore Employment Act* of 2010, Pub L No 111–147 enacted on 18 March 2010 [*FATCA*], see Chapter 9.

(Global Forum) from 1998 through 2014, and recent experiences in EOI between the United States and Switzerland.

Recently, the United States observed that bank transparency for tax purposes is necessary to restore integrity and stability to financial institutions.[12] This appears to be a new policy objective for transparency and information exchange in international taxation, one echoing the troubled international economic times of the present. In examining the complex subject of EOI, this book evaluates the effectiveness of strategies like TIEAs, Automatic Exchange, and *FATCA* as tools in the war against tax evasion. The research identifies deficiencies in TIEAs and more generally in EOI with tax havens that will impact Automatic Exchange and prescribes more effective arrangements to deal with these problems.

For governments and fiscal agencies the world over seeking to beat back tax cheats, this research analyzes the collective efforts of the OECD and the 121 nation members of the Global Forum from 1998 to 2014 to combat bank secrecy and offshore tax evasion. In so doing, this book offers insights into why TIEAs did not work and why Automatic Exchange is not the magic bullet that the G20 and OECD say it is, and provides strategies for governments that will help them win the war against tax evasion.[13]

For financial institutions and financial service providers, this book first and foremost offers a fundamental understanding of the new legal regimes surrounding global EOI and explains their interrelationship and policy objectives. The Common Reporting Standard for automatic exchange of information contains some of the most complex concepts and definitions used today in international tax law, and they will need to be well understood by employees in financial institutions and their professional advisers. Knowledge of and education about the sweeping legal regimes that surround EOI must be the first line of defence for institutions seeking to comply with the law. Reliance on technology

[12] United States, Congress, Joint Committee on Taxation, *Explanation of Proposed Protocol to the Income Tax Treaty between the United States and Switzerland* (Washington, DC: Joint Committee on Taxation, 2011) at 5, online: www.jct.gov/publications.html?func=startdown&id=3791. This is in addition to other policy reasons discussed below.

[13] For a detailed analysis of the OECD's war against tax havens, see Chapter 3. For recommendations for governments regarding EOI and tax evasion, see Chapter 11.

alone (e.g., software programs to implement *FATCA*) will not suffice to prepare global organizations to understand how these legal regimes and their extraterritorial enforcement by the United States may interact with their products, services, technology, systems, and clients. It is hoped that armed with the foundational knowledge in this book, banks and financial service providers in Canada, the United States, the European Union, and the 132-member Global Forum will be in a better position to develop new strategies so that they may avoid being the subject of a criminal investigation by the IRS and costly sanctions (which may potentially be in the millions or billions of dollars) imposed by the US Department of Justice. As explained further in the recommendations in Chapter 11, the key to success for banks and financial service providers is recognizing that the challenges they face are both multijurisdictional and multifunctional across their vast organizations.

For banks, law firms, accounting firms, trust companies, and other organizations in the wealth management industry, this book also provides critical insight into the international enforcement powers of CRA and the IRS in light of the new era of EOI. For wealth management organizations with US clients, in particular those located outside the United States, this book underscores the imperative to create professional practice policies around advising delinquent US account holders and their executors and heirs. The preparation of wills and testamentary trusts for high net worth families is no longer sufficient where the client's family members include US persons. Today, preserving wealth demands that estate planners and financial planners advise their clients to take an expert look at the integrity and efficiency of their tax and foreign-reporting affairs, in particular where there exists a legal structure with foreign entities. Many estate planners, financial advisers, and accountants, while expert in their respective fields, may lack the training to recognize and deal with the complex Canadian, US, and international tax and corporate tax rules, in particular those dealing with foreign corporations and their reporting, including the requirements of the *Bank Secrecy Act*.[14] Additionally, for tax and estate

[14] Pub L 91-508, Tit II, 84 Stat 1118, 10/26/1970, codified as amended at 12 USC 1829b, 12 USC 1951–1959 and 31 USC 5311–5314; 5316–5332 [*BSA*]. Regulations implementing Title II of the *BSA* (codified at 31 USC 5311 et seq) appear at 31 CFR part 103, and effective 1 March 2011, at 31 CFR Chapter X. For a discussion of the *BSA* and related policy issues, see Chapter 10.

professionals with private clients, due regard must be had for the application of the extremely complex Common Reporting Standard to privately held entities, including trusts, to ensure that the correct classifications are made. For professionals advising on private trusts, it is advisable to alert clients to the potentially invasive new reporting rules applicable to settlors, trustees, protectors, and beneficiaries alike and to take care that the trust structure is still advisable in light of the new rules under Automatic Exchange and that any reporting is done correctly.

Chapter 11 contains a number of bold recommendations for governments combatting international tax evasion and for the OECD. It also contains specific tax policy recommendations for Canada and the United States. For the United States, the inescapable conclusion is that *FATCA* is too costly and is easy to circumvent. The United States squanders its limited resources to administer US tax and information returns for millions of US expatriates who have lived in Canada, the United Kingdom, the European Union, and elsewhere for most, if not all, of their lives. Due to exclusions and credits in the *Internal Revenue Code*, these individuals file US individual tax returns with zero or little US taxes owing.[15] Both shamefully and illogically, budget cutbacks for the IRS Criminal Investigation division have resulted in an 11 percent attrition of front line staff members, bringing the division within the staffing levels of the 1970s.[16] Budgeted dollars allocated to enforce the *Code* against expatriates living in Canada and the United Kingdom who are not tax cheats could be used to prosecute tax evaders living in the United States (for example, undeclared account holders at HSBC — see discussion below), to pursue alternative strategies against tax havens (see recommendations in Chapter 11), and to target the use of the global financial infrastructure,

---

[15] See *Internal Revenue Code*, USC 26 (1986) of 1986, as amended, and the *Treasury Regulations* issued thereunder under §§ 901 and 911 [*Code*] dealing with the foreign earned income exclusion and the foreign tax credit respectively.

[16] See United States, Internal Revenue Service, Criminal Investigation, *Fiscal Year 2014 National Operations: Annual Business Report* (Washington, DC: IRS, 2014) at 2, online: www.irs.gov/pub/foia/ig/ci/REPORT-FY2014-IRS-CI-Annual-Report.pdf. Audit rates will continue to decline as Congress has not increased funding for enforcement: see Richard Rubin, "Thanks for Calling the IRS" *Wall Street Journal* (16–17 January 2016) B7.

including offshore tax havens, by international terrorist organizations (such as Hezbollah and ISIS) and international crime.[17]

Understanding the policy drivers behind EOI and the competing perspectives of developed and developing countries against tax havens is key to appreciating the foremost challenges that banks and financial service providers will face in the war being fought by the G20, the OECD, and NATO against tax evasion and the forces of international terrorism and crime. For almost fifty years, the American roots of our law, accounting, and wealth management clients in Canada, the European Union, and elsewhere, from draft dodgers to those "accidentally" born into US citizenship through birth abroad to a US national parent, did not matter. Times have changed.

2 Recent Events in International Tax Evasion and International Financial Crime

In February 2015, the *Guardian* reported (based on data from a massive cache of leaked secret bank account files) that the Swiss bank unit of one of the world's largest financial institutions — HSBC — helped wealthy clients dodge taxes, conceal assets, and circumvent tax authorities.[18] The leak was part of an ongoing international collaboration of journalists, including from the French daily *Le Monde* and the International Consortium of Investigative Journalists. The leaked files dealing with HSBC's Swiss private-banking arm related to accounts holding more

[17] See, for example, Devlin Barrett, "U.S. Intensifies Bid to Defund Hezbollah" *Wall Street Journal* (17 December 2015) A14, online: www.wsj.com/articles/u-s-intensifies-bid-to-defund-hezbollah-1450312498, describing the intensification by the United States of efforts against Hezbollah's financial network, based, in part, on leads developed in the Lebanese Canadian Bank case in 2011.

[18] David Leigh et al, "HSBC Files Show How Swiss Bank Helped Clients Dodge Taxes and Hide Millions" *Guardian* (8 February 2015), online: www.theguardian.com/business/2015/feb/08/hsbc-files-expose-swiss-bank-clients-dodge-taxes-hide-millions. See also Serge Michel, Fabrice Lhomme, & Gérard Davet, "'SwissLeaks': The Backstory of a Worldwide Investigation" *Le Monde* (2 August 2015, updated 2 September 2015), online: www.lemonde.fr/economie/article/2015/02/08/swiss-leaks-the-backstory-of-a-worldwide-investigation_4572334_3234.html.

than $100 billion.[19] Responding to the events amid a flurry of accusations that he should have known about the tax evasion scandal that engulfed HSBC's Swiss private bank, HSBC's chief executive, Stuart Gulliver, remarked, "Can I know what every one of 257,000 people is doing? Clearly I can't."[20] However, renowned management expert Professor Henry Mintzberg observed, "You can't excuse scandals by saying we have so many employees. You . . . have got to be on the ground to have a sense of what your organization is all about."[21] Writing for the *Financial Times*, Andrew Hill acknowledged that Gulliver was right but at the same time was being disingenuous, noting, "by using a combination of the right structure, the latest technology and, above all, by imbuing a company with the correct culture and reinforcing regular communication with visits to the shop floor, he or she should be able to limit the chance of a major scandal."[22] Notwithstanding the increased efforts of the United States to combat tax evasion (for example, in the case of the Swiss banks), there has been criticism of its efforts. The United States has been criticized for bringing few prosecutions against clients of HSBC despite having the leaked data files since 2010.[23] In addition the United States has also been criticized for its failure in the prosecution of UBS global private banking head Raoul Weil after the jury acquitted him following a short one-hour deliberation.[24]

Perhaps if the IRS were not weighed down by psychologically and financially traumatized retired grandmothers and grandfathers who have lived in Canada for over fifty years and who owe no taxes, it might have the resources to go after the real tax cheats with undeclared Swiss bank

[19] See Ryle et al, above note 1.

[20] Quoted in Andrew Hill, "When Is a Company Too Big to Manage?" *Financial Times* (27 February 2015) 9, online: www.ft.com/intl/cms/s/0/87395500-bdd2-11e4-8cf3-00144feab7de.html#axzz3vdYLgWNn.

[21] *Ibid.*

[22] *Ibid.*

[23] See Economist, "America the Not So Brave" *Economist* (23 May 2015), online: www.economist.com/news/finance-and-economics/21651887-america-has-led-global-assault-tax-dodgers-and-their-enablers.

[24] See *ibid.*

accounts at HSBC and elsewhere.[25] Indeed, the United States Taxpayer Advocate, Nina Olson, has called upon the IRS to stop terrorizing the entire country of Canada.[26] Winning the war on tax evasion needs innovation, resilience, motivation, and a fundamental change in international tax policy away from citizenship-based taxation, to shut down federal crime involving US tax laws and to fight the resurgence in global international terrorism and cybercrime.

On 12 March 2015 in Washington, DC, Commerzbank AG, a global financial institution with its worldwide headquarters in Frankfurt, Germany, together with its US branch, Commerzbank AG New York, entered into a deferred prosecution agreement for violations of the *International Emergency Economic Powers Act* and the *BSA*.[27] Commerzbank admitted and accepted responsibility for its criminal conduct in violation of both statutes.[28] Based on documents filed with the court since 2008 and continuing until at least 2013, Commerzbank New York violated the *BSA* and its implementing regulations by failing to maintain adequate policies, procedures, and practices to ensure its compliance with US law, including its obligation to detect and report suspicious activity.[29] As a result of the willful failure of Commerzbank New York to comply with US law, a multibillion-dollar securities fraud was operated through Commerzbank and Commerzbank New York.[30] Olympus Corporation (a Japan-based manufacturer of medical devices

---

[25] As explained in Chapter 10, the cost for older Canadians to comply with the older and even the current US voluntary disclosure programs can be staggering, and may force these retirees to dip into their RRSPs to fill out a myriad of US forms, including meaningless foreign trust reporting forms for certain savings accounts and their grandchildren's education funds, money they can never hope to make back. These individuals often have no ties to the United States and honestly comply with Canadian tax and reporting laws but must face onerous reporting rules, including those under the *BSA* if they have their spouse's power of attorney or joint accounts.

[26] See Federal Taxes Weekly Alert Newsletter, "National Taxpayer Advocate Suggests Changes to Offshore Voluntary Disclosure Initiative" (2012) 58 *Federal Taxes Weekly Alert Newsletter* at 3 (Checkpoint).

[27] See United States, Internal Revenue Service, Criminal Investigation, *Fiscal Year 2015 National Operations Annual Business Report* (Washington, DC: IRS, 2015) at 34–35, online: www.irs.gov/pub/foia/ig/ci/FY2015_IRS-CI_Annual_Report.pdf [IRS CI, *2015 Annual Report*]. For a discussion of the *BSA*, see Chapter 10.

[28] See IRS CI, *2015 Annual Report*, above note 27.

[29] *Ibid*.

[30] *Ibid*.

and cameras) used Commerzbank and Commerzbank New York to commit a massive accounting fraud involving Commerzbank's Singapore branch and affiliates and loaned money to off-balance-sheet entities formed by or for Olympus to perpetrate the fraud. Commerzbank New York transacted more than $1.6 billion in furtherance of the fraud. In addition, based on court-filed documents, Commerzbank AG processed billions of US dollar transactions through the US financial system on behalf of Sudanese and Iranian entities subject to US economic sanctions from 2002 to 2008.[31]

As noted below, while the Commerzbank scandal is hardly unique, international tax evasion and crime is becoming increasingly more sophisticated, and law enforcement agencies, including the IRS, face increased challenges from use of the "darknet" and virtual currency to disguise the flow of illegal funds.[32] In 2014, more than one billion records with personal information, including social security numbers, credit card data, health records, and photos, were snatched by cybercriminals.[33] Hackers are inspired by different objectives. Some hackers are motivated to engage in state-sponsored espionage while many attacks are carried out by global crime rings.[34] These elements operate in the shadows or hidden parts of the Internet known as the darknet, where their conduct, including wiring money from bank accounts, filing fake tax returns, and extortion, costs the global economy more than $400 billion a year.[35] In May 2015 in Manhattan, New York, Ross Ulbricht, aka Dread Pirate Roberts, of San Francisco, California, the creator and operator of the Silk Road

---

[31] *Ibid.*

[32] See *ibid* at 1. See also Max Colchester, "Under Scrutiny Standard Chartered Beefs Up Compliance" *Wall Street Journal* (10 August 2015) C3, online: www.wsj.com/articles/under-scrutiny-standard-chartered-beefs-up-compliance-1439213360, reporting that London-based bank Standard Chartered PLC hired a number of top compliance executives as it expects to deal with increased scrutiny of its global sanctions controls by US officials. In 2014, deficiencies in the bank's anti–money laundering systems at its New York branch resulted in a $300 million fine. In 2012, the bank settled allegations of sanctions violations with both the New York Department of Financial Services and the Department of Justice (*ibid*).

[33] See Andrew Tannenbaum, "To Prevent Cyberattacks, Share the Threat Data" *Wall Street Journal* (9 July 2015) A13, online: www.wsj.com/articles/to-prevent-cyberattacks-share-the-threat-data-1436482349.

[34] *Ibid.*

[35] *Ibid.*

website, was sentenced to life in prison and ordered to forfeit $183,962.[36] He was found guilty of distributing narcotics by means of the Internet, conspiring to commit computer hacking, conspiring to traffic in false identity documents, and conspiring to commit money laundering.[37]

The year 2014 marked one of the most significant criminal prosecutions (involving the IRS) of sanction evasion in US history when BNP Paribas, a global financial institution headquartered in Paris, agreed to plead guilty to conspiring to process $8.8 billion of transactions through the US financial system for Sudanese, Iranian, and Cuban entities subject to US economic sanctions.[38] Commenting on the guilty plea of BNP Paribas, US District Attorney Cyrus R Vance, Jr observed:

> The most important values in the international community — respect for human rights, peaceful coexistence, and a world free of terror — significantly depend upon the effectiveness of international sanctions. Today's guilty plea marks the seventh major case involving sanctions violations by a large international bank that my Office has pursued and resolved since 2009. These cases are critically important for international public safety and the security of our banking system, which is put at risk when it is used to further criminal activity. The seven investigations have revealed a series of widespread schemes to falsify the business records of financial institutions in Manhattan and have resulted in the forfeiture of approximately $12 billion in total.[39]

---

[36] See IRS CI, *2015 Annual Report*, above note 27 at 36.

[37] See *ibid*. Ulbricht created Silk Road in January 2011 and owned and maintained the website until law enforcement authorities closed it in October 2013. During its operation, Silk Road was used by thousands of drug dealers to distribute hundreds of kilograms of illegal drugs and other unlawful goods and services to more than 100,000 buyers and to launder hundreds of millions of dollars derived from these unlawful transactions. Ulbricht sought to anonymize transactions on Silk Road by operating on a special network of computers on the Internet (distributed around the world and designed to conceal the true IP addresses of the computers on the network) and through the use of a bitcoin-based payment system to conceal the identities and locations of the users transmitting and receiving funds through the site (*ibid*).

[38] See United States, Department of Justice, News Release 14-194, "BNP Paribas Agrees to Plead Guilty to Conspiring to Process Transactions through the U.S. Financial System for Sudanese, Iranian, and Cuban Entities Subject to U.S. Economic Sanctions" (30 June 2014), online: www.justice.gov/usao-sdny/pr/bnp-paribas-agrees-plead-guilty-conspiring-process-transactions-through-us-financial.

[39] *Ibid.*

Also in 2014, Credit Suisse agreed to plead guilty to criminal charges for helping thousands of US clients hide assets and income from the IRS and to pay a $2.6 billion settlement.[40] Senator Carl Levin criticized the settlement for not requiring the bank to "cough up" some of the names of those holding undeclared Swiss bank accounts.[41] IRS Criminal Investigation also led the case against Bank Leumi Group, a major Israeli international bank, which admitted to conspiring to aid and assist 1,500 US taxpayers to prepare and present false tax returns.[42] In 2014, Bank Leumi agreed to pay $270 million to the United States and $130 million to New York's Department of Financial Services.[43] A dozen or more Swiss banks are still under investigation.[44]

In addition to the bank prosecutions noted above, the United States has, for the first time, targeted the entire banking industry of a sovereign nation with the Department of Justice's Swiss Bank Program. Some 100 Swiss banks are participating in the program, which began in 2013 and which offers non-prosecution in exchange for cooperation and payment of penalties.[45] As of January 2016, seventy-eight Swiss banks have signed non-prosecution agreements with the US Department of Justice.[46] As of January 2016, the Department of Justice expects to collect more than $1.36 billion from eighty Swiss banks and other financial firms that have acknowledged assisting US taxpayers with undeclared accounts.[47] The deployment by the United States of its Swiss Bank Program is the

[40] *Ibid.* Under the settlement, $100 million will go to the Federal Reserve, more than $715 million will go to the New York Department of Financial Services, and $1.8 billion will go to the Department of Justice (*ibid*).

[41] *Ibid.*

[42] See United States, Department of Justice, News Release 14-1453, "Bank Leumi Admits to Assisting U.S. Taxpayers in Hiding Assets in Offshore Bank Accounts" (22 December 2014), online: www.justice.gov/opa/pr/bank-leumi-admits-assisting-us-taxpayers-hiding-assets-offshore-bank-accounts.

[43] See Robert W Wood, "Israel's Bank Leumi Settles U.S. Tax Charges for $400M, Gives Depositor Names" *Forbes* (22 December 2014), online: www.forbes.com/sites/robertwood/2014/12/22/israels-bank-leumi-settles-u-s-tax-charges-for-400m-gives-depositor-names/.

[44] See Economist, above note 23.

[45] For a description of the Swiss Bank Program, see Chapter 5, Section D(4).

[46] See *ibid.*

[47] See Laura Saunders, "U.S. Expects $1.36 Billion from Swiss Firms" *Wall Street Journal* (28 January 2016) C3.

first known use by a government of the threat of criminal prosecution against the entire banking industry of a foreign sovereign to procure foreign-based taxpayer information, impose and collect fines, and obtain cooperation in prosecuting US tax crimes.[48] The use of criminal prosecution by the United States against the Swiss banking industry evidences both a resolve and a power that the global banking and financial industries need to understand in setting international policies and strategies surrounding global EOI — the United States has the power to take what it wants.

Early in 2012, as part of an attempt to persuade the US government to drop its investigations into eleven banks (including Credit Suisse, Julius Baer, and Basler Kantonalbank), the Swiss government turned over to US authorities encrypted data on bank employees who allegedly served US clients suspected of tax evasion.[49] The data transfer was apparently made against a deadline set by the US government for the banks to comply or face possible criminal prosecution and amid the indictment of three employees of Switzerland's oldest bank, Wegelin, for conspiring with US taxpayers (and others) to hide $1.2 billion in accounts (and the related income they generated) from the IRS.[50] As of 2010, Wegelin, which had been founded in 1741, had approximately $25 billion in assets under management.[51] It allegedly aided and abetted US taxpayers who were committing tax evasion. The US Department of Justice alleged that from 2002 through 2011, Wegelin, and employees Michael Berlinka, Urs Frei, and Roger Keller (client advisers at the bank), had conspired with various US taxpayers to hide the existence of bank accounts held at Wegelin and the income generated in those accounts from the IRS. The Department of Justice also accused members of Wegelin's senior management of conspiring to capture the illegal business that UBS exited. Berlinka, Frei, and Keller are alleged to have advised various US taxpayer clients that their undeclared accounts would not be disclosed to the US authorities

[48] See *ibid.*

[49] See Lynnley Browning, "US Indicts Wegelin Bank for Helping Americans Avoid Tax" *Reuters* (3 February 2012), online: www.reuters.com/article/us-usa-tax-swiss-indictment-idUSTRE81203M20120203.

[50] See *ibid.*

[51] See *ibid.*

because of the bank's long tradition of secrecy and further persuaded US taxpayer clients to transfer assets from UBS to Wegelin, emphasizing that Wegelin, unlike UBS, did not have offices outside of Switzerland and was thus less vulnerable to the reach of US law enforcement.[52] Keller, a Swiss resident, is one of thirty-eight offshore bankers, lawyers, and advisers (some of whom worked for UBS and Credit Suisse) who have been indicted in the United States for tax crimes.[53] In February 2012, the United States criminally charged Wegelin, and a US District Court judge declared the bank a fugitive when it failed to appear in court under the indictment.[54] Shortly thereafter, Wegelin pleaded guilty, and in March 2013 it was sentenced by the US District Court for the Southern District of New York to pay $58 million in fines and restitution.[55]

In 2009, UBS paid approximately $780 million to defer prosecution and provided the United States with the names of 250 American account holders, breaking centuries of Swiss banking secrecy.[56] UBS later provided the names of an additional 4,450 American account holders under threats by the IRS to issue John Doe summonses seeking 52,000 client names.[57] The US government has since expanded its investigations into

[52] See United States, Department of Justice, News Release 12-041, "Manhattan U.S. Attorney Announces Indictment of Overseas Bank on U.S. Tax Charges" (2 February 2012), online: www.justice.gov/archive/usao/nys/pressreleases/February12/wegelinindictment.html. See also Kara Scannell & Haig Simonian, "Wegelin Charged with Aiding Tax Evasion" *Financial Times* (3 February 2012), online: www.ft.com/intl/cms/s/0/70aac594-4df5-11e1-b96c-00144feabdc0.html#axzz3vv83ZaBd.

[53] See David Voreacos & Karin Matussek, "Wegelin Banker Facing U.S. Tax Charge Said to Be Arrested" *BloombergBusiness* (5 February 2015), online: www.bloomberg.com/news/articles/2015-02-06/wegelin-banker-facing-u-s-tax-charge-said-to-be-arrested.

[54] See Reed Albergotti, "Wegelin's Fall to Tax-Haven Poster Child" *Wall Street Journal* (3 March 2013), online: www.wsj.com/articles/SB10001424127887323293704578334310421785672.

[55] See Nate Raymond, "Update 2-Swiss Bank Wegelin to Pay $58 MLN in US Tax Evasion Case" *Reuters* (4 March 2013), online: http://mobile.reuters.com/article/idUSL1N0BWKIK20130305.

[56] See David Voreacos & Carlyn Kolker, "U.S. Sues UBS Seeking Swiss Account Customer Names" (Update 3) *Bloomberg* (20 January 2009, updated 19 February 2009), online: www.bloomberg.com/news/articles/2009-01-20/billionaire-olenicoff-adds-racketeering-kurer-to-ubs-complaint.

[57] See Lynnley Browning, "I.R.S. to Drop Suit against UBS over Tax Havens" *New York Times* (26 August 2010) B6, online: www.nytimes.com/2010/08/27/business/global/27suisse.html?_r=0; Editorial, "Still Waiting for Those Names" *New York Times* (16 June 2010), online: www.nytimes.com/2010/06/17/opinion/17thu3.html.

international tax evasion to include, among other financial institutions, Credit Suisse and HSBC.[58]

These large-scale bank scandals reveal not only a commitment by the IRS and the US Department of Justice to enforce US laws but sadly an appalling (and one might add inexcusable) abdication of executive leadership on the part of a host of financial service providers in the global banking industry. These bank scandals also underscore an apparent indifference to the concept of integrity and to the weighty commitment to legal obligations to combat international crime, money laundering, and terrorism that financial institutions must shoulder in today's international regulatory environment. It is hoped that these events will serve as a wake-up call for rethinking (or, dare we say, initiating) strategic approaches to identifying the tax, legal, anti–money laundering, risk management, withholding compliance, technological, and other issues and challenges arising from the new hard and soft laws (e.g., the OECD Automatic Exchange rules) and facing financial institutions.

In Canada, the government is still failing to curtail the activities of persons that seek to evade the payment of tax. In truth, CRA cannot point to a single successful tax prosecution that is similar in fact to the many "foreign bank" tax evasion cases with serious penal outcomes that have occurred in the United States. Between 2006 and 2014 CRA is said to have audited more than 8,600 international tax cases and identified more than $5.6 billion in additional taxes that are being collected.[59] Apparently in 2013–2014 CRA resolved $46 billion in outstanding tax debt, and so far it has received more than 10,000 offshore voluntary disclosures.[60]

One of the more interesting Canadian developments is a group of civil tax cases slowly making its way through the Tax Court of Canada process. The operative word here is "slowly." Reported by an investigative team of journalists from the Canadian Broadcasting Corporation, these cases

[58] See Andrew Grossman, John Letzing, & Devlin Barrett, "Credit Suisse Pleads Guilty in Criminal Tax Case" *Wall Street Journal* (19 May 2014), online: http://online.wsj.com/news/articles/SB10001424052702304422704579571732769356894.

[59] See Cindy E Harnett, "Crackdown on Tax Evaders Urged; Victoria Family Allegedly Paid Little Tax after Receiving Millions from Off Shore Firm" *Times Colonist (Victoria)* (10 September 2015) A3, online: www.timescolonist.com/news/local/victoria-family-cited-in-cra-crackdown-on-tax-evasion-1.2055917.

[60] See *ibid.*

involve CRA's allegation that a wealthy West-Coast family paid almost no tax over a period of eight years by its participation in an offshore tax sham developed by Canada's KPMG (a leading accounting firm).[61] Essentially, the court documents allege that the Cooper family invested $26 million in 2002 and 2003 with the assistance of KPMG. The money was deposited with an offshore company based in the Isle of Man that was not registered in the name of the Coopers. The money is alleged to have been "gifted" to the company by the Coopers. In turn, and over the years, the Coopers allegedly received millions of dollars back from the company in the form of non-taxable gifts that were never reported on the Coopers' personal tax returns. The Coopers, for their part, contend that they received professional advice before gifting the money to the company. The cases (for the father and his two sons) have yet to be heard by a judge of the Tax Court, and so the outcome remains unknown and will probably not be known for years.[62] Remarkably, KPMG is representing the Coopers in their appeals in Tax Court.[63]

3 IRS Criminal Investigation

In the United States, the IRS Criminal Investigation division conducts criminal investigations into alleged violations of the *Code*, the *BSA*, and certain money laundering statutes. As warranted, the findings of these

[61] See Peter Mansbridge, "An Exclusive Report on the Off Shore Tax Plan the Canadian Revenue Agency Calls a Sham" (Byline Frederic Zalac, Marshall Cooper, André Lareau, & Dennis Howlett) *National* (10 September 2015, 10:00 pm EST); Harvey Cashore, Dave Seglins, & Frederic Zalac, "KPMG Off Shore 'Sham' Deceived Tax Authorities, CRA Alleges" (9 September 2015, updated 10 September 2015), online: www.cbc.ca/news/business/kpmg-offshore-sham-deceived-tax-authorities-cra-alleges-1.3209838; Dave Seglins, Harvey Cashore, & Frederic Zalac, "Federal Probe of KPMG Tax 'Sham' Stalled in Court" (10 September 2015, updated 18 September 2015), online: www.cbc.ca/news/business/federal-probe-of-kpmg-tax-sham-stalled-in-court-1.3210113.

[62] See the Tax Court of Canada pleadings in *Peter Marshall Cooper v R*, 2015-1070(IT)(G), Notice of Appeal filed 9 March 2015, Amended Reply filed 10 July 2015, online: http://cas-cdc-www02.cas-satj.gc.ca/tcc_docket/search_e.php?ap_id=163359; *Marshall Cooper v R*, 2015-1069(IT)G, Notice of Appeal filed 9 March 2015, Amended Reply filed 10 July 2015, online: http://cas-cdc-www02.cas-satj.gc.ca/tcc_docket/search_e.php?ap_id=163358; and *Richard Cooper v R*, 2015-1068(IT)G, Notice of Appeal filed 9 March 2015, Amended Reply filed 10 July 2015, online: http://cas-cdc-www02.cas-satj.gc.ca/tcc_docket/search_e.php?ap_id=163357.

[63] See Harnett, above note 59.

investigations are referred to the US Department of Justice, Tax Division, if it is a tax investigation, or the US Attorney, for all other investigations for criminal prosecution. In 2015, the investigative priorities for Criminal Investigation to enforce tax laws and support tax administration were the following:

- identity theft fraud
- abusive return preparer fraud and questionable refund fraud
- international tax fraud
- fraud referral program
- political/public corruption
- Organized Crime Drug Enforcement Task Force
- *Bank Secrecy Act* and Suspicious Activity Report review teams
- asset forfeiture
- voluntary disclosure program
- counterterrorism and sovereign citizens[64]

A stated goal of the federal criminal tax enforcement program is to protect the public interest in preserving the integrity of the US tax system of self-assessment through vigorous and uniform enforcement of its internal revenue laws.[65] This enforcement in turn has a very important deterrence effect on would-be criminals.[66] Tax crimes prosecuted by the US Department of Justice may include the following:

- attempt to evade or defeat tax[67]
- willful failure to collect or pay over tax[68]
- failure to file, supply information, or pay tax[69]
- fraudulent withholding exemption certificate[70]

---

[64] See IRS CI, *2015 Annual Report*, above note 27 at 2.

[65] United States, Department of Justice, "U.S. Attorneys' Manual" (Washington, DC: Department of Justice, 2015) at § 6-4.010, online: www.justice.gov/usam/united-states-attorneys-manual.

[66] See IRS CI, *2015 Annual Report*, above note 27 at 1.

[67] *Code*, above note 15, § 7201.

[68] *Code*, above note 15, § 7202.

[69] *Code*, above note 15, § 7203.

[70] *Code*, above note 15, § 7205(a).

- fraud and false statement[71]
- aid or assist false or fraudulent document[72]
- removal or concealment with intent to defraud[73]
- compromises and closing agreements[74]
- fraudulent returns, statements, or other documents[75]
- omnibus clause[76]
- offenses with respect to collected taxes[77]

Additional crimes include the following, among others:

- aiding and abetting[78]
- false, fictitious, or fraudulent claims[79]
- conspiracy to commit offense or to defraud the United States[80]
- false statements[81]
- tax money laundering[82]

Section 7201 of the *Code*, "attempt to evade or defeat tax," provides as follows:

> Any person who willfully attempts in any manner to evade or defeat any tax imposed by this title or the payment thereof shall, in addition to other penalties provided by law, be guilty of a felony and, upon conviction thereof, shall be fined not more than $100,000 ($500,000 in the case of a

[71] *Code*, above note 15, § 7206(1).
[72] *Code*, above note 15, § 7206(2).
[73] *Code*, above note 15, § 7206(4).
[74] *Code*, above note 15, § 7206(5).
[75] *Code*, above note 15, § 7207.
[76] *Code*, above note 15, § 7212(a).
[77] *Code*, above note 15, § 7215.
[78] 18 USC § 2.
[79] 18 USC §§ 286 & 287.
[80] 18 USC § 371.
[81] 18 USC § 1001.
[82] 18 USC § 1956(a)(1)(A)(ii).

corporation), or imprisoned not more than 5 years, or both, together with the costs of prosecution.[83]

"Tax evasion" is a phrase that is widely used in a non-technical way to refer to all manner of tax fraud.[84] Section 7201 defines a single crime — attempted evasion of tax — that can be committed in two distinct manners: (1) the willful attempt to evade or defeat the assessment of a tax and (2) the willful attempt to evade or defeat the payment of a tax.[85] Prosecutors do consider other charges (e.g., conspiring to defraud the United States, filing false tax returns, or endeavouring to obstruct the IRS) in contemplating whether the facts of a case may establish the crime of tax evasion by proving the existence of a tax due and owing, and willfulness.[86] The use of "tax evasion" in the title of this book is meant to encompass the crime of tax evasion under the *Code* and the Canadian *Income Tax Act* but also the related crimes (noted above) for which an individual taxpayer may be prosecuted. In 2015, IRS Criminal Investigation reported the following results:[87]

- investigations initiated: 3,853
- prosecution recommendations: 3,289
- informations/indictments: 3,208
- convictions: 2,879
- sentenced: 3,092
- incarceration rate: 80.8%

[83] *Code*, above note 15, § 7201.

[84] See United States, Department of Justice, Tax Division, *Criminal Tax Manual* (Washington, DC: Department of Justice, 2012) at § 8.02, online: www.justice.gov/tax/file/705911/download [*Criminal Tax Manual*].

[85] See *United States v Mal*, 942 F 2d 682 at 686–88 (9th Cir 1991); *United States v Dunkel*, 900 F 2d 105 at 107 (7th Cir 1990). To establish a violation of § 7201, the government must prove each of the following elements beyond a reasonable doubt: an affirmative act constituting an attempt to evade or defeat a tax or the payment thereof (*Sansone v United States*, 380 US 343 at 351 (1965)), an additional tax due and owing (*Boulware v United States*, 552 US 421 at 424 (2008)), and wilfulness (*Cheek v United States*, 498 US 192 at 193 (1991)).

[86] See *Criminal Tax Manual*, above note 84 at § 8.02. Discussion of the above-noted crimes is beyond the scope of this book. For a detailed explanation of US federal tax crimes, see Michael Saltzman & Leslie Book, *IRS Practice and Procedure* (Valhalla, NY: Thomson Reuters, 2012) (Checkpoint) (loose-leaf).

[87] IRS CI, *2015 Annual Report*, above note 27 at 2.

International collaboration is vital to Criminal Investigation's goals to combat offshore tax evasion and fraud committed by individuals because the means by which tax evasion and fraud may be committed today are of course not limited by a country's borders.[88] To this end, Criminal Investigation has special agent attachés strategically stationed in ten foreign countries.[89] These attachés work to build strong alliances with both foreign government and law enforcement partners to enable Criminal Investigation to develop international case leads as well as to support domestic investigations having an international dimension. In 2015, Criminal Investigation's Office of International Operations created the Investigation Development and Support Unit, which places the former International Lead Development Center, Offshore Voluntary Compliance group, and Counterterrorism Center under one management structure.[90] This new unit is situated in the Office of International Strategy and Policy and has the responsibility for conducting research on potential international criminal investigations. It also has liaisons with Interpol and the US International Organized Crime Intelligence and Operations Center for the purposes of combatting threats posed by international criminal organizations and assisting in joint investigations and the apprehension of fugitives.[91] In 2015, Criminal Investigation's Office of International Operations reported the following results:[92]

- investigations initiated: 186
- prosecution recommendations: 168
- informations/indictments: 166
- convictions: 145
- incarceration rate: 78.4%

The *BSA*, which the IRS administers, mandates the reporting of certain currency transactions conducted with a financial institution, disclosure of foreign bank accounts, and reporting of the transportation of

[88] See *ibid* at 33.

[89] See *ibid.*

[90] See *ibid* at 34.

[91] See *ibid.*

[92] *Ibid* at 40.

currency across US borders.[93] Criminal Investigation analyzes *BSA* data and collaborates with state and local enforcement agencies to combat *BSA* violations, money laundering, narcotics trafficking, tax evasion, and terrorist financing.

4 Outline of Study and Methodological Approach

A fundamental starting point for legal research, and tax research in particular, is, what should the legal scholar be striving to accomplish in her research?[94] Michael Livingston offers that the goal of tax scholarship should be to move beyond the normative focus of determining the "right" answer to tax problems under idealized and apolitical conditions — to encompass approaches (such as empirical studies, narrative projects, and an expanded normativity) that recognize that in the partisan nature of taxation, tax policy is one aspect of a broader set of political and social issues.[95] Livingston believes that what is needed in tax scholarship is not more argument but more understanding of the relationship between structure and outcomes, and the effectiveness (or ineffectiveness) of various historical strategies for promoting tax reform.[96] Livingston believes that the ultimate goal of tax scholarship "is the construction (or reconstruction) of a practical reason tax scholarship, in which lawyers borrow from various non-legal disciplines but retain an independent assertive scholarly role."[97] Diane Ring, in reflecting on

---

[93] See *ibid* at 41.

[94] See Michael A Livingston, "Reinventing Tax Scholarship: Lawyers, Economists, and the Role of the Legal Academy" (1998) 83 *Cornell Law Review* 365 at 406.

[95] *Ibid* at 368. Livingston, *ibid* at 399, observes further

> that normative scholarship corresponds to the argumentative, "law"-centered aspect of legal practice — the lawyer as advocate for a position based on a fixed set of facts. Empirical or descriptive scholarship emphasizes the "fact"-centered aspect — the lawyer's skill as information gatherer and weigher of competing evidence. By using both of these skills, academic lawyers will be better able to carve out a distinct territory for their scholarship and resist the encroachment of economists and other outsiders.

[96] *Ibid* at 400.

[97] *Ibid* at 409.

international tax scholarship, observes, "The vision of legal scholarship urged by Livingston and others as an exercise in practical reasoning continues to reflect the needs of a society which must integrate analysis, facts, values, and competing goals."[98] Ring argues that "a vital mission of legal scholarship is to influence, shape and guide the legal regimes, and failure to appreciate this distinction between law and other disciplines can breed confusion."[99] Like others, Ring also encourages international tax scholars to collaborate with others doing empirical work.[100] In writing on case study research in international tax law scholarship, Professor Allison Christians argues for a "heuristic approach to case study research, that is one that employs qualitative social science research methods with the primary goal of identifying new data and developing more theoretical approaches for the study of international tax law."[101]

Two separate studies reviewing legal research in Australia and Canada, the *Pearce Report*[102] (in Australia) and the *Arthurs Report*[103] (in Canada), categorized research as encompassing doctrinal research,[104] reform-oriented

---

[98] Diane M Ring, "The Promise of International Tax Scholarship and Its Implications for Research Design, Theory and Methodology" (2010) 55 *Saint Louis University Law Journal* 307 at 328–29. In commenting on Livingston's conception of "empirical" work, Ring, *ibid* at 312, notes that Livingston favours the goal of gathering and analyzing relevant information in useful ways for those designing policy and that he believes a rigid adherence to highly sophisticated methodologies from the social sciences is not essential.

[99] *Ibid* at 328.

[100] *Ibid* at 329.

[101] Allison Christians, "Case Study Research and International Tax Theory" (2010) 55 *Saint Louis University Law Journal* 331 at 332, exploring case study research in international tax law scholarship and arguing that legal scholars could significantly advance international tax theory by approaching case studies more explicitly and more methodically. Professor Christians, *ibid* at 338, notes that international tax law scholars using case studies should ask, what can be learned both about and from the event or phenomenon identified as the case?

[102] Dennis Pearce, Enid Campbell, & Don Harding, *Australian Law Schools: A Discipline Assessment for the Commonwealth Tertiary Education Commission* (Canberra: Australian Government Publishing Service, 1987) [*Pearce Report*], cited in Terry Hutchinson & Nigel Duncan, "Defining and Describing What We Do: Doctrinal Legal Research" (2012) 17 *Deakin Law Review* 84 at 101.

[103] Social Sciences and Humanities Research Council of Canada, *Law and Learning: Report to the Social Sciences and Humanities Research Council of Canada* (Ottawa: Ministry of Supply and Services, 1983) [*Arthurs Report*], cited in Hutchinson & Duncan, above note 102 at 102.

[104] Doctrinal research is described as "[r]esearch which provides a systematic exposition of the rules governing a particular legal category, analyzes the relationship between the rules, explains areas of difficulty and, perhaps, predicts future developments": see *Pearce Report*, above note 102, cited in Hutchinson & Duncan, above note 102 at 101.

research,[105] theoretical research,[106] and fundamental research.[107] Susan Bartie, in her examination of the scholarship about legal scholarship, observes that "a great deal of English scholarship builds upon the tenets of the core rather than discards them."[108] Bartie notes that this research process is captured by the concept of "doctrinalism" or "black letter law" and argues that these tenets have provided "an element of unity in legal scholarship over the past century or so."[109] As noted above, other methodologies for legal and tax scholarship include case study, empirical study, and combinations of these approaches, as urged by Livingston and others. Overall, the approach of the research undertaken for this book relies on comparative legal analysis. A critique of such traditional analytical approaches as a guide is that they do not necessarily provide a consistent theoretical framework for analysis.[110] For the most part, the doctrinal research method is used to expose and analyze the related source rules associated with TIEAs and the EOI process, including explaining legal and, where applicable, economic and political obstacles to (and opportunities for) policy reform. The doctrinal approach is consistent with the long-standing tradition of scholarship in law in general and with the bulk of international tax law literature where the purpose is to evaluate primary sources of tax law. The doctrinal approach is also appropriate for

[105] Reform-oriented research is described as "[r]esearch which intensively evaluates the adequacy of existing rules and which recommends changes to any rules found wanting": see *Pearce Report*, above note 102, cited in Hutchinson & Duncan, above note 102 at 101.

[106] Theoretical research is described as "[r]esearch which fosters a more complete understanding of the conceptual bases of legal principles and of the combined effects of a range of rules and procedures that touch on a particular area of activity": see *Pearce Report*, above note 102, cited in Hutchinson & Duncan, above note 102 at 101.

[107] Fundamental research is described as "[r]esearch designed to secure a deeper understanding of law as a social phenomenon, including research on the historical, philosophical, linguistic, economic, social or political implications of law": see *Arthurs Report*, above note 103, cited in Hutchinson & Duncan, above note 102 at 102.

[108] Susan Bartie, "The Lingering Core of Legal Scholarship" (2010) 30:3 *Legal Studies* 345 at 350, cited in Hutchinson & Duncan, above note 102 at 105.

[109] Bartie, above note 108 at 350, cited in Hutchinson & Duncan, above note 102 at 105.

[110] For an example of a Coasean transaction cost approach to international taxation, see Arthur Cockfield, "The Limits of the International Tax Regime as a Commitment Projector" (2013) 33 *Virginia Tax Review* 59. Professor Cockfield's article, *ibid* at 61, conceptualizes the international tax regime as a political and legal system striving to address transaction cost challenges, as described by Ronald Coase, and claims that it has an uneven record in reducing transaction costs for taxpayers and others.

this research due to the relatively brief timeline of the subject matter, limited amount of research, and unavailability of empirical data. In addition to using the doctrinal approach, the authors seek throughout this book to inform the reader with insights drawn from almost half a century of collective professional experience in the practice of tax law.

Difficulties in obtaining empirical data exist for a number of reasons. In the case of the United States, the latest tax gap, which is for 2006 and is defined as the amount of tax liability faced by taxpayers that is not paid on time, does not break down the tax revenue shortfall connected with offshore individual tax evasion.[111] The estimated gross tax gap for 2006 is $450 million, but no estimate is provided for an individual income tax amount relating to accounts or assets held offshore. There are no official estimates of the individual tax gap, and estimates for individual evasion are more difficult because the initial basis of the estimate is the amount of assets held abroad whose income is not reported to fiscal authorities and because individuals can and do purchase foreign investments outside the United States, such as stocks and bonds, or put money into foreign bank accounts and do not report the income to the IRS, even though such income is subject to US tax.[112] There is also little or no withholding information on such individuals regarding these kinds of investments, and such individuals can and do use structures such as trusts or shell corporations to evade tax on both foreign investments and investments made in the United States.[113] Moreover, as discussed in Chapter 5, US sourced investment income such as interest and capital gains is not subject to withholding taxes, and new techniques have developed to transform dividends into exempt interest (using derivatives).[114] In the case of tax havens, the amount of annual deposits held in a tax haven jurisdiction by non-resident individuals (collectively or on a country-by-country basis) is

[111] See United States, Internal Revenue Service, News Release, IR-2012-4 (6 January 2012), online: www.irs.gov/uac/IRS-Releases-New-Tax-Gap-Estimates;-Compliance-Rates-Remain-Statistically-Unchanged-From-Previous-Study.

[112] Gravelle, above note 2 at 16.

[113] *Ibid* at 21.

[114] *Ibid.*

not publicly available.[115] The general lack of empirical data surrounding the research topic makes efforts to hypothesize optimal solutions more difficult and highlights the need, identified in Chapter 11, to enhance information sharing with tax havens.

This book is composed of eleven chapters. This, first, chapter contains a snapshot of the problem of tax evasion internationally and in Canada. It also outlines the methodology of the research and the subjects examined in the book. Chapter 2 examines the theoretical foundations, including policy objectives, relating to international taxation, the use of treaties, and the role of EOI. A basic knowledge of these principles is important for understanding and considering the role played by EOI between countries in combatting international tax evasion. This knowledge is essential both for an appreciation of the role that TIEAs and EOI mechanisms are intended to play in the broader scheme of international tax law and for a subsequent evaluation of their effectiveness.

Chapter 3 begins by providing a background to the origins of the global initiatives on EOI in the OECD and to the policy objectives and goals of the projects on harmful tax competition and transparency. The research in this book is informed in Chapter 3 by a literature review of work by scholars who have focused on the OECD's earlier efforts (and political challenges) surrounding its harmful tax competition project, of which EOI through TIEAs was a component.[116] While authors have

---

[115] See Arthur Cockfield, "Summary of Oral Submissions [Presented to the Standing Committee on Finance, House of Commons]: Tax Evasion and Offshore Bank Accounts" (17 February 2011) [unpublished, archived online at http://arthurcockfield.com/wp-content/uploads/2011/04/Summary-of-Oral-Submissions-Cockfield-Finance-Feb172011.doc], acknowledging that empirical studies attempting to assess the amount of assets Canadian individuals have placed in offshore accounts for tax evasion purposes would be inhibited by a lack of available data due to the illegal and secret nature of the activities, and, in any event, are extremely scarce.

[116] See, for example, the following articles, which focus on the OECD's efforts against tax havens from approximately 1998 through 2007 but not implementation of the new OECD standards and the peer review process or the efficacy of TIEAs and the effort to combat tax evasion surrounding them: Lorraine Eden & Robert T Kudrle, "Tax Havens: Renegade States in the International Tax Regime?" (2005) 27:1 *Law and Policy* 100 at 122, examining the OECD's harmful tax competition project; Robert T Kudrle, "The OECD's Harmful Tax Competition Initiative and the Tax Havens: From Bombshell to Damp Squib" (2008) 8 *Global Economy Journal* 1, reviewing the OECD's harmful tax competition project against tax havens in the early years, with economic analysis of the Cayman Islands; Reuven S Avi-Yonah, "The OECD Harmful Tax Competition Report: A Retrospective after a Decade" (2009) 34 *Brooklyn Journal of International Law* 783, arguing that the OECD effort was successful on the basis of data showing no decline in individual or corporate tax

commented on different periods or aspects of the OECD's war on tax evasion, this is the first comprehensive review of that effort from 1998 to 2014 that includes such important developments in the field as the Global Forum and peer reviews, John Doe summonses, criminal prosecution, and *FATCA*. Chapter 3 evaluates whether or not TIEAs — the main instrument of the Global Forum — are an effective tool in the fight against tax evasion. A number of different criteria are used in evaluating TIEAs to determine whether or not they are an effective tool in the war on tax evasion and to gain a broader understanding of the EOI problem (one that potentially identifies interdisciplinary and multidisciplinary issues). Other empirical data that may be used to measure how TIEAs perform and the broader problems of EOI can be found in the recently released "grades" given to members of the Global Forum on implementing the OECD's standards on EOI and transparency.[117] TIEAs are also evaluated in the context of how they relate to and whether or not they

revenues in OECD member countries. See also Allison Christians, "Hard Law, Soft Law, and International Taxation" (2007) 25 *Wisconsin International Law Journal* 325, arguing that whether an international tax practice or norm is described as "hard" law, "customary" law, "soft" law, or no law at all does matter as those terms point to the need for further analysis regarding the legitimacy of institutional authority and expectations, and the transformative impact of globalization on the making of national tax law; Steven A Dean, "Philosopher Kings and International Tax: A New Approach to Tax Havens, Tax Flight, and International Tax Cooperation" (2007) 58 *Hastings Law Journal* 911, arguing that the OECD's cooperation commitments have done little to reduce tax flight; Arthur J Cockfield, "The Rise of the OECD as Informal 'World Tax Organization' through National Responses to E-commerce Tax Challenges" (2006) 8 *Yale Journal of Law & Technology* 136, which is a case study assessing national and international responses to tax challenges posed by cross-border e-commerce in which the OECD is identified as an informal world tax organization; Allison Christians, "Taxation in a Time of Crisis: Policy Leadership from the OECD to the G20" (2010) 5 *Northwestern Journal of Law & Social Policy* 19 [Christians, "Taxation in a Time of Crisis"], observing that despite the financial crisis of 2008–2009 and the need for developing countries to play a greater role in global tax policy, such a goal remains elusive in a world where tax policy is set and dominated by the wealthiest countries in the OECD. This book has also been informed at points throughout the research by other scholars and their insights relating to certain aspects of TIEAs and EOI: see, for example, Arthur J Cockfield, "Protecting Taxpayer Privacy Rights under Enhanced Cross-border Tax Information Exchange: Toward a Multilateral Taxpayer Bill of Rights" (2010) 42 *University of British Columbia Law Review* 420, recommending that governments consider adopting a multilateral agreement on taxpayer rights to ensure that tax information is transferred across borders with minimum standards of legal protection; Adrian Sawyer, "Peer Review of Tax Information Exchange Agreements: Is It More Than Just about the Numbers?" (2011) 26 *Australian Tax Forum* 397, observing that the information exchange mechanism under TIEAs is fundamentally flawed.

[117] See Chapter 3, Section F.

support the basic principles and policies of international tax and treaty law overviewed in Chapter 2. As discussed in more detail in Chapter 2, there are various contested scholarly visions for what is fair and efficient in designing an international tax regime. In her research on tax policy leadership concerning the OECD and G20, Professor Christians observes that on multiple occasions the OECD has articulated a blunt policy to shut down tax havens to protect the national revenue bases of the wealthiest countries in the world.[118] Tax havens and developing countries have virtually no role in determining the policy that impacts their fiscal and economic systems, which role is reserved for the rich countries' "club."[119] The OECD's harmful tax competition project raises many important political, international legal, and social issues, especially those relating to principles of fairness. One's views on these issues can be influenced by national interest perspectives. In the case of Canada, as explained further in Chapter 6, combatting international tax evasion is an important policy objective. In the case of a tax haven, the OECD's initiatives to compel tax haven cooperation (e.g., through the adoption of transparency and EOI standards and now Automatic Exchange) can be extremely burdensome and result in driving business, including legal business, from its economy, and thus harming the country's national interests. While it is important to acknowledge these issues, in the context of evaluating the capacity of TIEAs to be an effective tool against offshore tax evasion for Canada, this study follows a traditional approach that looks to generally accepted international tax policy goals and principles and as a result does not focus

[118] See Christians, "Taxation in a Time of Crisis," above note 116 at 27. Professor Christians, *ibid*, observes that although for more than a decade the United States together with other European countries framed the issue of tax evasion as an important global problem for reasons relating to economic efficiency and fairness, in the early 1990s and again in response to the economic crisis in 2008–2009, the OECD's stated policy goals were directed at shutting down tax havens to protect national revenue bases and address major fiscal problems that wealthy countries were experiencing as a result of the crisis.

[119] *Ibid* at 19–20 and 40. Professor Christians, *ibid*, argues that despite the emergence of the G20 as an economic leader, the OECD remains the market leader in developing tax standards and guidelines while the G20, rather than providing developing countries with a meaningful voice in the dialogue, provides an opportunity to syndicate OECD-made policy, and further that despite the need for developing countries to play a greater role in global tax policy, such a goal will remain elusive while the OECD dominates this role.

on themes of fairness and sovereignty relating to the OECD's and Global Forum's project.[120]

The research into TIEAs covers not only the history of the legal instrument itself but also the work of the Global Forum to implement the new EOI and transparency standards contained in the *Agreement on Exchange of Information on Tax Matters* (*Model TIEA*) including the results of its peer review process. Accordingly, the evaluation of TIEAs considers the policy objectives behind their development and implementation during the years 1998 through 2013 and whether or not TIEAs have measured up to these stated policy goals. The evaluation in Chapter 3 also incorporates a comparison between some of the major tools used by the United States and Canada, described in Chapters 4 and 5, and TIEAs to provide contextual meaning to the debate about how to overcome the information gap to bolster tax administration and fairness. Additionally, Chapter 3 evaluates TIEAs against the Canadian policy considerations for their use to crystallize where Canada is in meeting its goals relating to EOI and tax evasion and to make recommendations for the future. Chapter 3 also contains an empirical analysis of the peer review ratings released by the Global Forum in 2013 on the effectiveness of the implementation of the OECD standards on transparency and effective EOI. This empirical analysis highlights a lack of proper infrastructure in tax haven jurisdictions owing to tax policy, economic, political, and historical differences that validate earlier arguments by Professor Steven Dean in favour of cooperation through tax deharmonization.[121] The earlier markedly poor results of tax havens in the peer review process also underscore the lack of an essential ingredient in a successful campaign against tax evasion — motivation. Just as the OECD failed to grasp the advantages and importance of making tax havens true economic partners in the fight against tax evasion with TIEAs, so is it making the same mistake with Automatic Exchange.

[120] See, for example, Allison Christians, "Sovereignty, Taxation and Social Contract" (2009) 18 *Minnesota Journal of International Law* 99, where Professor Christians examines the OECD's work on harmful tax competition from a political philosophy perspective to identify the existence of a global social contract for taxation and to assess its content and implications.

[121] For a discussion of tax harmonization versus deharmonization see Chapter 6, Section D.

The primary aim of Chapters 4 and 5 is to explore the alternative mechanisms used by Canada and the United States to obtain foreign-based taxpayer information to combat tax evasion. These alternative mechanisms are generally used when residents commit tax evasion by failing to follow the voluntary foreign-reporting rules. This analysis provides a basis to evaluate the effectiveness of TIEAs against other information-gathering tools used by Canada and the United States, including John Doe summonses, criminal prosecution, and *FATCA*. Chapter 4 examines two principal questions. First, how does the Minister of National Revenue access taxpayer information, particularly foreign-based taxpayer information? Second, what statutory provisions and rights are engaged to protect a taxpayer's information, especially in relation to the right of privacy? Essentially, Chapter 4 examines CRA powers and tools that can be used to obtain taxpayer information for an audit, whether for civil purposes or a criminal investigation, particularly in non-voluntary situations. Chapter 5 exposes some of the broader underlying policy challenges to effective EOI by examining US legal efforts to obtain bank account information from UBS, including under its treaty with Switzerland and by using the weight of its domestic judicial system through John Doe summonses and the unprecedented use of the threat of criminal prosecution, which has brought some 100 Swiss banks into the Department of Justice's Swiss Bank Program. Chapter 5 also underscores the immense examination powers wielded by the IRS and their potential impact on US nationals living abroad, including the dangers of non-cooperation, such as criminal penalties.

Chapter 6 reviews the policy objectives of TIEAs from the perspectives of the OECD, the United States, and Canada. It also provides a comparative analysis of Canada's TIEA network, comparing the agreements with one another and also with the Global Forum's *Model TIEA* and Article 26, the EOI provision, of the 2010 *Model Tax Convention on Income and on Capital*.[122] Chapter 7 explains Article 26, which is the cornerstone EOI mechanism in double tax conventions used by Canada, the United States, and other OECD and developing countries. Chapter 8

[122] OECD, *Model Tax Convention on Income and on Capital* (OECD: Paris, 2010), online: www.oecd.org/tax/treaties/47213736.pdf [*Model Tax Treaty*].

provides policy background to the new standard in EOI — Automatic Exchange — as well as an overview of the rules of the OECD's initiative. Chapter 9 provides policy background to *FATCA* and an overview of the intergovernmental agreement entered into between Canada and the United States, highlighting existing concerns relating to its implementation. Chapter 10 provides a perspective on the US voluntary disclosure program for US persons living outside the United States and highlights strategic considerations relating to collection and enforcement issues concerning US citizens living in Canada, the European Union, and other OECD countries. Chapter 10 also describes the Canadian offshore voluntary disclosure process and provides insights for individuals confronting this subject in their financial and legal holdings, and their advisers. Chapter 11 endeavours to summarize what has been learned both about and from the study of TIEAs and EOI as well as identify future areas of study to advance the research undertaken in this book. Chapter 11 makes policy recommendations for how deficiencies, explained in Chapter 3, regarding TIEAs and EOI can be addressed and, possibly, overcome. Additionally, Chapter 11 makes policy recommendations regarding key aspects of Canadian and US international tax policy that relate to EOI.

The research in this book is conducted from the perspectives of Canadian laws and US laws, and is also focused on the rules established by the OECD relating to the *Model TIEA*, Article 26 of the *Model Tax Treaty*, and Automatic Exchange. It should be noted that the weight afforded to the analysis of each country's laws is not equal, nor is it intended to be. In particular, the research considers select legal rules within US tax and foreign-reporting laws. Particular emphasis in parts of this book is placed on three reporting systems unique to the United States: the qualified intermediary rules, the report of foreign bank and financial accounts rules, and *FATCA*. As described in greater detail in parts of this book, these US legal rules have had a significant impact on developments in international taxation including EOI both in the OECD and in the cross-border context between Canada and the United States. Chapter 6 focuses on Canadian tax policy and a comparative analysis of Canada's TIEA network, and hence no equivalent study is made of the US TIEAs in force. In Chapters 4 and 5, the rules of both countries relating to accessing foreign-based information are reviewed. However, emphasis is given to the use by the United States of its summons power and criminal prosecution powers as innovative approaches in the field of EOI. The timeline for this research is generally from 1998 through the end of 2015. It is also important to note that this research covers individual rather than corporate tax evasion, which is an important and controversial subject in international tax policy today.[123]

This book's primary audience is readers living and working in Canada, the European Union, and other Global Forum–member countries who, by their nationality or occupation, we trust will benefit from an understanding of our work in this undertaking. There is a saying: "You don't get angry at a storm, you just get out of the way." We believe and hope that the knowledge conveyed in these pages will help readers safely guide their government, organization, or client away from the storms of international tax evasion occurring in the new age of global information.

[123] See, for example, Tom Fairless, "EU Demands Back Taxes from Global Companies" *Wall Street Journal* (12 January 2016) B3, who notes that thirty-five multinationals will be required by the European Union to pay approximately $765 million in additional taxes in Belgium after a ruling that they benefited from an illicit tax break.

2

International Tax and the Roles of International Tax Policy and Tax Treaties

1 Introduction

This chapter examines the basic concepts in international tax law and the roles of international tax policy and tax treaties. It also reviews the principal theories in international tax policy and provides some commentaries on what scholars are saying today about these theories.

The interaction between taxpayers and multiple jurisdictions necessarily gives rise to many questions under international law, and international taxation. These transnational fact patterns also create complex economic, political, and legal choices for policy-makers, especially those focused on fiscal sovereignty. Some of these interesting questions and challenges are the following: What is the legal basis for either country to impose its fiscal laws upon the foreign activities of its residents and citizens? What is the legal basis for either country to impose its fiscal laws upon individuals who reside in a foreign country, or persons (e.g., corporations) that have been formed in a foreign jurisdiction? What happens when taxpayers are subject to the fiscal tax laws of two nations at the same time? What happens when the government of one country cannot ever learn about the foreign activities of its residents and citizens (especially when the taxpayers intentionally

D.S. Kerzner, D.W. Chodikoff, *International Tax Evasion in the Global Information Age*, DOI 10.1007/978-3-319-40421-9_2

decide to hide their foreign income, activities, or assets)? What happens to principles of fairness in a society when a government has, after providing a taxpayer with full rights of appeal under the law, obtained a judgment against the taxpayer but when the taxpayer's assets, which could satisfy the judgment in whole or in part, lie in another jurisdiction?

Answers to these questions from Canadian and US perspectives may be found in the domestic tax laws (including statutes, judicial decisions, and administrative positions) dealing with international law, conflicts of law, and tax treaties of both nations. As international taxation must concern itself with either foreign jurisdictions or foreign persons, or both, an understanding of the principles of law that may relate to these international aspects of taxation is important to understanding this subject and to understanding the role of exchange of information, which has become a vital subtopic in today's war against international tax evasion.[1] Increasingly, both the Canadian and the American governments, among others, have been concerned with enforcement of their fiscal laws to prevent erosion of their tax base, to combat illegal tax evasion and other criminal behaviour, and to maintain equity in the system. Information regarding the foreign accounts, entities, and income of taxpayers is a vital component to determining their compliance with Canadian and US reporting and tax laws. Once fiscal authorities can determine that a taxpayer is delinquent regarding these laws, enforcement measures (including those under domestic law, treaty law, and international law) may be undertaken.

2 Sources of International Law

2.1 International Tax and International Tax Law

International taxation concerns the fiscal relationship between a taxpayer and his personal ties with or economic activities in two or more nations.[2] Both Canada and the United States impose taxation on a worldwide

[1] See, for example, Chapter 3 for a historical background to the initiatives of the OECD on harmful tax competition.

[2] International taxation deals with the tax aspects of international commerce and investment: see Jinyan Li, Arthur Cockfield, & J Scott Wilkie, *International Taxation in Canada — Principles and Practices*, 2d ed (Markham, ON: LexisNexis, 2011) at 1.

basis on their residents. As a result, both countries tax income wherever it is earned. Primary liability for tax in Canada is based on residency. Individuals resident in Canada are taxed on their worldwide income. Corporations formed in Canada, which are also regarded under Canadian common law as managed and controlled in Canada are also taxed on their worldwide income.[3] In the United States, US citizens and resident aliens are taxed on their worldwide income. The United States, unlike Canada, is one of the few countries that uses nationality for jurisdiction to tax, in addition to residence. The tax laws of the United States are embodied chiefly in the *Internal Revenue Code*,[4] as amended, the *Treasury Regulations* issued thereunder, decisions of the courts, and current administrative interpretations together with tax treaties in force. Section 1 of the *Code* imposes a tax on the taxable income of every individual (see section 11 for every corporation), and section 61 includes income from whatever source derived. Unlike the Canadian test for residence, the US test is more precise. Whether an individual is a resident under the *Code*, and hence subject to tax on her worldwide income, is determined under a set of prescribed tests in the *Code*, for example, the permanent resident (green card) test and the substantial presence test.[5] Under US tax law, an individual who is a dual resident of Canada and the United States but who is considered a resident of Canada under the applicable tie-breaker provision contained under Article IV of the *Convention between Canada and the United States of America with respect to Taxes on Income and on Capital*[6] may be relieved of certain tax liabilities. Unfortunately, a US resident who is considered a resident of Canada under the tiebreaker rules must still comply with the onerous US reporting rules.[7] However,

[3] See Brian J Arnold, *Reforming Canada's International Tax System: Toward Coherence and Simplicity* (Toronto: Canadian Tax Foundation, 2009) at 13. The term "resident" is not defined in the *Income Tax Act*, RSC 1985, c 1 (5th Supp) [*Act*]. Rather, residence is determined on facts that under Canadian law may connect an individual to Canada and also on certain statutory provisions in the *Act* that may if met deem an individual to be resident in Canada. See, generally, ch 4, dealing with residence, in David S Kerzner, Vitaly Timokhov, & David W Chodikoff, eds, *The Tax Advisor's Guide to the Canada–U.S. Tax Treaty* (Toronto: Thomson Reuters Carswell, 2008) (loose-leaf).

[4] *Internal Revenue Code*, USC 26 (1986) [*Code*].

[5] *Code*, *ibid*, § 7701(b).

[6] Signed at Washington, DC, on 26 September 1980, as amended by the protocols signed on 14 June 1983, 23 March 1984, 17 March 1997, 29 July 1997, and 21 September 2007 [*Canada–US Tax Treaty*].

[7] See *Treasury Regulations* § 301.7701(b)-(7)(e), Example 1.

Canadian residents who are also US citizens continue to be subject to US tax and reporting obligations under the saving clause in Article XXIX (Miscellaneous Rules) of the *Canada–US Tax Treaty*. The presence of almost one million Canadians of US heritage in Canada, who are subject to the US tax and reporting laws, has created a monumental international tax policy problem.[8] Corporations formed in the United States are also taxed on their worldwide income.[9]

International tax evasion generally consists of a taxpayer's purposeful non-disclosure of income earned abroad that would otherwise be taxed under the tax laws of the two countries. Tax evasion is to be distinguished from tax avoidance or the legal use of a country's laws to reduce the taxes owing. Baron Tomlin remarked in the UK House of Lords case *Duke of Westminster v Commissioners of Inland Revenue*:

> Every man is entitled if he can to order his affairs so that the tax attaching under the appropriate Acts is less than it otherwise would be. If he succeeds in ordering them so as to secure this result, then, however unappreciative the Commissioners of Inland Revenue or his fellow tax-payers may be of his ingenuity, he cannot be compelled to pay an increased tax.[10]

Judge Learned Hand similarly observed in *Helvering v Gregory* with respect to the tax laws of the United States, "Any one may so arrange his affairs that his taxes shall be as low as possible; he is not bound to choose that pattern which will best pay the Treasury; there is not even a patriotic duty to increase one's taxes."[11]

The term "international tax law" is largely misleading insofar as it suggests that taxpayers involved in international transactions or who may have personal ties to more than one country are governed by a single body

---

[8] See Barry McKenna, "Flaherty Slams IRS over Cross-border Tax Crack Down" *Globe and Mail* (16 September 2011), in regard to new US information-reporting rules that have an extraterritorial impact on Canada's financial services community; *Foreign Account Tax Compliance Act*, enacted by Congress as part of the *Hiring Incentives to Restore Employment (HIRE) Act*, Public Law 111-147, and signed into law by the president on 18 March 2010 [*FATCA*].

[9] See Paul R McDaniel & Hugh J Ault, *Introduction to United States International Taxation*, 4th ed (The Hague: Kluwer Law International, 1998) at 53.

[10] (1935), 19 Tax Cas 490 (HL) at 520.

[11] 69 F 2d 809 at 810–11 (2d Cir 1934).

of law (or set of rules) that ultimately determines their tax liabilities and tax (and other legal) obligations. Rather, the term "international tax law" may refer to multiple sets of legal regimes that may apply to a taxpayer's fact pattern or, thinking domestically, to those provisions in the *Act* or *Code* that deal with international aspects of taxation. As an example using the forty-ninth parallel between Canada and the United States, taxpayers doing cross-border business or who may have personal ties to both countries (e.g., US citizens working in Canada) must confront multiple legal regimes — three distinct legal regimes in fact — to determine their tax liability and reporting obligations. These three separate but related regimes are the tax laws of Canada,[12] the tax laws of the United States,[13] and the tax laws contained in the *Canada–US Tax Treaty*.

2.2 Sovereignty and the Jurisdiction to Tax

The jurisdiction of both Canada and the United States to impose taxation arises from the broader concept under international law that recognizes the principle of territoriality among nations to prescribe and enforce their own laws.[14]

---

[12] See the *Act*, above note 3. For additional readings on international tax law in Canada, see, generally, Li, Cockfield, & Wilkie, above note 2; Vern Krishna, *Canadian International Taxation* (Toronto: Carswell, 1995) (loose-leaf).

[13] Further complexities are posed by complex distinctions in US tax law that may characterize transactions under tax principles differently from their legal form. Under the step transaction doctrine, for example, purely formal distinctions cannot obscure the substance of a transaction: see *McDonald's Restaurants of Illinois, Inc v Commissioner*, 688 F 2d 520 at 524 (7th Cir 1982). In addition to this substantial body of law, the harsher practical reality is that inbound commercial transactions and investments into the fifty states (and possessions) often require additional knowledge of the income tax, sales and use tax, and other special tax rules of these separate jurisdictions: see Jerome R Hellerstein & Walter Hellerstein, *State Taxation*, 3d ed (Boston: Warren, Gorham & Lamont, 1998) (loose-leaf). For additional readings on the international tax rules of the United States, see Boris I Bittker & Lawrence Lokken, *Federal Taxation of Income, Estates, and Gifts*, 3d ed (Valhalla, NY: Warren, Gorham & Lamont, 2005); Joel D Kuntz & Robert J Peroni, *U.S. International Taxation* (New York: Thomson Reuters RIA, 1991) (loose-leaf).

[14] See, generally, Hugh M Kindred & Phillip M Saunders, eds, *International Law Chiefly as Interpreted and Applied in Canada*, 7th ed (Toronto: Emond Montgomery, 2006) at 289: the principal corollaries of the sovereignty and equality of states are (1) a jurisdiction, *prima facie* exclusive over a territory and the permanent population living there, (2) a duty of non-intervention in the areas of exclusive jurisdiction of other states, and (3) the dependence of obligations arising from customary law and treaties on the consent of the obligor; *The Lotus Case* (1927), PCIJ (Ser A)

The federal tax jurisdiction of the Canadian Parliament arises from section 91(3) of the *Constitution Act, 1867* (formerly, *The British North America Act, 1867*), wherein Parliament has exclusive legislative authority to raise money "by any Mode or System of Taxation."[15] In the earlier case of *BC Electric Railway Co v R*[16] (dealing with withholding on dividend payments to foreign shareholders), the Privy Council recognized Parliament's taxing jurisdiction under section 91 of *The British North America Act* including the extraterritorial operation of Parliament's tax laws. This case is to be juxtaposed with the Supreme Court of Canada's later decision in *United States v Harden*.[17] In contradistinction to the support given to a sovereign's broad extraterritorial tax reach in *BC Electric Railway*, the Supreme Court in *Harden* followed a long-standing principle (often referred to as the "revenue rule") in refusing to enforce the revenue laws of another sovereign and thereby adopted a more limited conception of the reach of a sovereign's fiscal powers.[18] One commentator refers to these cases as illustrations of the "puzzle surrounding the notion of legal sovereignty."[19]

In the United States, the jurisdiction to impose tax arises from Article I, section 8 of the Constitution, granting Congress the power "to lay and collect taxes, duties, imposts and excises ...."[20] The Sixteenth Amendment in 1913 empowered congress "to levy and collect taxes on income, from whatever source derived, without apportionment among the several

No 10: a state requires the permission of another state for the extraterritorial application of its laws, e.g., for discovery of documents or witnesses, or enforcement of penal or tax laws; Fiona Beveridge, *The Treatment and Taxation of Foreign Investment under International Law: Towards International Disciplines* (Manchester: Manchester University Press, 2000) at 3. Ms Beveridge, *ibid* at 57–59, recognizes that a state may also exercise its jurisdiction to tax based on nationality.

[15] (UK), 30 & 31 Vict, c 3, reprinted in RSC 1985, Appendix II, No 5.

[16] [1946] AC 527 (JCPC) [*BC Electric Railway*].

[17] [1963] SCR 366 [*Harden*].

[18] The Supreme Court relied on the House of Lords decision in *Ministry of Finance v Taylor*, [1955] AC 491 (HL), and a decision of Learned Hand J in *Moore v Mitchell*, 30 F 2d 600 at 604 (2d Cir 1929).

[19] Edward M Morgan, *International Law and the Canadian Courts: Sovereign Immunity, Criminal Jurisdiction, Aliens' Rights and Taxation Powers* (Toronto: Carswell, 1990) at 116.

[20] This power was qualified by Article I, section 2 of the Constitution, requiring the apportionment of direct taxes. Ensuing legal and political battles, not discussed here, led to the adoption in 1913 of the Sixteenth Amendment.

States, and without regard to any census or enumeration." The issue of the validity of the power of the United States to tax its citizens who were domiciled in foreign lands came before the US Supreme Court in the case of *Cook v Tait*.[21] In reply to a taxpayer's complaint that the US government had acted beyond its territorial jurisdiction in taxing a US citizen/resident domiciled in Mexico, the Court observed:

> [The taxing power] is based on the presumption that government by its very nature benefits the citizen and his property wherever found . . . . Or, to express it another way, the basis of the power to tax was not and cannot be made dependent upon the situs of the property in all cases, it being in or out of the United States, and was not and cannot be made dependent upon the domicile of the citizen, that being in or out of the United States, but upon his relation as citizen to the United States and the relation of the latter to him as citizen. The consequence of the relations is that the native citizen who is taxed may have domicile, and the property from which his income is derived may have situs, in a foreign country and the tax be legal — the government having power to impose the tax.[22]

Regarding the enforcement of foreign tax laws, the late Professor Andreas F Lowenfeld at New York University observed that the *Restatement of the Law (Third) of Foreign Relations Law of the United States*[23] attempts to loosen the logjam created by the combination of precedent and reciprocity.[24] Section 483 of the *Restatement* provides that courts in the United States are not required to recognize or enforce the collection of foreign taxes, fines, or penalties. However, the commentary ("Nonrecognition not required but permitted") states, "No rule of the United States law or of international law would be violated if a court in the United States enforced a judgment of a foreign court for payment of

---

[21] 265 US 47 (1924).

[22] *Ibid* at 56.

[23] (1986) [*Restatement*].

[24] Andreas F Lowenfeld, *International Litigation and Arbitration* (St Paul, MN: West Publishing, 1993) at 47.

taxes or comparable assessments that was otherwise consistent with the standards" for enforcement of foreign country judgments.[25]

The competition between different sovereign jurisdictions and their taxing powers creates policy challenges in international tax law. Countries strive to manage these challenges primarily through their domestic tax laws and treaty networks and increasingly through international cooperation. The US application of its worldwide taxing jurisdiction to nationals (not just residents) can create conflict and tension in international tax policy. This can, for example, give rise to differences in defining who is a tax cheat. As explained in more detail below, this is the main problem that has led to the Canada–US dispute over *FATCA*.

3 Goals of International Tax Law

As mentioned above, Canada taxes its residents on a worldwide basis, on income earned from within Canada and income earned from foreign countries.[26] Similarly, the United States taxes its residents and its citizens on a worldwide basis.[27] Canada and the United States represent examples of countries that employ a worldwide or residence-based tax system. The aforementioned approach may be referred to as residence-based taxation.[28] In addition, both Canada and the United States (as well as many other countries) tax income that is sourced in their respective countries and earned by foreign individuals or persons (often referred to as sourced-based taxation).[29] This leads to the overlapping of two jurisdictions, where the residence-based and the sourced-based countries each

---

[25] *Restatement*, above note 23, § 483, commentary. The principles of comity would have to be satisfied before tax judgments could be enforced.

[26] See Li, Cockfield, & Wilkie, above note 2 at 11.

[27] See Paul R McDaniel, "Territorial vs. Worldwide International Tax Systems: Which Is Better for the U.S." (2007) 8 *Florida Tax Review* 283.

[28] See Li, Cockfield, & Wilkie, above note 2 at 11.

[29] See *ibid*.

have a claim to tax the same income, and gives rise to the problem of international double taxation.[30]

International juridical double taxation has been defined as

> the imposition of comparable taxes in two (or more) States on the same taxpayer in respect of the same subject matter and for identical periods. Its harmful effects on the exchange of goods and services and movements of capital, technology and persons are so well known that it is scarcely necessary to stress the importance of removing the obstacles that double taxation presents to the development of economic relations between countries.[31]

One of the primary goals of international tax policy is to relieve such double taxation through a "mediation" of the claims of residence and source countries so that this income is taxed only once.[32] More recently, the goal of ensuring that income is taxed at least once has been a renewed priority for Canada, the United States, and the other OECD countries.[33] To this end, one of the goals of international tax policy is the advancement of worldwide economic efficiency. This objective is said to involve two kinds of neutralities: capital export neutrality (CEN) and capital import neutrality (CIN).[34]

---

[30] See *ibid.* See also Michael J Graetz, *Foundations of International Income Taxation* (New York: Foundation Press, 2003) at 5 [Graetz, *Foundations*]. For a history of the work of the League of Nations relating to the use of treaties and fiscal evasion, see Arthur J Cockfield, "The Limits of the International Tax Regime as a Commitment Projector" (2013) 33 *Virginia Tax Review* 59.

[31] See OECD, *Model Tax Convention on Income and on Capital* (Paris: OECD, 2010) Introduction at para 1 [*Model Tax Treaty*]. For an in-depth discussion of international juridical double taxation, including circumstances giving rise to double taxation, general rules of international law, economic and legal aspects of the international distribution of taxation, and the avoidance of double taxation through treaties, see Klaus Vogel, *Klaus Vogel on Double Taxation Conventions*, 3d ed (London: Kluwer Law International, 1997).

[32] See *Model Tax Treaty*, above note 31 at Introduction.

[33] See *ibid.*

[34] See Michael J Graetz, "Taxing International Income: Inadequate Principles, Outdated Concepts, and Unsatisfactory Policies" (2001) 54 *Tax Law Review* 261 at 270–75 [Graetz, "Taxing International Income"].

CEN is reached when a taxpayer's decision with regard to investing at home or abroad is not influenced by taxes.[35] To achieve CEN, certain conditions or elements must be present. A pure worldwide system of taxation that taxes the income of its residents regardless of whether the income is domestic or foreign and irrespective of whether foreign income is repatriated to the residence state helps accomplish CEN by making the investment choice now dependent on factors other than tax.[36] By reducing the tax burden on income from investments, tax havens cause income to be shifted from its true geographic source to low tax jurisdictions and can hinder CEN.[37] Other elements or features that would be necessary to implement CEN are the need to not limit the foreign tax credit to the residence country's tax rate (e.g., where the source state has a higher tax rate than the residence state) and the need for the residence country to currently tax income earned by a foreign subsidiary.[38]

Under CIN, it is envisioned that all investment and business activity within a particular country will be subject to the same overall tax level regardless of the residence of the investor, be it foreign or local.[39] CIN is achieved when from a tax perspective, foreign and local businesses are in effect treated the same in the source state where the investment or

---

[35] See Arthur J Cockfield, *Examining Policy Options for the Taxation of Outbound Direct Investment* (Ottawa: Advisory Panel on Canada's System of International Taxation, 2008) at 7 [Cockfield, *Examining Policy Options*].

[36] See *ibid* at 7 and 11. In a model worldwide or foreign tax credit system, the incentive to shift income and business operations to a low cost or no tax jurisdiction would be reduced because regardless of the location of the investment, the residence state (e.g., the United States) would impose its income tax on the investor: see McDaniel, above note 27 at 298.

[37] See Jane G Gravelle, *Reform of U.S. International Taxation: Alternatives* (Washington, DC: Congressional Research Service, 2012) at 18.

[38] See Graetz, "Taxing International Income," above note 34 at 270–75. As a corollary, providing a foreign tax credit for rates greater than those of the residence state creates the problem of which income, foreign or domestic, such excess credits should be applied against. Using the credits against the domestic source income would undermine the tax base of the residence state, and using the credits against taxes from lower tax rate foreign source states would enable a multinational enterprise to proliferate foreign tax credit schemes that could create distortions weakening the worldwide or foreign tax credit system: see Lawrence Lokken, "Territorial Taxation: Why Some U.S. Multinationals May Be Less Than Enthusiastic about the Idea (and Some Ideas They Really Dislike)" (2006) 59 *SMU Law Review* 751.

[39] See Graetz, "Taxing International Income," above note 34 at 270–75.

business activity is taking place.[40] The goal of CIN may be realized in a world order where each country agrees to adopt a pure exemption tax system in regard to income earned therein.[41]

The reality is that there is a natural tension between economic and sovereignty interests in formulating international tax policy.[42] The objective of realizing CEN and CIN concurrently is not realistic given not only the existence of a multitude of sovereign nations, each with its own unique fiscal system, but also the proliferation of thousands of double income tax and now tax information exchange agreements with different substantive terms.[43] Moreover, tax rates are only a minute aspect of a country's fiscal laws. The notion that economic efficiency can be realized through CEN and CIN ignores, certainly in the Canadian and American experiences, the vast body of law that must ultimately be considered in determining a taxpayer's liability and obligations. For example, before one can even apply a tax rate, key threshold tax issues must be addressed from within the *Act* and the *Code* relating to such important wider fiscal subjects as the jurisdiction to tax, the definition of taxable income, the subject of non-recognition transactions, and tax treaties. Additionally, due regard must be had for the often extensive legal regime surrounding any one tax issue, arising from its judicial and administrative interpretation, and, certainly on the US side, the relevant legislative history. Taking into account a nation's history, the intrinsic values in a society that compose a nation's culture, and its political, economic, and international objectives and responsibilities, including the unique tax expenditure program of

---

[40] See Cockfield, *Examining Policy Options*, above note 35 at 7.

[41] As many countries employ a hybrid system subjecting foreign income to current residence state taxation, CIN may in practical terms be achieved where source states apply the same tax rates to active business income (*ibid*). However, as Professor Lokken, above note 38 at 751, notes, moving to an exemption system in a world with so many low cost tax choices would encourage US companies to move investments abroad and thereby sacrifice CEN.

[42] For an in-depth study of this subject within the NAFTA-country governments, see Arthur J Cockfield, *NAFTA Tax Law and Policy: Resolving the Clash between Economic and Sovereignty Interests* (Toronto: University of Toronto Press, 2005) [Cockfield, *NAFTA Tax Law and Policy*]. Among the many observations made by Professor Cockfield, *ibid* at 21, are that the NAFTA governments prefer sovereignty over economic goals but that NAFTA permits its signatories to largely formulate their own tax policies, including the use of bilateral tax treaties to address special cross-border tax problems.

[43] See Graetz, "Taxing International Income," above note 33 at 270–75.

the elected government, underscores why pursuit of economic efficiency through CEN or CIN as the principal purpose of international tax policy is flawed and inconsistent with our approach to income tax policy and our values as a democracy. Professor Graetz aptly describes the major problem with relying on CEN as a foundation for international tax policy as that of concentrating our focus on economic efficiency to the exclusion of the other social, economic, historical, cultural, and national security values of a nation, using the United States as an example. Professor Graetz advocates refocusing the discussion away from the sterile debate of CEN versus CIN and toward the question of how to best articulate an international tax policy that addresses the political as well as the economic considerations and needs of the American people.[44]

4 Tax Treaties

4.1 The General Role of Tax Treaties

Bilateral tax treaties (also known as double tax conventions) together with unilateral domestic measures, such as the foreign tax credit mechanism in both Canada[45] and the United States,[46] provide relief from double taxation for eligible taxpayers[47] in many instances through apportioning the right to tax exclusively to either the residence state or the source state, or by providing a mechanism to reduce the tax rate or liability that would otherwise apply under purely domestic law.[48] For example, one of the

---

[44] *Ibid* at 276–325.

[45] For an overview of Canada's foreign tax credit system, and partial exemption rules, see Kerzner, Timokhov, & Chodikoff, eds, above note 3, ch 24. For a detailed work on Canada's rules relating to the taxation of foreign accrual property income, exempt surplus, and foreign affiliates, see Angelo Nikolakakis, *Taxation of Foreign Affiliates* (Toronto: Carswell, 2000) (loose-leaf).

[46] For an overview of the US foreign tax credit mechanism, see Kerzner, Timokhov, & Chodikoff, eds, above note 3, ch 24.

[47] To ensure that a taxpayer is rightfully entitled to benefits under the *Canada–US Tax Treaty*, the taxpayer must meet certain eligibility requirements under Article IV (Residence) and more recently Article XXIXA (Limitation on Benefits). For an explanation of these provisions, see Kerzner, Timokhov, & Chodikoff, eds, above note 3, ch 4 and 29A.

[48] See Kerzner, Timokhov, & Chodikoff, eds, above note 3, ch 1.

most important provisions that helps to minimize foreign tax liability in international commerce in an OECD double tax convention is Article VII (Business Profits), which generally requires an enterprise of the residence state to have a minimum level of contact with the source state before becoming liable for taxes in the source state on a net basis. Traditionally in double tax conventions, this minimum contact is defined in the article describing a permanent establishment (see, e.g., Article V (Permanent Establishments) in the *Canada–US Tax Treaty*). Other articles in a double tax convention like the *Canada–US Tax Treaty* that may, depending on the facts, reduce or eliminate sourced-based taxation include Article X (Dividends), Article XI (Interest), Article XII (Royalties), Article XIII (Capital Gains), and Article XV (Employment Income). Hence, tax treaties promote investors' and businesses' abilities to engage in international commerce with some measure of predictability as to how their transactions will be taxed and provide, where offered by the treaty, some relief in the taxation rates that would otherwise apply. Tax treaties also assist in the fight against tax evasion and help promote effectiveness of administration and fairness to taxpayers through various provisions such as those on exchange of information, assistance in collection, mutual agreement procedures, and non-discrimination.

Historically, the *Canada–US Tax Treaty* that was signed in September 1980 replaced the then-existing tax convention between Canada and the United States dating from 1942. Since then, the *Canada–US Tax Treaty* has been enhanced by five protocols spanning over a quarter of a century, with the latest having been signed in September 2007.[49]

4.2 Tax Treaties and Their Interpretation under Canadian and US Law

Once enacted, treaties are considered to form part of the domestic law of both Canada and the United States respectively.[50] Legal issues arise around interpreting treaties generally, and this is particularly true of tax

---

[49] Fifth Protocol to the *Canada–US Tax Treaty*, signed on 21 September 2007.

[50] See Li, Cockfield, & Wilkie, above note 2; US Const Art VI, cl 2.

treaties. A general departure point for interpreting a treaty is to look at the plain language of the treaty and also to have regard to the intentions of the parties.[51] Regarding tax treaties in the United States, provisions of the *Code* require that in determining the application of US tax rules to a taxpayer, one must consider any applicable obligation under a US tax treaty.[52] The courts in both Canada and the United States also consider the ongoing commentaries to the OECD *Model Tax Treaty* in interpreting the language of a tax treaty.[53]

5 Residence-Based versus Sourced-Based Taxation

5.1 Worldwide Taxation versus Territorial Taxation

In a pure worldwide taxation system (also referred to as residence-based taxation), individuals and entities that are residents in or nationals of a country are subject to tax on their worldwide income, regardless of where that income is earned (at home or abroad).[54] As noted above, a funda-

[51] See Art 31 of the *Convention of the Law of Treaties*, 23 May 1969, 1155 UNTS 331 [*Vienna Convention*], providing that a treaty is to be interpreted in good faith in accordance with the ordinary meaning to be given to the terms of the treaty in their context and in light of its object and purpose; *Crown Forest Industries Ltd v Canada*, [1995] 2 SCR 802 at paras 22 and 44, observing that in treaty interpretation the process involves looking to the language used and the intentions of the parties. Under Art 32 of the *Vienna Convention, ibid*, one can also consider supplementary or preparatory work relating to the treaty in determining its interpretation. In addition, in Canada regard should be had to the provisions of the *Income Tax Conventions Interpretation Act*, RSC 1985, c I-4. Regarding the United States, see *Sumitomo Shoji America, Inc v Avagliano*, 457 US 176 at 180 (1982); *De Geofroy v Riggs*, 133 US 258 at 271 (1890).

[52] *Code*, above note 4, § 894(a). Generally, where a conflict arises between a section of the *Code* and a treaty, the later in time is to prevail: see *Code, ibid*, § 7852(d)(1); *Chae Chan Ping v United States*, 130 US 581 at 600 (1889).

[53] See, for example, *MIL (Investments) SA v Canada*, 2006 TCC 460 at para 85; *National Westminster Bank PLC v United States*, 44 Fed Cl 120 (1999).

[54] See Cockfield, *Examining Policy Options*, above note 35 at 4–5. In a near ideal worldwide taxation system, all foreign income, whether from business operations or passive investments, would face current taxation on an accrual basis such that no deferral of tax on foreign sourced income would be allowed, under the rationale that US, for example, income tax considerations would not impact the decision of whether to operate abroad in a branch or subsidiary format: see McDaniel, above note 27 at 288. Additionally, such a near ideal worldwide system would incorporate a foreign tax

mental challenge of the worldwide or residence-based tax system is the double taxation of income by the residence state and the source state.[55] To address this problem, many countries employ a foreign tax credit mechanism, an exemption mechanism,[56] or some combination of both.[57] While the United States does not currently employ an exemption system, Canada has utilized a hybrid of the two systems for many years, which taxes both the domestic and foreign (passive-type) investment income of its residents, but which offers to exempt certain foreign business income of foreign affiliate corporations.[58]

In a pure territorial taxation system (also referred to as sourced-based taxation), a country looks to tax only income sourced within its borders.[59]

---

credit for all foreign taxes paid by the US taxpayer on its foreign sourced income, with a per country limitation on active and passive baskets of income (*ibid*).

[55] As countries with an income tax system almost universally tax income arising within their jurisdiction and as only certain nations utilize a residence-based system, the challenge to mitigate the double taxation of income generally falls to the country using the worldwide or residence-based tax approach: see Graetz, *Foundations*, above note 30 at 12–13. For an additional discussion of residence- versus sourced-based taxation and general policy considerations of international taxation, see Jinyan Li, *International Taxation in the Age of Electronic Commerce: A Comparative Study* (Toronto: Canadian Tax Foundation, 2003) at 57–62.

[56] For an explanation of the exemption system used in Canada, see, generally, Nikolakakis, above note 45.

[57] Many countries use some combination of both systems, with few countries having either a pure exemption or credit system. Both Canada and the United States employ a form of antideferral mechanism relating to passive-type or investment income involving capital gains, dividends, interest, and royalties (foreign accrual property income in Canada and Subpart F income in the United States). It is believed that permitting a resident taxpayer to exempt this type of investment income would both erode the tax base and diminish fairness in the tax system as between taxpayers earning similar amounts of income (sometimes referred to as "horizontal equity": see discussion in Section 5.2, below in this chapter). Exempting such income would also inhibit a country's efforts to fairly apply a gradual rate of taxation to those residents or nationals who earn more income (sometimes referred to as "vertical equity": see discussion in Section 5.2, below in this chapter): see Brian J Arnold & Michael J McIntyre, *International Tax Primer*, 2d ed (The Hague: Kluwer Law International, 2002) at 44–45; Cockfield, *Examining Policy Options*, above note 35 at 5. As discussed above, Canada exempts certain active business income meeting specified requirements in addition to employing a foreign tax credit system. The United States does not employ an exemption system but rather a complex foreign tax credit mechanism. Additionally, the United States generally grants a deferral of taxation on certain defined business income earned by foreign corporations until dividends are repatriated. Investors that can significantly delay these distributions can, in effect, reduce the present value of the taxes on foreign profits (*ibid* at 46).

[58] Canada has utilized a hybrid system since 1976: see Cockfield, *Examining Policy Options*, above note 35 at 4–5.

[59] A near ideal territorial tax system would have attributes that include allowing a residence country to include foreign sourced investment income in the tax base (but exempt foreign business income

A territorial system does not look to tax income based on the ties that an individual or entity may have with a country, such as residence or place of formation or management. Unlike the worldwide system of taxation, foreign sourced income of taxpayers is excluded from their income.[60] Although Hong Kong has been a unique example of a jurisdiction employing a "pure" territorial tax system, as discussed above, most countries that employ some type of exemption mechanism exempt foreign active business income but not passive investment income.[61] For example, certain income earned by foreign subsidiaries and branch operations in Canada, France, and the Netherlands may be exempt from further domestic corporate income tax so that profits are taxed only by the country where the income is earned.[62] According to the US Joint Committee on Taxation, a territorial tax system arguably promotes economic efficiency better than a worldwide tax system because a territorial system treats all investments within a particular source country the same, regardless of the residency of the investor. This efficiency norm is referred to as capital import neutrality or, in the business community, "competitiveness."[63]

including dividends from foreign subsidiaries paid out of foreign business income), allowing foreign tax credit for foreign passive income, and disallowing foreign losses to offset domestic source income: see McDaniel, above note 27 at 290–91.

[60] For an explanation of the Canadian rules relating to source, see Li, Cockfield, & Wilkie, above note 2 at 62–64. For an explanation of the rules relating to sourcing under the *Code*, above note 4, §§ 861–65, see Bittker & Lokken, above note 13, ch 73.

[61] See Alex Easson, *Tax Incentives for Foreign Direct Investment* (The Hague: Kluwer Law International, 2004) at 45. Under the territorial tax system in Hong Kong, residents, including companies, are not taxed on their foreign sourced income. Some other countries, including France and Malaysia, apply a territorial system to companies but not to individual residents (*ibid*). See also Arnold & McIntyre, above note 57 at 44–45. The lack of a partial exemption system in the United States may have encouraged the expatriation of US multinational enterprises to low cost tax jurisdictions for various tax savings on foreign earnings by shifting the corporate group's foreign operations beyond the US taxing jurisdiction: see, generally, United States, Department of the Treasury, Office of Tax Policy, *Corporate Inversion Transactions: Tax Policy Implications* (Washington, DC: United States Government Printing Office, 2002).

[62] See United States, Congress, Joint Economic Committee, *Reforming the U.S. Corporate Tax System to Increase Tax Competitiveness* (Washington, DC: Joint Economic Committee, 2005) at 3–4.

[63] See United States, Congress, Joint Committee on Taxation, *The U.S. International Tax Rules: Background and Selected Issues relating to the Competitiveness of U.S. Business Abroad* (Washington, DC: Joint Committee on Taxation, 2003) at 4. See the discussion in Section 3, above in this chapter, for a description of capital import neutrality and capital export neutrality.

Some proponents of a worldwide tax system argue that a territorial tax system is, in fact, not more simple to operate than a worldwide system[64] and that, moreover, if the deficiencies in the current US tax system were addressed, the need to shift the current US international taxation approach to an exemption system would be removed.[65] A worldwide system, it can be argued, also preserves the tax base of the residence country more effectively than a pure territorial approach.[66] It has also been argued that in actual operation the worldwide system together with a foreign tax credit and exemption system often yields quite similar results in relieving double taxation.[67] This argument appears to rest on the presumption that the tax rates of the residence and the source state are comparable. However, low cost tax jurisdictions continue to attract US and other high-tax-country multinational enterprises for various purposes, including call centres, international trading, contract manufacturing, and research and development centres, which illustrates that in the real world the two existing systems are not really the same.

---

[64] One common countercriticism is that many, if not all, of the technical tax issues found in the worldwide system are also present in the territorial system, such as the need for rules on residential qualifications, source of income, source of expenses, allocation of expenses and deductions, outbound transfers of property, and transfer pricing in related party transactions. Additionally, shifting to an exemption system would not eliminate the need for antideferral rules, such as those found in the US Subpart F regime: see, for example, McDaniel, above note 27 at 293–94. See also Arnold & McIntyre, above note 57 at 44–45 (simplification benefits are often illusory).

[65] Professor Lawrence Lokken, above note 38, argues that deficiencies in the existing US worldwide system are not inherent in that system and that they distort its effectiveness by allowing many multinational enterprises to pay less tax than they would under an exemption system. Professor Lokken gives examples of a number of distortions in the *Code*, involving the check-the-box, foreign tax credit, and sourcing rules, which he points out are not inherent deficiencies in the system and can and should be fixed.

[66] See United States, Congress, Joint Committee on Taxation, *Background Materials on Business Tax Issues* (Washington, DC: Joint Committee on Taxation, 2002) at 53–56 [JCT, *Background Materials on Business Tax*].

[67] The distinction between the exemption and foreign tax credit systems may be exaggerated where a country permits exemption of foreign sourced income only if taxed "comparably" in the foreign jurisdiction: see, for example, Michael J Graetz & Michael M O'Hear, "The 'Original Intent' of U.S. International Taxation" (1997) 46 *Duke Law Journal* 1021 at 1064–65. See also Hugh J Ault, *Comparative Income Taxation: A Structural Analysis* (Boston: Kluwer Law International, 1997) at 381–82.

5.2 Horizontal Equity and Vertical Equity

Under the concept of horizontal equity, taxpayers resident in the residence state who earn the same or similar amounts of income (regardless of its source, domestic or foreign) should be subject to tax at a similar overall effective rate. As an illustration, Taxpayer #1, who lives in Toronto and who earns $100,000 in interest income from sources in a foreign country with a zero rate of tax, should be subject to a tax rate in Canada equivalent to the tax rate that Taxpayer #2, who lives in Ottawa and who earns $100,000 in interest income from sources in Canada, is subject to. If Taxpayer #1 could exclude her income because it was foreign sourced, both Canadian resident taxpayers would earn substantially the equivalent income economically, but the principle of horizontal equity would be violated because Taxpayer #1 would not be subject to tax on her income. A worldwide tax system helps to promote horizontal equity (and, as we shall see below, vertical equity as well).[68]

Both Canada and the United States employ a progressive income tax that generally taxes resident taxpayers earning more income at progressively higher marginal rates. A worldwide or foreign tax credit system helps promote the policy that higher income earners ought to carry a larger proportion of the tax burden. Under the concept of vertical equity, including foreign and domestic source income of a taxpayer helps to further the policy of a progressive income tax by applying the marginal rate system to the actual overall amount of income earned by a taxpayer.[69] As an illustration, take the horizontal equity example above: If Taxpayer #1 could exclude her income because it was earned abroad, she would be subject to a lower marginal rate of tax than Taxpayer #2, even though both taxpayers earned economically the identical income and should hence be in the same effective tax bracket. Plainly, a move toward an exemption system where investors were able to shift their income abroad would potentially violate both horizontal and vertical equity.[70]

---

[68] See JCT, *Background Materials on Business Tax*, above note 66 at 53–56; Cockfield, *Examining Policy Options*, above note 35 at 8; Graetz, "Taxing International Income," above note 34 at 301.

[69] See JCT, *Background Materials on Business Tax*, above note 66 at 53–56.

[70] See McDaniel, above note 27 at 301.

5.3 Internation Equity

In addition to theories that support economic efficiency and equities, as described above, within a sovereign country in the making of international tax policy, there is a theory that relates to the sharing of international tax revenues between nations.[71] Under internation equity, to be just, a nation contemplating its international tax policy should consider a fiscal delineation of its tax base and taxpayers in a way that fosters internation equity.[72] In reality, the best opportunity for this division of revenues between residence and source state to occur generally, and to factor in the domestic policy and equity concerns of both nations, is in the context of a tax treaty.[73] Tax treaties allow a country to ensure that its agreements to share revenue with foreign nations support its existing tax policy goals. Moreover, tax treaties can enable a country to foster larger diplomatic and foreign policy goals, which may include the promotion of international trade and investment to assist a developing nation, foreign aid, and humanitarian considerations.

Further Readings

Arnold, Brian J. *Reforming Canada's International Tax System: Toward Coherence and Simplicity* (Toronto: Canadian Tax Foundation, 2009).

Arnold, Brian J, & Michael J McIntyre. *International Tax Primer*, 2d ed (The Hague: Kluwer Law International, 2002).

Ault, Hugh J. *Comparative Income Taxation: A Structural Analysis* (Boston: Kluwer Law International, 1997).

Beveridge, Fiona. *The Treatment and Taxation of Foreign Investment under International Law: Towards International Disciplines* (Manchester: Manchester University Press, 2000).

[71] See Cockfield, *NAFTA Tax Law and Policy*, above note 42 at 20–21; Peggy B Musgrave, "Interjurisdictional Equity in Company Taxation: Principles and Applications to the European Union" in Sijbren Cnossen, ed, *Taxing Capital Income in the European Union: Issues and Options for Reform* (Oxford: Oxford University Press, 2000) 47; Nancy H Kaufman, "Fairness and the Taxation of International Income" (1998) 29 *Law and Policy in International Business* 145 at 188–201.

[72] See *ibid*.

[73] See Graetz, *Foundations*, above note 30 at 11.

Cockfield, Arthur J. *NAFTA Tax Law and Policy: Resolving the Clash between Economic and Sovereignty Interests* (Toronto: University of Toronto Press, 2005).

Easson, Alex. *Tax Incentives for Foreign Direct Investment* (The Hague: Kluwer Law International, 2004).

Graetz, Michael J. *Foundations of International Income Taxation* (New York: Foundation Press, 2003).

Kerzner, David S, Vitaly Timokhov, & David W Chodikoff, eds. *The Tax Advisor's Guide to the Canada–U.S. Tax Treaty* (Toronto: Thomson Reuters Carswell, 2008) (loose-leaf).

Kindred, Hugh M, & Phillip M Saunders, eds. *International Law Chiefly as Interpreted and Applied in Canada*, 7th ed (Toronto: Emond Montgomery, 2006).

Li, Jinyan, Arthur Cockfield, & J Scott Wilkie. *International Taxation in Canada — Principles and Practices*, 2d ed (Markham, ON: LexisNexis, 2011).

Morgan, Edward M. *International Law and the Canadian Courts: Sovereign Immunity, Criminal Jurisdiction, Aliens' Rights and Taxation Powers* (Toronto: Carswell, 1990).

Musgrave, Peggy B. "Interjurisdictional Equity in Company Taxation: Principles and Applications to the European Union" in Sijbren Cnossen, ed, *Taxing Capital Income in the European Union: Issues and Options for Reform* (Oxford: Oxford University Press, 2000).

3

The OECD's War on Offshore Tax Evasion 1996–2014

1 Introduction

In the late 1990s, the OECD increasingly took formal notice of a phenomenon occurring in select jurisdictions around the world that was causing serious harm to fiscal authorities (of members and non-members alike) and impeding the organization's aims to advance global economic growth and development. This phenomenon or problem manifested itself in places where financial institutions from Europe to the Caribbean could offer bank accounts on which little or no taxes were payable by the account holders. At the heart of this problem were the jurisdictions' strict secrecy laws that forbade, including under threat of criminal penalty, the disclosure of the account holders' identities. This combination of low taxes and bank secrecy offered citizens and residents of OECD member countries a unique investment service that their home country could not provide (or compete with) — a place to grow their wealth and hide both assets and income from tax authorities. These "tropical investment conditions" had serious global financial, economic, and political repercussions that the OECD recognized and began to take aim at. As explained in this chapter, the cannon that the OECD constructed in 2002 to destroy tax havens' bank

D.S. Kerzner, D.W. Chodikoff, *International Tax Evasion in the Global Information Age*, DOI 10.1007/978-3-319-40421-9_3

secrecy laws was a single-purpose bilateral treaty known as the *Agreement on Exchange of Information on Tax Matters*.[1] Automatic exchange of information (Automatic Exchange) was not yet the primary focus of the OECD during the period 1996 to 2013, and is discussed in Chapter 8.

This chapter begins by reviewing the goals of international tax and treaty law and considering the relationship between these goals and exchange of information (EOI) and to what extent EOI may be said to support these goals. After this, the chapter describes the nature of the perceived fiscal threat, facing the OECD member states and other countries, posed by tax havens and certain developed countries that offer preferential tax regimes. It then examines the stated policy objectives of the OECD surrounding EOI and of the Global Forum on Transparency and Exchange of Information for Tax Purposes (Global Forum), the United States, and Canada. The chapter concludes with an evaluation of the OECD's war on offshore tax evasion during the period 1998 to 2014.

2 EOI and the Goals of International Tax and Treaty Law

2.1 International Tax Policy

A primary goal of international tax policy has been to relieve double taxation that arises from the claims of residence and source countries so that income is taxed only once. More recently, a key goal of international tax policy has been to combat tax evasion.[2] The importance of this goal can be seen in recent efforts of the Global Forum and its peer review project, the announcement by the G20 in 2013 of its commitment to Automatic Exchange, and the promulgation and worldwide implementation by the United States of the *Foreign Account Tax Compliance Act*.[3] As explained in

[1] OECD, *Agreement on Exchange of Information on Tax Matters* (Paris: OECD, 2002) [treaty and commentary together: *Model TIEA*].

[2] See Chapter 2, Section 3.

[3] Enacted by Congress as part of the *Hiring Incentives to Restore Employment (HIRE) Act*, Public Law 111-147, and signed into law by the president on 18 March 2010 [*FATCA*].

more detail below, EOI by request as found in both double tax conventions (DTCs) and tax information exchange agreements (TIEAs) supports the goal of combatting international tax evasion by providing fiscal authorities in Canada and the United States (and elsewhere) with a legal mechanism to obtain foreign information regarding the offshore income of a tax resident under examination. Moreover, TIEAs fill a gap by allowing Canada and the United States to exchange tax information on a bilateral basis with foreign countries where economic and other circumstances may not justify a DTC (which has some thirty articles, including one on EOI).

Concepts of Neutrality and Equity

International tax policy has also been concerned with neutrality — capital export neutrality (CEN) and capital import neutrality (CIN) — to achieve greater worldwide economic efficiency. In addition to economic efficiency goals, international tax policy has also been concerned with principles of equity — horizontal and vertical equity, and internation equity.

As explained in Chapter 2, where a taxpayer makes an investment decision as to whether to invest domestically or internationally based on factors and considerations other than those relating to tax, CEN may be reached. Under CIN, investment and business activity within a given jurisdiction is subject to the same overall tax level, without regard to the residence or nationality of the investor. The goal of CIN may be realized in a world order where each country (including Canada and the United States) agrees to adopt a pure exemption tax system regarding income earned therein. As both Canada and the United States adopt a worldwide system of taxation for individuals rather than a sourced-based system, the question of whether or not TIEAs support CIN is not considered.

Where CEN is achieved, the incentive to shift mobile capital from a high cost tax jurisdiction to a low or no cost tax jurisdiction would be reduced. Non-tax motives such as lifestyle, asset protection, business, criminal activity–related, and other factors may still drive individuals to transfer capital abroad and away from their residence state. A major hurdle to achieving CEN has been the existence of harmful tax practices and tax havens. It is estimated that as of 2010 the money in offshore tax haven accounts totals more than $21 trillion.[4] In a system where weak information exchange mechanisms and poor transparency rules enable taxpayers who are taxed on a worldwide basis to hide their offshore income from the view of fiscal authorities, tax incentives will continue to motivate shifts in income, thereby hindering CEN. TIEAs can bolster countries' ability to administer and enforce their tax and criminal laws by facilitating the exchange of foreign tax information that can then be used in an examination of a taxpayer. As a result, it can be broadly said that DTCs and TIEAs help advance the goals of CEN by promoting EOI, which assists fiscal authorities in administering a system of worldwide taxation based on residence and citizenship, thereby reducing the attractiveness (i.e., the tax motivation) for the taxpayer of hiding income-producing assets in tax havens.

As explained in greater detail in Chapter 2, the concept of horizontal equity requires that taxpayers who are resident in one jurisdiction and who earn similar amounts of income (whether the source be domestic or foreign) should be subject to tax at a similar overall effective rate. Under the concept of vertical equity, including the income earned by a taxpayer both in his country of residence and outside that country supports the policy of a progressive income tax by enabling the fiscal authorities to apply a marginal rate system to all income earned by a taxpayer. The worldwide tax system, which is the basis for taxation in Canada and the United States, helps to promote both horizontal and vertical equity by assessing income tax on both domestic and foreign sourced income. However, one of the challenges facing both Canada and the United States in achieving horizontal and vertical equity in their respective tax systems arises when CRA and the IRS are unable to assess the foreign income earned by residents and citizens because, for example, that information is

[4] See Janet McFarland & Bill Curry, "Document Leak Reveals Widespread Use of Tax Havens" *Globe and Mail* (5 April 2013), online: www.theglobeandmail.com/report-on-business/economy/document-leak-reveals-widespread-use-of-tax-havens/article10797329/. The estimate is from a report by James S Henry, a former chief economist with the global consulting firm McKinsey & Company. According to the article in the *Globe*, *ibid*, the top five tax haven destinations for Canadian dollars in 2011 were Barbados ($53.3 billion), the Cayman Islands ($25.8 billion), Ireland ($23.5 billion), Luxembourg ($13.8 billion), and Bermuda ($13.2 billion). These figures do not specifically break down which amounts may be attributable to funds held offshore by multinational enterprises, or directly or indirectly (e.g., through nominee entities) to undeclared accounts of individuals.

hidden from them. DTCs and TIEAs allow a fiscal authority that meets the requirements for EOI upon request the ability to obtain foreign information that can be used to support administration and enforcement of a country's tax laws. In this way, EOI through tax treaties helps to bolster the goals of horizontal and vertical equity.

Another concept in international tax policy considered in Chapter 2 is internation equity, which involves the sharing of international tax revenues between countries. Under this concept, a nation can use tax treaties to share revenue with foreign nations, and pursue its foreign policy goals to offer broad assistance to developing nations. As discussed in Chapter 6, Canada offered a kind of carrot to induce tax havens to enter into TIEAs via the lure of increased investments from Canadian companies that would then be eligible to repatriate profits on an exempt basis. This economic incentive, however, is not equivalent to sharing revenues through the use of tax treaties. Moreover, as TIEAs are much more limited in scope and function in sharing information (compared to DTCs), in their existing form they would be a difficult vehicle for Canada or the United States to use to achieve the goals behind internation equity. In addition, many tax haven jurisdictions lack an income or capital tax, and this would make use of traditional vehicles for revenue-sharing opportunities, like DTCs, that could be used to support internation equity unrealistic. Hence, in their present form and use as highly specialized treaties, TIEAs do not appear to support the goals of internation equity.

Historical Legal Background: OECD *Model Tax Convention on Income and on Capital*

Tax treaties or DTCs assist governments and taxpayers alike through the promotion of a variety of related tax policy objectives. As noted in Chapter 2, a major function of DTCs is to relieve taxpayers from double taxation on foreign earned income in large part through apportioning the right to tax such income between the residence state and the source state. To accomplish this, tax treaties contain a series of highly complex mechanisms and rules. For example, the rules on residence aid in the determination of whether a taxpayer is a resident of a contracting state or, if the taxpayer is a resident under the domestic laws of both contracting states, of which jurisdiction has the primary right to tax the taxpayer. Another example of the rules used to apportion the taxing jurisdiction between a residence state and a source state is the tests under the business profits and permanent establishment rules that may determine under what circumstances an enterprise of one contracting state may become subject to income tax, on a net basis, in respect of transactions undertaken by that enterprise in the other contracting state (whether such transactions relate to goods, services, intellectual property, or other investments). As such, these tax treaties provide a measure of predictability in tax planning concerning international trade and investment for companies and individuals taking advantage of the mobility of today's workforce or for individuals who for personal reasons choose to live in multiple countries. Tax treaties also help promote additional goals such as effectiveness of administration and enforcement of a country's tax laws and taxpayer fairness.

The primary method for a country to obtain tax information that is in another jurisdiction is through the use of a bilateral treaty.[5] The OECD *Model Tax Convention on Income and on Capital* appears to provide two broadly based arguments for putting an EOI mechanism into a DTC: (1) to ensure that the convention is properly used and (2) to facilitate the administration of taxation in the contracting states in an age of increasing international commerce and e-commerce, whether or not related to the convention.[6] In furtherance of these objectives, it is envisioned that information will be exchanged by the contracting states, to the widest possible extent, to support the laying of the proper basis for the implementation of the domestic laws of each party and the convention.[7]

---

[5] See Steven A Dean, "The Incomplete Global Market for Tax Information" (2008) 49 *Boston College Law Review* 605 at 637 [Dean, "Incomplete Global Market"]: Professor Dean observes that countries rely on the treaty EOI mechanism to ensure access to information "that would otherwise lie out of their reach."

[6] OECD, Committee on Fiscal Affairs, *Model Tax Convention on Income and on Capital* (Paris, OECD) (loose-leaf) commentary to Art 26 at paras 1–2 [treaty and commentary together: *Model Tax Treaty*]. Historically, one of the four treaty models presented in a report to the League of Nations addressed the exchange of extraterritorial tax information: *Double Taxation and Tax Evasion: Report Presented by the Committee of Technical Experts on Double Taxation and Tax Evasion, League of Nations*, Doc C.216.M.85.1927.II (1927).

[7] See *Model Tax Treaty*, above note 6, Art 26(1) and commentary to Art 26 at para 5.

Article 26 of the *Model Tax Treaty* underwent a substantial revision in 2006 based on the use of the 2002 *Model TIEA*.[8] The commentary to Article 26(1) of the *Model Tax Treaty* provides, in part, that "[t]he competent authorities of the Contracting States shall exchange such information as is foreseeably relevant for carrying out the provisions of this Convention or to the administration or enforcement of the domestic laws concerning their political subdivisions."[9] The commentary also notes that the "foreseeable relevance" language is a standard intended to provide for EOI in tax matters of the widest possible extent but with the limitation that its scope not encompass "fishing expeditions" or requests that are unlikely to be relevant to the tax matters of a particular taxpayer.[10]

As noted in Chapter 2, international law generally prohibits a sovereign act of state on a foreign territory without the consent of the other sovereign.[11] This is particularly true of conducting discovery of documents or of persons in a foreign territory without the consent of that state. Professor Vogel notes that the proper implementation of a DTC necessitates by design information from foreign sources and, further, that the EOI provision was included to overcome barriers of international law that may otherwise frustrate the gathering of this foreign information.[12] More recently, between 2000 and 2010, the emphasis on EOI has been driven by the need to ratchet up the fight against increasing tax fraud and evasion.[13] EOI is also important in combatting money laundering and

[8] See Tonny Schenk-Geers, *International Exchange of Information and the Protection of Taxpayers* (Alphen aan den Rijn, NL: Kluwer Law International, 2009) at 77. The focus of this work is the EOI and related laws in the European Union. Schenk-Geers, *ibid* at 94, observes that since the commentary to the 1963 *Model Tax Treaty* (Art 26 at para 3) mentions exchange to benefit "the correct implementation of the Convention, and also of the internal laws of the Contracting States," the original intent of the EOI article was to create two separate objectives.

[9] *Model Tax Treaty*, above note 6, commentary to Art 26 at paras 1–2.

[10] *Ibid*, commentary to Art 26 at para 5. See Schenk-Geers, above note 8 at 94.

[11] See Chapter 2, Section 2.2.

[12] Klaus Vogel, *Klaus Vogel on Double Taxation Conventions*, 3d ed (London: Kluwer Law International, 1997) at 1403. Professor Dean in "Incomplete Global Market," above note 5 at 607, notes that the challenges relating to enforcement of tax laws are increased when sought-after information is foreign sourced.

[13] See Schenk-Geers, above note 8 at 75.

corruption.[14] Moreover, a new policy objective of bank transparency for tax purposes has been sounded against the backdrop of the global financial crisis, with the goal of restoring integrity and stability to financial institutions.[15] Although EOI is important to achieving multiple policy objectives, the overriding focus of this book will be on its use in combatting tax evasion.

Under Article 26 of the *Model Tax Treaty*, information may be exchanged generally in three different ways: (1) on request by a state with a special case in mind, (2) automatically by a state through systematic transmission usually concerning information about one or various categories of income, and (3) spontaneously by a state that acquires information through an examination that it believes may be of interest to the other state.[16]

3 The Gathering Storm: Harmful Tax Competition and the Problems Posed by Tax Havens and Preferential Regimes

Harmful tax competition (or harmful tax practices) refers to a collective behaviour by both tax havens and harmful preferential tax regimes whose aim is to "affect the location of financial and other service activities, erode the tax bases of other countries, distort trade and investment patterns and undermine the fairness, neutrality and broad social acceptance of tax systems generally."[17]

In more concise terms, harmful tax competition arises when a country uses its tax rules to lure (or poach)[18] geographically mobile activities

[14] See OECD, *OECD's Current Tax Agenda* (Paris: OECD, 2011) at 89–90 [*OECD 2011 Current Tax Agenda*].

[15] See United States, Congress, Joint Committee on Taxation, *Explanation of Proposed Protocol to the Income Tax Treaty between the United States and Switzerland* (Washington, DC: Joint Committee on Taxation, 2011) at 23, online: www.jct.gov/publications.html?func=startdown&id=3791.

[16] For a more detailed description of Art 26 of the *Model Tax Treaty*, above note 6, see Chapter 7.

[17] OECD, *Harmful Tax Competition: An Emerging Global Issue* (Paris: OECD, 1998) at 8 [*OECD 1998 Report*].

[18] See Robert T Kudrle, "The OECD's Harmful Tax Competition Initiative and the Tax Havens: From Bombshell to Damp Squib" (2008) 8 *Global Economy Journal* 1 at 4.

such as financial investment and services (including the provision of intangibles) from non-residents.[19] This tax competition encourages non-compliance with the tax laws of other nations[20] and can become harmful between countries by eroding the tax bases of nations, disrupting principles of tax neutrality, creating unfairness in the tax system, and distorting international trade and investment (including financial and real investment flows).[21] Overall, as honest taxpayers perceive that they are carrying a greater proportion of the tax burden and that their government is failing to effectively enforce its tax laws, confidence in the integrity and fairness of not only the tax system but also the government can decline.[22] With respect to services, one commentator observes that the critical service being sought by individual investors is secrecy, which has become the ultimate focus of the harmful tax competition project.[23] These harmful practices have been driven by the acceleration of global trade and investment.[24]

In 1996, the OECD Council directed the OECD to "develop measures to counter the distorting effects of harmful tax competition on investment and financing decisions and the consequences for national tax bases, and report back in 1998."[25] By providing a framework to eliminate harmful

[19] See Jinyan Li, Arthur Cockfield, & J Scott Wilkie, *International Taxation in Canada — Principles and Practices*, 2d ed (Markham, ON: LexisNexis, 2011) at 327. Hugh J Ault, "Reflections on the Role of the OECD in Developing International Tax Norms" (2009) 34 *Brooklyn Journal of International Law* 757 at 763, describes "harmful tax competition" as a circumstance "where one country's tax system can have a potentially negative impact on those of other countries." In 1996, the OECD ministers requested that the organization develop measures to counter the effects of harmful tax competition and report on its work in 1998 (*ibid* at 764). The *OECD 1998 Report*, above note 17, created the Forum on Harmful Tax Practices (*ibid* at 767). Professor Ault, *ibid*, refers to the recommendations of the *OECD 1998 Report* as, although not legally binding, a "soft" international undertaking that has created substantial peer pressure to act in accordance with the recommendations.

[20] See OECD, *The OECD's Project on Harmful Tax Practices: The 2001 Progress Report* (Paris: OECD, 2001) at 4 [*OECD 2001 Progress Report*].

[21] See *OECD 1998 Report*, above note 17 at 7–8. See also Kudrle, above note 18 at 5, observing that the roots of the harmful tax competition project lie chiefly in EU concerns that certain forms of intra-union competition were eroding the tax bases of member states, both individual and corporate. See also *OECD 2001 Progress Report*, above note 20 at 4.

[22] See *OECD 2001 Progress Report*, above note 20 at 4.

[23] *Ibid* at 5.

[24] See *OECD 1998 Report*, above note 17 at 15.

[25] OECD, Council at Ministerial Level, Communique (21–22 May 2006) at para 15(xv), cited in Diane M Ring, "Who Is Making International Tax Policy? International Organizations as Power Players in a High Stakes World" (2009) 33 *Fordham International Law Journal* 649 at 704.

tax practices, the OECD believed that all nations (including non-OECD, small, and poor) could promote healthy tax competition to achieve the OECD's aims to foster global economic growth and development.[26] With these objectives in mind, the OECD published its report in 1998 entitled *Harmful Tax Competition: An Emerging Global Issue.*[27] The *OECD 1998 Report* identified for the first time two key problems in the taxation of geographically mobile activities, notably tax havens and harmful preferential tax regimes.[28] The report created significant controversy among states and businesses that benefited from the existing system.[29] The report allowed the OECD to develop measures designed to counter harmful tax practices and ultimately provided the foundation for the OECD's work in this area.[30] The OECD identified the two primary contributors to these harmful tax practices as being tax havens and so-called preferential tax regimes.[31] It viewed tax havens (comprising for the most part sovereign countries or fiscally sovereign territories) as possessing four key identifying factors: (1) no or only nominal taxes, (2) lack of effective EOI, (3) lack of transparency (relating to the legislative, legal, or administrative provisions of a jurisdiction), and (4) investment with no substantial activities.[32]

The OECD further noted that the lack of effective EOI by tax havens denied fiscal authorities access to bank information that was critical to raising revenue and preventing tax avoidance and base erosion.[33] In addition

---

[26] See *OECD 2001 Progress Report*, above note 20 at 4.

[27] *OECD 1998 Report*, above note 17.

[28] See Reuven S Avi-Yonah, "The OECD Harmful Tax Competition Report: A Retrospective after a Decade" (2009) 34 *Brooklyn Journal of International Law* 783, citing OECD, *Revenue Statistics 1965–2007* (Paris: OECD, 2008) at 19 [*Revenue Statistics*]; Richard M Bird & Eric M Zolt, "Redistribution via Taxation: The Limited Role of the Personal Income Tax in Developing Countries" (2005) 52 *UCLA Law Review* 1627, arguing that the OECD effort was successful on the basis of data showing no decline in individual or corporate tax revenues in OECD member countries.

[29] For a detailed history and discussion of the opposition to the report, and in particular that of the United States, see Ring, above note 25.

[30] See OECD, *The OECD's Project on Harmful Tax Practices: 2006 Update on Progress in Member Countries* (Paris: OECD, 2006) at 2 [*OECD 2006 Report*].

[31] The OECD's work in this area was carried out primarily through the Forum on Harmful Tax Practices, which was a subsidiary body of the Committee on Fiscal Affairs: see OECD, *The OECD's Project on Harmful Tax Practices: The 2004 Progress Report* (Paris: OECD, 2004) at 4.

[32] *Ibid* at 23.

[33] *Ibid* at 24.

to preventing tax avoidance, effective EOI was also viewed by the OECD as key to allowing governments to ensure that their own tax laws were being followed, especially with the increasing regularity of cross-border transactions in a global economy.[34] The OECD noted that as taxpayers' level of foreign activities and investments expanded, reliance on effective EOI became more important to tax enforcement, citing the problems with the reliance of governments on taxpayers' use of their foreign-reporting systems.[35] The OECD further observed that the lack of transparency evidenced by these regimes, which prevented EOI, facilitated not only tax evasion but also other illegal activities such as money laundering.[36] In Canada, the Financial Transactions and Reports Analysis Centre of Canada (FINTRAC) is the government agency authorized to gather tax information from tax authorities under certain conditions relating to money laundering and terrorist investigations.[37] Estimates of annual US tax losses from individual evasion using tax havens in 2008 were $100 billion.[38]

In addition to tax havens, the OECD also identified both member and non-member countries with established tax policies to attract mobile financial and other service activities, which the OECD referred to as "harmful preferential tax regimes" because they had certain features that have the potential to create harmful tax competition. The four principal factors by which the OECD identified harmful preferential tax regimes were (1) no or low effective tax rates, (2) "ring fencing" of regimes, (3) lack of transparency, and (4) lack of effective EOI.[39] Some of the factors that the OECD considered indicators of harmful preferential tax

[34] *OECD 2001 Progress Report*, above note 20 at 5.

[35] *Ibid.*

[36] *Ibid.* See Arthur J Cockfield, "Protecting Taxpayer Privacy Rights under Enhanced Cross-border Tax Information Exchange: Toward a Multilateral Taxpayer Bill of Rights" (2010) 42 *University of British Columbia Law Review* 420, recommending that governments consider adopting a multilateral agreement on taxpayer rights to ensure that tax information is transferred across borders with minimum standards of legal protection.

[37] FINTRAC, online: www.fintrac.gc.ca/intro-eng.asp.

[38] See United States, US Senate Permanent Subcommittee on Investigations, *Staff Report on Tax Haven Banks and U.S. Tax Compliance* (Washington, DC: United States Government Printing Office, 2008) at 1.

[39] *OECD 1998 Report*, above note 17 at 27. Typically, in a ring-fencing situation, a jurisdiction limits tax advantages to non-residents (and also excludes resident companies), thereby protecting its own tax base from the harmful effects of its policies.

regimes included an artificial definition of the tax base, failure to adhere to international transfer pricing guidelines, exemption of foreign sourced income from taxation by the resident country, negotiable tax rate or tax base, existence of secrecy provisions, and access to a wide network of tax treaties.[40] A lack of transparency may arise, for example, because of the following: the regime's provision of favourable administrative rulings that are not based on treating similarly situated taxpayers equally and on well-known ruling criteria, the existence of special administrative practices that encourage corruption and discriminatory treatment, and the regime's failure to enforce its domestic fiscal laws.[41] Lack of transparency is also present if there is inadequate regulatory supervision or if the government does not have legal access to financial records to identify the owners of income and assets.[42] In 2000, the OECD threatened to publish a list of "uncooperative tax havens" (a so-called blacklist) as a means of inducing jurisdictions to agree to remove certain harmful tax practices.[43] By 2002, twenty-eight of the original thirty-five offshore jurisdictions on the "draft" uncooperative list had made various commitments around harmful tax practices and EOI, with only seven being named on the official list in 2002.[44] Lorraine Eden and Robert Kudrle noted that among the challenges facing the OECD's harmful tax competition project were (1) general ambivalence in the OECD membership toward tax havens and (2) the policy debate around national competitiveness and the desire to respect national sovereignty.[45]

---

[40] *Ibid* at 30–34.

[41] *Ibid* at 28–29.

[42] See *OECD 2001 Progress Report*, above note 20 at 5.

[43] See Avi-Yonah, above note 28 at 785. See also Lorraine Eden & Robert T Kudrle, "Tax Havens: Renegade States in the International Tax Regime?" (2005) 27 *Law and Policy* 100 at 122, noting that one problem faced by the OECD was a general ambivalence among OECD members toward tax havens, based in part on pressure for national competitiveness and respect for national sovereignty.

[44] See Avi-Yonah, above note 28 at 786. In commenting on the need for defensive measures to deal with uncooperative jurisdictions, Professor Ault, above note 19 at 771, recognizes that "establishing international norms" in some cases requires the combination of "cooperation and enforcement mechanisms."

[45] See Eden & Kudrle, above note 43 at 122, examining the OECD's harmful tax competition project and arguing that tax havens were initially viewed as renegade states in the international tax community and that the combination of globalization, an increase in the number of tax havens, and the Internet was ultimately a strong motivator for international action.

The initial aims of the harmful tax competition project were to (1) identify and eliminate harmful features of preferential tax regimes in OECD countries, (2) identify "tax havens" and seek their commitment to the principles of transparency and effective EOI, and (3) encourage other non-OECD countries' association with the project.[46] Of the forty-seven preferential tax regimes that had been identified as potentially harmful in 2000, eighteen regimes were abolished and fourteen were amended to remove their potentially harmful features while upon reconsideration thirteen were found not to be harmful.[47] Accordingly, the OECD concluded that its objectives regarding harmful preferential tax regimes in member countries had been addressed.[48] By 2004, all but a small handful of the tax havens had agreed in principle to follow transparency and effective EOI standards of the kind embodied in the OECD's *Model TIEA*, released in March 2002.[49] Ultimately, the OECD's focus shifted away from harmful tax competition to EOI and transparency.[50] Although not the focus of this study, as noted above, it is important to recognize that there are differing scholarly viewpoints of what is fair and efficient in designing international tax policy. From the vantage point of tax havens, the aims of the OECD's harmful tax competition project could be seen as dangerous to their unique political, social, and economic systems. Regarding the OECD's project, Allison Christians asks, "why should the principles and standards articulated by a relatively small and elite group of individuals frame the taxing rights of sovereign nations?"[51] Professor Christians observes that through its work on harmful tax competition the

[46] See *OECD 2006 Report*, above note 30 at 2–3.

[47] *Ibid* at 3–6.

[48] *Ibid* at 6.

[49] See Kudrle, above note 18 at 10: Professor Kudrle after conducting an economic analysis of certain tax haven data concludes that no significant impact from the project on tax evasion could be found. He theorizes that this is because investments in tax havens remain very easy to disguise and are difficult to detect.

[50] See Ring, above note 25 at 717.

[51] Allison Christians, "Sovereignty, Taxation and Social Contract" (2009) 18 *Minnesota Journal of International Law* 99. Professor Christians, *ibid* at 101–2, examines the OECD's work on harmful tax competition from a political philosophy perspective to identify the existence of a global social contract for taxation and to assess its content and implications, observing that the OECD's work "evidences an emergent vision of sovereignty that entails positive obligations or duties of nations in exercising the power to tax."

OECD has developed a theory of "sovereign duty" wherein the sovereign state in exercising its right to tax as a member of the global community must conform to certain universal principles established by the OECD..

4 The Problems Created by Bank Secrecy

The OECD identified tax havens as being one of the two primary contributors to harmful tax practices (the other being so-called preferential tax regimes). It further viewed tax havens as possessing four key identifying factors: (1) no or only nominal taxes, (2) lack of effective EOI, (3) lack of transparency, and (4) investment with no substantial activities.[52] Among these attributes, the critical one sought by individual investors, and the ultimate focus of the OECD's harmful tax competition project, was secrecy.[53] The *OECD 1998 Report* observed:

> these tax haven jurisdictions do not allow tax administrations access to bank information for the critical purposes of detecting and preventing tax avoidance which, from the perspectives of raising revenue and controlling base erosion from financial and other service activities, are as important as curbing tax fraud. Thus, the lack of effective exchange of information is one of the key factors in identifying a tax haven since it limits access by tax authorities to the information required for the correct and timely application of tax laws.[54]

Taxpayers use bank secrecy laws in foreign jurisdictions both to hide their illegal activities from governments and to escape tax. The bank secrecy laws of a tax haven or foreign jurisdiction impede access to and analysis of records of financial transactions by fiscal and law enforcement authorities. As a result, these bank secrecy laws can and do hinder the effective administration and enforcement of countries' laws.[55] In addition, bank

---

[52] *OECD 1998 Report*, above note 17 at 24.

[53] See Kudrle, above note 18 at 5.

[54] *OECD 1998 Report*, above note 17 at 15.

[55] See OECD, *Improving Access to Bank Information for Tax Purposes* (Paris: OECD, 2000) at 7. Without such records of financial transactions, a tax authority may be unable to determine and

secrecy laws distort the distribution of the tax burden and call into question the fairness of the tax system by allowing some taxpayers to evade paying tax on income earned in their offshore accounts.[56] Moreover, bank secrecy can create unjustified advantages between different categories of income such as mobile capital versus income derived from employment or immovable property.[57]

Allowing fiscal authorities to access valuable information about bank deposits and withdrawals can unlock a treasure trove of pathways to discovering a number of improprieties that may otherwise remain concealed, such as unreported legal or illegal income, false deductions, back-to-back loan transactions, sham transactions, and bribes or suspicious payments.[58] Permitting greater access to such bank information may also aid in the collection of tax liabilities.[59] In 2000, the OECD believed that the availability of jurisdictions with bank secrecy laws was exponentially compounding these problems and advocated the use of specific requests for information to facilitate direct or indirect access to bank information.[60]

5 The Global Forum and EOI

The OECD's Global Forum was established in 2000.[61] It developed the *Model TIEA* in 2002 to address the issues arising from the harmful tax practices project and in 2005 adopted standards on transparency that relate to the availability and reliability of information.[62] The primary

collect the correct amount of tax (*ibid* at 9). Denying access to bank records also greatly facilitates money laundering schemes that deal with the proceeds of crime to conceal their illegal origins (*ibid* at 25).

[56] See *ibid.*

[57] See *ibid.*

[58] See *ibid* at 8.

[59] See *ibid.*

[60] *Ibid* at 13.

[61] As of 2011, the Global Forum included 105 member jurisdictions and the European Union: see OECD, *Tax Transparency 2011: Report on Progress* (Paris: OECD, 2011) at 10 [*Tax Transparency 2011 Report*].

[62] See *OECD 2011 Current Tax Agenda*, above note 14 at 84. The 2002 *Model TIEA*, above note 1, includes a commentary on the agreement and provides both a bilateral and a multilateral approach to information exchange.

difference between the *Model TIEA*, the Council of Europe and the OECD's *Convention on Mutual Administrative Assistance in Tax Matters*,[63] and Article 26 of the *Model Tax Treaty* is that the *Model TIEA* is limited to EOI on request.[64] The main function of the Global Forum is to promote the effective implementation of the OECD's standards on transparency and EOI.[65] The OECD created these standards, which are primarily contained in Article 26 of the *Model Tax Treaty* and the *Model TIEA*.[66] The standards require the following:

- Exchange of information on request where it is "foreseeably relevant" to the administration and enforcement of the domestic laws of the treaty partner.
- No restrictions on exchange caused by bank secrecy or domestic tax interest requirements.
- Availability of reliable information and powers to obtain it.
- Respect for taxpayers' rights.
- Strict confidentiality of information exchanged.[67]

The Global Forum has broken these standards down further into ten essential elements of transparency and EOI for tax purposes, which are used in its peer review of participating jurisdictions.[68] The ten essential elements are as follows:

A Availability of Information

A.1. Jurisdictions should ensure that ownership and identity information for all relevant entities and arrangements is available to their competent authorities.

A.2. Jurisdictions should ensure that reliable accounting records are kept for all relevant entities and arrangements.

---

[63] 25 January 1988, EurTS No 127.

[64] See *OECD 2011 Current Tax Agenda*, above note 14 at 84.

[65] See *Tax Transparency 2011 Report*, above note 61 at 29.

[66] See OECD, *The Global Forum on Transparency and Exchange of Information for Tax Purposes, Information Brief* (Paris: OECD, 2013) at 6 [*Global Forum Information Brief*].

[67] *Ibid.*

[68] *Ibid.*

A.3. Banking information should be available for all account-holders.

B Access to Information

B.1. Competent authorities should have the power to obtain and provide information that is the subject of a request under an EOI agreement from any person within their territorial jurisdiction who is in possession or control of such information.

B.2. The rights and safeguards that apply to persons in the requested jurisdiction should be compatible with effective exchange of information.

C Exchanging Information

C.1. EOI mechanisms should provide for effective exchange of information.

C.2. The jurisdictions' network of information exchange mechanisms should cover all relevant partners.

C.3. The jurisdictions' mechanisms for exchange of information should have adequate provisions to ensure the confidentiality of information received.

C.4. The exchange of information mechanisms should respect the rights and safeguards of taxpayers and third parties.

C.5. The jurisdiction should provide information under its network of agreements in a timely manner.[69]

In 2010, the Global Forum began a rigorous peer review process "as the best practical way to guarantee effective implementation" of information exchange.[70] The ultimate stated goal of the Global Forum's work was to determine whether it had "improved transparency and made exchange

[69] *Ibid.*

[70] OECD, *Tax Transparency 2011 Report*, above note 61 at 40. Phase 1 of the peer review process assessed the quality of a jurisdiction's legal and regulatory framework for EOI while Phase 2 looked at the practical operation of that framework (*ibid* at 42).

of information more effective in practice."[71] In April 2011, the Global Forum released its peer review report for Canada, which concluded that the elements of effective EOI were in place, owing to Canada's long history of EOI for tax purposes.[72] As of 2013, 113 peer review reports had been completed and published.[73]

6 Prequel to Danger: The Peer Review Grades for Tax Havens

6.1 Commentary on the Peer Review Grades

A survey of the ratings provided by the peer review process and interpreted through the letter grades used in Table 3.1, above, reveals that as of the close of 2013, twenty-seven jurisdictions (representing slightly more than one-half of the forty-nine tax havens reviewed) were non-compliant or had failed to have the prescribed measures in place in at least one of the three major categories composing the OECD standards on transparency and effective EOI. In addition, most of the tax havens reviewed (over 85 percent) either had a failure in complying with one of the three major categories or were found to be deficient in one of the three major categories by being only partially compliant with the requirements of that category. Only seven jurisdictions were found to be either largely compliant or compliant in all three major categories. The major category with by far the greatest number of failures relating to the ten essential elements composing the OECD standards was availability of information, which reviews a jurisdiction's competencies in the subcategory areas of

[71] OECD, Global Forum on Transparency and Exchange of Information for Tax Purposes, *Progress Report to the G20 Leaders: Global Forum Update on Effectiveness and On-going Monitoring* (Paris: OECD, 2013) at Executive Summary [*G20 Progress Report*]. The Global Forum's delivery of the overall ratings was looked upon as a "watershed moment" in its evolution (*ibid*).

[72] OECD, *Global Forum on Transparency and Exchange of Information for Tax Purposes Peer Reviews: Canada 2011 — Combined: Phase 1 + Phase 2* (Paris: OECD, 2011) at 8, online: http://dx.doi.org/10.1787/9789264110458-en. The report, *ibid* at 51, notes that Canada has been exchanging information under its DTC network for almost seventy years. Aspects of this report are discussed in further chapters below.

[73] See *Global Forum Information Brief*, above note 66 at 4.

ownership and identity information relating to entities, maintenance of reliable accounting records, and availability of banking information for all account holders. Although beyond the scope of this study, as part of further research into transparency issues around EOI, a correlation analysis (e.g., a Spearman correlation analysis) of the data could be performed to determine how the three aspects of information asymmetry may be related to one another.

Table 3.1 Peer Review Grades for Tax Havens

Tax Haven[a]	Availability of Information[b]	Access to Information[c]	Exchange of Information[d]
Andorra	C[g]	C	A[e]
Anguilla	**F**[h]	C	A
Antigua and Barbuda	**F**	A	A
Aruba	C	C	C
Austria	**F**	C	C
Bahamas	C	A	A
Bahrain	C	C	A
Barbados	C	C	**F**
Belize	**F**	A	A
Bermuda	C	A	C
British Virgin Islands	**F**	**F**	A
Cayman Islands	C	A	A
Cook Islands	**F**	A	A
Costa Rica	**F**	A	C
Cyprus	**F**	**F**	C
Dominica	**F**	**F**	**F**
Gibraltar	**F**	A	A
Grenada	**F**	C	C
Guernsey	C	A	C
Hong Kong	C	A	C
Ireland	A	A	A
Isle of Man	A	A	B[f]
Israel	**F**	C	C
Jersey	C	B	B
Lebanon	**F**	**F**	**F**
Liberia	**F**	A	A
Liechtenstein	**F**	C	C
Luxembourg	**F**	**F**	**F**

(*continued*)

Table 3.1 (continued)

Tax Haven[a]	Availability of Information[b]	Access to Information[c]	Exchange of Information[d]
Macau	C	B	A
Malta	B	A	A
Marshall Islands	**F**	C	C
Mauritius	B	A	A
Monaco	B	C	C
Montserrat	**F**	A	A
Nauru	**F**	**F**	**F**
Netherlands	B	B	B
Niue	C	A	**F**
Panama	**F**	A	B
San Marino	B	A	A
Seychelles	**F**	A	C
Singapore	A	C	C
St Kitts and Nevis	C	A	A
St Lucia	**F**	C	C
St Vincent and the Grenadines	**F**	A	A
Switzerland	**F**	C	**F**
United Arab Emirates	C	C	C
United States	C	A	A
Uruguay	C	C	A
Vanuatu	**F**	**F**	**F**

a The list of tax havens comprises countries that were on the original OECD list of tax havens in 2000, jurisdictions that agreed at the time to eliminate harmful tax practices, and some additional jurisdictions.[74] Israel has been included based upon the recent investigations of the US Department of Justice into one or more Israeli banks,[75] and the United States has also been included based upon its long-standing regime exempting portfolio interest from taxation.[76]

b Availability of information is one of the three major categories that the peer review process used and generally refers to the standards of transparency and EOI as broken down by the Global Forum into their ten essential elements.[77]

[74] The list of tax havens was drawn primarily from the list compiled by Eden & Kudrle, above note 43 at Table 2 (Tax Havens and Their Linkages).

[75] See, for example, David Voreacos, "Bank Leumi Said to Avoid Guilty Plea in Ending Tax Probe" *Bloomberg* (9 June 2014), online: www.bloomberg.com/news/2014-06-08/bank-leumi-said-to-avoid-guilty-plea-in-settling-u-s-tax-probe.html (relating to the bank's Swiss operations).

[76] See discussion of exception for US bank deposits and portfolio interest in Chapter 5, Section Tax Exempt Bank Deposit Interest and Portfolio Interest.

[77] See Section 5, above in this chapter.

c Access to information is one of the three major categories that the peer review process used and generally refers to the standards of transparency and EOI as broken down by the Global Forum into their ten essential elements.[78]
d EOI is one of the three major categories that the peer review process used and generally refers to the standards of transparency and EOI as broken down by the Global Forum into their ten essential elements.[79]
e The grades A, B, C, and F have been created as part of the research for this book and are different from the rating system used by the Global Forum. An A grade signifies the receipt of a grade of "In place" for each element within the given category in Phase 1 and 2 of the peer reviews.[80]
f A B grade signifies the receipt of a grade of "Largely compliant" for a particular element in either Phase 1 or 2 of the peer reviews. This grade has been given only to jurisdictions that received a grade of "Largely compliant" or better for each element within the given category. For example, if under the availability of information category a jurisdiction received the grade "Largely compliant" for A.1. Ownership and the grade "In place" for the other elements in the same category (A.2. Accounting and A.3. Banking Information), the jurisdiction would here receive a B grade for that category overall.[81]
g A C grade signifies the receipt of a grade of "In place, but" or "Partially compliant" for a particular element in either Phase 1 or 2 of the peer reviews. This grade has been given only to jurisdictions that received a grade of "In place, but" or better for each element within the given category. For example, if under the availability of information category a jurisdiction received the grade "In place, but" for A.1. Ownership and the grade "In place" for the other elements in the same category (A.2. Accounting and A.3. Banking Information), the jurisdiction would here receive a C grade for that category overall.[82]
h An F grade signifies the receipt of a grade of "Not in place" or "Non-compliant" for any element within a category in either Phase 1 or 2 of the peer reviews, notwithstanding that the jurisdiction may have received a higher grade for another element within the same category.[83]

---

[78] *Ibid.*

[79] *Ibid.*

[80] The Global Forum initially published compliance ratings with the individual elements of the international standards in 2013 for jurisdictions that had completed only a Phase 1 review and those that had completed Phase 1 and 2 reviews: see *G20 Progress Report*, above note 71 at Annex 2. The list of ratings was updated in 2014: see, for example, OECD, *Report to G20 Leaders Brisbane, Australia* (Paris: OECD, 2014) at Annex 4.

[81] See note 80, above in this chapter.

[82] See *ibid.*

[83] See *ibid.*

7 The OECD and the Global Forum 1996–2014: Strikes, Spares, and Misses

7.1 Introduction

A review of the work of the OECD and the Global Forum in the period 1996 to 2014 reveals a series of separate but related and sometimes overlapping policy objectives regarding TIEAs and EOI. For evaluation purposes, discussion of these policies is divided into three phases: Phase I considers the purpose of the OECD and the Global Forum's work in addressing harmful tax practices in the early years, which led to the creation of TIEAs, Phase II considers the objectives of the *Model TIEA*, and Phase III considers the objectives of the Global Forum and the peer review process, relating to the advancement of the new standards of transparency and EOI as embodied in the *Model TIEA*. The work of the OECD and the Global Forum around TIEAs over the years 1998 to 2014 can be said to represent a story, the TIEA story.

It is important for the evaluation of TIEAs to acknowledge that the *Model TIEA* is part of a larger undertaking by the international community that has been directed at improving the EOI process, especially with tax havens. An examination of the effectiveness of the *Model TIEA* as an instrument to fight tax evasion that left out the history of the Global Forum's work in seeking the accession of non-member jurisdictions to its terms and in implementing the peer review process would inaccurately omit key elements of the TIEA story, elements that have the potential to make EOI more effective today. Therefore, this evaluation considers the merits of the TIEA story and its contribution to the war on tax evasion, rather than solely judging the TIEA instrument and nothing more.

7.2 Phase I: Recognizing Harmful Tax Competition — A Prelude to Action

The special environment of low taxes and bank secrecy fostered by tax haven jurisdictions created tax competition with OECD countries. This tax competition attracted geographically mobile financial and service activities (including the provision of intangibles), through the use, for example, of international trading companies and contract manufacturing, to low cost tax jurisdictions and away from OECD countries with the following harmful results: base erosion, distortion of international trade and investment flows, interference with the administration and enforcement of tax laws, and impairment of the principles of equity and neutrality with respect to those laws.

The OECD in its *OECD 1998 Report* identified the following factors as contributing to harmful tax practices and harmful tax competition: (1) no or nominal taxes, (2) lack of effective EOI, (3) lack of transparency, (4) investment with no substantial activities, and (5) ring fencing of regimes. The OECD found tax havens and so-called preferential tax regimes to be the primary villains responsible for generating these harmful tax practices. Tax cheats tend not to use voluntary foreign-reporting tools to report offshore income on their annual tax returns. As such, the ability of a fiscal authority conducting an audit or exam of a taxpayer suspected of tax avoidance or tax evasion to access foreign account information is key to the administration and enforcement of tax laws, especially with enhanced international trade, investment, and mobility of workers. OECD member countries faced three main legal obstacles to accessing foreign-based taxpayer information: (1) bank secrecy, (2) absence of a treaty EOI mechanism (as most tax havens did not have DTCs with OECD members), and (3) transparency issues relating to the legal and administrative procedures in a tax haven.

The overarching goal of the OECD at this stage was to promote healthy tax competition so that the OECD's aims of fostering global economic growth and development could be achieved. To achieve this overarching goal, the OECD sought to identify harmful tax practices and design a framework to eliminate them. The *OECD 1998 Report* permitted the OECD to create measures intended to counter harmful tax practices. The initial aims of the project were to (1) identify harmful preferential tax regimes, or member and non-member countries whose tax policies attracted mobile financial and service activities, which had the potential to create harmful tax competition, (2) identify tax havens and obtain their commitment to principles of transparency and effective EOI, and (3) encourage non-OECD countries' association with the project. By 2000, the OECD's harmful tax practices project, as carried out by the Forum on Harmful Tax Practices, had identified more than forty jurisdictions with harmful tax practices. By 2005, thirty-five of these jurisdictions had committed through formal documentation to adhere to the OECD standards. And by 2009, the last three remaining uncooperative jurisdictions (Andorra, Liechtenstein, and Monaco) had been removed from the OECD's list of uncooperative tax havens.

7.3 Phase II: The Global Forum and the *Model TIEA* — Taking Action

In 2000, the OECD established the Global Forum, and in 2002 the Global Forum developed the *Model TIEA* to address the issues arising from the harmful tax practices project and to create a legal instrument for effective EOI. The main function of the Global Forum was to promote the effective implementation of the OECD standards on transparency and EOI. The primary impediment to achieving this objective, which needed to be dealt with, was the bank secrecy laws in tax havens.

Allowing fiscal authorities access to offshore bank records was extremely important because opening this doorway could lead to a multitude of potential discoveries that could aid in the administration and enforcement of countries' tax laws. Such access could reveal whether or not the activities of a taxpayer under audit were legal or illegal, including possibly whether they were connected to money laundering, international crime, or terrorism. Additionally, access to bank records could reveal whether deposits in an account originated from tax-paid dollars or from activities, services, transactions, or intangibles that had not been reported to CRA, the IRS, or other fiscal authorities. Most immediately, bank records would identify the period and amounts of income for which a taxpayer had failed to comply with the appropriate foreign-reporting rules and income tax obligations of her residence country (or country of nationality in the case of the United States). The data could also be used to reveal the presence of potential nominee or straw companies, foundations, or conduit entities, set up to circumvent US reporting and withholding rules.

Fiscal authorities could also use bank account information to determine whether to apply various anti-avoidance rules designed to thwart tax avoidance, such as the general anti-avoidance rule or GAAR in Canada and the United States, legal regimes targeting tax shelters, conduit financing (including back-to-back loans), and treaty shopping, or other anti-avoidance regimes such as the substance over form doctrine, circular cash flow doctrine, sham transaction doctrine, and transfer pricing rules enabling a re-allocation of revenues and expenses. Hence, the OECD saw the dismantling of bank secrecy laws and the implementation of effective EOI with tax havens as vital to stopping tax avoidance, base erosion, and the unfair distribution of the tax burden, and to the raising of revenue.

Accordingly, the two main goals behind the *Model TIEA* were to (1) compel tax haven jurisdictions to enact legislation to override domestic bank secrecy rules, thereby allowing access to bank information, and (2) establish a standard for what constitutes effective EOI for purposes of the harmful tax competition project. This new standard marked a significant departure from the language in Article 26 (EOI) of the OECD *Model Tax Treaty*, which does not obligate a contracting state to provide information that is not obtainable under its laws.

The *Model TIEA* establishes standards of transparency and EOI that the OECD believed would address the issues arising from the harmful tax competition project. The OECD standard that calls for EOI on request where such information is foreseeably relevant to the administration and enforcement of the applicant party's laws is contained in Article 1 of the *Model TIEA*. This standard was chosen to allow for the widest possible pathway for information exchange without permitting a "fishing expedition." Article 5(1) of the *Model TIEA* provides that the requirement to exchange information arises when the information is requested, as distinct from Automatic Exchange or spontaneous exchange. As discussed below, it is this standard — that information be exchanged upon request, and not automatically — that marks the fatal flaw in the Global Forum's efforts to achieve effective EOI as a means to stop the consequences of harmful tax practices.

The standard addressing the availability of reliable information requires that data concerning ownership and identity information, including banking information, be available to the competent authority and, moreover, that the competent authority have the legal power to obtain that information from any person who is in possession or control of that information within its territorial jurisdiction. Article 5(4) of the *Model TIEA* addresses the requirements surrounding the availability of information by requiring each of the contracting parties to give an undertaking that it has the legal authority to obtain upon request the various categories of information enumerated in the article, including bank information and ownership information of listed entities, and to affirm that bank secrecy laws cannot be used as a legal or public policy barrier to withhold information held by banks and financial institutions. Article 5(1) also confirms that information held by the requested party is not to be withheld solely on the grounds that the conduct being investigated would not constitute a crime under its laws. Article 5(2) addresses the obligation of the requested party to use all available information-gathering measures where it does not possess the information sought and further clarifies that the obligation to furnish the requested information exists independently of any need for or interest in the information, for its own tax purposes, on the part of the requested party.

The OECD standards also call for respect for taxpayers' rights. This commitment can be found in Article 1 of the *Model TIEA,* which requires that the rights and safeguards of persons under the laws or administrative practice of the requested party are to remain applicable to the extent that they do not unduly prevent or delay effective EOI. The OECD standards also call for the strict confidentiality of information exchanged. This requirement is addressed in the confidentiality provisions contained in Article 8, which calls upon the requesting party to treat the information that it receives from the requested party with the same degree of secrecy as information obtained under its own domestic tax laws, and which further requires that information that it receives ought not to be disclosed except only to persons or authorities concerned with the administration or enforcement of the taxes covered by the agreement.

An overarching question in the debate on effective EOI and the use of TIEAs arises in connection with the global community's focus on achieving a victory against international tax evasion through cooperation and the implementation of a uniform set of rules and procedures. Professor Dean suggests that countries explore the merits of joining forces and cooperating to tackle international tax problems such as tax evasion through tax *de*harmonization.[84] Tax harmonization seeks to eliminate differences between tax systems from the perspective of the taxpayer.[85] Professor Dean observes that tax harmonization produces two key benefits: efficiency and legitimacy.[86] Like simplification, tax harmonization can potentially create efficiency by targeting the wasteful expenditures resulting from the complexities that arise with differing tax concepts and rules and that must be navigated by taxpayers operating in multijurisdictional environments.[87] Arriving at the gains of efficiency through cooperation, rather than by competition, leads to a high degree of engagement, commitment, and interaction between regimes that provides a process through which taxpayers and governments can participate in the resulting system.[88] This collaborative process of harmonization can result in an increased sense of legitimacy.[89]

Tax deharmonization also attempts to achieve efficiency and legitimacy but without requiring that nations' tax regimes mirror one another.[90] Professor Dean uses the example of two states desiring to introduce a carbon tax. Instead of making the two regimes match one another by issuing identical laws and establishing identical agencies, the two nations could agree to distribute those functions across their boundaries.[91] As with harmonization, the resulting international cooperation would reinforce legitimacy.[92] Professor Dean acknowledges that administrative deharmonization to address offshore tax evasion through TIEAs would present high transaction costs[93] and warns that whether a bargain between

[84] Steven A Dean, "More Cooperation, Less Uniformity: Tax Deharmonization and the Future of the International Tax Regime" (2009) 84 *Tulane Law Review* 125 at 127 [Dean, "More Cooperation"].

[85] See *ibid* at 139. As using the same language offers no assurance that tax laws will be interpreted and applied in an identical fashion, to achieve true tax harmonization, two or more nations would have to achieve a high degree of uniformity with respect to tax laws, tax rates, and the administration of those laws (*ibid*).

[86] *Ibid* at 150.

[87] *Ibid.*

[88] *Ibid* at 153.

[89] *Ibid.*

[90] *Ibid.*

[91] *Ibid.*

[92] *Ibid* at 154.

[93] *Ibid* at 157.

two states would be worthwhile would depend largely on the balance between the costs of implementing the arrangement and the benefits that it would produce.[94] A consideration for any tax haven entering into such an arrangement would be the potential losses to its economy that would result from investors fleeing the jurisdiction due to its new commitment to investigate tax cheats. Professor Daniel Thornton describes the incentive problem as follows:

> Two factors inhibit the elimination of tax havens: information asymmetry (Canada doesn't know about its residents' activities in the Caymans) and incentive problems (Canadian taxpayers benefit from hiding income and wealth).
>
> Double-tax conventions and tax treaties work as intended only if information is perfect, transaction costs are zero and everyone is an angel.
>
> Absent incentive problems, Tax Information Exchange Agreements can be used to enforce tax treaties only if the partner jurisdiction has the infrastructure and the political will to conduct the necessary investigations. This might be encouraged by offering to share tax collections with the Caymans.
>
> Unfortunately, incentives are also an issue. If the Caymans started intensively investigating suspected tax cheats and sharing the information with Canada, investors in the Caymans would flee to other jurisdictions, so the Caymans's shared revenues would diminish.[95]

7.4 Phase III: The Global Forum and the Peer Review Process

In 2009, the Global Forum was fundamentally restructured to respond to a call from the G20 leadership to secure the integrity of the financial system through the implementation of the highest standards of transparency.[96] In 2010, the Global Forum began an intensive peer review process

[94] *Ibid* at 133.

[95] Daniel B Thornton, "Tax-Raiding the Caymans Won't Solve the Incentive," Letter to the Report on Business editor, *Globe & Mail* (13 March 2015), online: www.theglobeandmail.com/report-on-business/rob-commentary/rob-letters/homework-for-economistsDOUBLEHYPHEN-and-other-letters-to-the-rob-editor/article23460086/.

[96] See OECD, *Global Forum on Transparency and Exchange of Information for Tax Purposes* (Paris: OECD, 2009).

to guarantee effective implementation of information exchange. By the end of 2013, this process had resulted in the issuance of 124 peer review reports (reviewing 100 jurisdictions) and the making of approximately 818 recommendations regarding the implementation of the OECD standards.[97] Also announced in 2013 was the publication of separate report cards that were to grade jurisdictions on their performance. These ratings showed that more than 85 percent of the tax havens reviewed had failed to be compliant with all three major categories composing the OECD standards and that over 50 percent of the tax havens had a failure grade in at least one of the three major categories.[98]

7.5 TIEAs, Information Exchange, and the American Experience

Objectives of TIEAs

As discussed in Chapter 6, below, US TIEAs are very similar to the OECD *Model TIEA*. Like the OECD and the Global Forum, the United States recognized the pivotal role that bank secrecy plays in assisting taxpayers to evade US taxation on their worldwide income. The United States developed TIEAs (some twenty years before the Global Forum) as a mechanism to counter bank secrecy and obtain foreign information on investment income of US taxpayers.[99] A further US objective in developing TIEAs was to promote international cooperation in criminal and civil tax matters through information exchange.[100]

As of 2013, the United States had entered into thirty bilateral TIEAs. They can be used by the IRS to assist in an examination or audit of a US taxpayer, by providing the means for a foreign country to lawfully transfer data to the IRS. In a limited way, US TIEAs have enabled the US tax authorities to combat bank secrecy, foster international tax cooperation, and receive US taxpayer investment information, thereby assisting

[97] See *Global Forum Information Brief*, above note 66 at para 9.

[98] See Section 6.1, above in this chapter.

[99] See Chapter 6, Section 2.2.

[100] See *ibid.*

the United States in the administration and enforcement of its tax laws. As discussed above in relation to the work of the Global Forum, TIEAs have their own unique drawbacks, and these are also very much present in the TIEA network developed by the United States (and, as noted below, Canada). However, in addition to TIEAs, the United States maintains an arsenal of homegrown remedies such as requests for information (IDRs), summonses, John Doe summonses, and the threat of criminal prosecution. As discussed in Chapter 5, the United States has successfully used some of these alternative unilateral measures to obtain foreign taxpayer information for many years.

John Doe Summonses versus TIEAs

As discussed in Chapter 5, the IRS possesses a selection of administrative measures that it can use to obtain foreign-based information about a taxpayer both under domestic law and under the US network of DTCs and TIEAs. In the case of UBS (discussed in Chapter 5), the IRS used both treaty and domestic law. Which tool is best to give the IRS access to the foreign-based information of a particular taxpayer will depend on all of the relevant facts and circumstances. Where the identity of the taxpayer is known to the IRS, the IRS may avail itself of its summons powers. Generally, where the identity of a taxpayer is known to the IRS and where it possesses additional information sufficient to make a request for information under a TIEA between the United States and a tax haven, the IRS may employ the TIEA EOI mechanism. But where tax evasion is suspected, particularly among a group of taxpayers whose identities are not known (as was the case with the IRS efforts to pursue tax cheats with its Offshore Credit Card Program and investigations of UBS, Wegelin, and CIBC FirstCaribbean International Bank), the IRS is unable to use its summons power or to rely on TIEAs.[101] In this scenario, where the identity of a taxpayer or group of taxpayers is unknown, the IRS has

[101] For a discussion of US international tax enforcement, the Offshore Credit Card Program, and investigations of UBS, Wegelin, and CIBC FirstCaribbean International Bank, see Chapter 5, Section 3.6 & 3.7.

successfully used the John Doe summons, coupled more recently with the threat of criminal prosecution.

The IRS may use the John Doe summons to identify taxpayers suspected of tax evasion provided that the United States can first establish that (1) the summons relates to the investigation of a particular person or ascertainable group, (2) there is a reasonable basis for believing that taxes have been avoided, and (3) the information is not readily available from other sources.[102] The John Doe summons arguably fulfills a vital need in the information exchange arena where foreign banks are suspected of holding unreported accounts of US persons. TIEAs categorically do not provide an alternative way for the United States to obtain information sought in a John Doe summons because they require specific, detailed information about the taxpayer and the offshore account. Moreover, this problem is also inherent in EOI mechanisms in DTCs, which generally do not allow for requests where little to no taxpayer information can be provided and where such requests run the risk of being challenged on the grounds that they are fishing expeditions. Furthermore, TIEAs are not built to accommodate group requests. As discussed in Chapter 5 in relation to the case of the Bank of Nova Scotia, and more recently UBS, Credit Suisse, and the Swiss banking industry, the US summons power has another advantage that TIEAs do not have: teeth in the form of civil and criminal sanctions.[103] The EOI mechanism alone, whether contained in a DTC or TIEA, cannot pose the same personal threat to bank officials or economic threat (including an existential threat) to corporations that the John Doe summons wields in the face of defiance or non-compliance. The indictment of Wegelin and the participation of some 100 Swiss banks in the Swiss Bank Program established by the United States in 2013 were the result of the use by the United States of its John Doe summons power. In circumstances where the United States suspects that offshore banks are harbouring undisclosed US accounts but where the United States lacks data to identify these account holders or their accounts, it is likely that

[102] See Chapter 5, Section 3.6.

[103] For a discussion of US international tax enforcement concerning the Bank of Nova Scotia, UBS, Credit Suisse, Wegelin, and the Swiss banking industry, see Chapter 5, Sections 3.5 and 4.

John Doe summonses will be used over a TIEA due to the key advantages that they offer in accessing foreign-based account information.

FATCA versus TIEAs

Secrecy has been a central theme (if not the main villain) in the story of improving information exchange to enhance tax administration and enforcement and, more recently, to combat international tax evasion. The OECD and the Global Forum alike recognized early on that bank secrecy had to be eliminated in tax haven jurisdictions to achieve any meaningful progress in the implementation of the OECD standards. The work of the Global Forum was chiefly devoted from 2002 through 2010 to achieving international acceptance of the new OECD standards and from 2010 to 2013, through the peer review process, to the proper implementation of those standards. A primary goal of the *Model TIEA* was to eliminate bank secrecy, which was viewed as a significant impediment to effective information exchange. However, as the *Model TIEA* is premised on EOI by request, an offshore account can remain a secret from the IRS (or other fiscal authority) until the IRS learns of its existence from a whistleblower or in the course of an audit. In May 2008, as a result of the revelations of whistleblower and former UBS executive Bradley Birkenfeld, the IRS learned that tens of thousands of US taxpayers maintained secret bank accounts in Swiss banks.[104] In enacting *FATCA* in 2010, the US Congress was taking direct aim at the abilities of US taxpayers to take advantage of the many flaws in the US reporting system (and qualified intermediary system) and EOI mechanisms, relied upon by the United States to administer and enforce its tax laws, that allow US taxpayers to hide their money from the IRS.[105]

---

[104] See Sandra R Brown, "IRS & the FBAR: International Focus for U.S. Tax Compliance" (20 November 2008) [unpublished] at 4–9. Birkenfeld pleaded guilty to conspiring to defraud the IRS by helping UBS clients evade US reporting laws: see United States, Department of Justice, News Release 08-850, "Banker Pleads Guilty to Helping American Real Estate Developer Evade Income Tax on $200 Million" (19 June 2008), online: www.justice.gov/archive/opa/pr/2008/June/08-tax-550.html.

[105] For a description of *FATCA* and a comparison of *FATCA* with the *Model TIEA*, see Chapter 9.

FATCA provides the US government with three significant advantages over TIEAs: (1) detailed information on accounts held directly and indirectly by US taxpayers, including data on investment income, (2) annual automatic exchange of the detailed account and investment information, and (3) teeth, in the form of a *FATCA* penalty (described below) imposed on foreign financial institutions (FFIs) that continue to hide US account holders. Despite these apparent advantages of *FATCA* over TIEAs, the signing and implementation of an intergovernmental agreement (IGA) between the United States and Canada represents a historical failure in international tax policy on the part of both nations. As Michael Livingston recognizes, tax policy is one aspect of a broader set of political and social issues, and what scholars need to reflect more upon is an understanding of the relationship between structure and outcomes and the effectiveness (or ineffectiveness) of various historical strategies for promoting tax reform.[106] Diane Ring, commenting on international tax scholarship and echoing the vision of Livingston, calls for the exercise of practical reasoning that reflects the needs of a society and integrates analysis, facts, values, and competing goals.[107]

As discussed in Chapter 9, the motivation for *FATCA* was primarily the discovery of large-scale tax evasion by Americans living in the United States with undeclared bank accounts in Swiss and other European banks, and their apparent success at circumventing the qualified intermediary and other US reporting systems. American taxpayers living in the continental forty-eight states and Alaska and Hawaii generally do not report and pay taxes on a worldwide basis to any other country or jurisdiction. So clearly, income earned by these individuals in undeclared tax haven accounts made

---

[106] Michael A Livingston, "Reinventing Tax Scholarship: Lawyers, Economists, and the Role of the Legal Academy" (1998) 83 *Cornell Law Review* 365 at 368. Livingston offers that the goal of tax scholarship should be to move beyond the normative focus of determining the "right" answer to tax problems under idealized and apolitical conditions — to encompass approaches (such as empirical studies, narrative projects, and an expanded normativity) that recognize that in the partisan nature of taxation, tax policy is one aspect of a broader set of political and social issues.

[107] Diane M Ring, "The Promise of International Tax Scholarship and Its Implications for Research Design, Theory and Methodology" (2010) 55 *Saint Louis University Law Journal* 307 at 327–28. In commenting on Livingston's conception of "empirical" work, Ring, *ibid* at 312, notes that Livingston favours the goal of gathering and analyzing relevant information in useful ways for those designing policy and that he believes a rigid adherence to highly sophisticated methodologies from the social sciences is not essential.

them tax cheats who were evading income tax and committing fraud. *FATCA* was designed to stop this. But to equate approximately one million Canadian residents who report worldwide income and pay taxes thereon to CRA with tax cheats, or to put them in the same class as the tax criminals for whom *FATCA* was created, is neither just nor right. To impose *FATCA* on Canada and to drive hundreds of thousands of Canadians of US heritage into the cannons of the IRS's unfair enforcement (described in Chapter 10) is inconsistent with the goals of equity (described above in this chapter) surrounding international tax law and EOI. Finally, as the vast majority of Americans in Canada file zero returns (i.e., returns with no US income tax owing), because of the credits and exclusions under the *Internal Revenue Code*, the *FATCA* program to identify Americans in Canada and enforce the *Code* against them is illogical, especially when it drives these individuals to renounce their citizenship in record numbers.[108] Chapter 10, below, describes the injustices and illogic of applying the US foreign-reporting rules (totalling some 7,000 pages) to Canadians, and of the voluntary disclosure programs.[109] Canada failed in implementing *FATCA* by not asking about or considering the financial and social consequences of what the IRS would do with the information that it received. Canada and the United States need to develop a cross-border tax policy solution that embraces what Livingston and others (like Michael Graetz)[110] have called for: an appreciation of the unique factual, historical, social, and political circumstances of one million Americans in Canada, many of whom have lived in Canada for most, if not all, of their lives.

Generally, the *Model 1 IGA* permits FFIs to identify US account holders and provide the required information, described in Article 2, to the tax authorities in the FATCA partner's jurisdiction.[111] The primary

[108] For most of the years from 2005 to 2014, making an appointment to expatriate at the Consulate General of the United States in Toronto required a couple of weeks' advance notice. As of January 2016, scheduling an appointment to expatriate requires ten months' advance notice.

[109] See Chapter 10, discussing US voluntary disclosure programs from 2009 to 2015.

[110] See Michael J Graetz, "Taxing International Income: Inadequate Principles, Outdated Concepts, and Unsatisfactory Policies" (2001) 54 *Tax Law Review* 261 at 276–325. Professor Graetz advocates that to best articulate an international tax policy, the political as well as the economic considerations and needs of the American people should be addressed.

[111] See United States, Department of the Treasury, *Model Intergovernmental Agreement to Improve Tax Compliance and to Implement FATCA* (Washington, DC: US Department of the Treasury,

difference between the *Model 1 IGA* and the *Model 2 IGA* is that under the latter FFIs must report identified US account holders directly to the IRS.[112] The *Model 1 IGA*, entered into by Canada, may be entered into with jurisdictions that have a preexisting DTC or TIEA with the United States.

From a policy perspective, the *Model TIEA* aimed at improving effective EOI and transparency standards for all members of the Global Forum as a means of combatting international tax evasion. *FATCA*, on the other hand, aimed at stopping international tax evasion by US taxpayers at the very source: the financial institutions maintaining unreported bank accounts. An FFI's failure to comply with the *FATCA* regime can trigger financial penalties so devastating that they would in effect bar the FFI from investing in the US marketplace. Although *FATCA*'s implementation is arguably the most draconian extraterritorial application of a single nation's regulatory regime, it has been the catalyst for the G20's call to implement Automatic Exchange as the new standard by 2017.[113]

While both the *Model TIEA* and *Model 1 IGA* embrace goals consistent with improving international tax administration, the *Model 1 IGA* emphasizes that its purpose is to build an infrastructure to support Automatic Exchange, albeit of a magnitude without any historical precedent. Providing the country tasked with the obligation of identifying and collecting account information with detailed guidance on the identification and collection processes gives the *Model 1 IGA* a significant leg-up over the approach of the *Model TIEA*, which focuses on establishing general pathways to enable information access, and is backed by the principles behind the OECD standards. *FATCA* is more specific.

Article 1 of the *Model 1 IGA* acknowledges that *FATCA* does not extinguish the EOI mechanism maintained by the United States under either a DTC or a TIEA with the other government.[114] For example, the

---

2012) [*Model 1 IGA*]; United States, Department of the Treasury, Press Release, "Treasury and IRS Issue Final Regulations to Combat Offshore Tax Evasion" (17 January 2013).

[112] See *Model 1 IGA*, above note 111; United States, Department of the Treasury, *Model 2 IGA, Preexisting TIEA or DTC* (Washington, DC: US Department of the Treasury, 2013) [*Model 2 IGA*].

[113] For a description of Automatic Exchange and an examination of the policy issues relating to the new standard, see Chapter 8.

[114] For a description of each article in the *Model TIEA*, see Chapter 6.

entering into of an intergovernmental agreement between Canada and the United States does not nullify Article XXVII (EOI) of the *Convention between Canada and the United States of America with respect to Taxes on Income and on Capital.* Moreover, the preamble to the *Model 1 IGA* expressly acknowledges the article in the DTC, *Convention on Mutual Administrative Assistance in Tax Matters*, or TIEA that authorizes EOI for tax purposes between the United States and the *FATCA* foreign partner.[115]

Article 1 of the *Model TIEA* provides that the contracting parties agree to exchange information that is "foreseeably relevant," so as to allow the widest possible pathway for information exchange without permitting so-called fishing expeditions or speculative requests.[116] This standard may still apply and be relevant to a request for information under a DTC or TIEA pursuant to an examination. *FATCA* has related but different goals. Automatic Exchange under *FATCA* seeks to counter offshore tax evasion by increasing voluntary compliance related to foreign earned income. To this end, *FATCA* provides the US Department of the Treasury with detection abilities that it did not have previously. These abilities include assisting the IRS to identify tax evasion involving income earned on foreign investments and to identify principal amounts that have not been declared as income of a taxpayer. While the "foreseeably relevant" standard may apply to the *Model TIEA*, which is premised on information by request and hence may be classified as reactive in its response to suspected tax evasion discovered by the IRS, *FATCA* is focused on detection and prevention of tax evasion and is really concerned with taking a proactive stance regarding tax evasion that the IRS may not have discovered.

FATCA requires financial institutions in jurisdictions that enter into a *Model IGA* with the United States either to endure the hardship of building a system that identifies and reports required data on financial assets owned directly or indirectly by US citizens to the US Department of the Treasury annually or to endure a decimating withholding penalty on investment income in the United States. Moreover, *FATCA* requires very precise information about account balances and investment income that can then be used by the IRS to identify and investigate tax evasion

---

[115] For a description of each article in the *Model 1 IGA*, see Chapter 9, Section 4.

[116] See Chapter 6, Section 3.

by US citizens and residents. The combination of annual automatic exchange of prescribed financial and account data with a severe penalty for non-compliance makes *FATCA* the most powerful information-gathering tool to be designed or deployed in the fight against tax evasion. And the United States has begun to deploy its "dreadnought" foreign information–gathering weapon — *FATCA*. As a result of *FATCA* and the successes of John Doe summonses and the threat of criminal prosecution in obtaining information on large groups of non-compliant taxpayers, TIEAs are likely to play only a marginal role in the US war on tax evasion. A notable flaw in *FATCA*, discussed in Chapter 10, is that Canadians are easily able to evade its reporting requirements.

7.6 TIEAs and Canada

In March 2007, Ottawa announced that it was going to deny the deductibility of interest paid by Canadian companies to banks in Canada on debt used to acquire the shares of a foreign affiliate unless the shares generated income that was actually taxed in Canada.[117] The primary motivation behind TIEAs was to use the information exchange mechanism to enforce these new rules that sought to trace interest (and other deductions) to the earning of exempt foreign sourced income.[118] In May 2007, Ottawa altered its interest deductibility proposal to target more aggressive financing structures such as the "double dip" structure.[119] The revised restrictions would disallow interest deductions only in the circumstance where funds borrowed in Canada could be traced to double dip financing structures, and would otherwise continue to allow the use of borrowed funds to invest in foreign affiliates.

In addition to restrictions on interest deductibility, the 2007 budget plan announced a number of initiatives under the banner "International Tax Fairness Initiative." The Department of Finance announced that it was going to (1) extend the exempt surplus regime previously reserved for countries that enter into a DTC with Canada to tax havens that

[117] See Chapter 6, Section 2.2.

[118] See *ibid.*

[119] See *ibid.*

enter into a TIEA with Canada, (2) improve its ability to collect tax information within its existing treaty network by applying the new OECD standards to any new treaties and future treaty revisions, (3) expand its capabilities to exchange information with non-treaty countries through TIEAs, (4) allocate additional funding for international audit and enforcement, and (5) create a panel of experts to advise the government on enhancing Canada's system of international taxation.[120] The budget plan observed that by extending the exempt surplus regime to non-treaty countries that sign a TIEA with Canada, Canadian firms would have greater scope to expand internationally into new and emerging markets in a tax competitive manner. It was further hoped that these changes would provide incentives for non-treaty countries to enter into a TIEA with Canada and induce Canadian multinational enterprises to locate and invest in those jurisdictions. The budget also sought to penalize jurisdictions that failed to agree to enter into a TIEA with Canada within five years of being approached by Ottawa, by subjecting income earned by foreign affiliates of Canadian companies in those jurisdictions to current taxation in Canada.[121]

In 2007 when the Canadian government was unveiling its plans for the use of TIEAs in the Canadian international tax system, there appeared to be a number of competing policy objectives concerning the deductibility of interest related to foreign affiliates, the promotion of international business expansion for Canadian multinational enterprises, and also non-compliant individual taxpayers resident in Canada. More recently, the government appeared to be relying on the creation of a TIEA network to provide CRA with an effective EOI tool to combat international tax evasion.[122] In 2008, the advisory panel to the Canadian government recommended the extension of the exemption system to all foreign active business income. In addition, the panel recommended removing the requirement that a foreign affiliate earn business income only from a jurisdiction that has a DTC or TIEA with Canada. Freeing the availability of the exempt surplus regime from the requirement that

[120] See *ibid.*
[121] See *ibid.*
[122] See *ibid.*

a DTC or TIEA be in place will, as Professor Arnold notes, help reduce the resources that the already overburdened government expends on maintaining Canada's treaty network.[123] That the government is overburdened is painfully evident in the area of information exchange where, as discussed above, in 2014 over 80 percent of Canada's treaties did not conform to the OECD standards. As Professor Arnold and others have noted, TIEA countries make poor substitutes for DTC countries in justifying the extension of the exempt surplus regime as most of Canada's TIEAs are signed with tax havens that have little to no income tax.[124] Moreover, delinking the exempt surplus regime from any requirement that a jurisdiction maintain a DTC or TIEA with Canada will help the government focus more on using TIEAs to combat individual tax evasion. Breaking the link between the entitlement to an exemption and a TIEA will mean reconsidering Canada's strategy to induce jurisdictions to enter into TIEAs. While it is true that without the TIEA requirement in the picture, the allure of exempt surplus in attracting Canadian foreign affiliates to invest in a jurisdiction would be gone, Canadian companies would still be free to set up shop in any low cost jurisdiction and reap the benefit of the exemption. There would also be no downside for the Canadian foreign affiliate or the jurisdiction if an agreement were not entered into within the five-year limit. As discussed below, regardless of whether or not Canada ultimately chooses to sever the link between the entitlement to exempt surplus and a DTC or TIEA, there are significant potential upsides to considering new incentives and strategies to induce tax havens to partner with Canada in fighting international tax evasion.

As of 2015, there were twenty-two TIEAs in force in Canada. In Chapter 6, a comparison of Canada's TIEAs with the *Model TIEA* will show that Canada's TIEAs consistently reflect adherence to the essential elements of EOI and transparency found in the OECD standards. Article 5(5) of Canada's TIEAs recalls that the object and scope of the TIEA as set forth in Article 1 is for the contracting parties to provide assistance through the EOI mechanism that is foreseeably relevant to

---

[123] Brian J Arnold, *Reforming Canada's International Tax System toward Coherence and Simplicity* (Toronto: Canadian Tax Foundation, 2009) at 320–22.

[124] *Ibid.*

the administration and enforcement of their domestic tax laws. To support this goal, Article 5(5) provides a detailed list of information that the applicant party must provide to the requested party to demonstrate the foreseeable relevance of the information so that the request will be consistent with the scope of the TIEA and not be a fishing expedition. Indeed, the commentary to the *Model TIEA* goes so far as to counsel that incomplete information requests are not within the spirit of the TIEA and should be avoided.

As a result of this continuing effort to build a TIEA network, Canada will generally have a legal mechanism to support the administration and enforcement of its tax laws. A key question is, will this mechanism work? Because Canada's TIEAs require CRA to provide a tax haven jurisdiction with much of the information that it is itself seeking in order to obtain bank account information relating to taxpayers suspected of tax avoidance or evasion, TIEAs are not an effective tool in combatting tax evasion. If TIEAs will not effectively combat tax evasion, will they at least assist Canada in the administration and enforcement of its tax laws? Given that the OECD standards and peer review process were designed to make EOI on request effective, that is certainly the expectation. However, there are still other factors that can impede this objective.

Regarding tracing the income or deductions of a Canadian foreign affiliate, an investigation may be complicated if accounts are held by nominee entities, including those with nominee shareholders, and if the TIEA partner jurisdiction either does not have an adequate infrastructure to access the ultimate information or lacks the political or economic incentive to complete the appropriate investigation. To complicate matters, a taxpayer may use multiple accounts, some disclosed to CRA and some not, for skimming the profits from its foreign operations (a variation of the old two-cash-registers trick, one for the government and one for untaxed income). Where a taxpayer has failed to comply with the foreign-reporting rules relating to foreign entities, for example, Form T1134 (Information Return relating to Controlled and Not-Controlled Foreign Affiliates) or Form T1135 (Foreign Income Verification Statement), then query whether CRA will have the requisite information to make a valid request under a TIEA, in particular under Article 5 (EOI upon Request), for all the relevant accounts? What if the investigation requires that the requested party obtain information from another tax haven jurisdiction where the nominee entity is set up? Generally, under Article 2 of Canada's TIEAs, a requested party is not obligated to provide information that is not in the possession or control of persons within its territorial jurisdiction.

Tax cheats can be devious and may deploy a host of decoys to complicate any investigation into their affairs. Furthermore, differences in the terms of Canada's TIEAs may prove a source of frustration in a request for information further to an audit. For example, in the TIEAs with Jersey, Guernsey, and the Isle of Man, there is no time limit within which to respond. Only an elusive "reasonable" time standard is stipulated. Most of Canada's other TIEAs not only stipulate a ninety-day turnaround time but also require the requested party to notify CRA of any problems or expected delays. TIEAs can support Canada's efforts to administer its tax rules and enforce its tax laws, and these efforts should be monitored and reviewed. But Canada's TIEAs represent the proverbial floor on information exchange, not the ceiling. There is tremendous upside potential to the EOI relationships that Canada can foster with tax havens in its TIEA network. The ultimate answer to the question of how well this newly created network will function to support CRA's efforts relating to tax administration and enforcement will depend in part on what Canada does to maximize the opportunities for collaboration with its TIEA partners. Although currently it is not certain exactly how the legal mechanism or platform of Automatic Exchange will operate or what precise role TIEAs will play, the relationships that Canada ultimately creates with tax havens will likely have a significant impact on the success of these new efforts.

In March 2013, Canadian Broadcasting Corporation news reported that since 2006 CRA audits of aggressive international tax cases had led to the identification of over $4.5 billion in unpaid tax.[125] The *Globe and Mail* reported that 2013 estimates of Canadian funds stashed in tax havens were $170 billion and further that the related loss of annual

[125] David Simms, "Offshore Tax Dodgers Coming under Greater Pressure" *CBC News* (21 February 2013, last updated 9 March 2013), online: www.cbc.ca/news/business/taxes/offshore-tax-dodgers-coming-under-greater-pressure-1.1353349.

revenue was thought to be $7.8 billion.[126] The flaw in the standard to exchange information by request requires Canada, like other jurisdictions that have implemented the OECD standards with tax havens, to retarget its information exchange collection efforts to make a renewed effort to combat tax evasion.

Other governments confronted with the reality that TIEAs do not provide an effective means to combat international tax evasion have been adapting their tax strategies in a manner that will result in both cash hauls and the potential for enhanced deterrence even though it may not lead to a clear win against tax evasion.[127] As explained in Chapter 5, the United States has been the government to most vigorously deploy a multifaceted approach to using information exchange to combat tax evasion, including turbo charging its TIEA network with the new *FATCA* foreign-reporting regime. Both Germany and the United Kingdom have entered into separate agreements with Switzerland to deal with previously undeclared assets of residents in those jurisdictions.[128] In 2013, the United Kingdom has also, on its own initiative (i.e., without the United States), entered into *FATCA*-style agreements to share information with its Crown dependencies, including Guernsey, the Isle of Man,

---

[126] Janet McFarland, "Canadians' Offshore Tax-Haven Holdings Rise 10 Per-cent to $170 Billion" *Globe and Mail* (2 May 2014), online: www.theglobeandmail.com/report-on-business/international-business/canadians-tax-haven-holdings-rise-10-per-cent-to-170-billion/article18400026/.

[127] See, for example, United Kingdom, Press Release, "New UK Multilateral Action to Combat Tax Evasion" (2 April 2013), online: www.gov.uk/government/news/new-uk-multilateral-action-to-combat-tax-evasion, describing an agreement between the United Kingdom, France, Germany, Italy, and Spain to develop and pilot multilateral tax information exchange under which information will be automatically exchanged between the five countries.

[128] Switzerland entered into a new tax agreement with the United Kingdom to strengthen relations around cross-border financial services and taxation, deal with previously undeclared assets, and agree to a final withholding tax on future investment income: see Francesco Carelli, "The New Tax Agreement between Switzerland and the United Kingdom — An Analysis" (2012) 52:6 *IBFD European Taxation Journal* 301. Under the agreement, relevant UK resident individuals may opt for either a one-time penalty payment or the release of their account details to UK tax authorities (Carelli, *ibid* at 3, citing Art 5(1) of the *Agreement between the United Kingdom of Great Britain and Northern Ireland and the Swiss Confederation on Cooperation in the Area of Taxation*, 6 October 2011, Treaties IBFD [*Switzerland–UK Agreement*]). Regarding the treatment of future income, relevant UK resident individuals have the option either to accept an anonymous final withholding tax remitted to the United Kingdom or to have the Swiss bank disclose income and capital gains derived from the assets to UK authorities (Carelli, *ibid* at 7, citing Art 19 and 22 respectively of the *Switzerland–UK Agreement, ibid*). Switzerland also signed a nearly identical agreement with Germany (Carelli, *ibid* at 1).

and Jersey.[129] As of January 2014, there is no public record of Canada having entered into or pursued some form of agreement with the Swiss government to address historical or ongoing tax cheating by Canadian residents. In addition, as of January 2014, there is no public record of Canada having entered into or pursued *FATCA*-style agreements with any tax haven or other jurisdiction apart from the United States.

As Steven Dean observes, winning today's war on tax evasion necessitates (1) creating a framework that acknowledges and accounts for the differences between OECD member (and other developed and developing) states and tax haven jurisdictions and (2) embracing new tools and strategies.[130] Dean notes that if tax evaders shared benefits of $100 in the form of unpaid taxes, a cooperative arrangement that allowed participating governments to collect and share that $100 would most of the time leave those governments collectively better off than they would be without such an arrangement.[131] Dean also notes that because the estimated US revenue losses attributed to tax flight are much greater than the GDP of a tax haven like the Cayman Islands, the likelihood is that a mutually beneficial intergovernmental deal could be struck at the expense of tax evaders.[132]

Canada's TIEAs provide that the incidence of costs incurred in providing assistance shall be agreed by the competent authorities of the contracting parties. At a minimum, and after carefully exploring financial alternatives, Canada should agree to a formula whereby it will share revenues derived from any collaboration with a TIEA partner under the existing EOI request standard. In conjunction with exploring avenues for economic

---

[129] The United Kingdom has separately agreed to Automatic Exchange with its Crown dependencies (Guernsey, the Isle of Man, and Jersey) and some of its overseas territories (Anguilla, Bermuda, the British Virgin Islands, the Cayman Islands, Gibraltar, Montserrat, and the Turks and Caicos Islands): see OECD, *A Step Change in Tax Transparency: OECD Report for the G8 Summit* (Paris: OECD, 2013) at 6, online: www.oecd.org/ctp/exchange-of-tax-information/taxtransparency_G8report.pdf.

[130] Dean, "More Cooperation," above note 84 at 127.

[131] *Ibid* at 132.

[132] *Ibid*, citing Joseph Guttentag & Reuven Avi-Yonah, "Closing the International Tax Gap" in Max B Sawicky, ed, *Bridging the Tax Gap: Addressing the Crisis in Federal Tax Administration* (Washington, DC: Economic Policy Institute, 2005). See also Steven A Dean, "Philosopher Kings and International Tax: A New Approach to Tax Havens, Tax Flight, and International Tax Cooperation" (2007) 58 *Hastings Law Journal* 911 [Dean, "Philosopher Kings"], advocating cooperation in sharing collected revenues between tax flight and tax haven jurisdictions.

cooperation with TIEA partners, Canada could also explore sharing the country's richness in education, health science, technology, agriculture, and human rights with tax haven jurisdictions in a manner that would make the EOI relationship more attractive and also support internation equity. Moreover, Canada should consider adopting its own *FATCA*-style agreements for Automatic Exchange on hidden (directly and indirectly) Canadian owned accounts with major tax havens. To bolster this effort, Canada should, after careful exploration, offer a financial reward to these Canadian *FATCA* partners for their efforts in identifying Canadian held accounts and in reporting all historical data on these accounts. A principal aim of *FATCA* and Automatic Exchange is to increase foreign tax compliance. The sooner Canada takes the initiative in the many opportunities immediately before it in the area of EOI, the faster TIEAs (with modifications) or the relationships that they have opened up can be used to effectively combat international tax evasion. Canada has not been a leader in the field of EOI, nor has it been an innovator. Canada has also not followed the leader as other countries have in seeking redress from Switzerland and in pursuing *FATCA*-style agreements to combat tax evasion. Rather, Canada has been more of a straggler in taking action in the EOI field, and even then it has been taking only the minimum action. In the grand scheme of Canada's international tax policy agenda, the government may decide to stay the course vis-à-vis information exchange, adapting when necessary, over time. The risk to this approach is not only the likelihood of the continued loss of billions of dollars in revenue each year but, more profoundly, that equity will no longer be a guiding light in the administration of the country's tax system.

8 Conclusion

The findings of this research regarding whether TIEAs work have been presented above with respect to (1) their compatibility with the goals of international tax and treaty law, (2) the stated policy objectives of the OECD and the Global Forum, and (3) the policy objectives of both the United States and Canada. Based on the foregoing analysis, it can be argued that the OECD ultimately achieved its stated objectives in Phase I by identifying tax practices causing harmful tax competition, tackling the preferential tax regimes, and aligning the tax havens with its new standards on transparency and EOI. These objectives were furthered in part by the work of the Global Forum in Phase II. However, on closer scrutiny a counterargument may also be made that the agreement by tax havens to adopt the OECD standards was more for show than for substance. Did the OECD or the Global Forum really believe that by signing the required number of TIEAs (twelve), a tax haven like the Cayman Islands could put itself on an equal footing, the white list, with the United Kingdom or Germany on the subject of harmful tax practices? The plain truth is that residents of OECD member countries who maintained unreported offshore accounts in tax havens continued to enjoy the same low tax rates and concealment of their identities from home governments after the tax havens were moved to the white list that they had enjoyed while the tax havens had been on the black or grey list. Of course, the flaw in the Global Forum's logic lies in the standard to exchange information on request, which guarantees the secrecy of the tax evader's bank account until the taxpayer at last loses the "audit lottery."

The problem with the OECD standards is that they prevent fiscal authorities from learning about tax evasion by limiting access to foreign bank account information to circumstances where tax authorities suspect that a taxpayer is failing to report offshore income. Accessing information under the *Model TIEA* requires that the requesting party provide to the requested party detailed information under Article 5(5). To cross the bridge that we have built with TIEAs, as Professor Cockfield observes, requires that Canadian and other authorities already possess evidence that a taxpayer is hiding information offshore in order to have the legal grounds required under the TIEA to make the request.[133] Put another way, as Professors Brodzka and Garufi comment, information on request is inadequate to effectively tackle international tax evasion because this standard presumes that the requesting state already knows

[133] Li, Cockfield, & Wilkie, above note 19 at 380: without evidence that a taxpayer is hiding income offshore, there will be no grounds for making a request, thereby complicating Canadian investigations into offshore tax evasion.

what it is looking for.[134] Despite this flaw, the Global Forum between 2002 and 2013 was able to address other barriers to effective exchange of information through the implementation of the OECD standards and the peer review process. There is no question that the collective work of the Global Forum in developing and implementing the OECD standards has resulted in new international norms in the arena of information exchange between governments. The *Model TIEA* was created to eliminate bank secrecy laws in tax havens as a means to end arguably one of the most powerfully harmful tax practices and impediments to effective EOI. The *Model TIEA* was also created to establish an effective EOI standard to address the additional problems (besides bank secrecy) identified in the harmful tax practices project. To the OECD's credit, the OECD standards as contained in the *Model TIEA* deny tax havens the right to withhold bank account information under either domestic secrecy laws or public policy grounds. To its further credit, the OECD standards also address historical challenges that the harmful tax practices project identified as impediments to effective EOI. Moreover, since 2005, more than 1,500 new bilateral agreements have been signed that allow for EOI in accordance with the OECD standards.[135] As a result of these achievements, the Global Forum has been able to compel tax havens to undertake to end bank secrecy and enact legislation bringing their laws and administrative procedures into conformity with the OECD standards contained in the *Model TIEA*.

Since its founding in 2000, the Global Forum has grown to include, as of 2013, 121 jurisdictions. Today, OECD member countries and non-member countries alike conducting audits or exams have an international legal procedure — the TIEA — to access foreign bank account information that largely did not exist a decade earlier. There is no question that the creation of the TIEA and its adoption by over 120 jurisdictions, including all tax havens, is a substantial achievement in the global war against tax evasion. Moreover, given both the dangers and the complexities posed by economic globalization, the international cooperation that

[134] Alicja Brodzka & Sebastiano Garufi, "The Era of Exchange of Information and Fiscal Transparency: The Use of Soft Law Instruments and the Enhancement of Good Governance in Tax Matters" (2012) 52:8 *IBFD European Tax Journal* (Checkpoint) at 10.

[135] See *G20 Progress Report*, above note 71 at Executive Summary.

has occurred as a result of the work of the Global Forum (including in the peer review process) should be recognized as an important achievement in the fight against tax evasion. Beyond the new legal standards and the quest to transform and build an infrastructure that will support transparency for EOI, there has also been an unprecedented degree of international cooperation and collaboration in the field of international taxation. The drive to Automatic Exchange will unquestionably be aided by these developments, which have mostly centred around TIEAs.

Beyond the hope that surrounds the work of the OECD and the Global Forum as the 121 or so members move toward the next generation of EOI standard and protocols, there is also fear. It is one thing to ask a nation to be able to respond to requests for exchanges of information. It is quite another to ask a nation to build and maintain a complex system to support the Automatic Exchange concerning financial information of taxpayers from dozens of nations. Based on the Global Forum's ratings released in 2013, more than 50 percent of tax haven jurisdictions failed to have in place effective measures relating to one or more of the following areas: ownership and identity information relating to entities, maintenance of reliable accounting records, and availability of banking information for all account holders. Moreover, most of the tax haven jurisdictions had at least one significant deficiency (being only partially compliant) in one of the major categories composing the OECD standards. The delivery of the Global Forum's ratings was to be a watershed or defining moment in the evolution of the organization, representing the completion of its original mandate, which sought to improve transparency and EOI.[136] There can be no doubt that the totality of the work of the Global Forum, including the hundreds of recommendations and the focus of the international community on the OECD Standards through the peer reviews, has resulted in progress. However, the story told by the ratings, especially concerning tax havens, must also be recognized. To this end, the OECD and the Global Forum should not ignore the infrastructure gap (including in legal and financial systems that enable the availability of information) on the closing of which the future success of EOI mechanisms, including Automatic Exchange, will depend. The

[136] See *ibid.*

original research of Stephen Dean looking at the question of tax flight early on in the work of the Global Forum and his recommendation that economic cooperation through tax flight treaties can provide another and more potent avenue through which to beat tax cheats appears to be supported by the data collected by the Global Forum in its own reviews. The optimism surrounding Dean's vision does not negate its challenges. Neither the *Model Tax Treaty* nor TIEAs provide a template for cooperation through tax deharmonization. Studies need to be performed on the tax and legal considerations in designing and implementing any kind of revenue sharing. These considerations will need to be analyzed in both the tax flight and the tax haven countries, and political factors will also need to be identified and taken into account.

What are the economic incentives for tax havens to expend millions and potentially billions of dollars to support the tax systems of OECD, developed, and developing nations? In her research on tax policy leadership concerning the OECD and G20, Allison Christians observes that on multiple occasions the OECD has articulated a blunt policy to shut down tax havens to protect the national revenue bases of the wealthiest countries in the world.[137] Tax havens and developing countries have virtually no role in determining the policy that impacts their fiscal and economic systems, which role is reserved for the rich countries' "club."[138] The OECD's harmful tax competition project raises many important political, international legal, and social issues, especially those relating to principles of fairness. One's views on these issues can be influenced by national interest perspectives.

[137] Allison Christians, "Taxation in a Time of Crisis: Policy Leadership from the OECD to the G20" (2010) 5 *Northwestern Journal of Law & Social Policy* 19 at 27. Professor Christians, *ibid*, observes that although for more than a decade the United States together with other European countries framed the issue of tax evasion as an important global problem for reasons relating to economic efficiency and fairness, both in the early 1990s and again in response to the economic crisis in 2008–2009, the OECD's stated policy goals were directed at shutting down tax havens to protect national revenue bases and address major fiscal problems that wealthy countries were experiencing as a result of the crisis.

[138] *Ibid* at 19–20 and 40. Professor Christians, *ibid*, argues that despite the emergence of the G20 as an economic leader, the OECD remains the market leader in developing tax standards and guidelines while the G20, rather than providing developing countries with a meaningful voice in the dialogue, provides an opportunity to syndicate OECD-made policy, and further that despite the need for developing countries to play a greater role in global tax policy, such a goal will remain elusive while the OECD dominates this role.

Steven Dean remarked that the US Department of the Treasury introduced TIEAs in the 1980s because it believed that they could reduce tax flight.[139] But as Professor Kudrle observed in 2008 after conducting an economic analysis of tax haven data, no significant impact from the OECD's project on tax evasion could be found. Professor Kudrle theorizes that a lack of transparency enables tax cheats to easily disguise their investments, which complicates efforts to detect tax evasion.[140] An economic study looking at data on cross-border bank deposits from 2009 to 2011 by Professor Johannesen found that the overall level of funds in offshore financial centres had barely changed.[141] Professor Reuven Avi-Yonah argues that the OECD effort was successful on the basis of data showing no decline in individual or corporate tax revenues in OECD member countries.[142] He observes that among OECD member countries, corporate taxes were 2.2 percent of GDP in 1975 and 3.9 percent in 2006.[143] He concludes that overall there is no indication that either individual or corporate tax revenues have gone down in OECD countries from tax competition and that the OECD's effort to curtail harmful tax competition is partly responsible for the OECD's success in taxing the rich through income taxes.[144] But if the OECD's war against tax evasion was successful, why did the G20 call upon the OECD and the Global Forum to move to Automatic Exchange? The recent use by the United States of the threat of criminal prosecution to pry the names of tens of thousands of tax cheats from Swiss banks and the threat of financial penalties against foreign financial institutions under *FATCA* illustrates that in some instances EOI does not work without threats of economic or criminal sanctions.

In an odd kind of way, it can be argued that through the introduction and promulgation of TIEAs the OECD assisted in maintaining the status

---

139 See Chapter 6, Section 2.2.

140 Kudrle, above note 18 at 10.

141 Niels Johannesen & Gabriel Zucman, "The End of Bank Secrecy? An Evaluation of the G20 Tax Haven Crackdown" (2014) 6:1 *American Economic Journal: Economic Policy* 65.

142 Avi-Yonah, above note 28.

143 *Ibid* at 791. Professor Avi-Yonah further notes (citing *Revenue Statistics*, above note 28 at 21) that individual taxes on income were 11.2 percent of GDP in 1975 and 13 percent in 2006.

144 Avi-Yonah, above note 28 at 791, citing Bird & Zolt, above note 28.

quo surrounding bank secrecy (through the information upon request standard) and thereby assisted both existing tax evaders and newcomers to the field. After all, from a US and Canadian standpoint, putting money in a jurisdiction that had signed a TIEA with Washington gave many tax cheats an over 95 percent chance of going undetected by audit.[145]

Separately, it is important to note that many of the significant movements against international tax evasion during the past five years have been the result of unilateral (versus multilateral) measures by some countries, like the United States and others, that are applying the threat of criminal, civil, and financial penalties to bolster their information exchange powers to combat tax evasion. Further back, the European Union had started its own original efforts with the *European Union Savings Directive*. Will information exchange with tax havens, whether through existing TIEAs or the new Automatic Exchange standard, really work without additional motivation? Should the OECD and the Global Forum have considered and incorporated into the new standard something along the lines of Dean's economic cooperation through tax revenue sharing with tax havens? Is the omission of some form of economic cooperation from the blueprint of information exchange another fatal flaw that will continue to benefit tax evaders? Can Canada afford to put all of its future efforts relating to EOI to combat tax evasion into one basket such as Automatic Exchange the way that it relied solely on TIEAs? Should Canada be doing more in light of the findings of this research?

The answers to these questions will be revealed over time. While the purpose of EOI mechanisms is generally to promote fairness and principles of equity in the tax system, as the case of *FATCA*'s implementation against Americans living in Canada reveals, a failure to consider the wider policy implications (political, historical, social, and economic) relating to the particular society involved can lead to the opposite result. This research demonstrates that international tax evasion is a highly complex subject. The law is a major piece of the puzzle, but the challenges facing TIEAs and EOI are multidisciplinary in nature, touching

[145] In 2012, individuals earning under $200,000 had a likelihood of being audited of under 3.5 percent. That figure rose to 12 percent for individuals earning over $1 million: see Tony Nitti, "What Are Your Odds of Being Audited by the IRS?" *Forbes* (25 March 2013), online: www.forbes.com/sites/anthonynitti/2013/03/25/what-are-your-odds-of-being-audited-by-the-irs/#71998544727f.

on law, politics, economics, history, and culture. Understanding how the law can be used to more effectively combat international tax evasion requires integrating the political, economic, social, and historical factors relevant to this discussion, only some of which have been touched upon in this research. The adage that you are only as strong as your weakest link certainly holds true in the fight against tax evasion, especially where so many jurisdictions are non-compliant with the OECD standards. The progress that the global fiscal community has achieved to date surrounding TIEAs offers hope for achieving more effective EOI under the new Automatic Exchange standard. Smarter nations will probably figure out that there is a payoff for not waiting and implement some form of economic cooperation to quicken the pace of information exchange on tax cheats. Policy-makers in this field may benefit from recognizing that motivation is an essential element for a successful outcome in the war against tax evasion, and its presence or absence in an EOI mechanism may mean the difference between winning and losing.

Further Readings

Ault, Hugh J. "Reflections on the Role of the OECD in Developing International Tax Norms" (2009) 34 *Brooklyn Journal of International Law* 757.

Avi-Yonah, Reuven S. "The OECD Harmful Tax Competition Report: A Retrospective after a Decade" (2009) 34 *Brooklyn Journal of International Law* 783.

Christians, Allison. "Case Study Research and International Tax Theory" (2010a) 55 *Saint Louis University Law Journal* 331.

Christians, Allison. "Hard Law, Soft Law, and International Taxation" (2007) 25 *Wisconsin International Law Journal* 325.

Christians, Allison. "Sovereignty, Taxation and Social Contract" (2009) 18 *Minnesota Journal of International Law* 99.

Christians, Allison. "Taxation in a Time of Crisis: Policy Leadership from the OECD to the G20" (2010b) 5 *Northwestern Journal of Law & Social Policy* 19.

Cockfield, Arthur J. "Protecting Taxpayer Privacy Rights under Enhanced Cross-border Tax Information Exchange: Toward a Multilateral Taxpayer Bill of Rights" (2010) 42 *University of British Columbia Law Review* 420.

Dean, Steven A. "More Cooperation, Less Uniformity: Tax Deharmonization and the Future of the International Tax Regime" (2009) 84 *Tulane Law Review* 125.

Dean, Steven A. "Philosopher Kings and International Tax: A New Approach to Tax Havens, Tax Flight, and International Tax Cooperation" (2007) 58 *Hastings Law Journal* 911.

Eden, Lorraine, & Robert T Kudrle. "Tax Havens: Renegade States in the International Tax Regime?" (2005) 27 *Law & Policy* 100.

Kudrle, Robert T. "The OECD's Harmful Tax Competition Initiative and the Tax Havens: From Bombshell to Damp Squib" (2008) 8 *Global Economy Journal* 1.

OECD. *Harmful Tax Competition: An Emerging Global Issue* (Paris: OECD, 1998).

OECD. *Tax Transparency 2011: Report on Progress* (Paris: OECD, 2011).

Sawyer, Adrian. "Peer Review of Tax Information Exchange Agreements: Is It More Than Just about the Numbers?" (2011) 26 *Australian Tax Forum* 397.

4

International Tax Enforcement in Canada

1 Introduction

Tax collection in Canada relies upon taxpayer self-assessment and self-reporting.[1] Section 150(1) of the *Income Tax Act* requires taxpayers to file a return of income.[2] Once the return is received by CRA, the Minister of National Revenue (Minister) is obligated by statute to conduct, "with all

[1] In the Supreme Court of Canada case *R v McKinlay Transport Ltd*, [1990] 1 SCR 627 [*McKinlay*], Wilson J stated that s 150(1) of the *Income Tax Act*, RSC 1985, c 1 (5th Supp) [*Act*], is based on the principle of self-reporting and self-assessment. This case had many important elements. For example, the Court held that the requirement to produce documents does not violate an individual's rights, as an unreasonable search and seizure, as protected by the *Canadian Charter of Rights and Freedoms*, Part I of the *Constitution Act, 1982*, being Schedule B to the *Canada Act 1982* (UK), 1982, c 11 [*Charter*]. Moreover, Wilson J, *McKinlay*, *ibid* at 649, indicated that "a taxpayer may have little expectation of privacy in relation to his business records relevant to the determination of his tax liability."

[2] *Act*, above note 1. A non-resident person or corporation that has a taxable capital gain, sells taxable Canadian property, or is subject to tax under Part I on taxable income earned in Canada must file a tax return similarly to a resident. Section 150(2) is directed at preventing abuse and states:

> Every person, whether or not the person is liable to pay tax under this Part for a taxation year and whether or not a return has been filed under subsection (1) or (3), shall, on demand sent by the Minister, file, within such reasonable time stipulated in the demand, with the Minister in prescribed form and containing prescribed information a return of the income for the taxation year designated in the demand.

D.S. Kerzner, D.W. Chodikoff, *International Tax Evasion in the Global Information Age*, DOI 10.1007/978-3-319-40421-9_4

due dispatch," a review of the tax return.[3] The Minister will then issue a Notice of Assessment.[4] Section 152(4) of the *Act* provides that the Minister may subsequently reassess the taxpayer's tax liability.[5]

The success of administering this system of taxation is dependent on two key factors: taxpayer honesty and information. As Cory J of the Supreme Court of Canada in *Knox Contracting Ltd v Canada* stated, "[t]he entire system of levying and collecting income tax is dependent upon the

---

Failure to comply with a demand can have serious consequences. Section 238(1) states:

> Every person who has failed to file or make a return as and when required by or under this Act or a regulation . . . is guilty of an offence and, in addition to any penalty otherwise provided, is liable on summary conviction to (a) a fine of not less than $1,000 and not more than $25,000; or (b) [such a fine] . . . and imprisonment for a term not exceeding 12 months.

There is also the possibility that a taxpayer could be charged with the offence of willful tax evasion under s 239(1)(d) of the *Act*. Section 239(1) states:

> Every person who has . . . (d) wilfully, in any manner, evaded or attempted to evade compliance with this Act or payment of taxes imposed by this Act . . . is guilty of an offence and, in addition to any penalty otherwise provided, is liable on summary conviction to (f) a fine of not less than 50%, and not more than 200%, of the amount of the tax that was sought to be evaded, or (g) both the fine described in paragraph 239(1)(f) and imprisonment for a term not exceeding 2 years.

Furthermore, s 239(2) states:

> Every person who is charged with an offence described in subsection 239(1) . . . may, at the election of the Attorney General of Canada, be prosecuted on indictment and, if convicted, is, in addition to any penalty otherwise provided, liable to (a) a fine of not less than 100% and not more than 200% of . . . the amount of the tax that was sought to be evaded, and . . . (b) imprisonment for a term not exceeding 5 years.

The differences between ss 238(1) and 239(1)(d) are significant, and CRA typically does not pursue a conviction under s 239(1)(d) unless there are facts that would likely result in a conviction: see *Sturgessv R* (1983), 83 DTC 5434 (TD), correcting the record (1984), 84 DTC 6525 (CA).

[3] *Act*, above note 1, s 152(1).

[4] *Ibid*, s 152(1). For CRA policy regarding the tax audit, see CRA, Information Circular 71-14R3, "The Tax Audit" (18 June 1984).

[5] *Act*, above note 1.

integrity of the taxpayer in reporting and assessing income. If the system is to work, the returns must be honestly completed."[6] Information is therefore a central element leading either to confirmation of a taxpayer's filing position or to the basis from which the Minister develops certain assumptions and challenges a taxpayer's tax reporting position. When a taxpayer's position is challenged by the government, we know that the first step is an audit and the eventual issuance by the Minister of an audit proposal letter leaving the taxpayer two choices: either accept the Minister's proposed assessing or reassessing position or challenge it. In many instances, a taxpayer will provide sufficient documentation and oral evidence to convince the Minister's auditor to either modify or reverse in its entirety the proposed audit position. However, there are also many other instances where even when the taxpayer responds, the Minister refuses to accept the taxpayer's submissions and where CRA consequently issues an assessment or reassessment in accordance with the initial audit proposal letter.

The question that we attempt to resolve in this chapter is twofold. First, how does the Minister access taxpayer information, particularly foreign-based taxpayer information? Second, what statutory provisions and rights are engaged to protect a taxpayer's information, especially in relation to the right of privacy? Essentially, we examine the powers and tools that CRA can use to obtain taxpayer information for an audit, whether for civil purposes or a criminal investigation, particularly in non-voluntary situations.

2 The Taxpayer's Obligations: It Starts with Books and Records

The *Act* contains many provisions that are intended to encourage and ensure compliance. For example, taxpayers are required to maintain books and records for various specified periods of time at their place of business or residence in Canada.[7] The *Act* requires that taxpayers maintain

[6] [1990] 2 SCR 338 at 350.

[7] *Act*, above note 1, s 230(1). For CRA policy regarding the retention and destruction of books and records, see CRA, Information Circular 78-10R5, "Books and Records Retention/Destruction" (June 2010). For a historical review, see also Michael G Quigley, "Controlling Tax Information: Limits to Record-Keeping and Disclosure Obligations" (1999) 47 *Canadian Tax Journal* 1.

these documents "in such form and containing such information as will enable the taxes payable under this Act or the taxes or other amounts that should have been deducted, withheld or collected to be determined."[8] As noted by the Supreme Court of Canada in *R v McKinlay Transport Ltd*, the *Act* contains provisions that are intended to limit the possibility that a taxpayer may attempt "to take advantage of the self-reporting system in order to avoid paying his or her full share of the tax burden by violating the rules set forth in the Act."[9] In fact, section 238(2) of the *Act* makes it a criminal offence for a taxpayer to fail to meet the record-keeping obligations of section 230(1) of the *Act*.[10]

3 Investigative Powers: Commencing with Section 231.1

3.1 Introduction

It is equally important for the Canadian state to possess broad investigative powers so that CRA can ensure compliance with the *Act*. Section 231.1(1) of the *Act* provides the Minister with broad powers to inspect, audit, and examine a taxpayer's records "and any document of the taxpayer or of any other person that relates or may relate to the information that is or should be in the books or records of the taxpayer or to any amount payable by the taxpayer under" the *Act*.[11] The *Act* further provides ministerial officials with the right to examine any property in

---

[8] *Act*, above note 1, s 230(1). For a case dealing with judicial review of a requirement to keep adequate books and records of a business, see *Merchant (2000) Ltd v Canada (AG)*, 2000 CanLII 15779 (FC).

[9] *McKinlay*, above note 1 at 641.

[10] *Act*, above note 1, s 238(2). See, for example, *Sidhu v MNR* (1993), 93 DTC 5453 (FCA).

[11] There is a great deal of literature on the scope of s 231.1. See, for example, Colin Campbell, *Administration of Income Tax 2015* (Toronto: Carswell, 2015); Ed Kroft, "Recent Developments in CRA's Reach for Information — Questions You Want Answered" (Paper delivered at the Ontario Tax Conference, 24 October 2011) [unpublished]; Carole Benoit, Susan Betts, & Andrew Kingissepp, "Taxpayer Access to Government Papers and Government Access to Taxpayer Papers" in *2012 Tax Dispute Resolution Conference Report: Proceedings of the Tax Dispute Resolution, Compliance, and Administration in Canada Conference* (Toronto: Canadian Tax Foundation, 2013) 19:1 [*2012 Tax Dispute Resolution Conference Report*].

an inventory of a taxpayer and obligates a taxpayer to provide reasonable assistance to CRA personnel and to answer all proper questions relating to either the administration or enforcement of the *Act*.[12] Section 231.1 also requires the owner or manager of a property or business to attend at the place of business with CRA personnel. Section 231.3(1) permits the Minister to apply for a search warrant to enter and search any building or place for documents or things and gives the Minister the right to seize documents or things.[13] But CRA will often, and now more commonly, seek to obtain a search warrant under section 487 of the *Criminal Code*.[14] A judge or other judicial officer can issue a warrant under the latter section if satisfied that there are reasonable and probable grounds to believe that an offence has been committed, there is evidence at the place to be searched, and the thing to be seized will provide evidence of the commission of a suspected offence. There is also the "general warrant" provision found in section 487.01 of the *Criminal Code*.[15] This section is purposely broad as it permits the use of any investigative procedure or technique to do anything that would constitute an unreasonable search and seizure if it were not statutorily permitted by this very section of the *Criminal Code*. The general warrant is particularly useful in situations where the investigators have grounds to believe that evidence exists and can be obtained but are not certain of the location of the evidence. A perfect example of this kind of evidence is electronically stored financial data.

The *Criminal Code* also contains a number of provisions that deal with the production of documents and different types of data. Section 487.012 permits a public officer to demand that a person preserve computer data in her possession.[16] A demand can be made on the basis

---

[12] *Act*, above note 1, s 231.1(1). See *James Richardson & Sons v MNR* (1982), 82 DTC 6204 (FCA) [*Richardson*]; *AGT Ltd v Canada (AG)* (1996), 96 DTC 6388 (FCTD), aff'd (1997), 97 DTC 5189 (FCA) [*AGT Ltd* CA], leave to appeal to SCC refused, [1997] SCCA No 314.

[13] *Act*, above note 1, s 231.3(1). A warrant under the *Act* must be issued by a judge of a provincial superior court or of the Federal Court, as opposed to a judge of an inferior court.

[14] *Criminal Code*, RSC 1985, c C-46, s 487. Regular warrants under s 487 may be issued by a justice of the peace or other judicial officer. A warrant under section 487.01 of the *Criminal Code*, *ibid*, more commonly referred to as the general warrant provision, must be issued by a provincial court judge.

[15] *Ibid*, s 487.01.

[16] *Ibid*, s 487.012.

of a reasonable belief that an offence has been or will be committed, whether under the *Act* or the *Criminal Code* (or, for that matter, any Act of Parliament). The demand must be premised on the reasonable belief that the data would be of assistance in an investigation. Section 487.013 of the *Criminal Code* provides for the making of a preservation order for computer data.[17] It is made by way of an *ex parte* application, and either a judge or a justice of the peace may order a person to preserve computer data. Section 487.014(1) creates the general production order, which allows a judge or justice of the peace to order a person to produce a document that is a copy of a document that is in his possession or control. More importantly, it permits a judge or justice of the peace to order a person "to prepare and produce a document containing data that is in the person's possession or control."[18] The *Criminal Code* contains further precise production order provisions in respect of transmission data and tracking data.[19] Section 487.018 provides that a financial institution may be ordered to prepare and produce a document that sets out the following information: "(a) either the account number of a person named in the order or the name of a person whose account number is specified in the order; (b) the type of account; (c) the status of the account; and (d) the date on which it was opened or closed."[20] A production order can be challenged. Section 487.0193 provides that a person, financial institution, or entity can apply in writing to the judge or justice of the peace who made the order to revoke or vary the order.[21]

Section 231.4(1) of the *Act* permits the Minister to make inquiries into a taxpayer's affairs, as deemed necessary, with reference to anything relating to the administration or enforcement of the *Act*.[22] The *Act* also gives

---

[17] *Ibid*, s 487.013.

[18] *Ibid*, s 487.014.

[19] *Ibid*, ss 487.016 & 487.017.

[20] *Ibid*, s 487.018.

[21] *Ibid*, s 487.0193.

[22] *Act*, above note 1, s 231.4(1). See the decisions in *Del Zotto v Canada (MNR)*, [1997] 2 FC 428 (TD) [*Del Zotto* TD], and Strayer J's dissent in the appeal, [1997] 3 FC 40 (CA) [*Del Zotto* CA], leave to appeal to SCC granted, [1999] 1 SCR 3 [*Del Zotto* SCC].

CRA officials the specific right to make copies of any document relating to the taxpayer or any other person.[23]

3.2 Failure to Comply and Its Consequences

The obvious questions arising from the wide scope of these CRA powers are the following: First, to what extent must a taxpayer comply with these various statutory obligations? Second, what are the consequences if a taxpayer fails to comply with these obligations?

Section 231.5(2) of the *Act* plainly states that "no person shall physically or otherwise, interfere with, hinder or molest an official . . . doing anything that the official is authorized to do under this Act . . . ."[24] A taxpayer is required to provide "all reasonable assistance" and to "respond to all proper questions."[25] Failure to provide the requested information can have multiple possible outcomes. First, the Minister could simply rely upon section 152 of the *Act* to reassess the taxpayer for additional taxes and/or financially penalize the taxpayer. Second, the failure to comply is a criminal offence. Therefore, under section 238 of the *Act*, the Minister could seek to prosecute the taxpayer for the failure to comply.[26] Specifically, section 238 states that every person who has failed to comply with section 231.1 of the *Act* is guilty of an offence and in addition to any other penalty that is otherwise provided is liable on summary conviction to a fine of not less than $1,000 and not more than $25,000, or both a fine and imprisonment for a term not exceeding twelve months.[27] Section 238(2) of the *Act* also permits a court to impose on the taxpayer an order to comply with the provision of the *Act* with which the taxpayer has failed to comply.[28] Third, under section 231.7(1) of the *Act*, CRA could seek a compliance order from a judge, which would order the taxpayer to provide any access, assistance, information, or document

[23] *Act*, above note 1, s 231.5(1).

[24] *Ibid*, s 231.5(2).

[25] *Ibid*, s 231.1(1)(d).

[26] *Ibid*, s 238.

[27] *Ibid*.

[28] *Ibid*, s 238.2.

sought by the Minister.[29] The failure to comply with this court order could lead CRA to submit an application to the court for another order finding the taxpayer in contempt of the initial order.[30]

4 Requirements to Provide Documents or Information: Section 231.2

4.1 Introduction

Whereas section 231.1 of the *Act* may be described as a polite way of seeking both taxpayer cooperation and information, section 231.2 may be best described as the "No more excuses, just provide us the information or else" approach. Sections 231.2(1)(a) and (b) permit the Minister to obtain any information or document from any person where that information or document is intended to be used for "any purpose related to the administration or enforcement of this Act."[31] In *Tower v MNR*, Malone J, speaking for the court, offered the following analysis when describing the meaning of section 231.2:

[29] *Ibid*, s 231.7(1). In the recent decision *Canada (National Revenue) v BP Canada Energy Co*, 2015 FC 714 [*BP Canada*], the Minister brought an application to the Federal Court seeking an order to compel BP Canada Energy Company to comply with a request to produce records with respect to an audit being carried out by CRA. The Minister had sought production of tax accrual or tax reserve working papers and issues lists prepared by BP's in-house accounting personnel that indicated certain tax positions and the possibility that there may be tax liabilities by way of contingent liabilities. After BP objected to producing the documents as requested by way of a request under s 231.1(1) of the *Act*, above note 1, the Minister sought a compliance order under s 231.7(1) of the *Act* that would force BP to provide the documents. BP argued that the Minister was involved in a fishing expedition and that producing the working papers would offend the fundamental tenets of a self-reporting tax system. The court disagreed and found that the working papers and issues lists were compellable. Justice Campbell of the Federal Court concluded, *BP Canada*, *ibid* at para 37, that he was "unable to give any weight to BP Canada's arguments." He further added, *ibid* at para 38, that an "audit is not [a fishing] expedition." Justice Campbell dismissed out of hand the bad faith argument raised by BP. It was his view, *ibid* at para 44, that "no supportable finding can be made on the existing evidence that the Minister's officials made the demands for the Issues List in bad faith." The court granted the compliance order under s 231.7(1) of the *Act* for the production of BP's working papers as requested by the Minister. See also *Canada (National Revenue) v Marshall*, 2006 FC 279, where the Minister was successful in obtaining a compliance order, and for the opposite result, *Canada (National Revenue) v Chamandy*, 2014 FC 354.

[30] *Act*, above note 1, s 231.7(4).

[31] *Ibid*, ss 231.2(1)(a) & (b).

> Paragraph 231.2(1)(*a*), when properly interpreted, empowers the Minister to compel a taxpayer to provide "information," meaning knowledge or facts. In order to exercise this power, the Minister must be able to ask questions to elicit the knowledge, facts or figures. The words "return of income or supplementary return" in paragraph (*a*) does [*sic*] not detract from this interpretation as the preceding word "including" means that the phrase is not exhaustive of the meaning of "information." These words enable the Minister not only to get the information regarding a taxpayer's income, but also to specify the form in which this information must be provided, i.e. a tax return containing prescribed information rather than in a letter. In my view, the Minister is therefore able to compel production of documents and records under paragraph 231.2(1)(*b*) and ask questions to elicit knowledge or facts under paragraph 231.2(1)(*a*).[32]

There has been much caselaw on the exact scope of section 231.2 of the *Act*.[33] One commentator has suggested that section 231.2 permits CRA to carry out fishing expeditions for documents or information.[34] What is clear from the court decisions is that there appear to be few limits or restraints on just how far CRA can "mine" for information, whether information in the form of documents or other types of information. In the case of *Lapointe v Canada*, for example, CRA sought from a bank all written entries in the various accounts belonging to the taxpayer.[35] The taxpayer argued that the information request was nothing more than a fishing expedition and sought to quash the requirement. The application was dismissed by the Federal Court.[36] One of the functions of section 231.2 is to permit CRA to gather information from a third-party record holder.

In the case of *Redeemer Foundation v Canada (National Revenue)*, the Supreme Court of Canada was called upon to examine CRA's audit powers, and in so doing, the Court commented upon the distinction between

[32] 2003 FCA 307 at para 20.

[33] See *McKinlay*, above note 1; *Fraser Milner Casgrain LLP v MNR*, 2002 FCT 912; *Richardson*, above note 12; *NM Skalbania Ltd v R* (1989), 89 DTC 5495 (BC Co Ct); *AGT* CA, above note 12; *MNR v Sand Exploration Ltd* (1995), 95 DTC 5469 (FCTD); *Artistic Ideas Inc v Canada Revenue Agency*, 2004 FC 573, aff'd 2005 FCA 68.

[34] See Michael Ziesmann, "Gone Fishing: An Analysis of CRA Powers and Policies relating to the Use of Fishing Expeditions in Information Gathering" (2008–2009) 58 *Canadian Tax Journal* 1.

[35] 2003 FCT 102.

[36] For a similar outcome, see *Bining v Canada*, 2003 FCT 689.

sections 231.1 and 231.2 of the *Act*.[37] The Redeemer Foundation was a charity that operated a forgivable loan program. CRA made a request for the list of donors for the 2001 and 2002 taxation years, and the Foundation complied with the request. CRA then asked the Foundation for a list of donors for the 2003 taxation year, and this time the Foundation refused, arguing that prior judicial authorization was required. The Foundation went to the Federal Court to seek judicial review of the Minister's decision to ask for donor information on the grounds that the request was a nullity because a court order had not been previously obtained by the Minister. At the Federal Court, the reviewing judge found that the CRA request was improper without prior judicial authorization and ordered the return of the donor information (the Minister was also precluded from acting upon the information by reassessing donors).[38] The Minister appealed the decision. The Federal Court of Appeal overturned the Federal Court's decision and dismissed the application for judicial review.[39] The Foundation then sought and obtained leave to appeal to the Supreme Court.

There was a discreet issue before the Supreme Court. Put simply, was the Minister permitted to request the identification of the Foundation's donors pursuant to section 231.1 in carrying out an audit of the Foundation, or was the Minister required to obtain judicial authorization under section 231.2(3) before requesting this information from the Foundation? In a 4:3 decision, the Court held that the Minister was entitled to the donor information and was not required to obtain judicial authorization before requesting the information. According to the majority of the Court, the Minister has broad powers under section 231.1 to inspect, audit, and examine taxpayers' records and any information that is or should be in taxpayers' books. It is what the Court had to say about 231.2 in general, the unlikely abuse of power by CRA, and the expectation of taxpayer privacy that gives a better understanding of the scope of CRA's investigative powers. Writing for the majority, McLachlin CJ and LeBel J stated the following with respect to the scope of section 231.2:

---

[37] 2008 SCC 46 [*Redeemer Foundation* SCC].

[38] *Redeemer Foundation v Canada (National Revenue)*, 2005 FC 1361.

[39] *Redeemer Foundation v Canada (National Revenue)*, 2006 FCA 325.

"The Minister may well need to obtain information about one or more taxpayers outside the context of a formal audit. Section 231.2 responds to this need, subject to a requirement for judicial authorization if the Minister is seeking information relating to unnamed persons from a third party record holder."[40] Moreover, the Court majority stated:

> The s. 231.2(2) requirement should not apply to situations in which the requested information is required in order to verify the compliance of the taxpayer being audited. Regardless of whether or not there is a possibility or a probability that the audit will lead to the investigation of other unnamed taxpayers, the CRA should be able to obtain information it would otherwise have the ability to see in the course of an audit.[41]

The majority of the Court reiterated that when it comes to business records relevant to the determination of a taxpayer's tax liability, the expectation of privacy is low:

> It is true that the broad wording of s. 231.1(1) provides a powerful tool that may reveal a great deal of information about transactions between the taxpayer under audit and third parties. However, this is business information. Taxpayers have a very low expectation of privacy in their business records relevant to the determination of their tax liability: *R. v. McKinlay Transport Ltd.*, [1990] 1 S.C.R. 627.[42]

Finally, the majority of the Court concluded that there is little risk in CRA's abusing its powers to issue requirements:

> There remains a concern that the CRA may attempt to investigate unnamed taxpayers under the "guise" of an audit. Use of the word "guise" implies that the taxpayer being audited is not really suspected of non-compliance and that the unnamed persons are the real targets. However, if an organization's charitable program is not valid, then both the charity *and* any of its donors who claim tax credits are non-compliant. The CRA has a valid interest in investigating both. The

[40] *Redeemer Foundation* SCC, above note 37 at para 15.

[41] *Ibid* at para 22.

[42] *Ibid* at para 25.

> same would be true of any other relationship involving reciprocal tax treatment. In our view, the risk seems minimal that the CRA would use its authority to audit a taxpayer who is not personally suspected of non-compliance merely to investigate other unnamed taxpayers for non-compliance.[43]

As a result of both the language of the *Act* and the caselaw, taxpayers in the domestic civil context do not have very much protection against the powers of CRA to demand the production of documents and other tax-related information. This is equally true where CRA requests information in the hands of a corporation that operates outside of Canada or where a foreign government seeks CRA's assistance in obtaining information from a Canadian company. In the former situation, the case *Canada v Crestbrook Forest Industries Limited* is illustrative.[44] In this case, the corporate taxpayer operated a paper mill in Canada and agreed to sell all of its production to two Japanese companies. As part of the joint venture agreement, the Japanese companies gained control of the Canadian company. The Japanese companies further agreed that there would be a reduction in the price charged to them by the Canadian company for production. The discount rate was between 5.6 and 6 percent, depending on the circumstances. The Minister alleged that the discount was excessive and that a 2 percent discount was reasonable. Therefore, the Minister sought to add back to the taxpayer's income for three years amounts that represented the 4 percent difference in the price charged by the Canadian company to the two Japanese companies. The Minister also assessed the taxpayer for additional Part XIII non-resident withholding tax on the 4 percent amounts. The taxpayer appealed to the Federal Court, Trial Division,[45] and during the course of the discovery, the company's representative was asked a number of questions concerning the role played by the two Japanese companies in establishing the discount rate. The representative attempted to obtain answers to these questions, but the two Japanese companies refused to answer. The Crown therefore brought

[43] *Ibid* at para 27.

[44] [1993] 3 FCR 251 (CA) [*Crestbrook* CA].

[45] *Canada v Crestbrook Forest Industries Limited*, 55 FTR 146 (TD).

an application seeking to obtain an order from the court compelling the taxpayer to obtain answers to the questions.

The associate senior prothonotary of the Federal Court ordered that only three of the twenty-two questions at issue be answered because the other nineteen questions had to do with matters that predated the execution of the joint venture agreement.[46] This decision was appealed, and the motions judge of the Federal Court, Trial Division upheld the prothonotary's ruling on the nineteen questions. However, the motions judge overturned the decision of the prothonotary on the three questions that postdated the execution of the joint venture agreement on the basis that it was not open to the court to compel a taxpayer to respond to a question the answer to which was in the hands of companies over which the taxpayer allegedly had no control. The Crown appealed this decision to the Federal Court of Appeal, and that court held that it was within the ability of the taxpayer to obtain answers to all twenty-two questions. The court concluded that "the commercial reality of the corporate arrangement was that the two Japanese companies were *de facto* engaged jointly in an enterprise in Canada using Crestbrook as their source of supply."[47] Thus, the two Japanese companies were obliged to provide the answers, or information, to the Minister.

In the situation where a foreign government seeks CRA's assistance in obtaining information from a Canadian company, the case *Pacific Network Services Ltd v MNR* is illustrative.[48] Here, the Minister issued requirements under section 231.2 of the *Act* to compel two corporate taxpayers (Pacific Network Services Ltd and Leader Direct Marketing Ltd) to provide corporate information including documents, and names and addresses of officers and shareholders. The requirements were issued for the purposes of Article 26 (Exchange of Information) of the 1975 *Convention between Canada and France for the Avoidance of Double Taxation and the Prevention of Fiscal Evasion with respect to Taxes on Income and Capital.*[49] The two corporate

[46] *Crestbrook* CA, above note 44.

[47] *Ibid* at para 10.

[48] *Pacific Network Services Ltd v MNR*, 2002 FCT 1158 [*Pacific Network*].

[49] 2 May 1975, Can TS 1976 No 30 (as signed on 2 May 1975, and amended by the protocols signed on 16 January 1987, 30 November 1995, and 2 February 2010), online: www.fin.gc.ca/treaties-conventions/france_-eng.asp [*Canada–France Tax Treaty*].

taxpayers sought judicial review, more particularly, a declaration that the requirements were invalid and unlawful. The taxpayers argued that the Minister had no authority under either Article 26 of the *Canada–France Tax Treaty* or section 231.2 of the *Act* to issue the requirements and, in the alternative, that the parts of the requirements that required them to provide information pertaining to their shareholders and officers were invalid since no authorization had been obtained from a judge in accordance with section 231.2(3) of the *Act*.[50] What is significant about this case is that the requirements had been prompted by the French government, which had asked for the information and sought the assistance of CRA in obtaining it. The court concluded that the requirements were valid. The taxpayers' main contention was that upon a plain reading of Article 26 of the *Canada–France Tax Treaty*, the Minister did not have the authority to issue a requirement under section 231.2 of the *Act*. This was soundly rejected by the court primarily because

> the plain words used in Article 26 of the *Canada–France Income Tax Convention* infer that when faced with a request for information from the other State, the requesting State is required not only to exchange information already gathered, but also to obtain information by use of administrative measures, such as a requirement under subsection 231.2(1) of the Act.[51]

Where a taxpayer fails to respond to a CRA requirement for information, there can be serious consequences for the taxpayer. These consequences are discussed in the next section.

4.2 Saying No: The Consequences of a Failure to Comply

As with section 231.1 of the *Act*, a failure to comply with a requirement under section 231.2 can prompt CRA to seek a compliance order under

[50] *Pacific Network*, above note 48 at para 6.

[51] *Ibid* at para 25. Compare with the decision of the Federal Court, Trial Division in *Montreal Aluminum Processing Inc v Canada (AG)* (1991), 91 DTC 5424 (FCTD), and the Federal Court of Appeal's overturning of the Trial Division's decision in *Montreal Aluminum Processing Inc v Canada (AG)* (1992), 92 DTC 6567 (FCA).

section 231.7(1).[52] In practice, it is common for a summary application to be made by lawyers from the Department of Justice on behalf of the Minister to the Federal Court, requesting that a judge order the person to provide any access, assistance, information, or documents sought by the Minister, assuming that the judge is satisfied that the person was required to provide access, assistance, information, or documents and failed to do so and that in the case of information or documents, they are not protected from disclosure by solicitor-client privilege. In seeking this order, the Minister must provide notice of the application, and it is mandated by statute that five clear days must pass before the court can hear the application. As with an application for an order in respect of section 231.1, the court can impose any conditions on an order in respect of section 231.2 that a judge deems appropriate.[53] Typically, the judge will impose a deadline to produce or will stipulate the actual number of days that a person has to produce the ordered information or documents. The failure or refusal to comply with an order of the court may lead to a judge's finding the person in contempt of court, following which the person will be subject to the processes and punishments of the court to which the judge is appointed.[54] A person can appeal the decision to impose the order, but an appeal does not suspend the execution of the order unless it is ordered by a judge of the court to which the appeal is made.[55] There have been many instances where the Federal Court has

[52] *Act*, above note 1, s 231.7(1). See *Canada (National Revenue) v Revcon Oilfield Constructors Incorporated*, 2015 FC 524; *Canada (National Revenue) v SML Operations (Canada) Ltd*, 2003 FC 868 [*SML Operations*]; *Canada (National Revenue) v Lee*, 2015 FC 634. In *SML Operations, ibid* at para 14, Tremblay-Lamer J set out the three requirements that must all be satisfied before a judge will exercise the discretion to order a person to provide the information or documents sought by the Minister:

1) The person against whom the order is sought was required under ss 231.1 or 231.2 to provide the access, assistance, information, or documents sought by the Minister.
2) Although "the person was required to provide the information or documents sought by the Minister, he or she did not do so."
3) The information or documents sought "are not protected from disclosure by solicitor-client privilege," as defined in the *Act*.

[53] *Act*, above note 1, s 231.7(3).

[54] *Ibid*, s 231.7(4).

[55] *Ibid*, s 231.7(5).

imposed a fine for contempt of court for failing to comply, and in some rare cases it has imposed imprisonment.[56]

Given the powers conferred upon the Minister and the Minister's officials by sections 231.1 and 231.2 of the *Act*, it is fair to say that taxpayers have little ability to withhold tax information. The *Act* contains further provisions to gain taxpayer information, which are discussed in the next sections.

5 Public Inquiries

What may surprise some readers is the existence of an inquiry provision in the *Act*. Section 231.4(1) provides the Minister with the power to authorize any person, whether a CRA official or someone else, to make any inquiry that the person deems necessary with reference to anything related to the administration or enforcement of the *Act*.[57]

The reality is that section 231.4 has been used infrequently by CRA. The provision was subject to a constitutional challenge in *Del Zotto v Canada*, in which the Supreme Court of Canada concluded that section 231.4 does not violate the protections against self-incrimination or unreasonable search and seizure contained in sections 7 and 8 of the *Charter*.[58] Essentially, the Supreme Court adopted the dissenting reasons of Strayer J of the Federal Court of Appeal.[59] Justice Strayer, in turn, had agreed with the reasoning of Rothstein J of the Federal Court, Trial Division (as he was then), who had held that the provisions of section 231.4 and the actual inquiry process were constitutional.[60] Justice Rothstein had found that the inquiry process was primarily regulatory in nature, therefore not criminal or quasi criminal, and therefore justifiable under the *Charter*.

---

[56] See, for example, *Canada (National Revenue) v Money Stop*, 2013 FC 133; *Canada (National Revenue) v Vallelonga*, 2013 FC 1155.

[57] *Act*, above note 1, s 231.4(1).

[58] *Del Zotto* SCC, above note 22; *Charter*, above note 1.

[59] *Del Zotto* FCA, above note 22.

[60] *Del Zotto* FCTD, above note 22.

6 Foreign-Based Information

6.1 Introduction

While at first blush it may seem inappropriate to say that when all else fails, CRA can resort to section 231.6 of the *Act* to obtain taxpayer information or documents, it is not far from the truth. In the normal course of conducting a taxpayer audit, the Minister will first ask politely for information,[61] after which the Minister will resort to the issuance of a requirement for information.[62] However, in this day and age of international business, it is more than likely that information or documents could exist that are located or available outside of Canada and that may be relevant to the administration or enforcement of the *Act*, including the collection of any monies payable under the *Act* by any person.[63]

Therefore, in certain instances, the Minister can rely upon section 231.6(1) of the *Act* to obtain foreign-based information or documents. This section requires the Minister to give notice to the taxpayer, either by serving the notice personally or by registered or certified mail, and whether a resident or non-resident if that taxpayer is carrying on business in Canada, it is required to provide any "foreign-based information or document."[64] But what is foreign-based information or a foreign-based document? The *Act* defines "foreign-based information or document" in section 231.6(1) as any information or document available or located outside Canada that may be relevant to the administration or enforcement of the *Act*. Section 231 defines the term "document" to include "a record."[65] And section 248(1) in turn defines the term "record" to include any other thing containing information, whether in writing or in any other form.[66]

One would presume that this definition is sufficiently broad to include information in electronic form stored on a computer server.

---

[61] See Section 3, above in this chapter.

[62] See Section 4, above in this chapter.

[63] *Act*, above note 1, s 231.6(1).

[64] *Ibid*, s 231.6(2).

[65] *Ibid*, s 231.

[66] *Ibid*, s 248(1).

From this presumption, one would further presume that the processes and procedures established in the *Act* with respect to the acquisition of foreign-based information would apply. However, in the recent case *eBay Canada Ltd v Canada (National Revenue)*, the Federal Court of Appeal found that information stored electronically on a computer server outside of Canada but accessible to a person in Canada is not "foreign-based information."[67] In *eBay*, the Minister issued a requirement under section 231.2 on eBay Canada Ltd and eBay CS Vancouver Inc to produce information identifying "Power Sellers" in Canada who had sold more than a certain volume of merchandise on eBay. The Minister sought this information and additionally requested the gross sales of these Power Sellers to determine whether the Power Sellers had complied with the *Act*. The appellants, eBay Canada and eBay Vancouver, challenged the Minister's use of section 231.2 to obtain this information, arguing that section 231.2 does not apply to their case because the information sought is foreign-based information and that as such the request for this information is subject to the comprehensive code found within section 231.6. The appellants further argued that it was important to determine whether the Minister had relied upon the correct section to request this information because section 231.2 permits the Minister, with judicial authorization, to require production of information relating to unnamed persons whereas section 231.6 does not allow for the imposition of a requirement to produce foreign-based information relating to unnamed persons.

The facts of the case were straightforward. The information regarding the identity of Canadian eBay sellers was stored as electronic records on servers in the United States. These records were maintained by Swisscorp, which was a wholly owned subsidiary of eBay United States. The sole question put before the lower court was whether the information sought by the Minister was "foreign-based" because it was available or located outside Canada even though the appellants had been able to access the information in Canada for use in the business but had not downloaded the information to their computers. Justice Hughes found that the information sought was not foreign-based information even though it was

[67] 2008 FCA 348 [*eBay* CA].

stored on servers outside of Canada.[68] He found that the information was also located in Canada because it could be readily accessed and used by the appellants. Therefore, the Federal Court concluded that the Minister was entirely correct in requiring the appellants to produce the information by way of a requirement issued under section 231.2, without being subject to the procedural demands imposed by section 231.6.[69]

This decision was appealed to the Federal Court of Appeal, which faced the same question as the Federal Court. The Federal Court of Appeal concluded that the information was not "foreign-based," and in so doing, it examined the scheme of section 231.6.[70] The section was enacted following the release of the Department of Finance's *The White Paper: Tax Reform 1987*.[71] The Department of Finance had made recommendations to change the law so that it would be much easier for the Minister to obtain information concerning cross-border transfer pricing. As the Court of Appeal noted, the language of section 231.6 deals with foreign-based information more generally and is not limited to production of information concerning international transfer pricing.[72] Furthermore, the court stated:

> The scheme of section 231.6 suggests that Parliament was concerned that it could be unduly onerous for a person to be required to produce material located outside Canada and in the possession of another person, and that the section may operate in an unduly extraterritorial manner. [In the con-

[68] *eBay Canada Ltd v Canada (National Revenue)*, 2007 FC 930 [*eBay* FC]. Justice Hughes issued reasons and partial judgment on 18 September 2007 dismissing eBay's principal arguments, but he delayed releasing his final decision dealing with whether there was enough evidence that the Minister required the information to audit Canadian Power Sellers for compliance with the *Act* until after the release of the Federal Court of Appeal's decision in *MNR v Greater Montreal Real Estate Board*, 2007 FCA 346 [*Greater Montreal*], leave to appeal to SCC refused, [2007] SCCA No 605. Following its release, and accepting written submissions from the parties in the case, Hughes J held that he was bound by the Federal Court of Appeal's decision in *Greater Montreal*, *ibid*, regarding the "good faith audit" test and that since the Minister in his view had met the test, his earlier *ex parte* order authorizing the requirement was affirmed but in amended form to include the information regarding the Power Sellers.

[69] *eBay* FC, above note 68.

[70] *eBay* CA, above note 67.

[71] Canada, Department of Finance, *The White Paper: Tax Reform 1987* (Ottawa: Department of Finance, 1987). See *eBay* CA, above note 67 at para 44.

[72] *eBay* CA, above note 67 at para 44.

> text of the case before the Court of Appeal, while] . . . these concerns may be taken into account on a review by a judge for unreasonableness, they are largely irrelevant to the information . . . that is the subject of the requirement in the present case.
>
> This is because, with the click of a mouse, the appellants make the information appear on the screens on their desks in Toronto and Vancouver, or anywhere else in Canada. It is as easily accessible as documents in their filing cabinets in their Canadian offices. Hence, it makes no sense in my view to insist that information stored on servers outside Canada is as a matter of law located outside Canada for the purpose of section 231.6 because it has not been downloaded. Who, after all, goes to the site of servers in order to read the information stored on them?[73]

Thus, the Federal Court of Appeal agreed with Hughes J in finding that the information was not foreign but within Canada for the purposes of section 231.2 of the *Act*.

6.2 Challenging a Demand for Foreign-Based Information

Section 231.6(4) of the *Act* states, "The person on whom a notice of a requirement is served under subsection 213.6(2) may, within 90 days after the service of the notice, apply to a judge for a review of the requirement."[74] The reviewing judge has the power to confirm the requirement, vary the requirement, or if the judge is satisfied that the requirement is unreasonable set aside the requirement.[75] Generally, the caselaw concerning challenges to a requirement for foreign-based information indicates that the courts are inclined to favour CRA's position. In other words, financial information must be produced.

In *Saipem Luxembourg SA v Canada (Customs and Revenue Agency)*, the CCRA (Canada Customs and Revenue Agency, now known as the Canada Revenue Agency or CRA) served upon Saipem Luxembourg SA

[73] *Ibid* at paras 47–48.

[74] *Act*, above note 1, s 231.6(4).

[75] *Ibid*, s 231.6(5).

a notice of requirement pursuant to section 231.6(2) of the *Act*, which demanded that Saipem produce for inspection all of its corporate records for two fiscal years (1999 and 2000).[76] The sole issue before the Court of Appeal was whether the requirement was so broad as to be unreasonable. If so, the court could set the requirement aside under section 231.6(5). Initially, the application was brought by Saipem to the trial level of the Federal Court, where Rouleau J dismissed Saipem's application, concluding that the test to be applied was whether the information sought by CCRA was relevant to the administration of the *Act*.[77] He also found that CCRA's duty to verify Saipem's tax liability required the production of the books and records sought by CCRA. In dismissing Saipem's application, Rouleau J never did state why he found the notice of requirement reasonable. Thus, it was not surprising that Saipem appealed the decision to the Federal Court of Appeal. In deciding in favour of the Minister, once again, Pelletier J, speaking for the Court of Appeal, framed the issue in the following manner:

> The issue before the reviewing Court is not the reasonableness of the Agency's intention to conduct an audit, but the reasonableness of the notice of requirement in light of the Agency's determination that an audit is required. Saipem's argument that the Agency could have obtained the documents it seeks by issuing a notice of requirement with respect to specific classes of documents seeks to question the reasonableness of conducting an audit. In the absence of some evidence of bad faith or other improper motive, the appropriateness of an audit is outside the mandate of the Court under subsection 231.6(5).[78]

The court held that CCRA's request for all of Saipem's corporate books and records was not unreasonable considering that the records were maintained outside Canada and that limiting access to those records would only handcuff CCRA's statutory right to conduct the audit as it saw fit. As a consequence of the Federal Court of Appeal's decision upholding

---

[76] 2005 FCA 218 [*Saipem Luxembourg* CA].

[77] *Saipem Luxembourg SA v Canada (Customs and Revenue Agency)*, 2004 FC 113.

[78] *Saipem Luxembourg* CA, above note 76 at para 34.

the lower court's findings and dismissing Saipem's application, Saipem sought leave to appeal to the Supreme Court, which was denied.[79]

In *Fidelity Investments Canada Ltd v Canada (Canada Revenue Agency)*, the applicant sought an order either varying or setting aside two notices of requirement.[80] It argued that the notices were too broad, CRA had not shown why it needed the information or that it was relevant for the purpose of administering the *Act*, the notices were in conflict with the provisions of the *Convention between Canada and the United States of America with respect to Taxes on Income and on Capital*, and the lack of any guarantee of protection of confidential information led to the inference that the notices were unreasonable.[81] The court concluded that the information sought by CRA was relevant to the conduct of an audit and that the conduct of an audit was relevant to the administration and enforcement of the *Act*. The court also stated that the existence of the *Canada–US Tax Treaty* did not overrule or restrict the Minister's right to obtain the requested information by means of notices issued under section 231.6 of the *Act*. The court determined that the financial statements at issue were confidential materials but nevertheless concluded that this was not a basis for restricting disclosure. The court went on to state that it did not believe that CRA was on a "fishing trip" for the purpose of using the financial statements other than for carrying out an audit of the applicant. Finally, the court stated that in general the Minister is subject to the obligation of acting in good faith.[82]

In *Soft-Moc Inc v Canada (National Revenue)*, CRA was conducting a transfer pricing audit and sought information from corporations in the Bahamas that provided services to Soft-Moc.[83] The evidence established that the corporations in question were owned by one person in the Bahamas and that the same individual owned 90 percent of the common shares of the Canadian company, Soft-Moc. CRA, therefore, issued a foreign-based

[79] *Saipem Luxembourg SA v Canada (Customs and Revenue Agency)*, 2005 CanLII 45789 (SCC).

[80] 2006 FC 551 [*Fidelity Investments*].

[81] 26 September 1980 (as amended by the protocols signed on 14 June 1983, 23 March 1984, 17 March 1997, 29 July 1997, and 21 September 2007) [*Canada–US Tax Treaty*]; *Fidelity Investments*, above note 80 at paras 18–19.

[82] *Fidelity Investments*, above note 80 at para 44.

[83] 2013 FC 291, aff'd 2014 FCA 10.

information requirement to Soft-Moc under section 231.6(2) of the *Act*. The requirement requested copious amounts of information from the Bahamian-based corporations including customer lists, employee lists, financial statements, and details of all of the services provided by each Bahamian company. The central argument of the applicant (Soft-Moc) was that the requirement should be set aside as unreasonable on the basis that it was overbroad in scope, it required the production of irrelevant material, and it requested material that could not be provided because it was confidential and proprietary, non-existent, or otherwise unavailable. The court held that the information was necessary to make determinations regarding the appropriate transfer pricing methodology and whether the transfer price paid was arm's-length, and to verify information.[84] The court had little sympathy for the applicant's arguments and found that the information requested was relevant to the transfer pricing audit and reasonable.[85]

All of these cases demonstrate that today the courts are more than likely to support CRA's efforts to obtain information that is linked to the administration and enforcement of the *Act*. In recent years, no taxpayer has been successful in challenging a foreign-based requirement issued by CRA.

6.3 Failure to Comply with a Notice of Requirement to Provide Foreign-Based Information

Section 236.1(8) of the *Act* provides that when a person fails to comply with a notice and when the notice is not set aside by a judge, any court having jurisdiction in a civil proceeding relating to the administration or enforcement of the *Act* shall on motion by the Minister prohibit the introduction by that person of any foreign-based information or document covered by that notice.[86]

In *Glaxo Smithkline Inc v Canada*, Bowie J dealt with a Crown motion for an order prohibiting Glaxo from introducing any foreign-based information or document covered by a foreign-based requirement for information or documents where there had not been substantial compliance

---

[84] *Ibid.*

[85] *Ibid.*

[86] *Act*, above note 1, ss 236.1(1) and 231.6(8).

with the requirement.[87] In a detailed analysis, he first dealt with the scope of the requirement. He stated as follows in considering the nature of foreign-based requirements:

> The legislation has been carefully crafted to provide that the requirement must be in writing, and that it must set out in writing the subject matter that it covers. It makes provisions for variation, but only by order of a judge. Parliament has clearly recognized that the certainty of a written instrument is necessary to define the scope of such a far-reaching requirement for documents and information. In my view, any variation of the terms of the requirement would also have to be in writing, and would have to express unequivocally the intention to vary the original document. . . . For purposes of this motion, I accept that a taxpayer served with a section 231.6 requirement could resist an order under subsection (8) if it were shown that a representative of the Minister had deliberately led the taxpayer's representative to believe the compliance in whole or in part would not be required of it, and the taxpayer, relying on that representation, had then failed to comply.[88]

What prompted a thoughtful analysis by the court was the appellant's argument that section 231.6(8) intrudes upon the right of an appellant to a fair hearing in accordance with the principles of fundamental justice. In illustrating the problem, Bowie J stated:

> if the documents that were the subject of an Order included two opinions of a scientist as to the quality of the product in issue, the second of which contradicted or qualified the first on the basis of an error in the original opinion, [the Crown] . . . could rely at trial on the first opinion and it would not be open to the Appellant to put the second opinion before the Court. This, it is argued, would deprive the Appellant of a fair hearing in accordance with the principles of fundamental justice.[89]

He thus concluded that section 231.6 "may, in some circumstances, give rise to an infringement of a taxpayer's right to a fair hearing."[90] Ultimately,

---

[87] 2003 TCC 258 [*Glaxo Smithkline*].

[88] *Ibid* at para 9.

[89] *Ibid* at para 17.

[90] *Ibid* at para 19.

the question for the court was, what would the appropriate remedy be? Justice Bowie noted that similar legislation existed in the United States.[91] In the case before him, he concluded that the appellant had made no attempt to comply with the requirement and that therefore there was no need for a reasonable cause exception: "All that is required is that the trial judge have the power to permit the Appellant to proffer evidence in rebuttal that would otherwise be excluded by section 231.6, if that is necessary to prevent injustice."[92] Therefore, Bowie J ordered that Glaxo would be prohibited from introducing at trial any foreign-based information or document covered by the notice otherwise than as rebuttal evidence, or in cross-examination, and only with leave of the trial judge.[93]

The lessons from this case and others are clear. There is virtually no privacy in respect of financial information related to tax compliance. Financial information must be disclosed to CRA. Failure to comply with a foreign-based requirement can have serious consequences for a taxpayer including being prohibited from admitting evidence in a tax court proceeding.

7 Criminal Provisions related to the Search for Information and Their Consequences

As we have demonstrated in our review of the provisions and the caselaw, the Minister has broad powers to obtain information and investigate a taxpayer's tax affairs under sections 231.1, 231.2, 231.4, 231.6, and 231.7 of the *Act*. Additionally, the Minister can apply under the *Act* for a search warrant authorizing any person to enter and search any building, receptacle, or place for any document or thing that may afford evidence of the commission of an offence under the *Act* and seize it, under certain court-imposed conditions.[94] Today, however, CRA's general practice is to

---

[91] Sanctions and penalties available under US tax laws for the failure to produce foreign-based information are discussed in Chapter 5.

[92] *Glaxo Smithkline*, above note 87 at para 22.

[93] *Ibid.*

[94] *Act*, above note 1, s 231.3(1).

obtain a search warrant under section 487 of the *Criminal Code* rather than rely on the warrant provision found in the *Act*.[95] These powers are not unrestricted, and in the context of a criminal investigation, the use of these powers is, to some degree, limited. The distinction between a civil audit and an investigation leading to criminal charges was addressed by the Supreme Court of Canada in the seminal case *R v Jarvis*.[96]

In *Jarvis*, CRA commenced an audit inquiry following a confidential tip. It was alleged that Mr Jarvis had not reported the sales of his late wife's artworks in his returns of income for the 1990 and 1991 taxation years. The CRA auditor advised Mr Jarvis that his returns had been selected for audit and asked him for his books and records. In the auditor's efforts to determine the validity of the tip, she gathered information from online searches and contacted a number of galleries in Calgary. Her research confirmed that there was some merit to the allegations raised by the lead source. The auditor then corresponded with the taxpayer and the taxpayer's accountant regarding obtaining more information. Later, the auditor with her supervisor (or team leader) held a meeting with the taxpayer. Mr Jarvis fully cooperated by answering questions and providing more detailed records of the sales and expenses relating to his late wife's artworks. Ultimately, the auditor reached the conclusion that Mr Jarvis had grossly omitted revenues from his returns of income for the 1990 and 1991 taxation years, and as a result, she referred the file to CRA's Special Investigations section. A Special Investigations officer was responsible for determining whether or not Mr Jarvis should be prosecuted for tax evasion. Even though the taxpayer made several requests as to the status of the file, the auditor deliberately withheld the fact that the file had been referred to the Special Investigations section.

The Special Investigations officer determined that there were reasonable and probable grounds to seek a search warrant to investigate Mr Jarvis for tax evasion. A warrant was obtained, and CRA conducted searches of the homes of Mr Jarvis and his accountant. Also the Special Investigations officer issued requirement letters pursuant to section 231.2(1) of the *Act* to various banks and obtained even more information. Mr Jarvis was

---

[95] *Criminal Code*, above note 14, s 487.

[96] 2002 SCC 73 [*Jarvis*].

finally charged with tax evasion under section 239 of the *Act*.[97] In his fight against these charges, Mr Jarvis argued that it was improper that CRA officers had obtained evidence using their inspection powers as it had been a warrantless investigation and that therefore his *Charter* rights had been violated.[98] The legal case resulted in mixed lower-court decisions, and ultimately leave was granted for the appeal to be heard by the Supreme Court.

The reasons for judgment of the Supreme Court were delivered by Iacobucci and Major JJ. The justices said that the central questions for the Court were as follows:

1) "Is there a distinction between [CCRA's] . . . audit and investigative functions under the [*Act*]?"
2) "If it is indeed correct to draw such a distinction, when does the CCRA exercise its audit function and when does it exercise its investigative function?"
3) "Finally, what are the legal consequences for the taxpayer when the CCRA exercises its investigative function?"[99]

In the analysis section of the reasons, the justices expanded upon the third question with the following questions: "To what extent do taxpayers under investigation for ITA [*Act*] offences benefit from the principle against self-incrimination under s. 7 of the *Charter*? Is a s. 8 violation made out where documents are obtained under colour of the ITA's 'audit powers' after a prosecutorial investigation has commenced?"[100] In a review of the regulatory framework, the justices stated:

---

[97] *Act*, above note 1, s 239. See also William Innes & Ralph Cuervo-Lorens, *Tax Evasion* (Toronto: Carswell, 1995) (loose-leaf); Johanne Charbonneau, "Tax Evasion from the Government's Perspective" in *2012 Tax Dispute Resolution Conference Report*, above note 11 at 22:1–22:12; Craig C Sturrock & Jessie Meikle-Kahs, "Tax Evasion from the Practitioner's Perspective" in *2012 Tax Dispute Resolution Conference Report*, above note 11 at 23:1–23:14; Marie Comiskey & Matthew Sullivan, "Avoidance, Deception and Mistake of Law: The *Mens Rea* of Tax Evasion" (2005–2006) 51 *Criminal Law Quarterly* 303.

[98] At the Supreme Court, the case focused on the violation of ss 7, 8, and 24(2) of the *Charter*, above note 1.

[99] *Jarvis*, above note 96 at para 1.

[100] *Ibid* at para 45.

> To be effective, self-enforcing regulatory schemes require not only resort to adequate investigation, but also the existence of effective penalties . . . . To this end, s. 238(1) sets out a summary conviction offence that is triggered by non-compliance with the filing requirements or with other of the Act's provisions — including ss. 231.1(1) and 231.2(1), and the documentary retention rules imposed by s. 230(1). Section 238's purpose is inherently pragmatic or instrumental: the offence exists "not to penalize criminal conduct but to enforce compliance with the Act" . . . .[101]

In reference to the general statutory purpose of section 239(1) of the *Act*, the justices stated:

> Section 239(1) creates a number of additional offences. It speaks of false or deceptive statements, destruction or alteration of documents, false or deceptive documents, wilful evasion of income tax, and conspiracy to engage in prohibited activities . . . . As a consequence, the s. 239(1) offences carry rather significant penalties. They may be proceeded on by way of summary conviction or by way of indictment at the election of the Attorney General . . . .[102]

Before either section 238 or 239 is engaged, it is critical, as it was in *Jarvis*, to first consider whether CRA is conducting an audit or an investigation. The audit process is administrative in nature and not a criminal process. As such, an audit does not trigger the taxpayer's *Charter* rights. However, the use of investigative functions is plainly different. These powers are used to investigate suspected schemes of tax evasion of a criminal nature. A successful investigation can lead to criminal charges. In turn, conviction can lead to fines or incarceration. Thus, when CRA is carrying out its investigative functions, it is in an adversarial relationship with the taxpayer. And this relationship brings with it a whole series of constitutional protections such as the protection against self-incrimination, the right to remain silent, the right to counsel, and potentially other *Charter* rights. Thus, in *Jarvis*, the Supreme Court squarely addressed how a trial judge should assess the situation where there is an audit requirement to provide

---

[101] *Ibid* at para 55.

[102] *Ibid* at para 56. See *Act*, above note 1, s 239(2).

information and documents when there is evidence of a possible concurrent criminal investigation. Justices Iacobucci and Major stated:

> In our view, where the predominant purpose of a particular inquiry is the determination of penal liability, CCRA officials must relinquish the authority to use the inspection and requirement powers under ss. 231.1(1) and 231.2(1). In essence, officials "cross the Rubicon" when the inquiry in question engages the adversarial relationship between the taxpayer and the state.[103]

The Court made it clear that there is no "special" or clear formula. Rather, the predominant purpose of the requirement must be assessed when all of the factors are considered in relation to that request. The Court did indicate that there are factors that can assist in ascertaining whether the predominant purpose engages the adversarial relationship:

> the trial judge will look at all factors, including but not limited to such questions as:
>
> (a) Did the authorities have reasonable grounds to lay charges? Does it appear from the record that a decision to proceed with a criminal investigation *could have* been made?
> (b) Was the general conduct of the authorities such that it was consistent with the pursuit of a criminal investigation?
> (c) Had the auditor transferred his or her files and materials to the investigators?
> (d) Was the conduct of the auditor such that he or she was effectively acting as an agent for the investigators?
> (e) Does it appear that the investigators intended to use the auditor as their agent in the collection of evidence?
> (f) Is the evidence sought relevant to taxpayer liability generally? Or, as is the case with evidence as to the taxpayer's *mens rea*, is the evidence relevant only to the taxpayer's penal liability?
> (g) Are there any other circumstances or factors that can lead the trial judge to the conclusion that the compliance audit had in reality become a criminal investigation?[104]

[103] *Jarvis*, above note 96 at para 88.
[104] *Ibid* at para 94.

In terms of privacy and the protection afforded by section 8 of the *Charter*, the Court maintained that taxpayers have "very little" privacy in the materials and records that they are obligated to maintain under the provisions of the *Act*.[105] In fact, the Court stated that if some evidence came to light as a result of information contained in the auditor's file, the investigators could later make use of it.[106]

In terms of the protection afforded by section 7 of the *Charter*, the Court was equally clear. If the predominant purpose of a CRA inquiry is the determination of penal liability, then the "full panoply" of *Charter* rights is engaged to protect the taxpayer.[107] In such a case, there are a number of consequences, which the Court outlined.[108] First, no further statements may be compelled from the taxpayer under section 231.1(1)(d) for the purpose of pursuing a criminal investigation. No written documents may be inspected or examined, and no documents may be demanded from the taxpayer or any third party for the purpose of carrying out a criminal investigation. The only way that CRA can inspect or examine written documents when engaging in a criminal investigation is by resorting to a warrant under section 231.3 of the *Act* or the now more common practice of obtaining a warrant under section 487 of the *Criminal Code*. Put simply, if CRA is carrying out an inquiry that has as its predominant purpose the determination of penal liability, CRA does not have "the benefit of the ss. 231.1(1) and 231.2(1) requirement powers."[109]

CRA can conduct parallel investigations; that is, CRA can simultaneously carry out a civil audit and a criminal investigation. But the justices of the Supreme Court added:

> if an investigation into penal liability is subsequently commenced, the investigators can avail themselves of that information obtained pursuant to the audit power prior to the commencement of the criminal investigation, but

---

[105] *Ibid* at para 95.

[106] *Ibid.*

[107] *Ibid* at para 96. For several different *Charter* rulings, see *R v Chen*, 2007 ONCJ 177; *R v Martin*, 2015 NSSC 8; *R v Mori*, [2015] DTC 5081 (Ont Ct J); *Stanfield v MNR*, 2005 FC 1010; *R v McCartie*, 2015 BCPC 254; *R v Dolinski*, 2014 ONSC 681; *R v McCartie*, 2015 BCPC 69.

[108] *Jarvis*, above note 96 at para 96.

[109] *Ibid.*

> not with respect to information obtained pursuant to such powers subsequent to the commencement of the investigation into penal liability.[110]

Simply put, there can be situations where information is transferred from the audit section to the investigations branch, and these would not engage the taxpayer's *Charter* rights so long as there has been no "commencement of the investigation into penal liability." The Court considered the possibility of a situation where an investigation had commenced but was at some later point in time stopped and where thereafter there was an audit with the issuance of a requirement. What should happen in this situation? The Court indicated that if there was evidence that the criminal investigation had in reality stopped, then the information could flow between the audit section and the investigations branch.

Justices Iacobucci and Major summarized the key points of the *Jarvis* case in the following manner:

1. Although the ITA is a regulatory statute, a distinction can be drawn between the audit and investigative powers that it grants to the Minister.
2. When, in light of all relevant circumstances, it is apparent that CCRA officials are not engaged in the verification of tax liability, but are engaged in the determination of penal liability under s. 239, the adversarial relationship between the state and the individual exists. As a result, *Charter* protections are engaged.
3. When this is the case, investigators must provide the taxpayer with a proper warning. The powers of compulsion in ss. 231.1(1) and 231.2(1) are not available, and search warrants are required in order to further the investigation.[111]

In terms of applying the law to the facts in *Jarvis*, the Court concluded that the auditor had not used her audit powers to obtain information for prosecutorial purposes.[112]

---

[110] *Ibid* at para 97.

[111] *Ibid* at para 99.

[112] *Ibid* at paras 100–4.

As the decision in *Jarvis* confirms, the determination of whether or not an audit has moved to a criminal investigation is a question of mixed fact and law. Thus, each case is fact specific, and no exact formula exists to determine whether a taxpayer's rights have been engaged by CRA's quest for information. The *Jarvis* decision also demonstrates the Court's recognition that audits and the statutory tools to conduct audits are highly intrusive on privacy. Yet this form of intrusion is permissible, and not an infringement of rights, when the aim of CRA is merely to audit the taxpayer and nothing more.[113]

8 Section 238

Among other offences, section 238 of the *Act* provides that every person who fails to comply with sections 230 to 232 or a compliance order under section 238(2) is guilty of an offence and therefore subject to (among other penalties provided by the *Act*) a summary conviction offence.[114] A finding of guilt by a court could result in a fine of not less than $1,000 and not more than $25,000, or both a fine and imprisonment for a term of not more than twelve months. This provision creates a strict liability offence. In the case of such offences, the Crown must prove only that the taxpayer (the accused) committed the prohibited act (in this case the failure to supply some form of information or document). The taxpayer's only defence is to demonstrate to the court that she exercised all reasonable care.[115]

---

[113] In the post-*Jarvis* world, much has been written on the case's impact: see, for example, David Stratas, "Crossing the Rubicon: The Supreme Court and Regulatory Investigations" 6 *Criminal Reports (Sixth Series)* 74; Tim Quigley, "The Impact of the *Charter* on the Law of Search and Seizure" (2008) 40 *Supreme Court Law Review*, 2d, 117; Jeffrey S Clarke, "R. v. Jarvis and Corporations" (2008) 54 *Criminal Law Quarterly* 167; David M Porter, "A Contextual Analysis of Section 8 *Charter* Rights in Regulatory Audits" (2002) 46 *Criminal Law Quarterly* 341; Chris Sprysak, "Life after Jarvis — Just How Much Help Must You 'Voluntarily' Give the Canada Revenue Agency?" (2005–2006) 43 *Alberta Law Review* 713; Christopher Sherrin, "Distinguishing *Charter* Rights in Criminal and Regulatory Investigations: What's the Purpose of Analyzing Purpose?" (2010) 48:1 *Alberta Law Review* 93; Croft Michaelson, "The Limits of Privacy: Some Reflections on Section 8 of the *Charter*" (2008) 40 *Supreme Court Law Review*, 2d, 87.

[114] *Act*, above note 1, s 238.

[115] See *R v Sault Ste Marie (City)*, [1978] 2 SCR 1299, Dickson J.

In *R v MacDonald*, a prosecution arose under section 238(1) of the *Act* where the taxpayer was charged with failing to comply with a notice to provide financial information about his business and personal income, contrary to section 231.2.[116] In the analysis portion of the decision, Bruce J noted that a failure to comply with a notice issued under section 231.2 is a strict liability offence.[117] Judge Bruce continued by stating that the *actus reus* of the offence charged under section 231.2 consists of the following elements:

1. the defendant is properly served with a notice to produce information.
2. the information demanded is for a purpose related to the administration or enforcement of the *Act*, including the collection of any amounts payable under the *Act*.
3. the time stipulated in the notice is a reasonable time for the provision of the information demanded.
4. the defendant failed to comply with the notice.[118]

In this case, the court concluded that the thirty-day period was not a reasonable time frame within which the defendant (taxpayer) could provide the many documents demanded by CRA in its notice. The court indicated that factors such as the nature, volume, and "custodial status of the documents or information" must be considered in determining what is a reasonable time.[119] Judge Bruce also noted that the Crown had produced no evidence to establish that the thirty-day period provided to the defendant was reasonable in the circumstances. Since the information request in this case had not been a simple one and since there was no evidence regarding the reasonableness of the time provided to comply, the court concluded that the time provided was not reasonable.[120] Consequently, Bruce J acquitted Mr MacDonald of the charge under section 238(1) of the *Act*.

---

[116] 2005 BCPC 398.

[117] *Ibid* at para 13.

[118] *Ibid* at para 16.

[119] *Ibid* at para 31.

[120] *Ibid* at para 34.

9 The Crime of Tax Evasion: Section 239

Section 239(1) of the *Act* contains five separate offence provisions.[121] Section 239(1)(a) creates the offence of making a false or deceptive statement in a return, certificate, statement, or answer filed or made as required by the *Act* or the regulations under the *Act*. The reference to a statement filed or made as required by the *Act* refers to requests for information made under section 231.2 of the *Act*.[122] Section 239(1)(b) creates the offence related to destroying, altering, mutilating, secreting, or otherwise disposing of the records or books of account belonging to the taxpayer.[123] Section 239(1)(c) essentially creates two offences, although they are closely related.[124] Both offences deal with the books and records of a taxpayer. First, it is an offence to make a false or deceptive entry in the books or records of account of a taxpayer. Second, it is an offence to omit entering a material particular in the books or records of account of a taxpayer. The key tax evasion provision is section 239(1)(d).[125] It states that every person who has wilfully, in any manner, evaded or attempted to evade compliance with the *Act* or the payment of taxes imposed by the *Act* is guilty of an offence. Section 239(1)(e) makes it an offence to conspire with any person to commit an offence described in sections 239(1)(a), 239(1)(b), 239(1)(c), and 239(1)(d).[126] Similarly to section 238, section 239 offences require prosecution in a provincial court, as these offences are a matter of criminal law. The Crown must prove both the *actus reus* and the *mens rea* for a successful prosecution under section 239.[127] This proof must result in a finding of guilt beyond a reasonable doubt.

---

[121] *Act*, above note 1, s 239(1). See *R v Burko*, 2011 ONSC 479 [*Burko*]. In tax evasion cases, it is up to the Crown to prove beyond a reasonable doubt that an accused voluntarily performed an act or engaged in a course of conduct that either attempted to avoid or avoided the payment of tax owing under the *Act*: see *R v Klundert* (2004), 187 CCC (3d) 417 (Ont CA) [*Klundert*].

[122] *Act*, above note 1, s 231.2.

[123] *Ibid*, s 239(1)(b).

[124] *Ibid*, s 239(1)(c).

[125] *Ibid*, s 239(1)(d). For an example of a decision where the criminal conviction was dependent upon the proof of *mens rea* in the form of willful blindness, see *R v Tempelman*, 2006 ONCJ 55.

[126] *Act*, above note 1, s 239(1)(e).

[127] As a succinct way to summarize the *actus reus* and *mens rea* of the crime of tax evasion, Myers J in *R v Porisky & Gould*, 2012 BCSC 67 at para 14, referred to the charge to the jury in *Klundert*,

The offences found in section 239 are punishable on summary conviction or, at the election of the Attorney General of Canada, on conviction by trial by indictment.[128] If convicted by summary trial, a taxpayer can face a fine of not less than 50 percent and not more than 200 percent of the amount of tax that was sought to be evaded or both a fine and a term of imprisonment of not more than two years. If incarceration is considered, the principles in section 718 of the *Criminal Code* will apply in respect of the sentencing conditions and the length of incarceration.[129] Section 239(2) of the *Act* gives the Attorney General of Canada the option of proceeding by indictment for every person who is charged with an offence described in sections 239(1) or 239(1.1). If the taxpayer is found guilty, then in addition to a substantial fine the

---

above note 121, wherein the Ontario Court of Appeal had stated as follows:

> In most cases of tax evasion, the trial judge will adequately describe the elements of the offence by instructing the jury that they must be satisfied beyond a reasonable doubt that the accused:

- did something or engaged in a course of conduct that avoided or attempted to avoid the payment of tax imposed by the Act;
- knew there was tax imposed by the Act; and
- engaged in the conduct for the purpose of avoiding or attempting to avoid payment of tax imposed by the Act or knowing that avoiding payment of tax imposed by the Act was a virtual certain consequence of his actions.

See also *Burko*, above note 121.

[128] *Act*, above note 1, ss 239(1) & 239(2). See *R v Bulua*, 2006 BCSC 1234; *R v Andrus*, 2013 BCPC 160.

[129] *Criminal Code*, above note 14, s 718:

> The fundamental purpose of sentencing is to protect society and to contribute, along with crime prevention initiatives, to respect for the law and the maintenance of a just, peaceful and safe society by imposing just sanctions that have one or more of the following objectives:

(a) to denounce unlawful conduct and the harm done to victims or to the community that is caused by unlawful conduct;
(b) to deter the offender and other persons from committing offences;
(c) to separate offenders from society, where necessary;
(d) to assist in rehabilitating offenders;
(e) to provide reparations for harm done to victims or to the community; and
(f) to promote a sense of responsibility in offenders, and acknowledgment of the harm done to victims or to the community.

taxpayer can face up to five years in prison.[130] Furthermore, the Crown can lay charges of fraud under section 380 of the *Criminal Code*, and a conviction resulting from a section 380 charge can lead to a maximum of fourteen years in prison.[131]

While the Special Investigations section of CRA is responsible for carrying out criminal investigations, the Public Prosecution Service of Canada is responsible for prosecuting the cases referred to it by CRA. This is not to say that CRA is not involved in the pretrial work and actual tax evasion trial. CRA personnel prepare and organize the evidence and assist in the preparation of the Crown's obligation to disclose its case before the actual trial, and CRA investigators are often called to testify as witnesses by the prosecutor at the trial. But it is ultimately the prosecutor who decides whether there are sufficient grounds to proceed with a prosecution. Two major considerations generally determine whether the Crown will proceed.[132] First, is the evidence such that there is a reasonable prospect of conviction? Second, if indeed there is a reasonable prospect of conviction, is it in the public interest for the prosecution to proceed? Another central factor that prosecutors will consider is whether the case is sufficiently important to merit the expenditure of finite government resources.

From our review of the law, it is clear that CRA has a broad range of powers to audit and investigate the financial affairs of taxpayers. However, there are limits on the use of these powers. There are protections against disclosure. The Supreme Court of Canada has firmly established that when an audit crosses "the Rubicon" and becomes an investigation, certain legal rights are triggered, and a taxpayer is entitled to certain statutory defences and *Charter* protections.[133] When CRA's investigative focus is in respect of criminal matters, it is easy to understand why these protections are raised. Unlike an audit, a criminal investigation can lead to a tax prosecution. In cases where the Crown is successful, a conviction can

[130] *Act*, above note 1, s 239(2).

[131] *Criminal Code*, above note 14, s 380. See *R v Watts*, 2015 ONSC 5597.

[132] Less experienced Crown prosecutors will rely on the Department of Justice's *Public Prosecution Service of Canada Deskbook* (Ottawa: AG of Canada, 2014), online: www.ppsc-sppc.gc.ca/eng/pub/fpsd-sfpg/fps-sfp/tpd/d-g-eng.pdf, to provide guidance on and a framework for the laying of charges, resolution discussions, and determining whether a case should proceed to trial.

[133] *Jarvis*, above note 96 at para 88.

lead to a sentence of incarceration, and the loss of the taxpayer's freedom. In the domestic context, there is always an uneasy balance between the government's objective of ensuring tax compliance, which can result in unwanted intrusions into a taxpayer's personal affairs, and respect for a taxpayer's guaranteed rights.

10 Information Exchange at the International Level: Canada–US Relations

Canada's efforts to comply with obligations owed to foreign states (such as the United States) raise concerns that there very well may be an erosion of existing individual rights. In 2010, the *Foreign Account Tax Compliance Act* was passed by the US Congress.[134] The purpose of *FATCA* is to prevent US citizens from hiding wealth in bank accounts outside the United States with the intention of evading US tax. To obtain the data required for this, the United States has sought, some would say forced, the cooperation of foreign governments to assist in obtaining account information guarded by foreign financial institutions. To this end, in February 2014, Canada and the United States entered into an intergovernmental agreement (IGA).[135] The *Canada–US IGA* commits certain financial institutions in Canada to provide CRA with account information of US persons. This information is then turned over to the IRS by way of provisions in the *Canada–US Tax Treaty*.[136] Some Canadian tax scholars have criticized this development for a number of reasons, raising concerns

[134] Subtitle A of Title V of the *Hiring Incentives to Restore Employment Act* of 2010, Pub L No 111–147, enacted on 18 March 2010 [*FATCA*].

[135] *Agreement between the Government of Canada and the Government of the United States of America to Improve International Tax Compliance through Enhanced Exchange of Information under the Convention between Canada and the United States of America with respect to Taxes on Income and on Capital* (5 February 2014), online: www.fin.gc.ca/treaties-conventions/pdf/FATCA-eng.pdf [*Canada–US IGA*].

[136] *Canada–US Tax Treaty*, above note 81.

that the *Canada–US IGA* and other statutory commitments will violate *Charter* rights and international law.[137]

In the next section, we consider statutory provisions and rights that are triggered when CRA seeks out taxpayer information both for domestic enforcement and for compliance with Canada's obligations to share taxpayer information with other states, particularly the United States.

11 Keeping It Confidential

A central feature of the Canadian tax system is the obligation of taxpayers to voluntarily disclose personal information. Parliament has recognized that to encourage this free flow of personal data, it must carefully guard the confidential nature of taxpayer information, and for this reason section 241(1) of the *Act* was enacted.[138] This section is intended to prevent the disclosure of confidential information obtained for the purposes of the *Act*. In *Slattery (Trustee of) v Slattery*, Iacobucci J of the Supreme Court of Canada described the importance of confidentiality in the Canadian tax system:

> Section 241 reflects the importance of ensuring respect for a taxpayer's privacy interests, particularly as that interest relates to a taxpayer's finances. Therefore, access to financial and related information about taxpayers is to be taken seriously, and such information can only be disclosed in prescribed

[137] See Allison Christians & Arthur J Cockfield, "Submission to Finance Department on Implementation of FATCA in Canada: Submission on Legislative Proposals relating to the Canada–United States Enhanced Tax Information Exchange Agreement" (10 March 2014), online: http://dx.doi.org/10.2139/ssrn.2407264; Allison Christians, "Country Report: Canada" in Eleonor Kristoffersson et al, eds, *Tax Secrecy and Tax Transparency: The Relevance of Confidentiality in Tax Law, Part 1* (Frankfurt am Main: PL Academic Research, 2013) 209; Arthur J Cockfield, "Protecting Taxpayer Privacy Rights under Enhanced Cross-border Tax Information Exchange: Toward a Multilateral Taxpayer Bill of Rights" (2010) 42 *University of British Columbia Law Review* 420; Arthur J Cockfield, "FATCA and the Erosion of Canadian Taxpayer Privacy: Report to the Office of the Privacy Commissioner of Canada" (1 April 2014), online: http://papers.ssrn.com/sol3/papers.cfm?abstract_id=2433198.

[138] *Act*, above note 1, s 241(1). See George Alatopulos, Bernardo Elizondo Rios, & Xiaolu Su, "Legislative and Regulatory Privacy Considerations in the Context of the Application of, and Amendments to, Section 241 of The Income Tax Act" *Confidentiality of Taxpayer Information* (Taxnet Pro) (November 2014) 1.

situations. Only in those exceptional situations does the privacy interest give way to the interest of the state.

. . . Parliament recognized that to maintain the confidentiality of income tax returns and other obtained information is to encourage the voluntary tax reporting upon which our tax system is based. Taxpayers are responsible for reporting their incomes and expenses and for calculating the tax owed to Revenue Canada. By instilling confidence in taxpayers that the personal information they disclose will not be communicated in other contexts, Parliament encourages voluntary disclosure of this information. The opposite is also true: if taxpayers lack this confidence, they may be reluctant to disclose voluntarily all of the required information . . . .[139]

Section 241(1) provides that no official or representative of a government entity will:

(a) knowingly provide, or knowingly allow to be provided, to any person any taxpayer information;
(b) knowingly allow any person to have access to any taxpayer information; or
(c) knowingly use any taxpayer information otherwise than in the course of the administration or enforcement of this Act . . . .[140]

Section 241(2) provides that no official or representative of a government entity is required, in connection with any proceedings, "to give or produce evidence relating to any taxpayer information."[141] Where an official or other authorized person contravenes section 241(1), that person is guilty of an offence and is liable on summary conviction to a fine of not more than $5,000, jail of up to twelve months, or both.[142] There are many exceptions to the confidentiality law. Under section 241(3), sections 241(1) and (2) do not apply to criminal proceedings initiated by the laying of an information or the preferring of an indictment under the *Act* or any proceedings relating to the administration or enforcement of

[139] [1993] 3 SCR 430 at 444.
[140] *Act*, above note 1, s 241(1).
[141] *Ibid*, s 241(2).
[142] *Ibid*, s 241(1).

the *Act*.[143] In terms of international relations, section 241(4)(e)(xii) permits officials to provide taxpayer information to a foreign government on the basis of the terms contained in a tax treaty or in a listed international agreement.

In June 2014, the *Act* was amended to include section 241(9.5).[144] This section permits designated officials to disclose to the police taxpayer information where there are reasonable grounds to believe that the information will provide evidence of a variety of serious criminal offences, including bribery of foreign officials, terrorism, and criminal organization offences. This amendment is extremely broad in scope, and it raises the prospect that the protection of taxpayers' privacy rights and, more generally, *Charter* rights will be jeopardized by the exercise of these statutory powers. Warrantless searches could be carried out for the purposes of the furtherance of an investigation and possible prosecution. Some observers believe that if such a situation occurs, taxpayers will likely raise court challenges on the basis that section 241(9.5) is arbitrary, is grossly disproportional, and lacks a rational connection to its legislative objective.[145] The courts have yet to be called upon to determine the appropriate balance between, on the one hand, the protection against unreasonable search and seizure, the protection against disclosure of taxpayers' biographical information, and the protection against self-incrimination and, on the other hand, the state's right to gather evidence leading to the laying of charges regarding the commission of serious criminal offences.[146] The concerns raised with the introduction of section 241(9.5) about the potential erosion of the specific right to privacy and encroachment on various other *Charter* rights must surely expand to include other recent amendments to the *Act* relating to the provision of information to CRA by certain financial institutions and its exchange with the IRS.

As discussed in greater detail in Chapter 9, *FATCA* was passed in 2010, and it imposes a heavy obligation on Canada's financial services industry. The failure of a financial institution or other affected party to meet

---

[143] *Ibid*, s 241(3).

[144] Bill C-31, *Serious Offences Amendment to Section 241 of the Income Tax Act*, 2nd Sess, 41st Parl, 2014; *Act*, above note 1, s 241(9.5).

[145] *Act*, above note 1, s 241(9.5).

[146] See Alatopulos, Rios, & Su, above note 138.

the *FATCA* reporting requirements would mean that it would face the imposition of a 30 percent withholding tax. In February 2014, Canada and the United States signed the *Canada–US IGA*, which sets out the methodology and obligations for providing and exchanging information with respect to reportable accounts.[147] Specifically, Article 2 of the *Canada–US IGA* imposes reciprocal obligations on each government to collect account holder information concerning reportable accounts at both Canadian and American financial institutions.[148] Article 4 of the *Canada–US IGA* sets out a number of conditions that if met will ensure compliance by financial institutions with the terms of *FATCA*.[149] Furthermore, Annex I to the *Canada–US IGA* describes the steps, or the due diligence procedures, that financial institutions must follow to determine which of their accounts are held by US persons.[150]

From the Canadian standpoint, Parliament enacted Part XVIII of the *Act*, entitled "Enhanced International Information Reporting," which contains sections 263 to 269.[151] These sections outline the due diligence procedures that certain financial institutions are obligated to employ, as proposed by the terms of Annex I to the *Canada–US IGA*, to identify US reportable accounts for the purposes of the *Canada–US IGA*. Canadian financial institutions are mandated by statute to search their records for the purpose of identifying accounts held by US persons. "Listed financial institution" is a term that is defined by section 263(1) of the *Act*.[152]

In the recent Federal Court case *Hillis and Deegan v Canada (AG)*, Martineau J explained some of the essentials of the statutory terms:

> Every reporting Canadian financial institution is compelled by law to submit itself to the due diligence procedures set out in subsections 265(2) and (3) of the ITA which apply in respect of pre-existing and new individual accounts, and to designate any US reportable account (see sections 264 and 265 of the ITA). Financial institutions already have a legal

[147] *Canada–US IGA*, above note 135.

[148] *Ibid*, Art 2.

[149] *Ibid*, Art 4.

[150] *Ibid*, Annex I.

[151] *Act*, above note 1, ss 263–269.

[152] *Ibid*, s 263(1).

> responsibility to determine where an account holder resides for tax purposes. If a customer has an existing account and there is an indication that they may be a US person, or if they are opening new bank accounts, their financial institution may ask them to provide additional information or documentation to demonstrate that they are not a US person (or to self-certify that they are or are not a US person for tax purposes). Indeed, every reporting Canadian financial institution shall keep, at the institution's place of business (or at such other place as may be designated by the Minister), records that the institution obtains or creates for the purpose of complying with Part XVIII of the ITA, including self-certifications and records of documentary evidence.
>
> The reporting institutions must annually file with the Minister — that is, with the CRA — prescribed information about each reportable account maintained by the financial institution, as well as prescribed information relating to payments made to non-participating financial institutions that held accounts at the financial institution in the calendar year (for 2015 and 2016 only). The information must be reported in an information return filed for each calendar year by May 2 of the following year (section 266 of the ITA) . . . . The CRA will then annually turn the information it collects over to the IRS in bulk "on an automatic basis pursuant to the provisions of Article XXVII of the [US–Canada Tax Convention]" . . . .[153]

In *Hillis and Deegan*, the plaintiffs sought a declaration that the *Canada–United States Enhanced Tax Information Exchange Agreement Implementation Act* and Schedule 3 of the *Economic Action Plan 2014 Act, No 1* were *ultra vires* or inoperative because their provisions were unconstitutional or infringed on the plaintiffs' *Charter* rights.[154] The plaintiffs also filed an amended statement of claim that added non-constitutional arguments, which became the focus of Martineau J's review and reasons for judgment. As stated by Martineau J, the summary trial dealt with the legality of the disclosure of US persons' personal information collected for the year 2014 by Canadian financial institutions for CRA. The information in question was scheduled to be shared by CRA with the US tax authorities on or before

---

[153] 2015 FC 1082 at paras 33–34 [*Hillis and Deegan*].

[154] *Canada–United States Enhanced Tax Information Exchange Agreement Implementation Act*, SC 2014, c 20; *Economic Action Plan 2014 Act, No 1*, SC 2014, c 20 [latter two acts together: *Implementation Act*]; *Hillis and Deegan*, above note 153 at paras 1 and 3.

30 September 2015. Hence, the plaintiffs sought a general declaration and injunction of a permanent nature that would prevent the collection of taxpayer information and its disclosure by CRA to the United States.

While the plaintiffs raised a series of arguments, the court was not convinced of the merits of any of them in terms of both the law and the evidence that was on the record before it. Justice Martineau stated:

> I agree with the defendants that the plaintiffs misread the IGA and the Canada–US Tax Treaty in a way that frustrates the intention of the parties. It is manifest that the authority to exchange automatically on an annual basis the information obtained by Canada pursuant to the terms of the IGA indeed derives from Article XXVII of the Canada–US Tax Treaty, which does not expressly prohibit such disclosure. The provisions of the IGA are clear. The IGA has force of law in Canada. Sections 266 to 269 of the ITA are compulsory. While all information exchanged is protected by the confidentiality provisions of the Canada–Tax Convention and the ITA, the exceptions created under subsection 241(4) of the ITA are applicable to the impugned provisions and the IGA.[155]

Even though Martineau J ultimately denied the declaratory and injunctive relief sought by the plaintiffs, he did acknowledge the following:

> True, a great number of Canadian taxpayers holding US reportable accounts are likely to be affected by a reporting system that in many quarters is considered unjust, costly and ineffective, considering that at the end of the day they are not likely to owe taxes to the US. In the absence of legislative provisions requiring all Canadian financial institutions (provincially and federally regulated) to automatically notify their account holders about reporting to the CRA under the IGA and Part XVIII of the ITA, these taxpayers may also be taken by surprise by any consequences that flow from such disclosure. The plaintiffs may find this deplorable, but apart from a constitutional invalidation of the impugned provisions or a change of heart by Parliament or Congress, or the governments of Canada or the US, there is nothing that this Court can judicially do today to change the situation. The impugned provisions have not been held to be

[155] *Hillis and Deegan*, above note 153 at para 65.

ultra vires or inoperative. Judicial courage requires that judges uphold the Rule of Law.[156]

The *Hillis and Deegan* case was the first legal challenge in Canada to the international exchange of information under the new provisions in Part XVIII of the *Act* and under the *Canada–US IGA*. A couple of noted tax scholars have pinpointed the serious challenges to taxpayer privacy and other rights posed by these new disclosure requirements. Professors Cockfield and Christians agree that the *Implementation Act*[157] and the *Canada–US IGA*[158] do not enhance the reciprocal tax information exchange between Canada and the United States. They posit that these legal relations will not create a workable regime for Canada that will improve its international tax enforcement efforts on a go-forward basis. In fact, after carrying out an exhaustive study of the legal arrangements between Canada and the United States, Cockfield and Christians reach some startling findings including that the *Implementation Act* and the *Canada–US IGA* will

- unduly harm the privacy rights and interests of all Canadians;
- unduly raise compliance costs for all Canadian financial institutions and Canadian taxpayers;
- unduly raise legal exposure for Canadian financial institutions, due to ongoing potential liability for mistakenly-transferred personal financial information;
- provide potentially sensitive commercial information held by Canadian firms to the United States that, if improperly revealed, could harm firm competitiveness;
- interfere with cross-border mobility of Canadian workers to the United States as these "green card holders" will be subject to costly tax compliance measures after they return to Canada;
- impede Canada's efforts to enforce its own tax laws and to cooperate on a global scale to promote the integrity of the income taxation system; and

[156] *Ibid* at para 76.
[157] *Implementation Act*, above note 154.
[158] *Canada–US IGA*, above note 135.

- violate the spirit and potentially the letter of a number of Canadian laws including the *Personal Information Protection and Electronic Document Act*, the *Privacy Act*, the *Access to Banking Services Regulations*, NAFTA, and others.[159]

It is possible, and even probable, that the plaintiffs in *Hillis and Deegan* will appeal Martineau J's decision to the three-judge panel of the Federal Court of Appeal. Aside from the *Hillis and Deegan* challenge, we have not seen a full-blown court challenge claiming that these new tax provisions infringe *Charter* rights.

Currently, there are few, if any, impediments to the exchange of information between Canada and the United States. An individual gets no advance notice and no way of ascertaining exactly what information has been shared between CRA and the IRS. An individual also has no control over the use of the information that has been shared. Furthermore, the new international agreements between Canada and the United States such as the *Canada–US IGA* and the amendments to the *Act* (sections 263 to 269) guarantee that certain financial institutions will supply account information to CRA and that CRA will, in turn, provide this data to the IRS. Canadian courts have already established that if an investigation as opposed to an audit is carried out by Canadian authorities in a foreign country, *Charter* protections and privacy rights do not apply.[160] The practical implications for US non-filers in Canada are discussed in Chapter 10.

12 Taxpayer Rights: Challenges to the Exchange of Information

It is clearly possible that a taxpayer's engagement of the rights guaranteed by the *Charter* could have some limiting effect on CRA's ability to share information with a foreign state. But this depends on many factors, such as the nature of the specific information shared with the foreign state and, possibly, how that information is used. The *Hillis and Deegan* case raised

[159] Christians & Cockfield, above note 137 at 1–2.

[160] *Schrieber v Canada (AG)*, [1998] 1 SCR 841.

the prospect that a court would hear *Charter* arguments based on sections 7, 8, and 15.[161] However, the court in that case put those arguments aside, and, therefore, Canadians are still waiting for the first *Charter* challenge in respect of the exchange of information agreement with the United States and the new provisions (sections 263 to 269) in Part XVIII of the *Act*.

Section 52 of the *Charter* is the starting point for appreciating this unique Canadian constitutional circumstance. Section 52 states, "The Constitution of Canada is the supreme law of Canada, and any law that is inconsistent with the provisions of the Constitution is, to the extent of the inconsistency, of no force or effect."[162] Is it likely that a court will find the provisions of international agreements with the United States or the new provisions of the *Act* inconsistent with the *Charter* and therefore of no force and effect? It is difficult to imagine that the provision of information, in and of itself, would contravene *Charter* rights for a number of reasons, including and most importantly the saving provision — section 1 — of the *Charter*. This section states, "The *Canadian Charter of Rights and Freedoms* guarantees the rights and freedoms set out in it subject only to such reasonable limits prescribed by law as can be demonstrably justified in a free and democratic society."[163] The international agreements and the *Act* contain safeguards to restrict disclosure. And there are serious consequences for those who have the responsibility of maintaining the proper confidentiality of this information if they improperly disclose it.

The combination of the need to share information between states for purposes of the administration and enforcement of the *Act* and the restrictions imposed on state actors with regard to sharing this information suggests that even if there were a contravention of a *Charter* right, such contravention would likely be saved by section 1 of the *Charter* because it would constitute a reasonable limit prescribed by law in a free and democratic society. Yet, it will be important to test this limit because such a serious encroachment on individual privacy and other rights requires the full scrutiny of the courts to ensure that, in practice and in fact, the exchange of information in such an all-encompassing manner is truly justified in a democratic society.

---

[161] *Hillis and Deegan*, above note 153.

[162] *Charter*, above note 1, s 52.

[163] *Ibid*, s 1.

13 Conclusion

It has been said about the evolution of the law that the pendulum can swing from one side to the other. In terms of the powers of the Canadian state and specifically the purpose and functions of CRA, it seems as though the courts today are more willing to provide greater latitude to CRA to pursue and obtain taxpayer information. In the context of civil matters, the right to privacy is given very minimal protection, and this lack of protection extends from the domestic to the international sphere. When a foreign state authority seeks financial information regarding a Canadian taxpayer and asks for CRA's assistance in obtaining it, CRA willingly acts.

Not all is lost for the Canadian taxpayer, however, as there are several circumstances that permit the taxpayer to at least raise a reasonable challenge to the potential invasion of privacy and disclosure of information. In the first place, the Minister must always seek information that is related to the administration or enforcement of the *Act*. It is therefore possible for a taxpayer to argue that the request or requirement for information lies outside of the statutory conditions for a request or requirement. Section 231.5(2) of the *Act* also provides a reasonable bar to the production of information. While a taxpayer must be compliant, what if the taxpayer is unable to comply? Plainly, the language of this section contemplates such situations.[164] Another possible basis for challenging the Minister's request or requirement for information is a taxpayer's claim of solicitor-client privilege. The *Act* does contain, in section 232, a definition of solicitor-client privilege. But solicitor-client privilege is also fully protected under the *Charter*.[165] Another bar to the production of information can arise where CRA's request or requirement for information crosses "the Rubicon" from a civil audit to a criminal investigation. According

---

[164] *Act*, above note 1, s 231.5(2).

[165] See *R v Lavallee, Rackel and Heintz*, 2002 SCC 61. Section 232 of the *Act*, above note 1, contains the solicitor-client privilege protection, and section 232(1), *ibid*, defines solicitor-client privilege as follows:

> the right, if any, that a person has in a superior court in the province where the matter arises to refuse to disclose an oral or documentary communication on the ground that the communication is one passing between the person and the person's lawyer in professional confidence, except that for the purposes of this section an accounting record of a lawyer, including any supporting voucher or cheque, shall be deemed not to be such a communication.

to the *Jarvis* predominant purpose test,[166] where this line is crossed, the taxpayer's *Charter* rights become fully engaged. Thus, to navigate through the potential invasion of privacy, taxpayers require an understanding of both the scope and the limits of CRA's investigative powers.

Further Readings

Antoine, Rose-Marie Belle. *Confidentiality in Offshore Financial Law*, 2d ed (Oxford: Oxford University Press, 2014).

Calderón, Jose M. "Taxpayer Protection within the Exchange of Information Procedure between State Tax Administrations" (2000) 28:12 *Intertax* 462.

Douvier, PJ. "Confidentiality of Taxpayer Information" *International Transfer Pricing Journal* (January 2000).

Fitzsimmons, Richard G. *Resolving Tax Disputes*, 2d ed (Toronto: CCH Canadian Limited, 2004).

Keen, Michael, & Jenny E Ligthart. "Information Sharing and International Taxation: A Primer" (2006) 13 *International Tax and Public Finance* 81.

Malherbe, J. "General Report IFA — Conference on Protection of Confidential Information in Tax Matters" (1991) 76:b *Cahiers de Droit Fiscal International.*

Rust, Alexander, & Eric Fort, eds. *Exchange of Information and Bank Secrecy* (Alphen aan den Rijn, NL: Kluwer Law International, 2012).

Urtz, C. "Confidentiality of Taxpayer Information" (2000) 7 *International Transfer Pricing Journal* No 2 (March/April 2000).

For further discussion on solicitor-client privilege, see Brian R Carr, "Solicitor-Client Privilege" in *Report of Proceedings of the Sixty-Second Tax Conference* (Toronto: Canadian Tax Foundation, 2011) 7:1; Dan Misutka, "Select Issues related to Solicitor-Client Privilege" in *2012 Tax Dispute Resolution Conference Report*, above note 11, 7:1; Adam M Dodek, *Solicitor-Client Privilege* (Markham, ON: LexisNexis, 2014); *Canada (Procureur général) c Chambre des notaires du Québec*, 2014 QCCA 552.

[166] *Jarvis*, above note 96.

5

International Tax Enforcement in the United States

1 Introduction

International tax enforcement may comprise an examination or investigation process, an enforcement or collections process, and, where warranted, a criminal prosecution process. This chapter will be of particular interest to professionals who work in wealth management, accounting, and law and who have clients with offshore or delinquent compliance issues concerning the tax or foreign-reporting laws of the United States. It explains the domestic administrative measures relied upon by the United States to obtain foreign-based taxpayer information for the purpose of conducting a civil audit or examination, or a criminal investigation. Without the ability to verify the foreign earned income of its citizens and residents, the United States would not be able to effectively or fairly administer its tax system, which is based on the taxation of worldwide income.[1] Hence, the focus of this chapter is on understanding the framework of legal powers granted to the fiscal authorities in the

[1] See United States, Congress, Joint Committee on Taxation, *Tax Compliance and Enforcement Issues with respect to Offshore Accounts and Entities* (Washington, DC: Joint Committee on Taxation, 2009) at 44 [JCT, *Enforcement Issues*].

D.S. Kerzner, D.W. Chodikoff, *International Tax Evasion in the Global Information Age*, DOI 10.1007/978-3-319-40421-9_5

United States to obtain taxpayer information for the administration and enforcement of their respective tax laws and to combat non-compliance related to offshore accounts, where this information is not currently in the government's possession, or is otherwise unobtainable from an unwilling taxpayer or record holder. As the Supreme Court of the United States observed in *United States v Arthur Young & Co*,

> Our complex and comprehensive system of federal taxation, relying as it does upon self-assessment and reporting, demands that all taxpayers be forthright in the disclosure of relevant information to the taxing authorities. Without such disclosure, and the concomitant power of the Government to compel disclosure, our national tax burden would not be fairly and equitably distributed. In order to encourage effective tax investigations, Congress has endowed the IRS with expansive information-gathering authority; § 7602 is the centerpiece of that congressional design.[2]

An understanding of these administrative measures is critical to grasping where tax information exchange agreements (TIEAs) and exchange of information (EOI) under double tax conventions (DTCs) fit into the information-gathering process and to evaluating their functionality in fighting tax evasion against alternative tools. This chapter is also important to the research in this book because it examines some of the legal, political, economic, and social problems connected to the EOI process. Moreover, it illustrates the range of domestic powers that the IRS can use against a taxpayer or third-party holder of information to inflict potential civil and criminal sanctions for failing to comply with its summons power, thereby creating serious consequences for uncooperative parties. As Professor Gianni admonishes, "since deficiencies asserted by the IRS are presumptively correct when litigated, taxpayers usually lose more than they gain by dragging their feet when asked for information."[3]

This chapter begins by reviewing the privacy rights and safeguards of taxpayers in the United States, including the vital interplay between these

[2] 465 US 805 at 815–16 (1984), cited in Monica Gianni, "IRS Investigative Authority" in Boris Bittker & Lawrence Lokken, *Federal Taxation of Income, Estates, and Gifts* (Thomson Reuters/WG&L) (Checkpoint) at 112.2.1 [Revised].

[3] Gianni, above note 2.

domestic rules and the obligations of governments to exchange information under TIEAs and DTCs. An understanding of these rights is important because, as discussed below, taxpayer privacy is a cornerstone both to administering the tax system domestically and to enabling effective EOI with treaty partners. This chapter also examines, perhaps for the first time in this research field, the use of criminal prosecution by the United States as a new means of bolstering EOI. Additionally, it examines the legal regime surrounding the use of the summons powers, including the John Doe "super" summons power, to obtain foreign-based information. The use of these two administrative measures either as an alternative to treaty-based EOI mechanisms or in conjunction with them serves to (1) illustrate how these measures differ from TIEAs and (2) reveal underlying political and legal problems with EOI mechanisms. To help illustrate the use of some of the tools being used to obtain foreign documentation, this chapter draws on the experience of the United States in obtaining foreign account information from UBS both under the United States' tax treaty with Switzerland and through such unilateral measures as the John Doe summons and the recent and new formalization of the threat of criminal prosecution. The UBS case study highlights the legal, political, and economic challenges that exist in the EOI field. And these challenges pose the broader policy questions of whether EOI works without incentives (be they sanctions or rewards) and whether one "policy size" (e.g., automatic exchange of information) will be effective in the war on tax evasion for all players.

2 Privacy Rights and Safeguards of Taxpayers

The question of whether or not information regarding taxpayers in America should be private is as old as the income tax itself.[4] Present rules on tax privacy provide that tax returns and tax return information are

[4] See Joshua Blank, "In Defense of Individual Tax Privacy" (2012) 61 *Emory Law Journal* 265 at 267, quoting Boris I Bittker, "Federal Income Tax Returns — Confidentiality vs. Public Disclosure" (1981) 20 *Washburn Law Journal* 479 at 480–81: when the income tax was first introduced in 1862 to pay for the American Civil War, the statute required the names of taxpayers and their liabilities

to be treated as confidential and prohibit the release, subject to limited exceptions, of taxpayer information by the federal government without the consent of the taxpayer.[5]

Taxpayer information that is to be treated as confidential is broadly defined to include the following: a tax or information return, a taxpayer's identity, the nature, source, or amount of a taxpayer's income, payments, receipts, deductions, exemptions, credits, assets, liabilities, net worth, tax liability, tax withheld, deficiencies, overassessments, and tax payments, and any other data received or collected by the Secretary of the Treasury (Secretary) with respect to a return or the determination of the existence, or possible existence, of liability (or the amount thereof) of any person under the *Code* for any tax, penalty, interest, fine, forfeiture, or other imposition, or offence.[6] Special rules govern the circumstances under which the IRS may disclose taxpayer information to foreign countries. A key exception to the non-disclosure rule of *Code* section 6103 is for the disclosure of tax information by the IRS to foreign tax authorities under a treaty or bilateral agreement. *Code* section 6103(k)(4) provides:

> A return or return information may be disclosed to a competent authority of a foreign government which has an income tax or gift and estate tax convention, or other convention or bilateral agreement relating to the exchange of tax information, with the United States but only to the extent provided in, and subject to the terms and conditions of, such convention or bilateral agreement.[7]

---

to be open to public access. In this article, Professor Blank examines the relationship between individual tax privacy and individual tax compliance, arguing that tax privacy allows the government to influence individuals' perceptions of its tax enforcement strengths without exposing its weaknesses, which would become apparent without appropriate measures of confidentiality.

[5] *Internal Revenue Code*, USC 26 (1986) of 1986, as amended, and the *Treasury Regulations* issued thereunder at § 6103(a) [*Code*]. Section 6103, relating to tax return privacy, was rewritten by Congress in 1976 in part to address privacy concerns following the Watergate scandal: see M Saltzman & L Book, *IRS Practice and Procedure* (Thomson Reuters/WG&L, 2012 ed) (Checkpoint) ch 2B and 4C. Although the *Privacy Act of 1974*, 5 USC ch 5 § 552a, provides certain safeguards against the invasion of personal privacy, *Code, ibid*, § 6103 expressly regulates the disclosure of tax return information (Saltzman & Book, *ibid*, ch 2B). Exceptions to the general rule of IRS non-disclosure may be made for a variety of reasons involving tax administration and law enforcement: see *Code, ibid*, §§ 6103(c)–(o); Blank, above note 4 at 279.

[6] *Code*, above note 5, §§ 6103(b)(1) & (2).

[7] *Ibid*, § 6103(k)(4).

Code section 6105 contains a general rule providing that tax convention information shall not be disclosed unless an enumerated exception applies.[8] Tax convention information generally includes information exchanged by the IRS with a foreign jurisdiction under a tax treaty or TIEA.[9] A key objective of section 6105 is to support good working relationships among treaty partners.[10] US tax treaties and TIEAs also contain a confidentiality provision that is similar to that contained in Article 26 of the *United States Model Income Tax Convention.*[11] Article 26(2) of the *US Model Tax Treaty* provides:

> Any information received under this Article by a Contracting State shall be treated as secret in the same manner as information obtained under the domestic laws of that State and shall be disclosed only to persons or authorities (including courts and administrative bodies) involved in the assessment, collection, or administration of, the enforcement or prosecution in respect of, or the determination of appeals in relation to, the taxes covered by the Convention, or the oversight of such functions. Such persons or authorities shall use the information only for such purposes. They may disclose the information in public court proceedings or in judicial proceedings.

Exceptions to the prohibition on disclosure of tax convention information permit information to be disclosed to persons or authorities (including courts and administrative bodies) that are entitled to such disclosures under a tax treaty,[12] and as provided under applicable procedures regarding applications for relief under a tax treaty.[13] Additionally, information

[8] *Ibid,* § 6105(b).

[9] See United States, *Conference Report to Accompany H.R. 4577,* HR Conf Rep No 106-1033 (2000) at 1012, online: www.congress.gov/106/crpt/hrpt1033/CRPT-106hrpt1033.pdf [US *Conference Report*]. The identities and information of taxpayers and the identities of countries involved in EOI are protected from public disclosure: *Code,* above note 5, § 6105. See also *Tax Analysts v Internal Revenue Service,* 217 F Supp 2d 23 at 28 (DDC 2002), citing *Tax Analysts v Internal Revenue Service,* 152 F Supp 2d 1 at 11 (DDC 2001).

[10] See US *Conference Report,* above note 9.

[11] 15 November 2006, Art 26(2), online: www.treasury.gov/press-center/press-releases/Documents/hp16801.pdf [*US Model Tax Treaty*].

[12] *Code,* above note 5, § 6105(b)(1).

[13] *Ibid,* § 6105(b)(2).

may be disclosed to federal, state, and local enforcement officers and employees who are directly involved in responding to or investigating any terrorist incident, threat, or activity.[14] The Secretary may also disclose information that does not relate to a particular taxpayer if the Secretary determines after consultation with the treaty partner that the disclosure would not impair tax administration.[15] As a general matter, under US law, the IRS is not required to notify a taxpayer before providing information in its possession to a foreign jurisdiction pursuant to a tax treaty or TIEA.[16]

A series of civil and criminal penalties may apply as a result of the violation of US confidentiality rules applicable to returns or return information as well as the unauthorized disclosure of information received as part of an exchange under a tax treaty or TIEA that violates *Code* section 6105.[17]

Under the *Right to Financial Privacy Act of 1978*, bank account information generally may not be disclosed to federal government authorities without notice to the customer, and the customer has the right to challenge such a disclosure.[18] However, an exception permits the disclosure of financial data for certain enforcement procedures under the *Code*, including summonses issued in response to requests for information under a treaty or TIEA.[19] The *RFPA* also expressly permits the disclosure of financial data on accounts held by non-residents to the US Department of the Treasury, in regard to withholding taxes.[20]

---

[14] *Ibid*, § 6105(b)(3).

[15] *Ibid*, § 6105(b)(4).

[16] See OECD, *Global Forum on Transparency and Exchange of Information for Tax Purposes Peer Reviews: United States 2011 — Combined: Phase 1 + Phase 2* (Paris: OECD, 2011) at 62, online: http://dx.doi.org/10.1787/9789264115064-en [OECD, *US Peer Review*].

[17] For example, pursuant to *Code*, above note 5, § 7213, the willful unauthorized disclosure of a return or return information may result in a felony crime subject to a fine of $5,000, imprisonment for five years, or both. Further, under *Code*, *ibid*, § 7213A, the willful unauthorized access to or inspection of returns or return information may result in a misdemeanour offence subject to a fine of $1,000, imprisonment for one year, or both.

[18] See, generally, *Right to Financial Privacy Act of 1978*, USC tit 12 §§ 3401–22 [*RFPA*].

[19] *Ibid*, §§ 3402 and 3413(c). See also OECD, *US Peer Review*, above note 16 at 67. In general, the *RFPA* also does not apply to information subject to a grand jury subpoena: see OECD, *US Peer Review*, above note 16 at 71.

[20] *RFPA*, above note 18, § 3413(k). See also OECD, *US Peer Review*, above note 16 at 67.

3 Administrative Procedures for Obtaining Taxpayer Information

3.1 Introduction

The IRS commands a powerful array of legal measures by which to compel the disclosure of information that is held by persons subject to its jurisdiction.[21] These same powers may also be used by the IRS to obtain information for the purpose of complying with an obligation that the United States has under a tax treaty or TIEA.[22] Such information may include information held by banks and financial institutions as well as information regarding the ownership of companies or other entities such as partnerships or trusts.[23]

3.2 Request for Information

The IRS may go about obtaining information from a taxpayer through a voluntary process that begins with the issuance of a Form 4564 (Information Document Request) (IDR). The IRS may also obtain information from a taxpayer through the formal issuance via the legal system of an administrative summons. (The summons process is described below.) Due to recent changes regarding the enforcement of IDRs, a taxpayer who becomes the subject of an examination conducted by an IRS agent is strongly urged to retain counsel as soon as possible.[24] The IDR enforcement process, which became effective as of 3 March 2014, is

---

[21] See OECD, *US Peer Review*, above note 16 at 67.

[22] See *ibid* at 65.

[23] See *ibid* at 61.

[24] The IRS has issued three new directives relating to IDRs: "Large Business & International Directive on Information Document Requests (IDRs)," 04-0613-004 (18 June 2013), online: www.irs.gov/Businesses/LBI-Directive-on-Information-Document-Requests; "Large Business and International Directive on Information Document Request Enforcement Process," 04-1113-009 (4 November 2013), online: www.irs.gov/Businesses/Corporations/Large-Business-and-International-Directive-on-Information-Document-Request-Enforcement-Process; "Large Business and International Directive on Information Document Requests Enforcement Process," 04-0214-004 (28 February 2014), online: www.irs.gov/Businesses/Large-Business-and-International-Directive-on-Information-Document-Requests-Enforcement-Process [February 2014 Directive].

initiated when in the absence of any granted extensions a taxpayer either fails to respond by the IDR due date or provides an incomplete response by the IDR due date.[25] The enforcement process has three graduated steps: (1) issuance of a delinquency notice (Letter 5077), (2) issuance of a pre-summons letter, and (3) issuance of a summons.[26] Of critical importance for the taxpayer and her counsel is that the enforcement process is mandatory and has no exceptions.[27] For persons with tax problems with the IRS, in terms of practical strategy, a lack of cooperation can lead to varying degrees of difficulty for the taxpayer. To begin with, failure to cooperate with an IRS agent during an examination could be an indication of civil fraud.[28] Under the new mandatory IDR enforcement process, a lack of cooperation in an IRS examination will dial up the intensity of the taxpayer's experience by turning a civil administrative process into a confrontation with the US federal justice system on a criminal level.[29]

3.3 Power to Issue Summonses: Section 7602

In *United States v Bisceglia*, the Supreme Court of the United States observed, "[Section] 7601 gives the Internal Revenue Service a broad mandate to investigate and audit 'persons who may be liable' for taxes and § 7602 provides the power to 'examine any books, papers, records, or other data which may be relevant . . . [and to summon] any person having possession . . . of books of account . . . relevant or material to such inquiry.'"[30] While *Code* sections 7601 and 7602 dealing with sum-

[25] See February 2014 Directive, above note 24.

[26] See *ibid.*

[27] See *ibid.*

[28] See *Klassie v United States*, 289 F 2d 96 (8th Cir 1961): taxpayer's giving false or incomplete records or being uncooperative with agent may be evidence of fraudulent intent; *Bradford v Commissioner of Internal Revenue*, 796 F 2d 303 (9th Cir 1986): non-cooperation with IRS, failure to file, and knowing failure to pay tax may be evidence of fraud.

[29] The IRS can apply for a district court order to arrest the taxpayer pending a contempt and enforcement hearing, and if the court orders enforcement, the summoned taxpayer will be held in contempt for further failure to comply: *Code*, above note 5, § 7604(b). The IRS may also recommend prosecution of the taxpayer for willful failure to comply with a summons: *Code*, *ibid*, § 7210.

[30] 420 US 141 at 145–46 (1975) [square brackets and ellipses in original], cited in Gianni, above note 2 at 112.2.1.

mons powers are concerned with IRS administrative investigations, it is important to note that where a tax matter is litigated in court, both the government and the taxpayer have access to a range of trial tactics that may be used to uncover and prove the facts at issue in the case, for example, motions for discovery and subpoenas to compel witnesses to appear and for the production of documents.[31] Under *Code* section 7602, the Secretary has broad powers to examine any books, records, or data that may be relevant or material to ascertaining the correctness of any return, making a return where none has been made, determining the liability of any person for any internal revenue, or collecting any such revenue.[32] Although beyond the scope of this book, the validity of these summons powers must be viewed in light of the immense body of administrative, criminal, and constitutional law that exists both within and outside the laws on taxation.[33] The IRS may choose to issue a formal summons after an unsuccessful IDR has been made. *Code* section 7602 authorizes the IRS to compel a taxpayer or third party by issuance of a summons to appear at a time and place named in the summons and to produce such records or data and to give such testimony under oath as may be relevant or material to the inquiry.[34] The IRS may issue a summons to the taxpayer, an officer or employee of the taxpayer, any person having custody of accounting books relating to the business of the taxpayer, or any other person with relevant records or data.[35] This summons power is available to the IRS in either a civil or a criminal tax-related investigation.[36] And these summons procedures may also be used in carrying out the obligations of the United States under a tax convention[37]

[31] See Gianni, above note 2 at 112.2.1.

[32] *Code*, above note 5, § 7602(a)(1).

[33] See Gianni, above note 2 at 112.2.1, noting among other doctrines and defences, the privilege against self-incrimination, claims that a summons is excessively broad or intended to harass a witness, and also the right to counsel.

[34] *Code*, above note 5, § 7602(a)(2).

[35] *Ibid.*

[36] See *Treasury Regulations*, 26 CFR § 301.7602-1(b)(1).

[37] See *United States v Stuart*, 489 US 353 at 359–60 (1989) [*Stuart*], affirming the validity of an administrative summons issued by the IRS pursuant to a request by Canadian authorities under Articles XIX and XXI of the *Convention between Canada and the United States of America with respect to Taxes on Income and on Capital*, 4 March 1942, 56 Stat 1405–1406, TS No 983, regardless

or TIEA.[38] Generally, the IRS is not required to notify a taxpayer before providing information in its possession to a foreign jurisdiction pursuant to a request under a treaty or TIEA.[39]

For a summons to be enforceable, the IRS need only demonstrate good faith in issuing the summons by showing that the summons (1) is issued for a legitimate purpose, (2) seeks information relevant to that purpose, (3) seeks information that is not already within the IRS's possession, and (4) satisfies all the administrative steps required by the *Code*.[40] This four-part good faith test also applies where a foreign government has requested that the IRS use its summons powers pursuant to a tax treaty or TIEA.[41] Only a "minimal" showing that a summons has been issued in good faith is required of the IRS,[42] and a heavy evidentiary burden must be met to successfully challenge the summons.[43] However, a summons may not be issued to a person under the *Code* where a Department of

---

of whether or not investigation by CRA was equivalent to a referral to the US Department of Justice under *Code*, above note 5, § 7602(c), and observing, *Stuart*, *ibid* at 356, "So long as the summons meets statutory requirements and is issued in good faith, as we defined that term in *United States v Powell*, 379 U.S. 48, 379 U.S. 57–58, 14 AFTR 2d 5942 (1964), compliance is required, whether or not the Canadian tax investigation is directed toward criminal prosecution under Canadian law."

[38] See *Barquero v United States*, 18 F 3d 1311 at 1314–15 (5th Cir 1994), confirming the IRS authority to issue a summons on behalf of a foreign government with which the United States has signed a TIEA, in support of a request by the competent authority of Mexico to serve IBC Bank a request for all the bank's records pertaining to a bank account held by a taxpayer, to determine his Mexican tax liability.

[39] See OECD, *US Peer Review*, above note 16 at 62. But see discussion in Section 3.4, below in this chapter: the IRS is obligated to notify a taxpayer regarding the issuance of a summons to a third party under *Code*, above note 5, § 7609.

[40] See *United States v Powell*, 379 US 48 (1964) [*Powell*]; *Stuart*, above note 37 at 359.

[41] See *Lidas, Inc v United States*, 238 F 3d 1076 (9th Cir 2001) at 1082, quoting *Stuart*, above note 37 at 360: to be entitled to enforcement in this instance, the IRS was not obligated to show the good faith of the requesting nation but, rather, that it was acting in good faith pursuant to *Powell*, above note 40, and compliant with applicable statutes.

[42] See *United States v Abrahams*, 905 F 2d 1276 at 1280 (9th Cir 1990) [*Abrahams*]. This showing is generally made by the submission of a declaration of the IRS agent who issued the summons: see *United States v Samuels, Kramer & Co*, 712 F 2d 1342 at 1345 (9th Cir 1983) [*Samuels, Kramer & Co*]; *Code*, above note 5, §§ 7603 & 7604, which provide rules relating to the service and the enforcement, respectively, of IRS summonses.

[43] See *Abrahams*, above note 42 at 1280. A party opposing enforcement will have to show that the summons was issued for an improper purpose such as harassing the taxpayer or putting pressure on the taxpayer to settle a collateral dispute: see *Powell*, above note 40 at 58.

Justice referral is in effect with respect to that person.[44] Such a referral is in effect with respect to any person if (1) the Secretary has recommended to the Attorney General a grand jury investigation or criminal prosecution of the person for an offence connected with the administration or enforcement of the internal revenue laws or if (2) any request has been made under *Code* section 6103(h)(3)(B) for the disclosure of any return or return information relating to the person.[45] The Supreme Court has recognized that certain evidentiary privileges such as attorney-client privilege are protected from intrusion.[46]

The US district courts have jurisdiction over actions brought to enforce IRS administrative summonses.[47] For US citizens living abroad, such actions would generally be brought in the District of Columbia.[48] Failure to comply with an administrative summons may involve multiple penalties, including a fine of up to $1,000, a prison sentence of up to one year, or both, and may also trigger civil contempt sanctions.[49] Additionally, the *Code* contains general penalties for any person who is required to pay any tax, make a return (including an information return), keep any record, or supply any information as specified in the *Code* or its regulations and who willfully fails to do so that may cause such person to be guilty of a misdemeanour carrying a fine of not more than $25,000 ($100,000 for corporations), imprisonment for not more than one year, or both.[50] Search warrants may be issued if they meet prescribed constitutional tests under the Fourth Amendment for probable cause and are supported by an oath or affirmation, and conform to standards of particularity with respect to persons to be searched or things to be seized.[51] However, as the IRS must obtain Department of Justice concurrence for search warrants, they are seldom used absent concern that a summons may trig-

[44] *Code*, above note 5, § 7602(d).

[45] *Ibid*, § 7602(d)(2)(A).

[46] See Gianni, above note 2 at 112.2.4, citing *United States v Euge*, 444 US 707 at 714 (1980). A more limited privilege arises in respect of tax practitioners (*ibid*).

[47] *Code*, above note 5, § 7604(a).

[48] *Ibid*, § 7701(a)(39).

[49] *Ibid*, § 7210. See also OECD, *US Peer Review*, above note 16 at 66.

[50] *Code*, above note 5, § 7203. See also OECD, *US Peer Review*, above note 16 at 66.

[51] See Gianni, above note 2 at 112.2.9.

ger the destruction of the records sought.[52] The Tax Division within the Department of Justice generally has the authority to approve the execution of search warrants in matters concerning the internal revenue laws. The Tax Division is responsible for overseeing all federal criminal tax enforcement and handles the investigation and/or prosecution of certain criminal tax cases.[53] Criminal tax violations encompass federal criminal charges arising not only under the internal revenue laws but also under related statutes.[54]

3.4 Notification Procedure for Third-Party Summonses: Section 7609

Before the passage of *Code* section 7609, the IRS possessed the authority to summon third parties for the purpose of obtaining taxpayer records without notifying the taxpayer. In enacting *Code* section 7609, Congress wished to afford taxpayers a measure of privacy protection by establishing certain notice procedures that the IRS must follow to summon a third-party keeper of records and to accord taxpayers a reasonable and speedy means to challenge a summons in certain situations.[55] Generally, a copy of the summons is to be provided to the taxpayer within three days of service being made.[56] Under *Code* section 7609, the taxpayer has the right to intervene in any proceeding with respect to the enforcement of such summons under *Code* section 7604 or to begin a proceeding to quash such summons within twenty days of notice being given.[57]

---

[52] See *ibid.*

[53] See United States, Department of Justice, "U.S. Attorneys' Manual" (Washington, DC: Department of Justice, 2015) at §§ 6-1.100 & 6-1.110, online: www.justice.gov/usam/united-states-attorneys-manual [USAM].

[54] See *ibid.*

[55] See United States, HR 10612 — *Tax Reform Act*, HR Rep No 658 at 307 (1975), reprinted in 1976 USCCAN 2897 at 3203; United States, HR 10612 — *Tax Reform Act*, S Rep No 938, pt 1 at 368–69 (1976), reprinted in 1976 USCCAN 3439 at 3798. See also *Code*, above note 5, § 7609(a), regarding notice provisions.

[56] *Code*, above note 5, § 7609(a)(1).

[57] *Ibid*, § 7609(b).

3.5 Production of Foreign-Based Information

Verification of foreign earned income is a central component of administering the US tax system, which is based on the taxation of worldwide income.[58] As a result, the United States utilizes a range of unilateral domestic legal measures to obtain foreign information. These tools can be divided into summons powers, which may be used to compel production of foreign-based documents, and penalty provisions, which may be used to persuade a taxpayer to comply with a request for information. These tools are discussed below in the following sections: 3.6, Summonses and Grand Jury Subpoenas; 3.7, John Doe Summonses; 3.8, Miscellaneous Sanctions and Penalties; and 4, Criminal Prosecution.

3.6 Summonses and Grand Jury Subpoenas

Subject to certain exceptions, only the Department of Justice Tax Division may authorize grand jury investigations of potential criminal tax violations and the designation of any individual or entity as a target of such an investigation.[59]

In contemplating whether or not to compel production of foreign-based documents, US courts have historically sought to balance the conflicting interests of the IRS in enforcing US tax laws and the foreign jurisdiction in maintaining its bank secrecy rules.[60] This balancing test is summarized in the *Restatement of the Law (Third) of Foreign Relations Law of the United States*, which provides as follows:

---

[58] See JCT, *Enforcement Issues*, above note 1 at 44.

[59] USAM, above note 53 at § 6-1.110.

[60] See JCT, *Enforcement Issues*, above note 1 at 44, noting that courts have tended to give greater weight to the interests of the United States in cases involving criminal activity, such as money laundering or drug dealing, than in cases solely concerned with tax evasion. See also the following cases, which are discussed below: *Societe Internationale v Rogers*, 357 US 197 (1958) [*Societe Internationale*]; *In re Grand Jury Proceedings, United States v Field*, 532 F 2d 404 (5th Cir 1976), cert denied, 429 US 940 (1976) [*Field*]; *United States v Bank of Nova Scotia*, 691 F (2d) 1384 (11th Cir 1982), cert denied, 462 US 1119 (1983) [*Bank of Nova Scotia*].

(a) A court or agency in the United States, when authorized by statute or rule of court, may order a person subject to its jurisdiction to produce documents, objects, or other information relevant to an action or investigation, even if the information or the person in possession of the information is outside of the United States;
(b) failure to comply with an order to produce information may subject the person to whom the order is directed to sanctions, including finding of contempt, dismissal of a claim or defense, or default judgment, or may lead to a determination that the facts to which the order was addressed are as asserted by the opposing party; and
(c) in deciding whether to issue an order directing production of information located abroad, and in framing such an order, a court or agency in the United States should take into account the importance to the investigation or litigation of the documents or other information requested; the degree of specificity of the request; whether the information originated in the United States; the availability of alternative means of securing the information; and the extent to which noncompliance with the request would undermine important interests of the United States, or compliance with the request would undermine important interests of the state where the information is located.[61]

In *Societe Internationale v Rogers*, the Supreme Court, in describing a fundamental rule of comity, held unanimously that a US district court could not ignore the interests of a foreign state in considering whether to compel production of documents located in that state.[62] In this case, the district court ordered the petitioner to make available a large number of bank records located in Switzerland.[63] The petitioner was a Swiss holding company that had brought an action to recover assets seized under the *Trading with the Enemy Act*. The petitioner sought to be relieved of this order because disclosure of the required bank records could lead to criminal sanctions for violating Swiss penal laws. The order was affirmed by

---

[61] (1986), § 441(1) [*Restatement*].

[62] *Societe Internationale*, above note 60.

[63] *Ibid* at 199–200.

the court of appeals. The Supreme Court held that, given the petitioner's good faith and efforts to comply with the order and weighing certain constitutional considerations, the district court's dismissal of the petitioner's complaint with prejudice had not been justified.[64] Justice Harlan, in delivering the opinion of the Court, observed:

> The findings below, and what has been shown as to petitioner's extensive efforts at compliance, compel the conclusion on this record that petitioner's failure to satisfy fully the requirements of this production order was due to inability fostered neither by its own conduct nor by circumstances within its control. It is hardly debatable that fear of criminal prosecution constitutes a weighty excuse for nonproduction, and this excuse is not weakened because the laws preventing compliance are those of a foreign sovereign . . . . Here, the findings below establish that the very fact of compliance by disclosure of banking records will itself constitute the initial violation of Swiss laws. In our view, petitioner stands in the position of an American plaintiff subject to criminal sanctions in Switzerland because production of documents in Switzerland pursuant to the order of a United States court might violate Swiss laws. Petitioner has sought no privileges because of its foreign citizenship which are not accorded domestic litigants in the United States courts. *Cf. Guaranty Trust Co. v. United States*, 304 U.S. 126, 304 U.S. 133–135. It does not claim that Swiss laws protecting banking records should here be enforced. It explicitly recognizes that it is subject to procedural rules of United States courts in this litigation and has made full efforts to follow these rules. It asserts no immunity from them. It asserts only its *inability* to comply because of foreign law.
>
> In view of the findings in this case, the position in which petitioner stands in this litigation, and the serious constitutional questions we have noted, we think that Rule 37 should not be construed to authorize dismissal of this complaint because of petitioner's noncompliance with a pretrial production order when it has been established that failure to comply has been due to inability, and not to willfulness, bad faith, or any fault of petitioner.
>
> This is not to say that petitioner will profit through its inability to tender the records called for . . . . It may be that, in the absence of complete disclosure by petitioner, the District Court would be justified in drawing

[64] *Ibid* at 208–13.

> inferences unfavorable to petitioner as to particular events. So much, indeed, petitioner concedes. But these problems go to the adequacy of petitioner's proof, and should not, on this record, preclude petitioner from being able to contest on the merits.[65]

In *United States v Field*, the Court of Appeals for the Fifth Circuit found that a subpoena compelling Anthony R Field to testify before a grand jury did not violate either the Constitution or the rules of international comity.[66] The grand jury in the Southern District of Florida was investigating possible criminal violations of US tax laws and the use of foreign banks to evade US tax enforcement and conceal crimes.[67] Mr Field was a Canadian citizen and the managing director of Castle Bank and Trust Company (Cayman), Ltd, located in Grand Cayman Island, British West Indies. He was served with a subpoena at the Miami International Airport on 12 January 1976, asking him to appear before a grand jury on 20 January. Mr Field refused to answer questions about his role at Castle and about its clients for fear of incriminating himself in violation of his Fifth Amendment rights and also for fear that his testimony would violate the Cayman Islands' bank secrecy laws. The district court held him in contempt and he appealed.[68] The Court of Appeals noted that if Mr Field had demonstrated that the content of his answers could be used as evidence against him in a foreign prosecution, there would have been a difficult question concerning Fifth Amendment protection against self-incrimination.[69] However, the court found that the subpoena was not an attempt to obtain information from him that would later be used against him in a criminal case and that the Fifth Amendment is not relevant where a foreign state makes the act of testifying a criminal offence.[70] The court next considered Mr Field's claim that international comity demanded that enforcement of the subpoena be declined. The court observed, "The Restatement position requires a balancing of the

[65] *Ibid* at 211–13 [footnote omitted].

[66] *Field*, above note 60 at 405.

[67] *Ibid* at 405–8.

[68] *Ibid* at 406.

[69] *Ibid.*

[70] *Ibid* at 407.

several factors in determining whether the United States or, in this case, the Cayman Islands' legal command will prevail."[71] The court noted that the important factors to be weighed were the relative interests of the states, as between obtaining information about the violation of US tax laws and the protection of the right to privacy incorporated into the Cayman Islands' bank secrecy laws.[72] The court concluded that to refuse to require Mr Field's testimony would "significantly restrict the essential means that the grand jury has of evaluating whether to bring an indictment."[73] The court further observed, "If this court were to countenance Mr. Field's refusal to testify it would significantly restrict the ability of the grand jury to obtain information which might possibly uncover criminal activities of the most serious nature."[74]

In *United States v Bank of Nova Scotia*, the court enforced a grand jury subpoena against a Canadian chartered bank calling for production of financial data maintained in the Bahamas in violation of that jurisdiction's bank secrecy laws.[75] The court subsequently fined the Canadian bank $1.8 million.[76] In this case, a federal grand jury issued a subpoena on The Bank of Nova Scotia to produce records of a bank customer as part of a tax and narcotics investigation that it was conducting.[77] The requested records were in the Bahamas and Antigua. The subpoena was served on the bank's agency in Miami in September 1981. The district court held the bank in civil contempt after its Miami agent formally declined to produce the documents in an appearance before the grand jury.[78] The bank contended that complying with the subpoena would require it to violate

[71] *Ibid* [footnote omitted].

[72] *Ibid.*

[73] *Ibid.*

[74] *Ibid* at 409.

[75] *Bank of Nova Scotia*, above note 60. The bank, *ibid* at 1386, declined to comply with the document request, asserting that compliance without the customer's consent or an order of a Bahamian court would violate Bahamian bank secrecy laws and, moreover, would violate due process under *Societe Internationale*, above note 60, on the rationale that it would be unfair, because of the bank's lack of purposeful involvement or responsibility in the subject matter, to require a "mere stakeholder" to incur criminal liability in the Bahamas.

[76] *Bank of Nova Scotia*, above note 60 at 1386.

[77] *Ibid.*

[78] *Ibid* at 1387.

Bahamian bank secrecy laws such that the subpoena's enforcement would violate due process under *Societe Internationale*.[79] The court rejected the bank's claim, noting that *Societe Internationale* does not stand for the proposition that a lawfully issued grand jury subpoena can be resisted on constitutional grounds where compliance would violate foreign criminal laws.[80] The court found that the bank had not made a good faith effort to comply with the subpoena.[81] The bank further argued that the principle of comity prevented enforcement of the subpoena.[82] Here, the court observed, "Comity is 'a nation's expression of understanding which demonstrates due regard both to international duty and convenience and to the rights of persons protected by its own laws.'; *Somportex Limited v. Philadelphia Chewing Gum Corp*., 453 F.2d 435 (3rd Cir. 1971), cert. denied, 405 U.S. 1017, 92 S.Ct. 1294, 31 L.Ed.2d 479 (1972).[83]"

In rejecting the bank's comity argument, the court upheld the balancing test found in *Field*, where the court had upheld contempt penalties against a non-resident alien in the United States who was an officer of a bank in the Grand Cayman Island and who had been subpoenaed to testify before a grand jury investigating the use of offshore bank accounts held by US citizens to evade income taxes and conceal crimes.[84] The bank argued that *Field* was distinguishable from the facts in its case on several grounds including that unlike in *Field*, the bank was not under investigation and further that the government "could avoid rather than provoke disrespect for the sovereignty of a friendly nation" through the alternative of applying for an order of judicial assistance permitting a disclosure from the Supreme Court of the Bahamas.[85] Regarding the first contention, the court observed that the fact that in *Field*, Castle Bank and Trust Company (Cayman), Ltd had been under investigation simply did not impact the

[79] *Societe Internationale*, above note 60; *Bank of Nova Scotia*, above note 60 at 1388.

[80] *Bank of Nova Scotia*, above note 60 at 1389. The court noted, *ibid* at 1388–89, that *Societe Internationale*, above note 60, held only that dismissal of the plaintiff's case was not supported where the plaintiff had acted in good faith, was unable to comply due to foreign law, and was nevertheless entitled to a hearing on the merits of the case.

[81] *Bank of Nova Scotia*, above note 60 at 1389.

[82] *Ibid.*

[83] *Ibid* at 1390.

[84] *Field*, above note 60 at 405–9.

[85] *Bank of Nova Scotia*, above note 60 at 1390.

court's analysis, which was concerned with the offshore accounts and tax evasion.[86] Regarding the second contention, the court noted that "[a] pplying for judicial assistance . . . is not a substantially equivalent means for obtaining production because of the cost in time and money and the uncertain likelihood of success in obtaining the order."[87]

As discussed above, the IRS authority to investigate using its administrative summons power ends when the Secretary has made a recommendation that the Attorney General prosecute or conduct a grand jury investigation of the person for an offence connected with the administration or enforcement of the internal revenue laws.[88] While the IRS may generally use the administrative summons, after a referral to the Department of Justice and while a referral to the department is in effect, the IRS may not rely on the administrative summons and must consider the grand jury subpoena and the search warrant to compel evidence.[89] The IRS Criminal Investigation division may make a referral after special agents have conducted an investigation using the summons powers found in *Code* section 7602. The US government may obtain evidence abroad by using the subpoena power against an entity present in the United States (e.g., a corporation formed in Delaware or a branch of a foreign corporation) that has a legal relationship with the foreign-based entity holding the records being sought.[90] A grand jury or criminal trial subpoena may also be used to obtain evidence located in a foreign jurisdiction.[91] The US government has used its power to compel production of foreign-based documents in a variety of different legal situations.[92] For example, the US government has been successful in compelling the

---

[86] *Ibid.*

[87] *Ibid* at 1390–91.

[88] *Code*, above note 5, § 7602(d)(2)(A)(i). See Section 3.3, above in this chapter.

[89] *Code*, above note 5, § 7206(d); Saltzman & Book, above note 5 at 12.05[4][d][ii].

[90] See, for example, *United States v Toyota Motor Corp*, 561 F Supp 354 (CD Cal 1983) [*Toyota Motor Corp*]; *In re Grand Jury Proceedings (Bank of Nova Scotia)*, 740 F 2d 817 at 821 and 832–33 (11th Cir 1984); *In re Marc Rich & Co, AG*, 736 F 2d 864 at 867 (2d Cir 1984); *In re Grand Jury Proceedings (Bank of Nova Scotia)*, 691 F 2d 1384 at 1385–86 (11th Cir 1982).

[91] USAM, above note 53 at § 9-13.525.

[92] For a further discussion of US summons power, see Richard E Andersen, *Analysis of United States Income Tax Treaties* (New York: Thomson Reuters, 2003) (online), ch 24; Saltzman & Book, above note 5, ch 13.

production of bank documents situated in a Central American branch of a US bank[93] and in a Caribbean branch of a Canadian chartered bank.[94]

It has been more than thirty years since the Court of Appeals for the Eleventh Circuit in *Bank of Nova Scotia* rejected the bank's argument that the US government should avoid disrespecting the sovereignty of a friendly nation (the Bahamas) and instead of seeking to enforce the subpoena should pursue relief through judicial assistance procedures. The court roundly rejected this alternative because of its unpredictable cost, in time and money, and the lack of certainty of success, observing:

> The judicial assistance procedure does not afford due deference to the United States' interests. In essence, the Bank asks the court to require our government to ask the courts of the Bahamas to be allowed to do something lawful under United States law. We conclude such a procedure to be contrary to the interests of our nation and outweigh the interests of the Bahamas.[95]

At the time that the court decided the *Bank of Nova Scotia* decision, the US government would not have a TIEA with the Bahamas for another twenty-one years, and it is interesting to wonder whether it would have been used had it been in existence earlier and with what measure of success, or would unilateral measures have still been the "catch of the day."[96]

---

[93] See *First Nat'l City Bank of NY v IRS*, 271 F 2d 616 (2d Cir 1959), cert denied, 361 US 948 (1959), cited in Saltzman & Book, above note 5, ch 13: court held that the bank's records in a Panama branch were subject to government subpoena and that the bank's membership in the Federal Reserve System affirmed the bank's obligations notwithstanding any contravention of Panamanian law.

[94] See *Bank of Nova Scotia*, above note 60 (see discussion above in this section).

[95] *Ibid* at 1391.

[96] See *Agreement between the Government of the Commonwealth of the Bahamas and the Government of the United States of America for the Provision of Information with respect to Taxes and for Other Matters* (25 January 2002, entered into force 31 December 2003), online: www.bahamas.gov.bs/wps/wcm/connect/5661db08-6979-464b-be2e-aef37ae9eab5/US%2BBahamas%2B25%2BJan%2B2002.pdf?MOD=AJPERES. See also *The Bahamas and the United States of America Tax Information Exchange Agreement Regulations*, c 349B, online: http://laws.bahamas.gov.bs/cms/images/LEGISLATION/SUBORDINATE/2004/2004-0103/TheBahamasandtheUnitedStatesofAmericaTaxInformationExchangeAgreementRegulations_1.pdf.

The US government was also successful in compelling a Japanese corporation to provide information relating to a transfer pricing and tax examination of its wholly owned US subsidiary.[97] And in *United States v Vetco*, the US government successfully used its subpoena power against a US parent to obtain corporate records maintained by its Swiss subsidiary.[98] In this case, the Court of Appeals for the Ninth Circuit enforced IRS summonses for records of a US firm's wholly owned Swiss subsidiary in a tax fraud case, noting that the treaty between Switzerland and the United States did not preclude the use of IRS summonses to obtain the records.[99] In balancing the competing interests, as set forth in the *Restatement*, between the possibility of criminal liability in Switzerland related to compliance and enforcement of the summons, the court found that the interests of the United States in enforcing the summons outweighed the contrary interests of Switzerland.[100] Additionally, the US government used its power to compel the return of funds located in a foreign jurisdiction to the United States[101] and to order the freezing of financial assets situated in a foreign jurisdiction.[102] Prosecutors may also obtain a court order to compel an account holder to direct its bank in a foreign jurisdiction to disclose to the prosecutor financial information that may

[97] See *Toyota Motor Corp*, above note 90. The District Court determined that it had personal jurisdiction over the Japanese parent corporation in an action brought under *Code*, above note 5, § 7604, to enforce two summonses issued during the course of an audit of the parent's US subsidiary, observing that "[n]othing in the language of section 7602 precludes issuance of a summons against a foreign parent corporation possessing information relevant to the taxation of its subsidiary" (*Toyota Motor Corp*, above note 90 at 83-1149). Having found that *Code*, above note 5, §§ 7402(b) and 7604(a) conferred jurisdiction over the case, the court in *Toyota Motor Corp*, above note 90 at 83-1150, proceeded to examine due process limitations on jurisdiction under the constitution: see also *United States v Toyota Motor Corp*, 569 F Supp 1158 at 1163 (CD Cal 1983), cited in Saltzman & Book, above note 5, ch 13: District Court ordered an IRS summons for documents located in Japan to be partially enforced.

[98] 691 F 2d 1281 (9th Cir 1981) [*Vetco*].

[99] *Ibid* at 81-1547.

[100] *Ibid.* See *Restatement*, above note 61, § 441(1). But see *United States v First National Bank of Chicago*, 699 F 2d 341 (7th Cir 1983), cited in Saltzman & Book, above note 5, ch 13: Court of Appeals for the Seventh Circuit denied enforcement of an IRS summons for bank records in Greece.

[101] See *United States v McNulty*, 446 F Supp 90 (ND Cal 1978), cited in Saltzman & Book, above note 5, ch 13.

[102] See *United States v First National City Bank*, 379 US 378 (1965), cited in Saltzman & Book, above note 5, ch 13.

otherwise be protected by foreign privacy or secrecy laws.[103] Furthermore, federal law enforcement attorneys may use subpoenas issued to US citizens or residents who are living abroad in connection with any federal proceeding, be it criminal or civil, together with sanctions under Title 28 (Judiciary and Judicial Procedure) of the *United States Code*.[104]

As discussed further below, a survey of recent US government enforcement efforts to obtain information on the use of offshore accounts (in particular with John Doe summonses) appears to echo the preference noted by the Court of Appeals for the Eleventh Circuit in *Bank of Nova Scotia* decades ago in favour of homegrown remedies over the complexities and shortcomings of legal alternatives under international law and treaties.[105]

3.7 John Doe Summonses

Code section 7602 confers a broad authority on the IRS to compel production of documents and information in an examination of civil or criminal violations provided that the case has not been referred to the Department of Justice for prosecution.[106] Such power is particularly useful when a taxpayer has been identified and when an offshore transaction has been chosen for audit. But the United States has acknowledged that stronger administrative measures are needed where the identity of the taxpayer is not known and where tax evasion is suspected, such as with secret bank accounts held in an offshore tax haven.[107] The John Doe summons has been used by the IRS in a number of high-profile cases. In 2000, the IRS initiated the Offshore Credit Card Program in an effort to identify taxpayers hiding unreported income in offshore banks and issued John Doe summonses to financial businesses to learn the identity of US residents holding credit or debit cards issued by offshore financial institutions.[108]

[103] See, for example, *Doe v United States*, 487 US 201 at 215–18 (1988).

[104] 28 USC §§ 1783–84.

[105] *Bank of Nova Scotia*, above note 60.

[106] *Code*, above note 5, § 7602. See *United States v LaSalle National Bank*, 437 US 298 (1978).

[107] See JCT, *Enforcement Issues*, above note 1 at 48.

[108] *Ibid* at 49.

In the latter situation, the IRS has successfully used the John Doe summons to identify the taxpayer.[109] In 2008 and 2009 respectively, the IRS used John Doe summonses on UBS and First Data Corporation regarding the processing of payments involving offshore accounts.[110] In 2011, the IRS used a John Doe summons on HSBC Bank USA, NA regarding thousands of potential unreported offshore accounts at HSBC India.[111] And in 2013, the IRS used a John Doe summons to seek information about US taxpayers who may hold offshore bank accounts at CIBC FirstCaribbean International Bank.[112]

Procedurally, before obtaining a John Doe summons, the United States must seek judicial review in an *ex parte* proceeding,[113] where it must establish that (1) the summons relates to the investigation of a particular person or ascertainable group (or class) of persons, (2) there is reasonable basis for believing that taxes have been avoided, and (3) the information is not readily available from other sources.[114] Once the summons has been served, the summoned party may not seek judicial review of the *ex parte* ruling but may challenge the summons based on the *Powell* factors.[115] In the context of a John Doe summons issued on the US branch of a foreign bank, as in the case of *Bank of Nova Scotia*, the prospect of civil contempt of court sanctions for recalcitrant banks can be very costly.[116] The existence of a treaty containing an EOI mechanism

---

[109] *Ibid.*

[110] See Scott D Michel, Zhanna A Ziering, & Young Ran Kim, "Offshore Account Enforcement Issues" (2014) 16 *Journal of Tax Practice and Procedure* 49 at 74.

[111] See *ibid.*

[112] See United States, Department of Justice, Tax Division, News Release 13-488 "Court Authorizes Service of John Doe Summons Seeking the Identities of U.S. Taxpayers with Offshore Accounts at Canadian Imperial Bank of Commerce's FirstCaribbean International Bank" (30 April 2013), online: www.justice.gov/opa/pr/court-authorizes-service-john-doe-summons-seeking-identities-us-taxpayers-offshore-accounts [Service of John Doe Summons News Release].

[113] See *Code*, above note 5, § 7609(h).

[114] *Ibid*, § 7609(f).

[115] See JCT, *Enforcement Issues*, above note 1 at 48; *Samuels, Kramer & Co*, above note 42; *Powell*, above note 40.

[116] See Michel, Ziering, & Kim, above note 110 at 7; *Bank of Nova Scotia*, above note 60.

does not bar the United States from seeking enforcement of a John Doe summons.[117]

3.8 Miscellaneous Sanctions and Penalties

Admissibility of Documentation Maintained in Foreign Countries: Section 982

As noted above, the IRS may formally request, for example using Form 4564 (Information Document Request), information located outside of the United States.[118] Where a taxpayer fails to substantially comply with such a document request (typically within ninety days of its mailing), the IRS may sanction the taxpayer by prohibiting the introduction of that document by the taxpayer in any civil court proceeding having jurisdiction of the examined item.[119]

Information with respect to Certain Foreign-Owned Corporations and Foreign Corporations Engaged in US Business: Sections 6038A and 6038C

The potential reporting requirements facing US corporations with foreign ownership and foreign corporations engaged in US business can be staggering, especially if a foreign partnership is involved.[120] Beyond these reporting requirements, the IRS may issue administrative summonses that carry a sanction for non-compliance that permits the IRS to determine the federal tax liability of the entity and file a return for the taxpayer based on limited information, which can be a financial disaster.[121]

---

[117] See Marie Therese Yates et al, "Death of Information-Exchange Agreements? Part 3" (2011) 22 *Journal of International Taxation* 48 at 61, citing *Vetco*, above note 98 at 1286.

[118] See Section 3.2, above in this chapter.

[119] *Code*, above note 5, § 982(a).

[120] *Ibid*, §§ 6038A, 6038C, and 1446, and the regulations thereunder.

[121] *Ibid*, §§ 6038A(e), 6038C(d), and 6020(b).

Tax Court — Production of Records in the Case of Foreign Corporations, Foreign Trusts or Estates, and Non-resident Alien Individuals: Section 7456(b)

In the case of proceedings before the US Tax Court, the IRS may upon motion ask the court to order any foreign corporation, foreign trust or estate, or non-resident alien individual that has filed a petition with the Tax Court to produce any documents wherever situated.[122] Failure to comply with such an order by the court may lead the court to issue an order to strike the proceedings of the petitioner, dismiss the proceedings against the petitioner, or render a judgment against the petitioner.[123]

4 Criminal Prosecution

4.1 Introduction

This section examines the use by the United States of the threat of criminal prosecution to elicit foreign-based information, notably the names of unreported offshore account holders. Although criminal prosecution, or the threat of criminal prosecution, does not appear to be listed as an enumerated procedure for obtaining taxpayer information in texts dealing with the broad subject of tax administration, it has nevertheless emerged in recent years as an important tool in the US arsenal for obtaining foreign documentation to combat tax evasion.[124] As described below, the agreement in 2013 between the United States and Switzerland regarding a non-prosecution program (also read as the threat of criminal prosecution) marks a watershed moment in the EOI process.[125] Under the

[122] *Ibid*, § 7456(b). See also *Hongkong and Shanghai Banking Corp v Commissioner*, 85 TC 701 (1985).

[123] *Code*, above note 5, § 7456(b).

[124] See, for example, the following treatises, which do not currently list criminal prosecution as a means to access foreign-based taxpayer information: Saltzman & Book, above note 5 at 4.06, Gianni, above note 2; Andersen, above note 92, ch 24.

[125] See Lynnley Browning, "Swiss Agree on Penalties for Banks That Aided Tax Cheats" *New York Times*(29August2013)B2,online:http://dealbook.nytimes.com/2013/08/29/u-s-and-switzerland-reach-deal-on-bank-penalties/?_r=0. Since 2009, the United States has prosecuted more than thirty banking

non-prosecution program, in exchange for agreeing to provide account information on American clients, paying billions of dollars in penalties, and making other significant undertakings, certain Swiss banks may escape criminal prosecution by the US government.[126]

4.2 A Case Study in Criminal Prosecution: UBS

Introduction

In February 2009, Switzerland's largest bank, UBS, entered into a deferred prosecution agreement with the United States and agreed to release information regarding its account holders.[127] Under the *UBS DPA*, UBS agreed to waive indictment and consent to a one-count information in the US District Court for the Southern District of California charging UBS with participating in a conspiracy to defraud the United States and its agency the IRS in violation of 18 *United States Code* section 371.[128] UBS further agreed to pay the United States the sum of $780 million, composed of $380 million in disgorgement of profits from maintaining its cross-border business in the United States from 2001 to 2008 and $400 million for federal backup withholding tax that UBS had been required to withhold for the years with respect to certain disclosed accounts together with interest, penalties, and other amounts for restitution for unpaid taxes and interest for undeclared US taxpayers who had been actively assisted by UBS.[129] The agreement was made in response to a legal procedure commenced by the US Department of Justice against UBS that sought the disclosure of account documents for a large number

professionals and sixty-eight US account holders, including the deferred prosecution agreement with one Swiss bank and the indictment of another Swiss bank: see United States, Department of Justice, News Release 13-975 "United States and Switzerland Issue Joint Statement regarding Tax Evasion Investigations" (29 August 2013), online: www.justice.gov/opa/pr/2013/August/13-tax-975.html [DOJ News Release re Tax Evasion Investigations].

126 See DOJ News Release re Tax Evasion Investigations, above note 125.

127 See *United States of America v UBS AG*, 09-60033-CR-COHN (SD Fl) [*UBS DPA*].

128 See *ibid* at 1.

129 See *ibid* at 3.

of UBS clients.[130] In admitting to its participation in criminal activities, UBS acknowledged that from 2000 and continuing until 2007 it had participated in a scheme to defraud the IRS through its private bankers and managers in the US cross-border business.[131]

Background on the US Qualified Intermediary (QI) System

Taxation of US Sourced Investment Income Earned by Foreign Persons

A review of the QI System helps provide yet more detail on the complex picture that we are attempting to draw, so that one may see how TIEAs and EOI fit into the current and ever-shifting landscape of information sharing to combat international tax evasion. When looking at the QI system, one sees third-party non-governmental financial institutions that perform the important function of US withholding agents under a complex but fallible foreign tax and reporting system. One might also see US taxpayers and their straw foundations and nominee corporations manipulating the system, with the assistance of their wealth advisers, so as to masquerade as foreign taxpayers. These tax evaders, and their advisers, seek to qualify for tax exemptions and reductions (under the *Code* or a treaty) on US sourced income, or simply to evade all reporting to the IRS of any investment income.

The abuse of the QI system, for example by UBS and LGT Bank (see below), further illustrates the vital role played by bank secrecy laws and nominee foreign entities in hiding both the existence of offshore accounts and their income from fiscal authorities. The US Department

[130] See Baker & McKenzie Voluntary Disclosure Steering Committee, "Undeclared Money Held Offshore: U.S. Voluntary Compliance Programs" (Part 2) (2010) 21 *Journal of International Taxation* 36 at 46.

[131] See *UBS DPA*, above note 127 at 2. UBS actively assisted US individual taxpayers to establish accounts at UBS in ways designed to conceal the individuals' ownership or beneficial interests in these accounts, including by creating offshore companies. As a result of the efforts of UBS's private bankers and managers, US taxpayers were able to evade US reporting requirements and engage in securities trading and other financial transactions such as using credit or debit cards linked to the offshore corporate accounts (*ibid*).

of the Treasury relied on this tax and reporting system to provide accurate information to ensure the proper withholding of income while permitting reductions thereon only for taxpayers qualifying under the complex domestic legal regime or a treaty. Not only did the system permit banks and US taxpayers to evade its rules, but it also blocked reporting of information on income earned by foreign taxpayers, whose names were not revealed to the IRS, to their governments.

General Taxation and Withholding of US Sourced Investment Income

As noted above, a state has exclusive jurisdiction over its territory, which includes its power to tax income that has its source within its sovereign boundaries.[132] Both the residence-based and sourced-based taxation models acknowledge and acquiesce to the right of a sovereign to tax income arising within its territory.[133] Both Canada and the United States generally tax domestically sourced income earned by foreign persons and foreign corporations.[134]

Foreign persons generating income from US sources are potentially subject to one of two US federal taxation regimes or both. Under the first regime, if a foreign person or corporation carries on trade or business in the United States, federal income tax is imposed on its *net* income, wherever

[132] See Chapter 2, Section 2.2.

[133] Both Canada and the United States recognize the right of other countries to impose tax on investment-type income arising within the source state generally under the *Income Tax Act*, RSC 1985, c 1 (5th Supp) [*Act*], and the *Code* by providing a foreign tax credit mechanism to reduce double taxation and through the use of their extensive treaty networks: see Chapter 2, Section 2.2.

[134] The taxation of foreign persons and corporations on a gross withholding basis turns in part on whether or not the income is domestic sourced as opposed to foreign sourced. For example, regarding the sourcing rules under the *Act*, above note 133, see Part XIII, and regarding the sourcing rules under the *Code*, above note 5, see §§ 861–865. The character of the income (e.g., dividends, interest, or royalties) must also be determined as not only may different domestic tax rules apply but, depending on the characterization of the income, different treaty provisions may apply. For example, under US jurisprudence, interest has been broadly defined by the courts as representing the cost of using borrowed money, the amount that one has contracted to pay for the use of borrowed money, compensation for the use or forbearance of money, and the equivalent of rent for the use of funds: see, for example, *Snyder v Commissioner*, 93 TC 529 at 546 (1989). For a general discussion of the source and characterization rules pertaining to passive investment income under Canadian and US tax law, see David S Kerzner, Vitaly Timokhov, & David W Chodikoff, eds, *The Tax Advisor's Guide to the Canada–U.S. Tax Treaty* (Toronto: Thomson Reuters Carswell, 2008) (loose-leaf) ch 10, 11, & 12.

derived, that is effectively connected with the US trade or business.[135] Under the second regime, a flat tax of 30 percent (which can be reduced pursuant to US treaty obligations) is imposed on a foreign person's or corporation's gross income from "interest, . . . dividends, rents, salaries, wages, premiums, annuities, compensations, remunerations, emoluments, and other fixed or determinable annual or periodical gains, profits, and income" (FDAP) but only to the extent that the amount is from sources within the United States and is not effectively connected with the conduct of trade or business within the United States by such person or corporation.[136]

The QI system described below relates to US sourced FDAP-type income subject to the flat tax of 30 percent. (A lower rate may apply under the *Code* or a tax treaty.[137]) The *Code* and the regulations thereunder generally provide that tax on FDAP income earned by a foreign person or corporation is withheld at the source by the foreign person's or corporation's withholding agent and is deposited with the IRS.[138] Generally, the withholding at the source fully satisfies the non-resident taxpayer's US tax liability, and no tax return needs to be filed solely on account of FDAP income.

Under the US withholding regime, a payor of FDAP income is required to report the payments on Form 1099 in the absence of an applicable exception.[139] If a payment is reportable on Form 1099, a Form

---

[135] *Code*, above note 5, §§ 871(b) and 882(a).

[136] Under *ibid*, §§ 871(a) and 881(a), a 30 percent tax is applied to FDAP income of non-resident aliens and foreign corporations.

[137] See *ibid*, reg §§ 1.1441-6(a) and 1.1441-1(b), relating to certificate requirements.

[138] See *ibid*, §§ 1441 & 1442, requiring withholding at the source for payments to non-resident aliens and foreign corporations respectively; *ibid*, § 7701(a)(16), defining withholding agent for purposes of § 1442. The 30 percent tax on FDAP income is to be withheld by the withholding agent under the complex rules under §§ 1441 & 1442 and the regulations thereunder. Special withholding rules also apply under § 1445 for withholding in connection with § 897 (*Foreign Investment in Real Property Tax Act*) and under § 1446 for certain payments to foreign partners. For a detailed description of the US withholding tax regime, see Carol P Tello, *U.S. Withholding and Reporting Requirements for Payments of U.S. Source Income to Foreign Persons* (Washington, DC: Tax Management, 2002); Marnin Michaels, *International Taxation: Withholding* (Thomson Reuters/WG&L, 2011/2012 ed) (Checkpoint).

[139] See, generally, *Code*, above note 5, §§ 6041, 6042, 6045, 6049, 6050N, and the regulations thereunder. See also United States, Internal Revenue Service, *Withholding of Tax on Nonresident Aliens and Foreign Entities* (Publication 515) (Washington, DC: US Treasury, 2015), online: www.irs.gov/pub/irs-pdf/p515.pdf [IRS, *Withholding of Tax*].

W-9 identifying the individual as a US citizen or US person must be obtained.[140] If a payor does not receive a Form W-9, the payor must generally apply backup withholding under *Code* section 3406 and report the payment on Form 1099.[141] No Form 1099 reporting is required if the payee is a foreign person.[142] A payor may treat a person as foreign if the payor can reliably associate the payment with documentation establishing that the person is the beneficial owner[143] of the income or a foreign payee.[144] A payor of these types of income must also report the payments on Form 1042-S.[145] Where the withholding agent fails to withhold, it becomes liable under *Code* section 1463 for the tax (except for portions paid by the recipient of interest). There is no backup withholding applicable to payments to foreign beneficial owners or foreign payees.[146]

In addition, the payee remains liable for the tax and is required to file a US income tax return. It is important to note that the mechanisms provided under the *Code* to escape withholding are a convenience afforded to the taxpayer. If a taxpayer wishes to claim a refund due to a right to an exemption under the *Code* or an entitlement to a lower withholding rate under an applicable treaty, the taxpayer may have to file a non-resident tax return declaring that right or entitlement.

Tax Exempt Bank Deposit Interest and Portfolio Interest

Since 1921, for almost a century, foreign persons have been entitled to receive tax-free interest payments from US banks on their deposits.[147]

---

[140] See IRS, *Withholding of Tax*, above note 139.

[141] See *ibid.*

[142] See *ibid.*

[143] The beneficial owner in the context of the withholding rules is defined as the person who is the owner of the income for tax purposes and who beneficially owns that income: see *Code*, above note 5, reg § 1.1441-1(c)(6). For a discussion of the legal concept of beneficial ownership as it relates to the true owner of investment income for Canadian withholding tax purposes, see *Prévost Car Inc v R*, 2008 TCC 231, aff'd 2009 FCA 57 (*sub nom R v Prévost Car Inc; MNR v Prévost Car Inc*); *Velcro Canada Inc v Canada*, 2012 TCC 57, additional reasons 2012 TCC 273.

[144] *Code*, above note 5, reg § 1.1441-1(c)(6).

[145] *Ibid.*

[146] *Ibid.*

[147] See *ibid*, §§ 871(i) and 881(d). See also *ibid*, §§ 1441(c)(10) and 1442(a).

More recently, since 1984, portfolio interest on various government Treasury bills, notes, and bonds and corporate bonds has been paid tax free to foreign owners of these securities (i.e., a withholding tax is not applied by the US government to cross-border payments to non-residents).[148] By contrast, interest paid on these accounts and investments to US residents and citizens is subject to the highest personal federal and state tax rates.[149]

A contributing factor to the United States' being regarded as a tax haven derives in part from the special exemption from taxation for interest payments to foreign persons but also from the fact that generally the United States does not require any reporting of these payments except for those paid to Canadian residents.[150] This lack of reporting on interest payments to non-residents is going to change under the new *Foreign Account Tax Compliance Act* regime, described in Chapter 9.[151] As described above, tax information is generally confidential under the *Code*.[152] As a result, and in the absence of some treaty request for information, hundreds of billions of dollars belonging to foreign persons could be invested in the

[148] In 1984, Congress repealed the 30 percent withholding tax imposed by *Code, ibid*, §§ 871 and 881 with respect to certain US sourced interest paid on portfolio debt, referred to as "portfolio interest": see United States, Joint Committee on Taxation, *General Explanation of the Revenue Provisions of the Deficit Reduction Act of 1984* (Washington, DC: Joint Committee on Taxation, 1984) at 391–92, online: www.jct.gov/publications.html?func=startdown&id=3343. Congress feared a US withholding tax could impair the ability of US corporations to raise capital in the Eurobond market. See also Peter E Pront & Roger M Zaitzeff, "Repeal of the United States Withholding Tax on Interest Paid to Foreigners" (2012) 3 *Berkeley Journal of International Law* Article 1. Portfolio interest generally refers to interest payments made to a non-resident alien or individual or foreign corporation (owning less than 10 percent of the payor entity) pursuant to certain debt obligations (either in bearer form or registered form) that are sold exclusively to non-US persons. The portfolio interest exemption rules contain various formalities that are designed to prevent the debt obligations from being held by US persons: see *Code*, above note 5, §§ 871(h), 881(c), and 163(f)(2)(B). See also *ibid*, §§ 1441(c)(9) and 1442(a).

[149] For example, a 39.6 percent federal rate: see Luke Landes, "Updated: 2013 Federal Income Tax Brackets and Marginal Rates" *Forbes* (5 January 2013), online: www.forbes.com/sites/money-builder/2013/01/05/updated-2013-federal-income-tax-brackets-and-marginal-rates/.

[150] See Marshall J Langer, "Harmful Tax Competition: Who Are the Real Tax Havens?" (2000) *Tax Notes International* 2831. Langer, *ibid* at 2834, notes that for many years the instructions to Form 1042-S required banks to identify and report only Canadian holders of accounts, but not other foreign persons. See also *Code*, above note 5, § 6103.

[151] Enacted by Congress as part of the *Hiring Incentives to Restore Employment (HIRE) Act*, Public Law 111-147, and signed into law by the president on 18 March 2010 [*FATCA*].

[152] See Section 2, above in this chapter; Langer, above note 150.

United States without a requirement that income on these investments be reported to foreign tax authorities.[153]

Professor Langer further points out that the dichotomy between the interest exemption and the high rates of tax in the United States has created an incentive for US citizens and residents to game the system by falsely claiming to be non-resident aliens.[154] Langer describes a fictional uncle Juan who opens a US bank account and puts his US resident nephew Jimmy on the account as a signing authority. Jimmy, who is the true beneficial owner of the account, makes all of the deposits and withdrawals. Since the account is registered to uncle Juan, not only will the bank pay tax-free interest, but on uncle Juan's death the account balance will go to Jimmy free of estate taxes.[155] Back in 2000, Langer asked rhetorically, how many billions of dollars of US bank deposits have been structured in this way?[156] Fast forward to the UBS and LGT Bank scandals described below.

Objectives of the QI Program

Generally, as described above, the United States imposes a 30 percent withholding tax on US sourced investment (FDAP) income earned by foreign persons. The QI program focuses on encouraging foreign financial institutions (FFIs) to report US sourced income to the IRS and withhold taxes on that income under US tax law. This objective was frustrated by systemic difficulties that existed in the prior withholding regulations and by the substantial growth in the flows of cross-border investment.[157]

---

[153] See Langer, above note 150 at 2831.

[154] *Ibid* at 2834.

[155] *Ibid* at 2837. Foreign-held US bank deposits are also exempt from US estate tax: see *Code*, above note 5, § 2105(b)(1). Langer, above note 150, also points out that residents of Japan and Ireland have set up fraudulent schemes to benefit from interest exemption programs for non-residents in their respective countries.

[156] Langer, above note 150.

[157] See United States, Joint Committee on Taxation, *Description of Revenue Provisions Contained in the President's Fiscal Year 2010 Budget Proposal: Part Three — Provisions related to the Taxation of Cross-border Income and Investment* (Washington, DC: Joint Committee on Taxation, 2009) at 150–86, online: www.jct.gov/publications.html?func=startdown&id=3579 [JCT, *Taxation of Cross-border Income and Investments*]: US custodians were exposed to a substantial risk of

The IRS explained the scope and purpose of the QI program at its initiation as allowing financial institutions greater self-regulation to act as qualified intermediaries in jurisdictions with which the United States has a tax treaty or TIEA in place.[158] The QI program helped coax FFIs into participating by allowing them to escape the 30 percent withholding penalty without providing their clients' names in contravention of foreign bank secrecy rules.[159] The United States offered FFIs three primary benefits for accepting the new QI program: (1) foreign client anonymity from competing US financial institutions, (2) maintenance of bank secrecy on non-disclosure of clients from the IRS, and (3) availability of treaty benefits for non-US persons on applicable investments.[160]

Mechanics of the QI System

The procedures governing the QI system are generally contained in a lengthy document as well as in various Treasury regulations.[161]

---

withholding tax liability that might exceed their custodial business profits and that stemmed from their inability to know whether the beneficial owner of a payment was a US person (and hence subject to backup withholding without a Form W-9), or whether such a person was a foreign person entitled to treaty benefits. For a discussion of the prior withholding regulations, see ABA Tax Section Committee on US Activities of Foreigners and Tax Treaties, "Report on Consolidating and Simplifying the Withholding Rules and Procedures under Sections 1441 through 1446" (1994) 47 *Tax Law* 425.

[158] See United States, Internal Revenue Service, Announcement 2000-48 "Supplemental Information on Revenue Procedure 2000-12 for Prospective Qualified Intermediaries" (Washington, DC: US Treasury, 2000), online: www.irs.gov/pub/irs-drop/a-00-48.pdf: the foundation for permitting this self-regulation was the confidence that the Department of the Treasury and the IRS had at the time in the know-your-customer rules existing in applicable jurisdictions. To date, approximately 7,000 FFIs have entered into QI agreements: see United States, Permanent Subcommittee on Investigations, Committee on Homeland Security and Governmental Affairs, *Tax Haven Banks and U.S. Tax Compliance* (Washington, DC: Committee on Homeland Security and Governmental Affairs, 2008) at 25, online: www.hsgac.senate.gov/download/report-psi-staff-report-tax-haven-banks-and-us-tax-compliance-july-17-2008 [*2008 Tax Haven Report*].

[159] See *2008 Tax Haven Report*, above note 158 at 22.

[160] See Itai Grinberg, "The Battle over Taxing Offshore Accounts" (2012) 60 *UCLA Law Review* 304 at 325.

[161] See United States, Internal Revenue Service, Revenue Procedure 2000-12 (2000-4 IRB 387) "Application Procedures for Qualified Intermediary Status under Section 1441; Final Qualified Intermediary Withholding Agreement" (Washington, DC: US Treasury, 2000), online: www.irs.gov/pub/irs-drop/rp-00-12.pdf [Rev Proc 2000-12]; *Code*, above note 5, reg § 1.1441-1ff.

To participate, an FFI must enter into a sixty-five-page agreement with the IRS in which it agrees to act as a US withholding agent.[162] This agreement also requires that the FFI have know-your-customer (KYC) procedures in place to ensure that it verifies and documents beneficial owners of accounts.[163] Generally, an FFI must obtain certain documentation from all of its clients who buy or sell US securities through any account for which the FFI is designated as a QI participant, typically a Form W-9 for US clients or a Form W-8BEN for foreign clients.[164] If the FFI receives a Form W-9, the FFI agrees to file an annual Form 1099 with the IRS, reporting the client's name, taxpayer information, and reportable amounts.[165] On the other hand, where a non-US person provides a Form W-8BEN, there is no requirement to file a Form 1042-S with the IRS, reporting account information.[166] Instead, the FFI calculates the reportable amounts of US sourced income paid to all of its non-US accounts in the QI program and files a single Form 1042 for each category of investment income, remitting any withheld taxes (e.g., dividend withholding taxes) to the IRS on an aggregate basis.[167] As the Form 1042s filed by QI participants for non-US account holders are without client names or client specific information, the practical effect of the QI program is the preservation of bank secrecy for these clients.[168]

[162] See Rev Proc 2000-12, above note 161: some of the components of the agreement are "Section 1. Purpose and Scope," "Section 2. Definitions," "Section 3. Withholding Responsibility," "Section 4. Private Arrangement Intermediaries," "Section 4A. Special Rules for Related Partnership and Related Trusts," "Section 5. Documentation Requirements," "Section 6. Qualified Intermediary Withholding Certificate and Disclosure of Account Holders to Withholding Agent," "Section 7. Tax Return Obligations," "Section 8. Information Reporting Obligations," "Section 9. Adjustments for Over- and Under-withholding; Refunds," "Section 10. External Audit Procedures," "Section 11. Expiration, Termination and Default," and "Section 12. Miscellaneous Provisions."

[163] See *ibid.*

[164] See *ibid.*

[165] See *ibid.*

[166] See *ibid.*

[167] See *ibid.* Accounts not designated by the FFI as QI accounts are subject to the reporting of individual client names to the US financial institution, which in turn reports and remits taxes to the IRS. The QI program also contains auditing procedures using third-party auditors.

[168] See *2008 Tax Haven Report*, above note 158 at 23.

QI System Reporting Problems Revealed

Between 2000 and 2007, approximately 100 FFIs were terminated from the QI program for failing to comply with their reporting obligations.[169] In a study concluded in December 2007, the US Government Accountability Office (GAO) noted that FFIs were manipulating their QI reporting obligations to avoid reporting US client accounts.[170] The GAO warned that US persons could evade taxes by masquerading as foreign corporations and further observed:

> U.S. tax law enables the owners of offshore corporations to shield their identities from IRS scrutiny, thereby providing U.S. persons a mechanism to exploit for sheltering their income from U.S. taxation. Under current U.S. tax law, corporations, including foreign corporations, are treated as the taxpayers and the owners of their assets and income. Because the owners of the corporation are not known to IRS, individuals are able to hide behind the corporate structure.[171]

The flaws in the QI system foreshadowed by Professor Langer and referenced by the GAO are illustrated by the QI reporting of UBS of Switzerland and LGT Group of Liechtenstein (which includes LGT Bank, LGT Treuhand, a trust company, and other affiliates).[172]

From approximately 2000 to 2007, UBS failed to disclose to US tax authorities that it maintained accounts in Switzerland for thousands of US clients with billions of dollars in assets.[173] It is estimated that of the

---

[169] See *ibid* at 25.

[170] United States, Government Accountability Office, *Report to the Committee on Finance, U.S. Senate: Tax Compliance — Qualified Intermediary Program Provides Some Assurance That Taxes on Foreign Investors Are Withheld and Reported, but Can Be Improved* (GAO-08-99) (Washington, DC: Government Accountability Office, 2008), online: www.gao.gov/assets/280/270593.html.

[171] *Ibid* at Highlights and 3.

[172] LGT Group (online: www.lgt.com/en/lgt-group/) is the wealth and asset management group of the princely House of Liechtenstein and is the largest family-owned private wealth and asset manager in Europe, wholly owned by the Prince of Liechtenstein Foundation. LGT Group is headquartered in Liechtenstein and has approximately thirty-one offices in Asia, Europe, the Middle East, North America, and South America.

[173] See *2008 Tax Haven Report*, above note 158 at 9.

20,000 accounts that UBS is reported to have held for US clients, 19,000 were undeclared accounts, which were not disclosed to the IRS.[174] The undeclared accounts were estimated to have contained assets with a total value of approximately $20 billion.[175] Although UBS was a QI, it failed to file Form 1099s reporting these US owned accounts to the IRS.[176] In a November 2002 letter sent by UBS to its clients, it openly counselled them on how they could avoid the disclosure of their accounts to US tax authorities:

> UBS (as all other major Swiss banks) has asked for and obtained the status of a Qualified Intermediary under U.S. tax laws. The QI regime fully respects client confidentiality as customer information are only disclosed to U.S. tax authorities based on the provision of a W-9 form. Should a customer choose not to execute such a form, the client is barred from investments in US securities but under no circumstances will his/her identity be revealed. Consequently, UBS's entire compliance with its QI obligations does not create the risk that his/her identity be shared with U.S. authorities.[177]

According to UBS, after it had disclosed its QI disclosure requirements, many of its US clients chose to sell their US securities (worth some $2 billion) to avoid detection under the QI system.[178] Moreover, UBS helped its clients establish offshore nominee or straw entities to hold these undisclosed accounts to avoid US reporting, including accounts that still invested in US securities.[179]

Similarly, LGT Bank assisted US clients by advising them to use Liechtensteinian foundations to hide the beneficial ownership of their accounts, and, further, after it became a QI, it assisted US clients to evade

---

[174] See *ibid.*

[175] See *ibid.*

[176] See *ibid.*

[177] Quoted in *ibid* at 10.

[178] See *ibid.*

[179] See *ibid* at 11. The *2008 Tax Haven Report*, *ibid*, noted that while these actions may not have been per se violations of the QI program, they were aimed at circumventing its purpose, resulting in tax evasion by UBS's US clients.

US reporting by divesting those accounts of US securities.[180] Some of the recommendations made by the *2008 Tax Haven Report* to strengthen the QI program included requiring QI participants to utilize their KYC information to identify beneficial owners of accounts[181] and requiring domestic or foreign financial institutions to file Form 1099s for all US taxpayer clients and accounts beneficially owned by US persons, even if an account is titled in the name of a foreign corporation, trust, or other entity and regardless of whether the account holds US securities.[182] The report also suggested that banks that either impede US tax enforcement or fail to disclose accounts held by US clients have their QI status revoked or be prohibited from doing business with US financial institutions.[183]

Illusions of EOI: The United States, Switzerland, and UBS

A key flashpoint between the United States and Switzerland was Article 26 (EOI) itself of the *Convention between the United States of America and the Swiss Confederation for the Avoidance of Double Taxation with respect to Taxes on Income*.[184] At the time of the onset of the UBS bank scandal (2007–2008), the EOI parameters in both the *US–Switzerland Tax Treaty* and the *Convention between Canada and Switzerland for the Avoidance of Double Taxation with respect to Taxes on Income and on Capital*[185] were

[180] See *ibid* at 5. See also *ibid* at 5–8, for a description of assets hidden in the bank by some of its US clients, for example, Marsh accounts ($49 million).

[181] *Ibid* at 16. Both UBS and LGT Bank would rely on a Form W-8BEN offered by a foreign nominee for certification of non-US status notwithstanding that the banks knew that the beneficial owners were US citizens as a result of information obtained through their internal KYC rules: see JCT, *Taxation of Cross-border Income and Investments*, above note 157 at 167.

[182] *2008 Tax Haven Report*, above note 158 at 16. Under the existing requirement, the obligation to file a Form 1099 applied only if the account held US securities.

[183] *Ibid* at 17.

[184] Signed at Washington, 2 October 1996, together with a Protocol to the Convention, 2 October 1996, S Treaty Doc No 105-8 (entered into force 19 December 1997) at Art 26, online: www.irs.gov/pub/irs-trty/swiss.pdf [*US–Switzerland Tax Treaty*].

[185] 5 May 1997, Can TS 1998 No 15 (entered into force 21 April 1998) at Art 25, online: www.fin.gc.ca/treaties-conventions/switzerland-suisse-eng.asp [*Canada–Switzerland Tax Treaty*]:

1. The competent authorities of the Contracting States shall exchange such information (being information which is at their disposal under their respective taxation laws in the normal course of administration) as is necessary for carrying out the provisions of this Convention concerning

significantly more restrictive than those in the internationally agreed-upon standard.[186] Article 26 of the *US–Switzerland Tax Treaty* provided:

1. The competent authorities of the Contracting States shall exchange such information (being information available under the respective taxation laws of the Contracting States) as is necessary for carrying out the provisions of the present Convention or for the prevention of tax fraud or the like in relation to the taxes which are the subject of the present Convention. In cases of tax fraud,

(a) the exchange of information is not restricted by Article 1 (Personal Scope) and
(b) if specifically requested by the competent authority of a Contracting State, the competent authority of the other Contracting State shall

---

taxes covered by the Convention. Any information so exchanged shall be treated as secret and shall not be disclosed to any persons other than those concerned with the assessment and collection of the taxes covered by the Convention. No information as aforesaid shall be exchanged which would disclose any trade, business, industrial or professional secret or trade process.
2. In no case shall the provisions of this Article be construed so as to impose on a Contracting State the obligation to carry out administrative measures at variance with the regulations and practice of that or the other Contracting State or which would be contrary to its sovereignty, security or public policy or to supply particulars which are not obtainable under its own legislation or that of the State making application.

The treaty contained a "minor information clause," which limited EOI to that "necessary" for carrying out the terms of the treaty itself, rather than for the administration or enforcement of the requesting state's domestic tax laws: see Gilles Larin & Alexandra Diebel, "The Swiss Twist: The Exchange-of-Information Provisions of the Canada–Switzerland Protocol" (2012) 60 *Canadian Tax Journal* 1. Canada's new protocol with Switzerland was signed on 22 October 2010 and entered into force on 16 December 2011 (*ibid* at 15). The new protocol allows for requests for the purposes of the administration or enforcement of domestic laws but is limited to taxes covered by the treaty (so requests relating to the enforcement of the goods and services tax are excluded) (*ibid* at 20). Switzerland has also agreed to permit Canada to make requests, which are clearly not fishing expeditions, that identify a person using means other than the person's name and address (*ibid* at 38–40).

[186] See *United States v UBS AG*, 09-20423 MC-GOLD (SD Fl 19 February 2009) (Amicus Brief of Government of Switzerland), petition to enforce John Doe summons at 7, citing *Bilateral Tax Treaties and Protocol: Hearing before the Committee on Foreign Relations*, 105th Cong 43–44 (1977) (statement of Kenneth J Kies, chief of staff, Joint Committee on Taxation), online: www.bj.admin.ch/dam/data/bj/wirtschaft/fallubs/amicus-brief-e.pdf.

provide information under this Article in the form of authenticated copies of unedited original records or documents.[187]

The language in Article 26 of the *US–Switzerland Tax Treaty* made EOI conditional upon its being for (1) a task necessary for carrying out the provisions of the convention or (2) the prevention of tax fraud or the like. Generally under Swiss law, a person who, to commit tax avoidance, makes use of forged or falsified records so as to mislead tax authorities may be guilty of tax fraud.[188] Tax avoidance, by contrast, involves persons who intentionally or through negligence fail to pay all or a part of their taxes due.[189] In the context of the IRS efforts to procure information on the many thousands of secret UBS accounts held by individual American taxpayers, the refusal of Switzerland to exchange information in the absence of tax fraud was a significant impediment.[190]

The United States negotiated with Switzerland a 1996 Protocol that was designed to expand the circumstances under which the Swiss authorities could exchange information to include tax fraud or fraudulent conduct in both civil and criminal situations.[191] The 1996 Protocol included the following definition of "tax fraud": "fraudulent conduct that causes or is intended to cause an illegal and substantial reduction in the amount of tax paid to a contracting state."[192] In 2003, due to apparently rather limited EOI in practice, the United States negotiated a memorandum of understanding (MOU) with Switzerland that provided descriptions of conduct constituting "tax fraud or the like" and examples of fact patterns dealing with fraud.[193] Although the language in the 1996 convention

[187] *US–Switzerland Tax Treaty*, above note 184 at Art 26.

[188] See Larin & Diebel, above note 185 at 12–13.

[189] See *ibid.*

[190] See concerns of IRS Commissioner Barry Shott, noted below in this section.

[191] See United States, Congress, *Joint Committee on Taxation, Explanation of Proposed Protocol to the Income Tax Treaty between the United States and Switzerland* (Washington, DC: Joint Committee on Taxation, 2011) at 23, online: www.jct.gov/publications.html?func=startdown&id=3791 [JCT, *Proposed Swiss Protocol*].

[192] *US–Switzerland Tax Treaty*, above note 184, Protocol at para 10.

[193] See *Mutual Agreement of January 23, 2003, regarding the Administration of Article 26 (Exchange of Information) of the Swiss–U.S. Income Tax Convention of October 2, 1996*, online: www.treasury.gov/press-center/press-releases/Pages/mutual.aspx [*Mutual Agreement re Article 26*]; JCT, *Proposed Swiss Protocol*, above note 191 at 23.

referred to a narrow scope for EOI, as necessary "for carrying out the provisions of the present Convention," in the 2003 memorandum of understanding, the United States and Switzerland agreed to memorialize additional understandings in reference to Article 26 including the understanding that ". . . Article 26 of the Convention and paragraph 10 of the Protocol will be interpreted to support the tax administration and enforcement efforts of each Contracting State to the greatest extent possible."[194]

Historically, the United States has cited a combination of factors that it says have ultimately resulted in the Swiss authorities' declining to exchange information, including lack of proof of fraud, lack of domestic interest in the information being sought, and bank secrecy laws.[195] In 2008, the United States found itself confronting an epic tax evasion problem involving more than 50,000 US clients of UBS, and it was virtually no more able to obtain information on the account holders than it would have been had Article 26 of the *US–Switzerland Tax Treaty* (together with its protocol and MOU) not existed. A separate treatise could be written about EOI and the affairs of Switzerland, the United States, and UBS, and likely will be. Such a work could focus on analyzing in detail how the various domestic legal, political, regulatory, and economic factors contributed to building the dam that restricted the flow of information through the *US–Switzerland Tax Treaty* to US authorities to a trickle, before the use of legal action. Such research could also focus on the language of the *US–Switzerland Tax Treaty* and its protocol and MOU, and the relationship of those instruments to internal Swiss considerations and the conflict as a whole. Such a substantial undertaking is beyond the scope of this book, and for the purpose of this research it is enough to conclude that on the facts the EOI mechanism during the UBS crisis did not work before the use by the United States of the threat of criminal prosecution to bust open the Swiss dam. As discussed immediately below, the failure of the EOI mechanism led the United States to take unprecedented measures to secure taxpayer information in the fight against tax evasion.[196]

[194] See *Mutual Agreement re Article 26*, above note 193 at para 1.

[195] See JCT, *Proposed Swiss Protocol*, above note 191 at 34.

[196] See Section 4.4, below in this chapter.

It was not until 2009 that Switzerland finally announced it would adopt the OECD's standards on information exchange in its tax treaty regime and eliminate the current limitation on assistance to "tax fraud or the like."[197] The United States and Switzerland signed a new protocol on 23 September 2009 containing rules similar to those in recent US tax treaties and the 2010 OECD *Model Tax Convention on Income and on Capital*, including a new Article 26 (EOI) conforming to the OECD standards.[198]

In consideration of UBS's entry into the *UBS DPA*, the United States recommended to the court that prosecution of UBS on the criminal information be deferred for the period of the longer of eighteen months from the date of execution, the resolution of the John Doe summons enforcement action commenced by the IRS on 1 July 2008 (seeking records for US persons who maintained accounts with UBS in Switzerland), or the completion of UBS's exit from its US cross-border business.[199] The *UBS DPA* allowed UBS to defend against any efforts to enforce the John Doe summons, including to argue that Swiss law is a bar to compliance with the John Doe summons, but with the understanding that if UBS failed to comply with an enforcement order after all of its appellate remedies had been exhausted, the United States may find UBS to be in material violation of the agreement.[200]

[197] See *United States v UBS AG*, above note 186 at 9; Switzerland, Federal Department of Finance, "Switzerland to Adopt OECD Standard on Administrative Assistance in Fiscal Matters" (13 March 2009), online: www.news.admin.ch/message/?lang=en&msg-id=25863.

[198] See United States, Senate, Treaty Doc 112-1, *Protocol Amending Tax Convention with Swiss Confederation* (26 January 2011), online: www.congress.gov/treaty-document/112th-congress/1/document-text; JCT, *Proposed Swiss Protocol*, above note 191. As of February 2016, the protocol had not been ratified by the United States. One area of concern regarding the proposed protocol is the Swiss position on requests that do not name the taxpayer, such as in the context of the UBS case and the John Doe summons, and whether other means of identification will be admissible in the future or whether a more litigious pathway will be required (*ibid* at 35). See also OECD, *Model Tax Convention on Income and on Capital* (OECD: Paris, 2010), online: www.oecd.org/tax/treaties/47213736.pdf [*Model Tax Treaty*].

[199] See *UBS DPA*, above note 127 at 10. Additionally, under the *UBS DPA*, *ibid*, UBS agreed to waive indictment and all rights to a speedy trial pursuant to the Sixth Amendment to the Constitution, USC tit 18 § 3161, and Federal rule of criminal procedure 48(b). See also Lynnley Browning, "I.R.S. to Drop Suit against UBS over Tax Havens" *New York Times* (26 August 2010) B6, online: http://nyti.ms/1TxGYwW.

[200] See *UBS DPA*, above note 127 at 9.

On 19 February 2009, one day after entering into the *UBS DPA*, the United States took legal action to enforce the John Doe summons commenced by the IRS the previous year, in July 2008, and order UBS to release documents on 52,000 secret accounts of US clients holding about $14.8 billion in assets.[201] UBS took the position that Swiss law prohibits the bank from disclosing documents located in Switzerland.[202] Although the timing of the enforcement action appeared at odds with the apparent progress of the events of the day before, the United States believed that the enforcement of the summons served on UBS was necessary to counter the roadblocks relating to bank secrecy put up by the Swiss authorities.[203] As of the date of the enforcement action, UBS had provided the names of only 323 American account holders.[204] As discussed above, failure by a third party to comply with a summons enforcement order could result in contempt of court sanctions, including criminal penalties.[205]

A major problem in obtaining the information sought by the US government was that the *US–Switzerland Tax Treaty* did not provide an alternative way to obtain the information sought in the John Doe summons in the UBS case.[206] During the UBS controversy, Deputy Commissioner (International), Large and Mid-size Business Division of the IRS, Barry Shott was the US competent authority. Commissioner Shott was involved

---

[201] See *ibid*. See also William P Barrett & Janet Novack, "52,000 Had Secret UBS Accounts" *Forbes* (19 February 2009), online: www.forbes.com/2009/02/19/ubs-fraud-offshore-personal_finance-taxes_ubs.html; United States, Department of Justice, "United States Asks Court to Enforce Summons for UBS Swiss Bank Account Records" (19 February 2009), online: www.justice.gov/opa/pr/united-states-asks-court-enforce-summons-ubs-swiss-bank-account-records.

[202] JCT, *Proposed Swiss Protocol*, above note 191 at 26. As part of the *UBS DPA*, above note 127, UBS was permitted by the Swiss banking regulators to transfer under Swiss law approximately 250 names of US clients suspected of fraudulent conduct: see JCT, *Proposed Swiss Protocol*, above note 191 at 26, n 19, citing Lee Sheppard, "Don't Ask, Don't Tell, Part III: UBS's Sweet Deal" *Tax Notes* (2 March 2009) at 1050.

[203] See Barrett & Novack, above note 201, quoting IRS agent Daniel Reeves: the IRS had formally asked the Swiss government for information relating to tax enforcement under the treaty, but no records had been produced in response to this request.

[204] See *ibid*: the names of these US account holders were provided on US records and identified Americans who had wired funds from the United States to Switzerland.

[205] See Anand Sithian, "'But the Americans Made Me Do It!': How *United States v. UBS* Makes the Case for Executive Exhaustion" (2011) 25 *Emory International Law Review* 681.

[206] See *US–Switzerland Tax Treaty*, above note 184; declaration of Barry B Shott in *United States v UBS AG*, above note 186 at 5.

with the Swiss competent authority and had a dialogue with his counterpart in Switzerland. According to Commissioner Shott, part of the difficulties encountered by the United States stemmed from the refusal of the Swiss government to exchange information about a taxpayer unless the taxpayer had committed an affirmative act of deception (such as the falsification of a document), rather than merely failing to report the existence of an account or income earned in that account.[207] Moreover, Commissioner Shott observed that the efforts of the IRS under Article 26 of the *US–Switzerland Tax Treaty* to obtain taxpayer information were hampered because the Swiss applied the article so as to provide the IRS with assistance only in response to a specific request that named a particular taxpayer, whereas the IRS focus with UBS was on learning the identities of taxpayers not known to the United States.[208]

As of 21 January 2009, Switzerland had, in response to a formal treaty request made on 16 July 2008, made final determinations to provide requested records to the IRS on only twelve accounts out of as many as 52,000 undeclared bank accounts that UBS maintained for US holders.[209] Moreover, the transmission of information by the Swiss government on the twelve account holders was subject to the appeal rights of those account holders, to litigate in a Swiss court against the information exchange.[210] Regarding the situation concerning EOI between Switzerland and the United States, Commissioner Shott observed, "In sum, the Swiss Government has not provided any records sought under the Treaty Request, and it is not clear when, if ever, it will."[211] Commissioner Shott also noted (regarding the original summons request) that although the United States had a mutual legal assistance treaty with Switzerland, which had entered into force on 23 January 1977, the IRS was not able to use this treaty mechanism to obtain information sought

[207] Declaration of Barry B Shott in *United States v UBS AG*, above note 186 at 5. As noted above, Switzerland relied on a narrower interpretation of tax fraud under its domestic law notwithstanding its understandings with the United States, which expressly authorized EOI in scenarios giving rise to a broader interpretation of tax fraud that encompassed tax evasion.

[208] *Ibid.*

[209] See *ibid* at 6.

[210] See *ibid.*

[211] *Ibid.*

in the John Doe summons because the assistance treaty applied only to criminal investigations.[212]

The threat of sanctions carried by the Florida lawsuit to enforce the John Doe summons and of a larger confrontation between the two sides (involving the US Department of State, Department of the Treasury, and the Federal Reserve System) was averted in a historic agreement between the United States and Switzerland in August 2009 to disclose the names of 4,450 UBS account holders.[213] Under the *UBS Agreement*, Switzerland agreed to process under the then existing *US–Switzerland Tax Treaty* a request by the United States for information regarding US clients of UBS based on criteria established in the annex to the agreement.[214] A number of lawsuits were filed in Switzerland to challenge the transfer of UBS data, but almost all of the 4,450 data requests have since been honoured.[215]

4.3 Wegelin and Other Swiss Banks

In February 2012, the United States criminally charged Wegelin, and a US district court judge declared the bank a fugitive when it failed to appear in court under the indictment.[216] The bank's closure and sale occurred just after the indictment of three of its bankers in January

[212] Declaration of Barry B Shott in *In the Matter of the Tax Liabilities of: John Does*, 08-21864 (SD Fla 1 July 2008) at 5, online: www.justice.gov/tax/BShott_Decl_UBS_AG.pdf.

[213] See Lynnley Browning, "Swiss Ruling Jeopardizes Deal for UBS Clients' Names" *New York Times* (23 January 2010) B2, online: http://nyti.ms/1LamsRO. See also *Agreement between the United States of America and the Swiss Confederation on the Request for Information from the Internal Revenue Service of the United States of America regarding UBS AG, a Corporation Established under the Laws of the Swiss Confederation* (19 August 2009), online: www.irs.gov/pub/irs-drop/us-swiss_government_agreement.pdf [*UBS Agreement*].

[214] *UBS Agreement*, above note 213, at Art 1. Under Art 2, *ibid*, the United States agreed to withdraw its enforcement action.

[215] For a description of the legal challenges involved in the transfer of UBS account data to the United States, see Mathew Allen, "Legal Challenge to UBS Data Handover Fading" *swissinfo.ch* (7 November 2011), online: www.swissinfo.ch/eng/Specials/Rebuilding_the_financial_sector/Spotlight_on_banking_secrecy/Legal_challenge_to_UBS_data_handover_fading.html?cid=31510472.

[216] See Reed Albergotti, "Wegelin's Fall to Tax-Haven Poster Child" *Wall Street Journal* (4 March 2013), online: http://on.wsj.com/ZToCck.

2012.[217] Shortly thereafter, Wegelin pleaded guilty, and in March 2013 it was sentenced by the US District Court for the Southern District of New York to pay $58 million in fines and restitution.[218] Wegelin became the first foreign bank to be indicted for assisting US taxpayers to commit tax evasion.[219]

As one journalist has observed in commenting on the rare time in recent history when a corporation has gone out of business as a result of charges brought by US authorities, "[c]riminal indictments and guilty pleas can do that."[220] In the broader context of criminal scandals involving large banks, prosecution agreements have also become more common, for example, in the Libor-rigging scandals.[221] Following close on the heels of Wegelin's guilty plea, in January 2013 the IRS obtained authorization to issue a John Doe summons on UBS to determine the identity of US taxpayers holding accounts at Wegelin.[222] Another journalist has observed that the indictments are helping the IRS get more data from

---

[217] See Robert W Wood, "With Indictments, IRS Will Get More Data from Swiss" *Forbes* (4 February2012),online:www.forbes.com/sites/robertwood/2012/02/04/with-indictments-irs-will-get-more-data-from-swiss/.

[218] See Nate Raymond, "Update 2 — Swiss Bank Wegelin to Pay $58 Million in US Tax Evasion Case" *Reuters* (4 March 2012), online: http://reut.rs/WrLXV7.

[219] See Halah Touryalai, "Tale of Two Swiss Banks: Why Wegelin Failed and UBS Survived Tax Evasion Charges" *Forbes* (4 January 2013), online: www.forbes.com/sites/halahtouryalai/2013/01/04/tale-of-two-swiss-banks-why-wegelin-failed-and-ubs-survived-tax-evasion-charges/. From 2002 through 2011, Wegelin conspired with US taxpayers to hide from the IRS both the existence of their bank accounts held in Switzerland and the income generated from those accounts. In addition, Wegelin at the height of the UBS scandal actively pursued undeclared UBS account holders exiting the latter bank and seeking a haven from the IRS: see United States, Department of Justice, News Release 13-002 "Swiss Bank Pleads Guilty in Manhattan Federal Court to Conspiracy to Evade Taxes" (3 January 2013), online: www.justice.gov/usao/nys/pressreleases/January13/WegelinPleaPR.php.

[220] See Touryalai, above note 219.

[221] See *ibid*, noting that in the recent Libor-rigging scandal, Barclays paid approximately $450 million to settle charges but also obtained a non-prosecution agreement and that UBS paid $1.5 billion over Libor rigging and also obtained a non-prosecution agreement.

[222] See United States, Department of Justice, News Release 13-033 "Court Authorizes IRS to Seek Records from UBS relating to U.S. Taxpayers with Swiss Bank Accounts" (28 January 2013), online: www.justice.gov/usao/nys/pressreleases/January13/WegelinSummonsPR.php: the summons seeks records of Wegelin's US correspondent account at UBS, to enable the IRS to determine the identity of the US taxpayers who hold or held interests in accounts at Wegelin and possibly other Swiss banks that used the correspondent account.

the Swiss.[223] The US government has expanded its investigations into international tax evasion to include, among other financial institutions, Credit Suisse and HSBC.[224] In 2014, Credit Suisse agreed to plead guilty to criminal charges for helping thousands of US clients hide assets and income from the IRS and to pay a $2.6 billion settlement.[225]

4.4 The US Swiss Bank Program

By the summer of 2013, a number of Swiss banks, including some of the largest, were under investigation by the US Department of Justice for assisting American clients to evade taxes, particularly in the aftermath of the US offensive against UBS and Wegelin.[226] These investigations have enabled the US government to obtain information to pursue American tax evaders.[227] Moreover, these investigations have pressured the Swiss government into entering a historic program with the US Department of Justice, which is designed to put pressure on other Swiss banks to cooperate with the Department of Justice in investigating US tax cheats and avoid criminal prosecution in connection with establishing and facilitating the use of secret offshore accounts to commit tax evasion.[228] Some 100 Swiss banks are participating in the Swiss Bank Program.[229] The program represents a monumental development in the formalization of the use of criminal prosecution by the United States as a tool to drive the flow of data through the EOI channel. As a result of this ingenuity,

[223] Wood, above note 217.

[224] See Andrew Grossman, John Letzing, & Devlin Barrett, "Credit Suisse Pleads Guilty in Criminal Tax Case" *Wall Street Journal* (19 May 2014), online: http://on.wsj.com/Sad4mI.

[225] See *ibid.* Under the settlement, $100 million will go to the Federal Reserve, more than $715 million will go to the New York State Department of Financial Services, and $1.8 billion will go to the Department of Justice (*ibid*). Senator Carl Levin criticized the settlement for not requiring the bank to "cough up" some of the names of those holding undeclared Swiss bank accounts (*ibid*).

[226] Banks under investigation included Basler Kantonalbank, Credit Suisse, Julius Baer, Neue Zürcher Bank, Pictet, and Zürcher Kantonalbank: see John Letzing, "Swiss Banks Near Deal on U.S. Tax Cheats" *Wall Street Journal* (11 July 2013), online: http://on.wsj.com/12kJPMD. Credit Suisse is Switzerland's second-largest bank by assets (*ibid*).

[227] See *ibid.*

[228] See *ibid.* See also DOJ News Release re Tax Evasion Investigations, above note 125.

[229] See Economist, "Tackling Tax Evasion: America the Not So Brave" *Economist* (23 May 2015), online: http://econ.st/1BdD1BS.

some Swiss banks, to mitigate potential Department of Justice penalties, are offering compensation to (or in some cases offering to pay the legal fees of) American clients with undisclosed accounts to come forward and make voluntary disclosures to the IRS.[230]

A key stated goal behind the Program for Non-prosecution Agreements or Non-target Letters for Swiss Banks, or Swiss Bank Program, is to provide a path for Swiss Banks not currently the subject of criminal investigation to assist the US Department of Justice in its law enforcement efforts.[231] The Swiss Bank Program is available to any Swiss bank not currently under formal criminal investigation that is requesting either a non-prosecution agreement (generally for banks that believe they have committed tax-related offences ("Category 2" banks)[232] or a non-target letter (generally for banks that believe they have not committed tax-related offences or banks with a domestic client base ("Category 3" or "Category 4" banks).[233] Participating Swiss banks must comply with onerous information-sharing and other program requirements.[234] As of

[230] See John Letzing, "Swiss Banks Use Carrot and Stick in Addressing Hidden Accounts" *Wall Street Journal* (18 July 2014), online: http://on.wsj.com/1pleN3b.

[231] See United States & Switzerland, "Joint Statement between the U.S. Department of Justice and the Swiss Federal Department of Finance" (29 August 2013), online: www.justice.gov/iso/opa/resources/8592013829164213235599.pdf; United States, Department of Justice, "Program for Non-prosecution Agreements or Non-target Letters for Swiss Banks" (29 August 2013), online: www.justice.gov/iso/opa/resources/8592013829164213235599.pdf ["Swiss Bank Program"].

[232] See "Swiss Bank Program," above note 231, Part II, which classifies a bank as a Category 2 bank if it is not a Category 4 bank and if it has reason to believe that it may have committed tax-related offences under USC tit 18, Crimes and Criminal Procedure [Title 18], or the *Code*, above note 5, or monetary transactions offences under the *Bank Secrecy Act*, USC tit 31 §§ 5314 or 5322 [*Bank Secrecy Act*], in connection with certain undeclared US related accounts held by the Swiss bank during the applicable periods described in the program.

[233] See "Swiss Bank Program," above note 231, Part III, which classifies a bank as a Category 3 bank if it is not a Category 4 bank and if it has not committed any tax-related offences under Title 18, above note 232, or the *Code*, above note 5, or monetary transactions offences under the *Bank Secrecy Act*, above note 232, §§ 5314 or 5322, in connection with certain undeclared US related accounts held by the Swiss bank during the applicable periods described in the program; "Swiss Bank Program," above note 231, Part IV, which classifies a bank as a Category 4 bank if it meets certain prescribed requirements and is a financial institution with a local client base.

[234] See "Swiss Bank Program," above note 231, for program details, including information-sharing obligations, a description of the penalty regime, and application of the 20, 30, and 50 percent penalty categories. For additional detailed requirements relating to Category 2 banks, see United States, Department of Justice, Tax Division, "The Tax Division's Further Comments about the *Program for Non-prosecution Agreements or Non-target Letters for Swiss Banks*" (5 June 2014), online:

January 2016, the Department of Justice had announced seventy-eight non-prosecution agreements executed as a result of its efforts under the Swiss Bank Program.[235] Based on the specific terms of the non-prosecution agreement entered into between the Department of Justice and a particular bank, the Department of Justice agrees that it will not prosecute the participating bank for any tax-related offences under Title 18 or the *Code* or any monetary transactions offences under *Bank Secrecy Act* sections 5314 and 5322 in connection with undeclared US related accounts held by the bank during the applicable period.[236]

5 Conclusion

Chapters 4 and 5 have reviewed the alternative approaches and tools available to governments in Canada and the United States to access foreign-based taxpayer information. For an evaluation of the role played by TIEAs and EOI in DTCs, it is important to understand how these mechanisms differ from administrative or unilateral methods for obtaining foreign-based information. In addition, both Canada and the United States have detailed rules about the privacy rights surrounding the sharing of taxpayer information. And Article 26 of the *Model Tax Treaty*, which forms the basis for the information exchange provisions in the tax treaties of both Canada and the United States (and many other countries), also has requirements around taxpayer privacy rights.[237] The signif-

www.justice.gov/sites/default/files/tax/legacy/2014/06/05/Further_Comments_on_Program_for_NonProsecution_Agreements_NonTarget_Letters_ for_Swiss_Banks.pdf.

[235] For a list of the seventy-eight Swiss banks with the accompanying non-prosecution agreements and statements of facts, see United States, Department of Justice, Tax Division, "Non-prosecution Agreements Executed under the Swiss Bank Program," online: www.justice.gov/tax/swiss-bank-program.

[236] Title 18, above note 232; *Code*, above note 5; *Bank Secrecy Act*, above note 232. For an example of the terms of a non-prosecution agreement entered into by the Department of Justice, see United States, Department of Justice, Tax Division, "Banque Bonhôte & Cie SA, Department of Justice Swiss Bank Program — Category 2, Non-prosecution Agreement" (28 October 2015), online: www.justice.gov/opa/file/790411/download, describing, among other numerous and complex details, the agreement to pay millions of dollars in penalties and cooperate with the Department of Justice in any criminal tax investigations of and proceedings against US undeclared account holders.

[237] See *Model Tax Treaty*, above note 198 at Art 26.

icant increase in the exchange (and re-exchange) of taxpayer information that is expected to occur with the implementation of both *FATCA* and automatic exchange of information (Automatic Exchange) creates additional risk that taxpayers' information may be shared or used inappropriately, whether within or outside government agencies. Ensuring privacy around taxpayer information needs to remain a top priority of the international community to ensure confidence and participation in information exchange between countries. Given the political, economic, legal, and social differences that characterize the 121 jurisdictions composing the Global Forum on Transparency and Exchange of Information for Tax Purposes (Global Forum), discussed in Chapter 3, it will be difficult to eliminate the risks associated with confidentiality and EOI.

The summons power, which for the United States is found in *Code* section 7602, works ideally where a taxpayer has been identified and where an offshore transaction has been selected for examination. Similarly, TIEAs also work well where a government has identified a taxpayer that it suspects of non-compliance and has detailed information concerning that taxpayer's offshore account. However, in circumstances where tax evasion is suspected but where the identity of the taxpayer or group of taxpayers is not known, the IRS has successfully used the John Doe summons to obtain foreign documentation. Recently, this unilateral measure has been used against UBS, Wegelin, HSBC, and CIBC FirstCaribbean International Bank. The John Doe summons has illuminated some of the shortcomings of treaties and TIEAs (and judicial assistance measures) when it comes to EOI, such as added time, added expense, political roadblocks, bank secrecy, and design flaws that do not favour group requests. It is likely that the United States will continue to avail itself of the John Doe summons as an effective unilateral measure to obtain production of foreign-based information. A major advantage of the John Doe summons over TIEAs or EOI in DTCs is the ability to obtain information relating to a large group of unknown taxpayers who, for example, may have accounts at a bank under investigation. As discussed in Chapter 3, in the context of EOI mechanisms such requests can conflict with safeguards against fishing expeditions in the *Agreement on Exchange of Information on Tax Matters* (*Model TIEA*) and the *Model Tax Treaty*. Given the recent revelations of large-scale tax evasion involving financial institutions, serious consideration should be given to modifying Article 26 of the *Model Tax Treaty* to permit John Doe–style group requests, with appropriate safeguards to prevent fishing expeditions. Such a modified Article 26 would have facilitated requests from the United States to Switzerland regarding various Swiss bank scandals involving US customers with undeclared accounts. From the perspective of lawyers and financial advisers in the wealth management industry in Canada, the European Union, and elsewhere, the inescapable message for their non-compliant US clients is that the IRS maintains a most powerful set of administrative weapons to compel information, with a potentially devastating downside for non-cooperation in the form of criminal sanctions. Professionals in this industry need to rethink how advice is provided to US private clients in Canada, the European Union, and elsewhere with undeclared foreign accounts and assets, and delinquent US tax and information returns.

The extent to which the United States will continue to rely on the threat of criminal prosecution in conjunction with administrative efforts to obtain foreign documentation is less certain. The threat of criminal prosecution against UBS in 2009 resulted in the *UBS Agreement* initially, and the threat of criminal prosecution against the Swiss financial-institution community as a whole in 2013 resulted in the historic Swiss Bank Program, which comprises some 100 Swiss financial institutions, most of which have entered into historical non-prosecution agreements with the US Department of Justice. A scenario involving some 100 Swiss banks lining up for the privilege of paying the US government billions of dollars in penalties for having maintained secret undeclared bank accounts for US citizens would not have been imaginable a decade ago. And that, furthermore, these banks would agree to assist the IRS with obtaining the names of the account holders and cooperate in criminal prosecution efforts against certain account holders would have been equally unthinkable. The recent use of criminal prosecution by the United States may persuade financial institutions and foreign governments to be more cooperative with foreign document requests in the future, for fear of winding up in the US Department of Justice's firing line. The UBS and other Swiss bank scandals raise the broader question of how well information exchange agreements work when the requested state is unwilling to comply and must be threatened with legal and economic harm. What about countries that lack the financial power (dwindling as it may be) of the US financial centres requesting information? The will that was lacking on the part of the Swiss may in the future be lacking in other governments for different reasons, be they political, economic, or both. Incentives, for example, in dealing with tax havens or developing countries, may enhance the outcome in EOI especially under TIEAs, DTCs, and Automatic Exchange, which is explored in Chapter 8. For banks and financial service providers in Canada, the European Union, and other regions that have significant US expatriate communities, the unasked question is, can the United States unleash its dreadnought criminal prosecution program against us? Here, in Canada? There is no doubt that the answer is yes. The grand policy failure of Canadian and other financial institutions in dealing with these newly unleashed extraterritorial powers of the United States has been the conscious choice to ignore the plight of their delinquent US citizen clients and account holders. The danger and risk for Canadian and other financial institutions in the European Union and elsewhere lies in being re-active instead of pro-active in creating unique strategies to resolve and mitigate the circumstances surrounding such clients, which if ignored may give rise to the imposition of penalties against these financial institutions by the United States just as surely as certain other circumstances gave rise to the imposition of penalties against members of the Swiss banking industry.

Like the general summons power in *Code* section 7602, TIEAs and the EOI upon request in DTCs require the government to be aware of substantial details regarding a taxpayer's potential non-compliance before taking action. The new standard for Automatic Exchange, provides tax authorities with an automatic flow of information on various types of investments without this handicap or flaw, which has helped provide cover for tax cheats. Underlying the potential benefits expected of Automatic Exchange is the belief that overall it will be a more effective tool to combat tax evasion and will ultimately result in an increase in voluntary compliance associated with foreign earned income. As discussed in Chapter 3, there are a number of uncertainties regarding the Automatic Exchange program's rollout to and operation in the global community. Given the complexity of the new regime and the difficulties and delays experienced by many countries in implementing the former standard, 2017 is not a realistic target date for completing the required transformations for all community members. Even Canada did not start entering into TIEAs in earnest until almost eight years after the *Model TIEA* had been adopted in 2002. Additionally, the results of the Global Forum's peer review process, which concerned the attempts of tax haven jurisdictions to adapt to the less stringent current OECD standards, suggest continued problems surrounding EOI in the infrastructure area.

From the perspective of governments worldwide seeking to combat international tax evasion, the answer is clear: there is no magic bullet. Rather, a country seeking to be successful in defeating tax cheats will need to employ multiple strategies. A number of countries are employing a simultaneous combination of strategies, programs, and tools to combat tax evasion, choosing from among various options including the following: unilateral administrative measures (e.g., John Doe summonses, criminal prosecution), tax treaties, TIEAs, *FATCA*, intergovernmental agreements (with multiple countries), offshore voluntary disclosure programs (e.g., the IRS 2012 Offshore Voluntary Disclosure Program), special bilateral agreements (like those entered into with Switzerland by the United Kingdom and Germany to address historical and future bank secrecy problems), US Swiss Bank Program non-prosecution agreements, the *European Union Savings Directive*, the Joint International Tax Shelter Information & Collaboration Network, CRA's Stop International Tax Evasion Program, and the US Simultaneous Examination Program and Simultaneous Criminal Investigation Program. In the quest to defeat offshore tax evasion, progress in the development, improvement, and use of administrative and international countermeasures should be welcomed, especially where perfection in the EOI realm seems, at least for the foreseeable future, to be elusive. However, as this drama unfolds and intensifies (with *FATCA*, Automatic Exchange, and more leaks?), it is clear that achieving progress in obtaining taxpayer information requires a country's tax authorities to adapt, be resilient, be assertive, be self-serving, be creative, and be steadfast.

Further Readings

Kristoffersson, Eleonor et al, eds. *Tax Secrecy and Tax Transparency: The Relevance of Confidentiality in Tax Law, Part 1 and Part 2* (Frankfurt am Main: PL Academic Research, 2013).

Larin, Gilles, & Alexandra Diebel. "The Swiss Twist: The Exchange-of-Information Provisions of the Canada–Switzerland Protocol" (2012) 60 *Canadian Tax Journal* 1.

Schenk-Geers, Tonny. *International Exchange of Information and the Protection of Taxpayers*, (Alphen aan den Rijn, NL: Kluwer Law International, 2009).

6

The Role of Canada's Tax Information Exchange Agreements in the Fight against Offshore Tax Evasion

1 Introduction

This chapter begins by reviewing the policy objectives behind tax information exchange agreements (TIEAs), while giving particular consideration to the objectives set by the OECD. The goals of Canada and the United States with respect to TIEAs are also reviewed. This chapter then examines how Canada's TIEAs function as vehicles for the exchange of information (EOI) between Canada and foreign jurisdictions. Select articles dealing with the EOI process in Canada's TIEAs are described and then compared against (1) the OECD *Agreement on Exchange of Information on Tax Matters*,[1] (2) each other (i.e., other Canadian TIEAs in force), and (3) the TIEA between the United States and the Cayman Islands.[2] The *US–Caymans TIEA* is used as an example of a US TIEA because of the Cayman Islands'

[1] See OECD, *Agreement on Exchange of Information on Tax Matters* (Paris: OECD, 2002) [treaty and commentary together: *Model TIEA*].

[2] See *Agreement between the Government of the United States of America and the Government of the United Kingdom of Great Britain and Northern Ireland, including the Government of the Cayman Islands, for the Exchange of Information relating to Taxes* (27 November 2001), online: http://www.oecd.org/unitedstates/35514531.pdf [*US–Caymans TIEA*].

D.S. Kerzner, D.W. Chodikoff, *International Tax Evasion in the Global Information Age*, DOI 10.1007/978-3-319-40421-9_6

ongoing high-profile as a tax haven.[3] By looking at Professor Steven Dean's analysis of tax harmonization versus tax deharmonization, this chapter examines an important overarching question in the debate on effective EOI and the use of TIEAs regarding the global community's focus on achieving a victory against international tax evasion through cooperation around the implementation of a uniform set of rules and procedures. The conclusion provides a summary of the results of the comparative analysis.

A TIEA is a bilateral agreement between two governments for the purpose of exchanging information with respect to taxes.[4] As of February 2016, twenty-two TIEAs were in force between Canada and other jurisdictions.[5] In broad strokes, a TIEA is a treaty made out of a single double-tax-convention article on EOI. By contrast, Canada has ninety-six full-blown tax treaties in force.[6] In terms of the legislative process in Canada, a TIEA is tabled in the House of Commons for a period of twenty-one sitting days, and following any questions or debate, the government ratifies the treaty by signing an order in council, and there is no additional legislative process involved.[7]

---

[3] The Cayman Islands was listed as one of the top five tax haven destinations for Canadian dollars with $25.8 billion invested in 2011: see Janet McFarland & Bill Curry, "Banking: Document Leak Reveals Widespread Use of Tax Havens" *Globe and Mail* (4 April 2013), online: http://fw.to/YW5XUuW.

[4] See *Model TIEA*, above note 1, Preamble. The *Model TIEA* is presented as both a multilateral instrument and a model for bilateral treaties or agreements. This chapter examines the latter model, which is used by Canada and the United States.

[5] See Canada, Department of Finance, "Tax Information Exchange Agreements," online: www.fin.gc.ca/treaties-conventions/tieaaerf-eng.asp, where the full texts of Canada's TIEAs can be found.

[6] See Canada, Department of Finance, "Notices of Tax Treaty Developments," online: www.fin.gc.ca/treaties-conventions/treatystatus_-eng.asp. For an excellent discussion of the history of Canada's tax treaties, including an explanation of the use of tax treaties and important policy considerations, see Brian J Arnold, *Reforming Canada's International Tax System: Toward Coherence and Simplicity* (Toronto: Canadian Tax Foundation, 2009) at 319–70.

[7] See OECD, *Global Forum on Transparency and Exchange of Information for Tax Purposes Peer Reviews: Canada 2011 — Combined: Phase 1 + Phase 2* (Paris: OECD, 2011) at 57–58, online: http://dx.doi.org/10.1787/9789264110458-en [*Canada Peer Review Report*].

2 The Policy behind TIEAs

2.1 The OECD's Response to Bank Secrecy

The OECD identified tax havens as being one of the two primary contributors to harmful tax practices (the other being so-called preferential tax regimes).[8] It further viewed tax havens as possessing four key identifying factors: (1) no or only nominal taxes, (2) lack of effective EOI, (3) lack of transparency, and (4) investment with no substantial activities.[9] Among these attributes, the critical one sought by individual investors, and the ultimate focus of the OECD's harmful tax competition project, was secrecy.[10] The *OECD 1998 Report* observed:

> these tax haven jurisdictions do not allow tax administrations access to bank information for the critical purposes of detecting and preventing tax avoidance which, from the perspectives of raising revenue and controlling base erosion from financial and other service activities, are as important as curbing tax fraud. Thus, the lack of effective exchange of information is one of the key factors in identifying a tax haven since it limits access by tax authorities to the information required for the correct and timely application of tax laws.[11]

Taxpayers use bank secrecy laws in foreign jurisdictions both to hide their illegal activities from governments and to escape tax. The bank secrecy laws of a tax haven or foreign jurisdiction impede access to and analysis of records of financial transactions by fiscal and law enforcement authorities. As a result, these bank secrecy laws can and do hinder the effective administration and enforcement of countries' laws.[12]

---

[8] See Chapter 3, Section 4.

[9] OECD, *Harmful Tax Competition: An Emerging Global Issue* (Paris: OECD, 1998) at 24 [*OECD 1998 Report*].

[10] See Robert T Kudrle, "The OECD's Harmful Tax Competition Initiative and the Tax Havens: From Bombshell to Damp Squib" (2008) 8 *Global Economy Journal* 1 at 5.

[11] *OECD 1998 Report*, above note 9 at 15.

[12] See OECD, *Improving Access to Bank Information for Tax Purposes* (Paris: OECD, 2000) at 7. Without such records of financial transactions, a tax authority may be unable to determine and collect the correct amount of tax (*ibid* at 9). Denying access to bank records also greatly facilitates money laundering schemes that deal with the proceeds of crime to conceal their illegal origins (*ibid* at 25).

In addition, bank secrecy laws distort the distribution of the tax burden and call into question the fairness of the tax system by allowing some taxpayers to evade paying tax on income earned in their offshore accounts.[13] Moreover, bank secrecy can create unjustified advantages between different categories of income such as mobile capital versus income derived from employment or immovable property.[14]

Allowing fiscal authorities to access valuable information about bank deposits and withdrawals can unlock a treasure trove of pathways to discovering a number of improprieties that may otherwise remain concealed, such as unreported legal or illegal income, false deductions, back-to-back loan transactions, sham transactions, and bribes or suspicious payments.[15] Permitting greater access to such bank information may also aid in the collection of tax liabilities.[16] In 2000, the OECD believed that the availability of jurisdictions with bank secrecy laws was exponentially compounding these problems and advocated the use of specific requests for information to facilitate direct or indirect access to bank information.[17]

As the OECD observed, the lack of effective EOI by tax havens denies fiscal authorities access to bank information that is critical to raising revenue and preventing tax avoidance and base erosion.[18] "Information exchange" is a term of art that refers to "agreed international standards on transparency and effective exchange of information."[19] The OECD has broken down the international standards on transparency and EOI into ten essential elements grouped under the following categories: (1) availability of information, (2) access to information, and (3) EOI.[20] The EOI category breaks down into the following elements: (1) EOI mechanisms should provide for effective EOI, (2) the jurisdiction's network of information exchange mechanisms should cover all relevant

[13] See *ibid.*

[14] See *ibid.*

[15] See *ibid* at 8.

[16] See *ibid.*

[17] *Ibid* at 13.

[18] *OECD 1998 Report*, above note 9 at 24.

[19] Adrian Sawyer, "Peer Review of Tax Information Exchange Agreements: Is It More Than Just about the Numbers?" (2011) 26 *Australian Tax Forum* 397 at 405, observing that the information exchange mechanism in TIEAs is fundamentally flawed.

[20] See OECD, *Tax Transparency 2011: Report on Progress* (Paris: OECD, 2011) at 53.

partners, (3) the jurisdiction's mechanisms for EOI should have adequate provisions to ensure the confidentiality of information received, (4) the EOI mechanisms should respect the rights and safeguards of taxpayers and third parties, and (5) the jurisdiction should provide information under its network of agreements in a timely manner.[21]

The initial aims of the OECD's harmful tax competition project were to (1) identify and eliminate harmful features of preferential tax regimes in OECD countries, (2) identify "tax havens" and seek their commitment to the principles of transparency and effective EOI, and (3) encourage other non-OECD countries' association with the project.[22] In 2000, the OECD established the Global Forum on Transparency and Exchange of Information for Tax Purposes, which developed the *Model TIEA* in 2002 to address the issues arising from the harmful tax practices project.[23] The lack of effective EOI was viewed by the OECD as one of the key factors determining harmful tax practices.[24]

A primary objective of the *Model TIEA* was to compel tax haven jurisdictions to enact laws to override their bank secrecy rules.[25] Professor Sawyer observes that the OECD was focused on the goal of proliferating TIEAs by encouraging tax haven jurisdictions to sign the required minimum of twelve agreements to be removed from the OECD's blacklist.[26] The blacklist identified jurisdictions that did not meet the OECD's standards on transparency and EOI.[27] Tax havens that entered into at least twelve TIEAs had, instead, the respectable aura of "white country"

---

[21] See *ibid.*

[22] See OECD, *The OECD's Project on Harmful Tax Practices: 2006 Update on Progress in Member Countries* (Paris: OECD, 2006) at 2–3.

[23] See *ibid*; OECD, *OECD's Current Tax Agenda* (Paris: OECD, 2011) at 84. The *Model TIEA* emerged from work by the OECD to address harmful tax practices and develop a legal instrument that could be used to establish effective EOI: see *Model TIEA*, above note 1, Introduction at para 3. See also David E Spencer, "OECD Model Agreement Is a Major Advance in Information Exchange" (2002) 13 *Journal of International Tax* 1 (Checkpoint) at 2; Sawyer, above note 19 at 399.

[24] See *Model TIEA*, above note 1, Introduction at para 3, citing *OECD 1998 Report*, above note 9.

[25] See Spencer, above note 23 at 2. See also Nathan Boidman, "New TIEAs Extend the Playing Field for Canada's Multinational Enterprises" (2010) 59 *Tax Notes International* 209 at 212 [Boidman, "New TIEAs"], describing Canada's TIEA efforts to learn about Canadian account holders' undisclosed income by rewarding tax haven jurisdictions with Canadian investment.

[26] Sawyer, above note 19 at 403.

[27] See *ibid.*

status bestowed upon them.[28] The *Model TIEA* was intended to establish the standard for what constitutes effective EOI for purposes of the harmful tax competition project.[29] Article 5 (EOI upon Request) of the *Model TIEA* requires that each contracting party have the authority to obtain upon request information held by banks and other financial institutions notwithstanding local bank secrecy and confidentiality laws. This standard marked a significant change from the language in Article 26 (EOI) of the OECD *Model Tax Convention on Income and on Capital*, which did not require a contracting state to supply information that was not obtainable under its laws.[30] In 2005, the OECD added new paragraph 5 to Article 26 of the *Model Tax Treaty*, which provides, "In no case shall the provisions of paragraph 3 be construed to permit a Contracting State to decline to supply information solely because the information is held by a bank, other financial institution, nominee or person acting in an agency or a fiduciary capacity or because it relates to ownership interests in a person." Although the *Model TIEA* represented an important first step toward improving cooperation with respect to EOI, as discussed in Chapter 3, it was not an effective weapon against tax evasion.

In April 2013, one of the last remaining outposts for bank secrecy, Luxembourg announced its decision to exchange information on EU holders of bank accounts in its jurisdiction with the rest of the European Union.[31] This move ends the decades-long policy that has made this jurisdiction of less than 100,000 persons one of the largest financial centres in Europe. Although Luxembourg was urged by the European

---

[28] For a detailed review of the OECD's tax haven lists, see Dries Lesage, "The G20 and Tax Havens: Maintaining the Momentum?" (Symposium on Governing the Global Economy: The Role of the G20, delivered at the University of Toronto, Munk School of Global Affairs, 18 June 2010) [Unpublished].

[29] See *Model TIEA*, above note 1, Introduction at para 6.

[30] OECD, Committee on Fiscal Affairs, *Model Tax Convention on Income and on Capital* (Paris: OECD, 1992) (loose-leaf) at Art 26, before 2005 [convention and commentary together: *Model Tax Treaty*].

[31] See Vanessa Mock, "Luxembourg to Disclose Bank-Account Data" *Wall Street Journal* (11 April 2013). This move leaves Austria as the only EU member state that does not share foreign clients' data with their home state. Austria believes that automatic information exchange involves a grave interference with individual privacy rights and, instead, remits a 35 percent withholding tax on interest income earned in Austrian banks, without disclosing the account holders' identities: see David Jolly & James Kanter, "Austria, under Pressure, Defends Bank Secrecy Rules" *New York Times* (13 April 2013) B2, online http://nyti.ms/20Xp1Zn.

Union to end its practice for years, the move came as a result of its negotiation of the implementation of information exchange with the United States under the *Foreign Account Tax Compliance Act*.[32] The United States has chosen to ratchet up the fight against tax evasion by upgrading its TIEA system through the implementation of *FATCA*, which in turn has led to the drive toward a new standard for Automatic Exchange between countries.[33] In March 2013, the Cayman Islands announced that it would be entering into a new information exchange agreement with the United States under *FATCA*.[34]

2.2 The Policy behind Canada's TIEAs

By way of background, the United States first began using TIEAs in the early 1980s and now has over twenty such agreements.[35] In the US context, a TIEA is an "executive agreement" entered into by the administration without the consent or advice of the Senate.[36] The United States recognized that bank secrecy played a crucial role in assisting taxpayers to evade US income taxes.[37] TIEAs were developed as a tool to enable the United States to obtain foreign tax information on investment income of US taxpayers.[38] In the early 1980s, the US Department of the Treasury

---

32 Enacted by Congress as part of the *Hiring Incentives to Restore Employment (HIRE) Act*, Public Law 111-147, and signed into law by the president on 18 March 2010 [*FATCA*]. See Mock, above note 31.

33 See Chapter 8.

34 On 15 March 2013, the Cayman Islands' government announced that it would adopt the *Model Intergovernmental Agreement to Improve Tax Compliance and to Implement FATCA* (*Model 1 IGA*) in response to *FATCA*: see Patrick Temple-West, "Cayman Islands, Costa Rica Sign Pacts with U.S." *Reuters* (29 November 2013), online: http://reut.rs/18skFED.

35 See United States, Congress, Joint Committee on Taxation, *Explanation of Proposed Protocol to the Income Tax Treaty between the United States and Luxembourg* (Washington, DC: Joint Committee on Taxation, 2011) at 22.

36 *Ibid.*

37 See Steven A Dean, "More Cooperation, Less Uniformity: Tax Deharmonization and the Future of the International Tax Regime" (2009) 84 *Tulane Law Review* 125 at 135–36 [Dean, "More Cooperation"], advocating economic cooperation in sharing tax revenues over tax harmonization.

38 See *ibid* at 136; Bruce Zagaris, "The Procedural Aspects of U.S. Tax Policy towards Developing Countries: Too Many Sticks and No Carrots?" (2003) 35 *George Washington International Law Review* 331 at 332–34.

suggested that TIEAs could reduce tax flight by building information bridges to tax havens with which the United States had no tax treaties.[39] A further objective of TIEAs was the promotion of international cooperation in criminal and civil tax matters through the EOI process.[40]

As of February 2016, Canada had entered into ninety-six tax treaties and signed twenty-two TIEAs. A generally held view is that Canada initially climbed onto the TIEA bandwagon in 2007 to support the OECD's harmful tax competition project and combat tax evasion.[41] While this ultimately became a key policy driver behind the government's support of TIEAs, in 2007 the government's primary motivation with respect to TIEAs was to use information exchange to enforce new rules that sought to trace interest and other deductions to the earning of exempt foreign sourced income through, for example, double dip cross-border financing structures.[42] In addition to combatting tax evasion, as described below,

---

[39] See Steven A Dean, "The Incomplete Global Market for Tax Information" (2008) 49 *Boston College Law Review* 605 at 642 [Dean, "Incomplete Global Market"].

[40] See United States, Congress, Joint Committee on Taxation, *Explanation of Proposed Protocol to the Income Tax Treaty between the United States and Switzerland* (Washington, DC: Joint Committee on Taxation, 2011) at 29.

[41] See Canada, Department of Finance, *The Budget Plan 2007* (Ottawa: Department of Finance, 2007), online: www.budget.gc.ca/2007/pdf/bp2007e.pdf, acknowledging that the "greatest challenges CRA faces in enforcing Canada's tax laws are in respect of income earned in countries with which Canada does not have a tax treaty" (*ibid* at 243) and proposing to extend the exemption for dividends received out of active business income earned by foreign affiliates resident in treaty countries to also include active business income earned by foreign affiliates resident in countries that have agreed to a TIEA with Canada (*ibid* at 422). See also Boidman, "New TIEAs," above note 25 at 212, describing Canada's TIEA efforts to learn about Canadian account holders' undisclosed income by rewarding tax haven jurisdictions with Canadian investment; Sandra Slaats, "Financing Foreign Affiliates: An Overview of the Canadian Proposals and the Rules in Selected Countries" (2007) 55 *Canadian Tax Journal* 676 at 679, observing that although the rationale for extending exempt surplus status to countries willing to sign a TIEA, including pure tax havens, is not exactly clear, it may be motivated by the desire to obtain information to combat tax evasion by Canadian individual investors.

[42] See Jinyan Li, Arthur Cockfield, & J Scott Wilkie, *International Taxation in Canada — Principles and Practices*, 2d ed (Markham, ON: LexisNexis, 2011) at 380. For further policy discussion surrounding interest deductions and the exempt surplus regime, see Arthur J Cockfield, "Finding Silver Linings in the Storm: An Evaluation of Recent Canada–US Crossborder Tax Developments" CD Howe Institute Commentary No 272, Tax Competitiveness Program (September 2008) at 10, online: www.cdhowe.org/pdf/Commentary_272.pdf, observing that in 2007 Ottawa had initially proposed denying interest deductions for any interest expense that could be traced to earnings-exempt foreign sourced income. See, generally, Tim Edgar, Jonathan Farrar, & Amin Mawani, "Foreign Direct Investment, Thin Capitalization, and the Interest Expense Deduction: A Policy Analysis" (2008) 56 *Canadian Tax Journal* 803, discussing interest deductibility restrictions relating

TIEAs enabled multinational enterprises to obtain preferred tax benefits by expanding the list of low tax jurisdictions that they could invest in.[43] Canada continues to embrace the notion that concluding TIEAs demonstrates its commitment to combatting international tax evasion and ensuring tax fairness by adhering to the standards developed by the OECD.[44] This new policy has also required that all new treaties and revisions to existing treaties include the OECD standards.[45] It is quite shocking to note that approximately eighty of Canada's ninety-two tax treaties fail to contain paragraph 5 (the anti–bank secrecy clause) of Article 26 of the *Model Tax Treaty*, which, as described above, was the centrepiece of the harmful tax competition project.[46]

Certain parallels may be found between the tax policy behind Canada's network of comprehensive tax treaties and that behind its ever-expanding TIEA network. In his research on Canada's tax treaty system, Professor Brian Arnold observes that from 1972 (when Canada had sixteen treaties in force) to 2008 (when Canada had eighty-six comprehensive tax treaties in force), the country's treaty network grew at an extraordinary rate.[47] He links this large-scale expansion (400 percent over

to both inbound and outbound investment and comparing the approaches of multiple jurisdictions. For a technical review of double dips and the revised proposal on interest deductibility, see Geoffrey S Turner, "Finance's May 14, 2007 Revised Interest Deductibility Proposals — An 'Anti-double-dip Initiative'" *Tax Topics* (5 July 2007) 1 at 1.

[43] See Advisory Panel on Canada's System of International Taxation, *Final Report: Enhancing Canada's International Tax Advantage* (Ottawa: Department of Finance, 2008) at 27 [Advisory Panel on International Taxation].

[44] See *ibid.*

[45] See Canada, Department of Finance, News Release, "Canada Signs Tax Information Exchange Agreement with Liechtenstein" (31 January 2013), online: http://news.gc.ca/web/article-eng.do?nid=718269. While in the sense that many of these countries have high tax rates and would not be ideal locations for tax evaders, it is true that they are not tax havens, the treaty list includes a number of jurisdictions widely regarded as tax havens, including countries where EOI may be useful to combat other crimes such as money laundering and terrorism (e.g., Austria, Cyprus, Luxembourg, Pakistan, and the United Arab Emirates).

[46] For a list of the eighty double tax conventions that Canada has signed and that do not contain either para 5 (anti–bank secrecy clause) or para 4 (which obligates a requested state to obtain the requested information even if it does not need that information for its own tax administration purposes) of Art 26 of the *Model Tax Treaty*, above note 30, see OECD, Global Forum on Transparency and Exchange of Information for Tax Purposes, "OECD Canadian Agreements," online: Exchange of Tax Information Portal www.eoi-tax.org/jurisdictions/CA#agreements.

[47] Arnold, above note 6 at 320–21.

thirty-five years) to the introduction of the foreign affiliate rules in 1972.[48] Canada also used the exempt surplus tax advantage to lure foreign countries into signing tax treaties with the prospect of Canadian investment.[49]

By the numbers, Professor Arnold observes that while many of these countries are indeed major trading partners, many of them (like Armenia, Ivory Coast, Kurdistan, and Kyrgyzstan) are in fact only minor trading partners.[50] He believes that Canada does not need so many comprehensive treaties (citing Australia, which has about forty-four, and the United States, which has about sixty) and that this large number is a mistake because it puts unnecessary pressure on Canada's treaty network.[51] As explained below, he believes that the path to correcting this approach is linked to Canada's policy on territorial versus worldwide taxation, which involves the complex rules on exempt surplus contained in the *Income Tax Act*.[52]

Income earned by a Canadian taxpayer through a foreign corporation is taxed under a set of rules known as the foreign affiliate rules.[53] These rules can be incredibly complex, and no attempt to summarize them is made here. Basically, under this regime, where a corporation formed in Canada owns a foreign affiliate that is resident and carries on its business in a country with which Canada has a tax treaty, active business income earned by that foreign affiliate is generally not taxable in Canada on repatriation, if deemed exempt surplus.[54] Accordingly, under Canada's

---

[48] *Ibid*: Professor Arnold explains that before the enactment of the foreign affiliate rules, Canada-based multinational enterprises could repatriate profits from foreign corporations on an exempt basis. However, under the new foreign affiliate rules (which required foreign affiliates to be residents of and doing business in countries with which Canada had a tax treaty), continuing this economic treatment would be very difficult, and hence the exigency to expand the Canadian treaty network.

[49] See H Kerr, K McKenzie, & J Mintz, eds, *Tax Policy in Canada* (Toronto: Canadian Tax Foundation, 2012); ch 12 at 40–41.

[50] Arnold, above note 6 at 322, observing that if Canada adopted a complex exemption system, this would eliminate the need to enter into a tax treaty with every jurisdiction that a Canadian company carries on active business with.

[51] *Ibid.*

[52] *Ibid.* See also *Income Tax Act*, RSC 1985, c 1 (5th Supp) [*Act*].

[53] For a detailed explanation of the foreign affiliate regime, see, generally, Angelo Nikolakakis, *Taxation of Foreign Affiliates* (Toronto: Carswell, 2000) (loose-leaf).

[54] See Advisory Panel on International Taxation, above note 43 at 22. These rules apply where the Canadian taxpayer, either alone or with related investors, owns at least a 10 percent direct or indirect interest in any class of shares of the foreign corporation (*ibid* at 21).

quasi-territorial approach to international taxation, Canada-based multinational enterprises with foreign affiliates are able to invest in foreign countries that have a tax treaty with Canada and repatriate actual or deemed "active business" profits back to Canada without further taxation to the Canadian parent.[55] However, if a foreign affiliate is not resident or does not carry on business in a country with which Canada has a treaty, the so-called credit method applies, and a tax credit is allowed for underlying foreign income and withholding taxes attributable to the income.[56]

The centrepiece of the Canadian TIEA initiative unveiled in the 2007 budget lay in an economic carrot and stick incentive approach to inducing tax havens to enter into TIEAs with Canada.[57] Canada hoped to entice tax haven jurisdictions into signing TIEAs with Ottawa with the lure of increased investments by Canadian multinational enterprises in the various island economies. In a nutshell, here is how it worked. The March 2007 federal budget proposed similar tax treatment (repatriation of profits under the exempt surplus model) for Canada-based multinational enterprises that invested in tax haven jurisdictions that had entered into a TIEA with Canada.[58] In the absence of such treaties, profits of Canadian subsidiaries based in jurisdictions such as Bermuda or the Cayman Islands, which do not qualify as "exempt surplus," are classified as "taxable surplus" and on repatriation to Canada are subject to tax on credit basis.[59] From an international tax policy perspective, the linkage between TIEAs and an exemption for active business income signalled the government's intention to expand the existing exemption system.[60] Canada appeared to be more focused on providing Canada-based multinational enterprises with additional low-tax-cost jurisdictions to utilize

[55] See Nathan Boidman, "Draft Regs for Novel Use of TIEAs" (2008) 51 *Tax Notes International* 228 [Boidman, "Draft Regs"].

[56] See Advisory Panel on International Taxation, above note 43 at 21.

[57] See Boidman, "Draft Regs," above note 55 at 228.

[58] See Boidman, "New TIEAs," above note 25 at 210. However, as Edgar, Farrar, & Mawani, above note 42 at 7, and others have noted, with the new extension of exempt surplus status to TIEAs, which are primarily being signed with jurisdictions that have little to no income tax, the presence of a tax treaty has become a poor proxy for a level of tax in a foreign country sufficient to justify exempt treatment.

[59] See Edgar, Farrar, & Mawani, above note 42 at 7.

[60] See Kerr, McKenzie, & Mintz, above note 49 at 12:40.

than on obtaining tax information on taxpayers hiding money offshore.[61] The flip side, or stick, of Canada's TIEA policy was that the Canadian parent company of a foreign affiliate would be subject to tax on an accrual basis on profits (including active business income) earned in tax haven jurisdictions that generally failed to conclude a TIEA within five years from the start of negotiations or the date on which Canada proposed negotiations, whichever occurred first.[62]

Canada signed its first TIEA, of twenty-two, with the Netherlands Antilles in 2009, and it is negotiating TIEAs with additional jurisdictions.[63] Canada continues to rely on the economic incentive described above to induce tax havens to enter into TIEAs.[64] Moreover, Canada relies on TIEAs to provide effective EOI to combat international tax evasion and to promote horizontal and vertical equity in the Canadian tax system.[65]

In 2008, the Advisory Panel on Canada's System of International Taxation recommended an extension of the exemption system for all foreign active business income, based on a number of considerations including that the system currently exempts most active business income repatriated to Canada.[66] Based on this recommendation, the advisory panel also believed that the exemption system should be detached from both tax treaties and TIEAs.[67]

---

[61] See Boidman, "New TIEAs," above note 25 at 210: "In other words, for Canadian-based MNEs that, in general, are fully compliant with Canada's tax laws, the significance of the signing of the TIEAs has nothing to do with information that will be exchanged thereunder. Rather, TIEAs can serve to make such countries an attractive place for Canadian companies to carry on business." An interesting parallel to note is that, as Professor Arnold observes, above note 6 at 321, the primary impetus behind Canada's entering into tax treaties after 1972 was the exemption for dividends from foreign affiliates.

[62] See Boidman, "New TIEAs," above note 25 at 210–11. See also Patrick Marley & Susan Wooles, "Canada's Tax Information Exchange Agreements: Impact on Tax Planning" (2010) 39 *Tax Management International Journal* 606 at 606–8.

[63] See Canada, Department of Finance, News Release, "Canada Signs Tax Information Exchange Agreement with Liechtenstein" (31 January 2013), online: http://news.gc.ca/web/article-eng.do?nid=718269; see also note 5, above in this chapter.

[64] See Canada, Department of Finance, "Tax Treaties and Tax Information Exchange Agreements," online: Canada's Economic Action Plan http://actionplan.gc.ca/en/initiative/tax-treaties-and-tax-information-exchange-agreements.

[65] See *ibid.*

[66] See Kerr, McKenzie, & Mintz, above note 49 at 12:40. See also Arnold, above note 6 at 322.

[67] See Advisory Panel on International Taxation, above note 43 at 27.

3 Analysis and Comparison of Canada's TIEA Network

The aim of this section is to examine Canada's TIEAs and compare them to the OECD *Model TIEA*, each other, and a TIEA used by the United States. The following format is used for the comparison: (1) the text of the applicable article from the *Model TIEA* is reproduced, (2) a table is presented indicating whether the language of the article in each of a selected group of Canada's TIEAs tracks the *Model TIEA* or is different, and (3) commentary is provided describing the purpose of the article together with a conclusion regarding any notable similarities or distinctions.[68]

3.1 Article 1: Object and Scope of the Agreement

Article 1 of the *Model TIEA* provides as follows:

> The competent authorities of the Contracting Parties shall provide assistance through exchange of information that is foreseeably relevant to the administration and enforcement of the domestic laws of the Contracting Parties concerning taxes covered by this Agreement. Such information shall include information that is foreseeably relevant to the determination, assessment and collection of such taxes, the recovery and enforcement of tax claims, or the investigation or prosecution of tax matters. Information shall be exchanged in accordance with the provisions of this Agreement and shall be treated as confidential in the manner provided in Article 8. The rights and safeguards secured to persons by the laws or administrative practice of the requested Party remain applicable to the extent that they do not unduly prevent or delay effective exchange of information (Table 6.1).[69]

---

[68] Peter Blessing has used tables to compare provisions in the double tax conventions of the United States, and the use of tables to compare Canada's TIEAs in this section is inspired by Blessing's approach: see RE Andersen, *Analysis of United States Income Tax Treaties* (Thomson Reuters/WG&L, with updates through August 2015) (Checkpoint) (Blessing is the original author of this work). The legal instruments examined here, TIEAs, are altogether different from those examined in Blessing's work, and the format of the tables, organization of the data, and analysis are original to this study.

[69] *Model TIEA*, above note 1 at Art 1.

Table 6.1 Article 1 — Object and Scope of the Agreement

TIEA	Notes
Canada–Anguilla	b
Canada–Aruba	a
Canada–Bahamas	a
Canada–Bermuda	b, c
Canada–Cayman Islands	a
Canada–Costa Rica	a
Canada–Dominica	a
Canada–Guernsey	d, e
Canada–Isle of Man	d, e
Canada–Jersey	a, e
Canada–Liechtenstein	a
Canada–Panama	a
Canada–San Marino	f
Canada–St Kitts and Nevis	a
Canada–St Lucia	a
Canada–St Vincent and the Grenadines	a
Canada–Turks and Caicos Islands	b
Canada–Uruguay	a
US–Cayman Islands	g, h

Notes:

a Agreement contains identical or substantially similar language to the *Model TIEA*.

b Same as "a" except that the article notably does not contain the last sentence stating that individual rights and safeguards are not to unduly prevent or delay the effective EOI between the parties' competent authorities.

c The article's language uses the narrower scope of "information that is relevant," rather than "foreseeably relevant."

d Same as "a" except that in a new last sentence, the requested party agrees to use its best endeavours to ensure that effective EOI is not unduly prevented or delayed.

e The language of Article 2 (Jurisdiction) is added to Article 1.

f Same as "a" except that the contracting parties acknowledge that the rights and safeguards of individuals under the laws and administrative practice of the requested party remain applicable, without any limitation. To further dilute the importance of EOI, the article contains no language regarding the requested party's affirmation that its safeguards for taxpayers shall not unduly prevent or delay effective EOI.

g Additionally, a requested party is not obligated to provide information that is neither held by its authorities nor in the possession of nor obtainable by persons who are within its territorial jurisdiction.

h In lieu of the term "foreseeably relevant," the *US–Caymans TIEA* uses the broader standard "information that may be relevant" found in the *United States Model Income Tax Convention*.[70]

Commentary on Article 1

Article 1 of the *Model TIEA* describes the nature of the agreement as providing assistance in tax matters via EOI for the administration and enforcement of the tax laws of the contracting parties.[71] Article 1 sets forth certain expectations regarding the scope of and circumstances involving EOI by the contracting parties so as to strike a balance between rights granted to persons in the requested party's jurisdiction and the need for effective information exchange.[72] To this end, the contracting parties agree to EOI that is foreseeably relevant to the administration and enforcement of the laws of the applicant party relating to taxes covered by the agreement.[73] The foreseeable relevance standard is aimed at providing the widest possible bridge for information exchange without allowing fishing expeditions, for example, speculative requests for information that have no apparent connection to an open inquiry or investigation.[74] Article 1 also acknowledges that while the requested party may have laws granting rights to persons in its jurisdiction (e.g., notification requirements), such rights and safeguards are not to be applied in a manner that unduly prevents or delays effective EOI.[75]

---

[70] United States, Internal Revenue Service, *United States Model Income Tax Convention* (Washington, DC: Department of the Treasury, 2006) at Art 26, online: www.treasury.gov/press-center/press-releases/Documents/hp16801.pdf [convention and technical explanation together: *US Model Tax Treaty*].

[71] See *Model TIEA*, above note 1, Commentary to Art 1 at para 2.

[72] See *ibid*, Commentary to Art 1 at para 6.

[73] See *ibid*, Commentary to Art 1 at para 3.

[74] See *ibid*. In accepting this standard, the contracting parties acknowledge that information may be requested during an ongoing investigation and before the arrival of a definite assessment of the value of that information to the investigation: see *ibid*, Commentary to Art 1 at para 4; *Canada Peer Review Report*, above note 7 at 52.

[75] See *Model TIEA*, above note 1, Commentary to Art 1 at para 3.

While there appears to be a digression from the "foreseeably relevant" standard in the TIEA with Bermuda, overall, according to the *Global Forum on Transparency and Exchange of Information for Tax Purposes Peer Reviews: Canada 2011*, Canada's TIEAs meet the "foreseeably relevant" standard described in the 2005 commentary to Article 26 of the *Model Tax Treaty* and the *Model TIEA*.[76] The broader language in the *US–Caymans TIEA* derives from section 7602 of the *Internal Revenue Code*, authorizing the IRS to examine "any books, papers, records, or other data which may be relevant or material . . . ."[77]

3.2 Article 2: Jurisdiction

Article 2 of the *Model TIEA* provides as follows: "A Requested Party is not obligated to provide information which is neither held by its authorities nor in the possession or control of persons who are within its territorial jurisdiction." (Table 6.2)[78]

Commentary on Article 2

Article 2 adds further clarity to the scope of the responsibilities of the parties to the *Model TIEA*. It encompasses issues of sovereignty relating to the boundaries in which a requested party is agreeing to be responsible for its undertakings to provide information within the framework of the TIEA. Generally, a requested party is not obligated to provide information that its government agencies do not hold. Furthermore, a requested party is not obligated to provide information that is not in the possession or control of persons within its territorial jurisdiction.[79] Canada's TIEAs are consistent with the language and intent of Article 2 of the *Model TIEA*, and they are uniform as compared to one another (with the exceptions noted

[76] *Canada Peer Review Report*, above note 7 at 54. See also *Model Tax Treaty*, above note 30, Commentary to Art 26.

[77] USC 26 (1986) of 1986, as amended, and the *Treasury Regulations* issued thereunder at Chapter 4. See also *US Model Tax Treaty*, above note 70 at Art 26.

[78] *Model TIEA*, above note 1 at Art 2.

[79] See *Model TIEA*, above note 1, Commentary to Art 2 at para 7. Article 7 (Possibility of Declining a Request) may apply (see *ibid*).

above). Although the *US–Caymans TIEA* contains different wording, the meaning conveyed is in substance similar to that in Canada's TIEAs.

Table 6.2 Article 2 — Jurisdiction

TIEA	Notes
Canada–Anguilla	a
Canada–Aruba	a
Canada–Bahamas	a
Canada–Bermuda	a
Canada–Cayman Islands	a
Canada–Costa Rica	a
Canada–Dominica	a
Canada–Guernsey	b
Canada–Isle of Man	b
Canada–Jersey	b
Canada–Liechtenstein	a
Canada–Panama	a
Canada–San Marino	a
Canada–St Kitts and Nevis	a
Canada–St Lucia	a
Canada–St Vincent and the Grenadines	a
Canada–Turks and Caicos Islands	a
Canada–Uruguay	a
US–Cayman Islands	c

Notes:

a Agreement contains identical or substantially similar language to the *Model TIEA*.

b Agreement provides alternative language: "a requested Party is not obliged to provide information which is neither held by its authorities nor in the possession of nor obtainable by persons who are within its territorial jurisdiction." This is a lower standard. By eliminating the word "control" and inserting alternative wording, it permits the requested party in its discretion to exclude information that is not obtainable by persons in its jurisdiction.

c Agreement provides alternative language:

> information shall be provided in accordance with this Agreement by the competent authority of the requested party:
>
> a) without regard to whether the person to whom the information relates is, or whether the information is held by, a resident or national of a party; and
> b) provided that the information is present within the territory, or in the possession or control of a person subject to the jurisdiction, of the requested party.[80]

[80] *US–Caymans TIEA, above note 2 at Art 2.*

3.3 Article 3: Taxes Covered

Article 3 of the *Model TIEA* provides as follows:

1. The taxes which are the subject of this Agreement are:

    a) in country A, ______________________;
    b) in country B, ______________________.

2. This Agreement shall also apply to any identical taxes imposed after the date of signature of the Agreement in addition to or in place of the existing taxes. This Agreement shall also apply to any substantially similar taxes imposed after the date of signature of the Agreement in addition to or in place of the existing taxes if the competent authorities of the Contracting Parties so agree. Furthermore, the taxes covered may be expanded or modified by mutual agreement of the Contracting Parties in the form of an exchange of letters. The competent authorities of the Contracting Parties shall notify each other of any substantial changes to the taxation and related information gathering measures covered by the Agreement (Table 6.3).[81]

Commentary on Article 3

Under Article 3, each contracting party may decide which taxes within its tax regime it agrees to exchange information on.[82] The taxes listed by each contracting party need not be the same (e.g., Party A may list direct taxes while Party B may list only indirect taxes).[83] Although both parties may agree to waive a category of income, a contracting party that decides to omit any or all of the four categories of direct taxes (i.e., income or profits, capital, net wealth and estate, and inheritance or gift taxes) would nevertheless be obligated to respond to requests for information with respect to the taxes listed by the other contracting

---

[81] *Model TIEA*, above note 1 at Art 3.

[82] See *ibid*, Commentary to Art 3.

[83] See *ibid*, Commentary to Art 3 at para 9.

Table 6.3 Article 3 — Taxes Covered

TIEA	Notes
Canada–Anguilla	b, c, d
Canada–Aruba	f, g
Canada–Bahamas	h, i
Canada–Bermuda	b, j
Canada–Cayman Islands	e, j
Canada–Costa Rica	f, g, k
Canada–Dominica	i, l
Canada–Guernsey	m, n, o
Canada–Isle of Man	m, p, q
Canada–Jersey	m, o, r
Canada–Liechtenstein	a, f, s
Canada–Panama	a, f
Canada–San Marino	t
Canada–St Kitts and Nevis	t
Canada–St Lucia	u
Canada–St Vincent and the Grenadines	t
Canada–Turks and Caicos Islands	c, b, v
Canada–Uruguay	a, u
US–Cayman Islands	w

Notes:

a Agreement follows the terms of Article 3(2) in the *Model TIEA*.

b Agreement generally applies to any identical or substantially similar taxes imposed after the date of signature. Although the competent authorities of the parties are to notify each other of any substantial changes to the taxation and related information-gathering measures covered, there is no provision to expand or modify the taxes covered by mutual agreement.

c Canadian taxes covered are income, capital, and goods and services tax.

d Anguillan taxes covered are property tax, stamp duty, accommodation tax, and vacation and residential asset levy.

e Agreement has no provision for mirroring the terms of Article 3(2) in the *Model TIEA*.

f Canadian taxes covered are all taxes imposed or administered by the government of Canada.

g For the foreign contracting party, taxes covered include all taxes imposed or administered by the foreign contracting party.

h Canada and the Bahamas agree that the taxes covered are all existing taxes imposed or administered by the respective government of each contracting party.

i Agreement generally follows the terms of Article 3(2) in the *Model TIEA*. The TIEA shall apply to any identical or substantially similar taxes imposed in addition to or in place of the existing taxes after the date of signature.

j Taxes covered are all taxes on income and on capital imposed or administered by each contracting party respectively.

k Agreement applies to any identical or substantially similar taxes imposed after the date of signature. Competent authorities agree to notify each other of any significant changes that have been made in the taxation laws of the parties. There is no provision to modify the taxes covered.
l Similar to "f" and "g" except with the following limitation: "at the date of signature of this Agreement."
m Canadian taxes covered are taxes on income and on capital imposed or administered by the government of Canada.
n For Guernsey, taxes covered are income tax and dwellings profits tax.
o Agreement applies to any identical taxes imposed after the date of signature in addition to or in place of existing taxes, or any substantially similar taxes if the parties so agree. The competent authorities agree to notify each other of substantial changes in the laws that may affect the obligations of that party under the TIEA. There is no provision to expand or modify the scope of taxes covered.
p For the foreign contracting party, taxes covered are taxes on income or profits.
q Agreement also applies to any other taxes if the parties agree. The competent authority of each party shall notify the other of substantial changes to the laws that may affect the obligations of that party under the TIEA.
r For the foreign contracting party, taxes covered are taxes on income and goods and services.
s Liechtensteinian taxes covered include the personal income tax, corporate income tax, corporation taxes, real estate capital gains tax, wealth tax, coupon tax, estate, inheritance, and gift taxes, and value-added tax.
t Contracting parties agree that the taxes that are the subject of the TIEA are all taxes imposed or administered by each party respectively including any taxes imposed or administered after the date of signature.
u Contracting parties agree that the taxes that are the subject of the TIEA are all taxes imposed or administered by each party respectively including any identical or substantially similar taxes imposed or administered after the date of signature.
v For the Turks and Caicos Islands, taxes covered include stamp duty, passenger tax, and hotel and restaurant tax.
w Taxes covered are federal income taxes plus any other types of taxes as the parties may agree.

party.[84] Further to Article 3(2), the agreement applies automatically to all "identical taxes," and to "substantially similar taxes" if the competent authorities so agree. And further to Article 3(2), the meaning of "identical" should be construed very broadly.[85] Additionally, the taxes

[84] See *ibid*, Commentary to Art 3 at para 8.

[85] See *ibid*, Commentary to Art 3 at para 14.

covered under the agreement may be expanded or modified if the contracting parties so agree.[86]

The definition of taxes for Canada varies between TIEAs, and there is no uniform definition. The definition of taxes for the foreign countries varies widely, dependent in part on the unique characteristics of the socio-economic system of each particular jurisdiction. As many of the Caribbean and the Central and Latin American countries have no income tax and as, further, they have taxes with no corresponding tax in Canada, for example, the tourism taxes, it is unlikely that CRA would have information to exchange that would be of interest to the fiscal authorities in many of these countries.

Not all of Canada's TIEAs parallel Article 3 of the *Model TIEA* in providing a mechanism to incorporate taxes to be covered after the TIEA comes into force. The definition of taxes covered in respect of Canada varies broadly, but in each instance, at a minimum it encompasses federal income taxes, which are generally the taxes at issue with tax evasion. The broadest language in favour of Canada appears in the TIEAs with San Marino, St Lucia, and Uruguay, which cover all taxes imposed by the contracting parties both now and after enactment of the TIEA. The *US–Caymans TIEA* contains language similar to that in many of Canada's TIEAs in that it includes federal income taxes plus the ability to expand taxes covered by the contracting parties through an exchange of letters.

3.4 Article 4: Definitions

Article 4 of the *Model TIEA* provides as follows:

1. For the purposes of this Agreement, unless otherwise defined:
    a) the term "Contracting Party" means country A or country B as the context requires;
    b) the term "competent authority" means
        i) in the case of Country A, ______________________;
        ii) in the case of Country B, ______________________;

[86] See *ibid*, Commentary to Art 3 at para 11.

c) the term "person" includes an individual, a company and any other body of persons;
d) the term "company" means any body corporate or any entity that is treated as a body corporate for tax purposes;
e) the term "publicly traded company" means any company whose principal class of shares is listed on a recognised stock exchange provided its listed shares can be readily purchased or sold by the public. Shares can be purchased or sold "by the public" if the purchase or sale of shares is not implicitly or explicitly restricted to a limited group of investors;
f) the term "principal class of shares" means the class or classes of shares representing a majority of the voting power and value of the company;
g) the term "recognised stock exchange" means any stock exchange agreed upon by the competent authorities of the Contracting Parties;
h) the term "collective investment fund or scheme" means any pooled investment vehicle, irrespective of legal form. The term "public collective investment fund or scheme" means any collective investment fund or scheme provided the units, shares or other interests in the fund or scheme can be readily purchased, sold or redeemed by the public. Units, shares or other interests in the fund or scheme can be readily purchased, sold or redeemed "by the public" if the purchase, sale or redemption is not implicitly or explicitly restricted to a limited group of investors;
i) the term "tax" means any tax to which the Agreement applies;
j) the term "applicant Party" means the Contracting Party requesting information;
k) the term "requested Party" means the Contracting Party requested to provide information;
l) the term "information gathering measures" means laws and administrative or judicial procedures that enable a Contracting Party to obtain and provide the requested information;
m) the term "information" means any fact, statement or record in any form whatever;

n) the term "criminal tax matters" means tax matters involving intentional conduct which is liable to prosecution under the criminal laws of the applicant Party;
o) the term "criminal laws" means all criminal laws designated as such under domestic law irrespective of whether contained in the tax laws, the criminal code or other statutes.

2. As regards the application of this Agreement at any time by a Contracting Party, any term not defined therein shall, unless the context otherwise requires, have the meaning that it has at that time under the law of that Party, any meaning under the applicable tax laws of that Party prevailing over a meaning given to the term under other laws of that Party.[87]

Article 4(1): Definition of "Person" (Table 6.4)

Commentary on Article 4(1): Definition of "Person"

The definition of "person" is intended to be very broad to avoid excluding certain entities or other organizational structures and thereby jeopardizing the object and purpose of the TIEA.[88] In addition to individuals and companies, the definition includes any other organizational structures such as trusts, foundations, partnerships, and collective investment funds or schemes.[89] The standard of Article 4(1) also acknowledges that in countries where an estate is recognized as a distinct entity, it is a "person" as well.[90] The definition of "person" in Canada's TIEAs is generally uniform and identical to that in the *Model TIEA*, and it is similar to that in the *US–Caymans TIEA*.

---

[87] *Ibid* at Art 4.

[88] See *ibid*, Commentary to Art 4 at paras 16, 19, & 20.

[89] See *ibid*: the term "person" also includes organizational structures such as unincorporated associations.

[90] See *ibid*, Commentary to Art 4 at paras 21 and 38.

Table 6.4 Article 4(1) — Definition of "Person"

TIEA	Notes
Canada–Anguilla	a
Canada–Aruba	a
Canada–Bahamas	a
Canada–Bermuda	a
Canada–Cayman Islands	a
Canada–Costa Rica	a
Canada–Dominica	a
Canada–Guernsey	a
Canada–Isle of Man	a
Canada–Jersey	a
Canada–Liechtenstein	a, b
Canada–Panama	a
Canada–San Marino	a
Canada–St Kitts and Nevis	a
Canada–St Lucia	a
Canada–St Vincent and the Grenadines	a
Canada–Turks and Caicos Islands	a
Canada–Uruguay	a
US–Cayman Islands	c

Notes:
a Definition is identical or substantially similar to that in the *Model TIEA*.
b Definition includes "dormant inheritance."
c Definition uses "a natural person" in lieu of "an individual."

Article 4(1): Definition of "Company" (Table 6.5)

Commentary on Article 4(1): Definition of "Company"

The definition of "company" in the *Model TIEA* is identical to that in the *Model Tax Treaty*,[91] and the definition is uniform in Canada's TIEAs in force thus far. The term "company" is not defined in the *US–Caymans TIEA*.

[91] *Model Tax Treaty*, above note 30.

Table 6.5 Article 4(1) — Definition of "Company"

TIEA	Notes
Canada–Anguilla	a
Canada–Aruba	a
Canada–Bahamas	a
Canada–Bermuda	a
Canada–Cayman Islands	a
Canada–Costa Rica	a
Canada–Dominica	a
Canada–Guernsey	a
Canada–Isle of Man	a
Canada–Jersey	a
Canada–Liechtenstein	a
Canada–Panama	a
Canada–San Marino	a
Canada–St Kitts and Nevis	a
Canada–St Lucia	a
Canada–St Vincent and the Grenadines	a
Canada–Turks and Caicos Islands	a
Canada–Uruguay	a
US–Cayman Islands	b

Notes:
a Definition is identical or substantially similar to that in the *Model TIEA*.
b The term is not defined in the agreement.

"Information gathering measures" typically include requiring the presentation of records for examination, gaining direct access to records, copying the same, and interviewing persons having knowledge, possession, control, or custody of pertinent information.[92] Information gathering measures are aimed at obtaining the requested information.[93] The definitions of "information" and "information gathering measures" are uniform in Canada's TIEAs in force thus far, and the definitions in Canada's TIEAs are consistent with those in the *Model TIEA* and similar to those in the *US–Caymans TIEA*.

[92] See *ibid*, Commentary to Art 4 at para 32.

[93] See *ibid*.

Table 6.6 Article 4(1)—Definitions of "Information" and "Information Gathering Measures"

TIEA	Notes
Canada–Anguilla	a
Canada–Aruba	a
Canada–Bahamas	a
Canada–Bermuda	a
Canada–Cayman Islands	a
Canada–Costa Rica	a
Canada–Dominica	a
Canada–Guernsey	a
Canada–Isle of Man	a
Canada–Jersey	a
Canada–Liechtenstein	a
Canada–Panama	a
Canada–San Marino	a
Canada–St Kitts and Nevis	a
Canada–St Lucia	a
Canada–St Vincent and the Grenadines	a
Canada–Turks and Caicos Islands	a
Canada–Uruguay	a
US–Cayman Islands	a

Notes:
a Definitions are identical or substantially similar to those in the *Model TIEA*.

Article 4(1): Definitions of "Information" and "Information Gathering Measures" (Table 6.6)

Commentary on Article 4(1): Definitions of "Information" and "Information Gathering Measures"

The definition of "information" is very broad and includes any fact, statement, or record in any form whatever.[94] "Record" includes, but is not limited to, an account, an agreement, a book, a chart, a table, a diagram, a form, an image, an invoice, a letter, a map, a memorandum, a plan, a return, a telegram, a voucher, and also information maintained in electronic format.[95]

[94] See *Model TIEA*, above note 1, Commentary to Art 4 at para 33.

[95] See *ibid.*

Article 4(2): General Rule of Interpretation (Table 6.7)

Commentary on Article 4(2): General Rule of Interpretation

Only a fraction of the terms used in the *Model TIEA* are actually defined. Article 4(2) is a default rule generally providing that any term used in the TIEA but not defined therein will be given the meaning that it has under the law of the contracting party that is applying the TIEA (unless the context requires otherwise).[96] Canada's TIEAs are generally consistent with the *Model TIEA* in how they address terms that are not defined, and they are generally uniform with one another. The *US–Caymans TIEA* does not have a similar provision.

Table 6.7 Article 4(2) — General Rule of Interpretation

TIEA	Notes
Canada–Anguilla	a
Canada–Aruba	a
Canada–Bahamas	a
Canada–Bermuda	a
Canada–Cayman Islands	a
Canada–Costa Rica	a, b
Canada–Dominica	a
Canada–Guernsey	a
Canada–Isle of Man	a
Canada–Jersey	a
Canada–Liechtenstein	a, b
Canada–Panama	a
Canada–San Marino	a
Canada–St Kitts and Nevis	a
Canada–St Lucia	a
Canada–St Vincent and the Grenadines	a
Canada–Turks and Caicos Islands	a
Canada–Uruguay	a
US–Cayman Islands	c

Notes:
a Article 4(2) is identical or substantially similar to the *Model TIEA*.
b Contracting parties may agree upon a common meaning through their competent authorities.
c Agreement contains no similar provision.

[96] See *ibid*, Commentary to Art 4 at para 38.

3.5 Article 5: EOI upon Request

Article 5 of the *Model TIEA* provides as follows:

1. The competent authority of the requested Party shall provide upon request information for the purposes referred to in Article 1. Such information shall be exchanged without regard to whether the conduct being investigated would constitute a crime under the laws of the requested Party if such conduct occurred in the requested Party.
2. If the information in the possession of the competent authority of the requested Party is not sufficient to enable it to comply with the request for information, that Party shall use all relevant information gathering measures to provide the applicant Party with the information requested, notwithstanding that the requested Party may not need such information for its own tax purposes.
3. If specifically requested by the competent authority of an applicant Party, the competent authority of the requested Party shall provide information under this Article, to the extent allowable under its domestic laws, in the form of depositions of witnesses and authenticated copies of original records.
4. Each Contracting Party shall ensure that its competent authorities for the purposes specified in Article 1 of the Agreement, have the authority to obtain and provide upon request:

   a) information held by banks, other financial institutions, and any person acting in an agency or fiduciary capacity including nominees and trustees;
   b) information regarding the ownership of companies, partnerships, trusts, foundations, "Anstalten" and other persons, including, within the constraints of Article 2, ownership information on all such persons in an ownership chain; in the case of trusts, information on settlors, trustees and beneficiaries; and in the case of foundations, information on founders, members of the foundation council and beneficiaries. Further, this Agreement does not create an obligation on the Contracting Parties to obtain or provide ownership information with respect to publicly traded companies

or public collective investment funds or schemes unless such information can be obtained without giving rise to disproportionate difficulties.

5. The competent authority of the applicant Party shall provide the following information to the competent authority of the requested Party when making a request for information under the Agreement to demonstrate the foreseeable relevance of the information to the request:

   (a) the identity of the person under examination or investigation;
   (b) a statement of the information sought including its nature and the form in which the applicant Party wishes to receive the information from the requested Party;
   (c) the tax purpose for which the information is sought;
   (d) grounds for believing that the information requested is held in the requested Party or is in the possession or control of a person within the jurisdiction of the requested Party;
   (e) to the extent known, the name and address of any person believed to be in possession of the requested information;
   (f) a statement that the request is in conformity with the law and administrative practices of the applicant Party, that if the requested information was within the jurisdiction of the applicant Party then the competent authority of the applicant Party would be able to obtain the information under the laws of the applicant Party or in the normal course of administrative practice and that it is in conformity with this Agreement;
   (g) a statement that the applicant Party has pursued all means available in its own territory to obtain the information, except those that would give rise to disproportionate difficulties.

6. The competent authority of the requested Party shall forward the requested information as promptly as possible to the applicant Party. To ensure a prompt response, the competent authority of the requested Party shall:

   a) Confirm receipt of a request in writing to the competent authority of the applicant Party and shall notify the competent authority of the applicant Party of deficiencies in the request, if any, within 60 days of the receipt of the request.

b) If the competent authority of the requested Party has been unable to obtain and provide the information within 90 days of receipt of the request, including if it encounters obstacles in furnishing the information or it refuses to furnish the information, it shall immediately inform the applicant Party, explaining the reason for its inability, the nature of the obstacles or the reasons for its refusal (Table 6.8).[97]

Table 6.8 Article 5 — EOI upon Request

	Notes					
TIEA	Art 5(1)	Art 5(2)	Art 5(3)	Art 5(4)	Art 5(5)	Art 5(6)
Canada–Anguilla	a	d	e	f	h, i	m
Canada–Aruba	a, q	d	e	f	h	m
Canada–Bahamas	a	d	e	f	h, i	n, p
Canada–Bermuda	a	d	e	f	h, j, k	m
Canada–Cayman Islands	a	d	e	f	h	m
Canada–Costa Rica	a	d	e	f	h	n
Canada–Dominica	a	d	e	f	h	m
Canada–Guernsey	a, b, c	d	e	f, g	h, i, k	o, p
Canada–Isle of Man	a, b, c	d	e	f, g	h, i, k	o
Canada–Jersey	a, b, c	d	e	f, g	h, i, k	o
Canada–Liechtenstein	a	d	e	f	h, i	n
Canada–Panama	a	d	e	f	h	l
Canada–San Marino	a	d	e	f	h	m
Canada–St Kitts and Nevis	a	d	e	f	h, k	m
Canada–St Lucia	a	d	e	f	h	m
Canada–St Vincent and the Grenadines	a	d	e	f	h	m
Canada–Turks and Caicos Islands	a	d	e	f	h, i	m
Canada–Uruguay	a	d	e	f	h, i	l
US–Cayman Islands	a	d	e	f, g	h, r	o

Notes:

a Article 5(1) is identical or substantially similar to the *Model TIEA*.

b Similar to "a," but the requesting party must first exhaust all domestic means as a precondition for a request.

[97] *Ibid* at Art 5.

Table 6.8 (Continued)

c Similar to "a," but the requesting party may make a request only when unable to obtain the requested information by other means without disproportionate difficulty.
d Article 5(2) is identical or substantially similar to the *Model TIEA*.
e Article 5(3) is identical or substantially similar to the *Model TIEA*.
f Article 5(4) is identical or substantially similar to the *Model TIEA*.
g Similar to Article 5(4) of the *Model TIEA* except that it specifies "information regarding" the "legal and beneficial ownership of" instead of just "ownership of."
h Article 5(5) is identical or substantially similar to the *Model TIEA*.
i Similar to "h," but it also requests the period of time for which the information is requested.
j In addition to the information requested in "a", Article 5(5) affirms that there is no obligation on the parties to obtain or provide information relating to a period more than six years before the tax period under consideration or any information unless the applicant party demonstrates that it has pursued all means available except those that would give rise to disproportionate difficulties.
k Similar to "h," but it also requests the reasons for believing that the information is foreseeably relevant to the requesting party's tax administration and enforcement regarding the identified person. Regarding Bermuda, see paragraph 6 of the protocol to Canada's TIEA with Bermuda.[98]
l Article 5(6) is identical or substantially similar to the *Model TIEA*.
m Similar to "l" except that confirmations of receipt are to be immediate and that, if applicable, estimates of needed additional time are to be provided.
n There is no time limit to acknowledge or respond — an elusive "reasonable time" standard.
o There is no time limit to provide the information requested — an elusive "reasonable period" standard.
p There is no time limit to acknowledge or respond — an elusive "use its best endeavours to forward the requested information . . . with the least possible delay" standard. This is a grand failure to follow the *Model TIEA*.
q Agreement authorizes spontaneous EOI under Article 6.
r Similar to "h" except that Article 5(5)(d) imposes a "reasonable" standard on the grounds for the requesting party's belief that the requested information is held in the requested party's jurisdiction, and that the language in Article 5(5)(g) of the *Model TIEA* regarding a statement that the requesting party has pursued all means available in its own territory to obtain the information is omitted.

[98] See *Canada Peer Review Report*, above note 7 at 54.

Commentary on Article 5

Article 5(1) establishes that the requirement to exchange information arises when the information is requested, as distinct from automatic exchange or spontaneous exchange.[99] Under the *Convention between Canada and the United States of America with respect to Taxes on Income and on Capital*, information may be, and is, exchanged in three different ways: upon request, automatically, and spontaneously.[100] Automatic exchange involves information regarding various categories of income having their source in one contracting state and received in the other contracting state being transmitted systematically to the other contracting state.[101] In spontaneous EOI, a contracting state may provide to the other state at its discretion information acquired through an investigation that it views to be of interest to the other state.[102] The commentary to the *Model TIEA* invites the contracting parties to consider expanding their cooperation on information exchange to include both automatic and spontaneous exchanges of information.[103] In addition, Article 5(1) confirms that EOI is not restricted by a dual criminality requirement and that information relating to a criminal matter may not be withheld solely because such matter would not constitute a crime under the laws of the requested party.[104] None of Canada's TIEAs contain a dual criminality requirement restriction of EOI.[105]

The language of Article 5(1) in Canada's TIEAs is consistent with that in the *Model TIEA*, and it is generally uniform throughout Canada's TIEAs. The language of Article 5(1) in Canada's TIEAs is also similar to that in the *US–Caymans TIEA*. It is noteworthy that Article 6 in Canada's

[99] See *Model TIEA*, above note 1, Commentary to Art 5 at para 39.

[100] 26 September 1980 (as amended to the protocols signed on 14 June 1983, 23 March 1984, 17 March 1997, 29 July 1997, and 21 September 2007) at Art 27 (EOI). See also *Model Tax Treaty*, above note 30 at Art 26 (EOI).

[101] See *Model Tax Treaty*, above note 30, Commentary to Art 26 at para 9.

[102] See *ibid.*

[103] See *Model TIEA*, above note 1, Commentary to Art 5 at para 39.

[104] See *ibid*, Commentary to Art 5 at para 40.

[105] See *Canada Peer Review Report*, above note 7 at 56.

TIEA with Aruba permits contracting parties to exchange information on a spontaneous basis.

Article 5(2) requires a requested party to use all relevant information-gathering measures (e.g., local administrative or judicial procedures) to obtain the requested information where the data in its own possession is inadequate.[106] Moreover, Article 5(2) ensures that the obligation to exchange the requested information exists independently of whether the requested party needs the information for its own tax purposes.[107] The language of Article 5(2) in Canada's TIEAs is consistent with that in the *Model TIEA* and uniformly permits information to be exchanged notwithstanding that the requested party may not have a domestic tax interest in the requested information for its own tax purposes.[108] The language of Article 5(2) in Canada's TIEAs is also similar to that in the *US–Caymans TIEA*.

Article 5(3) strives to assist a requesting party with its evidentiary or legal requirements regarding the information that it is seeking (e.g., depositions of witnesses and authenticated copies of original records).[109] To the extent allowable under its laws, a requested party should provide the information in the format requested.[110] The language of Article 5(3) in Canada's TIEAs is consistent with that in the *Model TIEA*, is generally uniform in this regard, and is similar to that in the *US–Caymans TIEA*.

Article 5(4) contains a central undertaking by each contracting party to ensure that its competent authority has the legal means to obtain and provide the information agreed to under the TIEA. Article 5(4) establishes that bank secrecy cannot be used as a legal or public policy barrier to obtaining information held by banks and other financial institutions.[111] In addition, Article 5(4) provides that the contracting parties must have the authority to obtain and provide ownership information, including on legal and beneficial ownership of various legal entities.[112]

[106] See *Model TIEA*, above note 1, Commentary to Art 5 at paras 41–42.

[107] See *ibid*, Commentary to Art 5 at para 43.

[108] See *Canada Peer Review Report*, above note 7 at 55.

[109] See *Model TIEA*, above note 1, Commentary to Art 5 at para 44.

[110] See *ibid*.

[111] See *ibid*, Commentary to Art 5 at para 46.

[112] See *ibid*, Commentary to Art 5 at paras 50–51.

As discussed in Chapter 4, the *Act* provides Canada with sufficient information access powers to enable it to respond to an EOI request under a TIEA.[113] Canada's TIEAs meet the obligation under Article 5(4)(a) of the *Model TIEA* with regard to forbidding a requested jurisdiction to decline to supply information solely for the reason that it is held by a financial institution, nominee, or person acting in an agency or a fiduciary capacity.[114] Also the language of Article 5(4) in Canada's TIEAs is uniform, and it is similar to that in the *US–Caymans TIEA*. Although some of Canada's TIEAs use the terminology "legal and beneficial ownership of" in lieu of just "ownership of," the former is implied in the commentary to the *Model TIEA*.[115]

Article 5(5) recalls the object and scope of the TIEA as set forth in Article 1: the contracting parties are to provide assistance through EOI that is foreseeably relevant to the administration and enforcement of their domestic tax laws. Article 5(5) enumerates the types of information that an applicant party must provide to the requested party to demonstrate the foreseeable relevance of the information requested and so that the request will be consistent with the agreed-to scope of the TIEA and not a fishing expedition.[116] Notwithstanding that Article 5(5) contains important procedural requirements, the parties are called upon to interpret them liberally so that effective EOI is not frustrated.[117]

To meet the foreseeable relevance standard, an information request should generally contain the data enumerated in Article 5(5)(a)–(g) inclusive. The procedural requirements in Article 5(5) refer to information that may be held by any government agency or authority of the requested party.[118] And it is expected that a request should only ever be contemplated when an applicant does not have a convenient means to obtain the

[113] Regarding the *Act*, above note 52, see Chapter 4, Section 11. See also *Canada Peer Review Report*, above note 7 at 51 and 57.

[114] See *Canada Peer Review Report*, above note 7 at 55.

[115] See *Model TIEA*, above note 1, Commentary to Art 5 at paras 50–51.

[116] See *ibid*, Commentary to Art 5 at para 57.

[117] See *ibid*. As an example, a party that is seeking account information but lacks the name of the account holder may be permitted to provide an account number or similar identifying information: see *ibid*, Commentary to Art 5 at para 58.

[118] See *ibid*, Commentary to Art 5 at para 62.

information within its own jurisdiction, and, to the extent applicable, an applicant should explain in its request that the means available to it to obtain the information would give rise to disproportionate difficulties.[119] Incomplete information requests are not within the spirit of the *Model TIEA* and are to be avoided.[120] With regard to information that is requested in a specific form, all of Canada's TIEAs have a mechanism to allow for information to be provided in a specific form to the extent allowable under the domestic laws of the requested jurisdiction.[121]

Although there appear to be variations in the language of Article 5(5) in some of Canada's TIEAs, the OECD's *Canada Peer Review Report* concluded that overall Canada's TIEAs meet the foreseeably relevant standard described in the 2005 commentary to Article 26 of the *Model Tax Treaty* and the 2002 commentary to the *Model TIEA*.[122] The language of Article 5(5) in Canada's TIEAs is mainly uniform although some TIEAs contain the additional requirement that the applicant party justify a request by stating its reasons for believing that the information is foreseeably relevant to its tax administration and enforcement, which is dealt with in Article 1 and ostensibly covered again in Article 5(5). Hence, this additional requirement makes the process more burdensome than it ought to be and potentially provides the requested party with an opportunity to question the completeness or validity of the request.

Article 5(6) is a timing mechanism designed to focus the requested party on dealing with the information request promptly. Thus, the requested party agrees to generally comply with the information request within a ninety-day period, failing which the requested party is to advise the applicant party of any deficiencies in the request (within sixty days) or reasons for its inability to comply with the request.[123] A delayed response may prejudice the applicant party's interests in the relevant case.[124] And notably, Canada's TIEAs with the Bahamas, Costa Rica, Guernsey, the Isle of Man, Jersey, and Lichtenstein deviate from the OECD *Model TIEA*

---

[119] See *ibid*, Commentary to Art 5 at para 63.

[120] See *ibid*, Commentary to Art 5 at para 64.

[121] See *Canada Peer Review Report*, above note 7 at 57.

[122] *Ibid* at 54.

[123] See *Model TIEA*, above note 1, Commentary to Art 5 at para 65.

[124] See *Canada Peer Review Report*, above note 7 at 64.

standard by utilizing an elusive time frame work—"reasonable time" or "best endeavours." These deviations should be considered inconsistent with the purpose, spirit, and objective of the *Model TIEA*. The *US–Caymans TIEA* likewise uses a "reasonable period" standard.

3.6 Article 6: Tax Examinations Abroad

Article 6 of the *Model TIEA* provides as follows:

1. A Contracting Party may allow representatives of the competent authority of the other Contracting Party to enter the territory of the first-mentioned Party to interview individuals and examine records with the written consent of the persons concerned. The competent authority of the second-mentioned Party shall notify the competent authority of the first-mentioned Party of the time and place of the meeting with the individuals concerned.
2. At the request of the competent authority of one Contracting Party, the competent authority of the other Contracting Party may allow representatives of the competent authority of the first-mentioned Party to be present at the appropriate part of a tax examination in the second-mentioned Party.
3. If the request referred to in paragraph 2 is acceded to, the competent authority of the Contracting Party conducting the examination shall, as soon as possible, notify the competent authority of the other Party about the time and place of the examination, the authority or official designated to carry out the examination and the procedures and conditions required by the first-mentioned Party for the conduct of the examination. All decisions with respect to the conduct of the tax examination shall be made by the Party conducting the examination (Table 6.9).[125]

Commentary on Article 6

Article 6(1) is designed to permit officials of the applicant party to conduct their investigation directly in the territory of the requested party provided that the applicant party obtains the prior permission of the

[125] *Model TIEA*, above note 1 at Art 6.

Table 6.9 Article 6 — Tax Examinations Abroad

TIEA	Notes
Canada–Anguilla	a, b
Canada–Aruba	a
Canada–Bahamas	c
Canada–Bermuda	c
Canada–Cayman Islands	a
Canada–Costa Rica	c
Canada–Dominica	a
Canada–Guernsey	c
Canada–Isle of Man	a
Canada–Jersey	c
Canada–Liechtenstein	c
Canada–Panama	d
Canada–San Marino	a
Canada–St Kitts and Nevis	a
Canada–St Lucia	a
Canada–St Vincent and the Grenadines	a
Canada–Turks and Caicos Islands	b, c
Canada–Uruguay	c
US–Cayman Islands	a

Notes:
a Article 6 is identical or substantially similar to the *Model TIEA*.
b Fourteen days' notice in advance of examinations or meetings is to be given.
c Similar to "a" except that tax examinations abroad are allowed "to the extent permitted under [the Contracting Party's] domestic law."
d Agreement contains no similar provision.

requested party and the persons concerned.[126] This procedure should be distinguished from the power of the authorities in the requested party to compel disclosure of any information, which is not encompassed by this rule.[127] This procedure also serves the interests of the requested party, which may have limited resources, by sparing it a potentially costly burden while permitting it to retain full control of the process.[128]

Article 6(2) allows a requested party to permit foreign tax officials to attend a tax examination initiated by the requested party. It is not recommended that an applicant party request to have its representatives present

[126] See *ibid*, Commentary to Art 6 at para 66.

[127] See *ibid*.

[128] See *ibid*.

under this procedure except in rare situations, for example, where the foreign examination is part of a larger investigation concerning domestic enterprises and residents or is of great importance to solving other domestic tax cases of the applicant party.[129] On the whole, the language of Article 6 in Canada's TIEAs is uniform and conforms to that in the *Model TIEA*. The language of Article 6 in Canada's TIEAs is also substantively similar to that used in the *US–Caymans TIEA*.

3.7 Article 7: Possibility of Declining a Request

Article 7 of the *Model TIEA* provides as follows:

1. The requested Party shall not be required to obtain or provide information that the applicant Party would not be able to obtain under its own laws for purposes of the administration or enforcement of its own tax laws. The competent authority of the requested Party may decline to assist where the request is not made in conformity with this Agreement.
2. The provisions of this Agreement shall not impose on a Contracting Party the obligation to supply information which would disclose any trade, business, industrial, commercial or professional secret or trade process. Notwithstanding the foregoing, information of the type referred to in Article 5, paragraph 4 shall not be treated as such a secret or trade process merely because it meets the criteria in that paragraph.
3. The provisions of this Agreement shall not impose on a Contracting Party the obligation to obtain or provide information, which would reveal confidential communications between a client and an attorney, solicitor or other admitted legal representative where such communications are:

    (a) produced for the purposes of seeking or providing legal advice or
    (b) produced for the purposes of use in existing or contemplated legal proceedings.

4. The requested Party may decline a request for information if the disclosure of the information would be contrary to public policy (ordre public).

[129] See *ibid*, Commentary to Art 6 at para 67.

5. A request for information shall not be refused on the ground that the tax claim giving rise to the request is disputed.
6. The requested Party may decline a request for information if the information is requested by the applicant Party to administer or enforce a provision of the tax law of the applicant Party, or any requirement connected therewith, which discriminates against a national of the requested Party as compared with a national of the applicant Party in the same circumstances (Table 6.10).[130]

Commentary on Article 7

Article 7 enumerates the grounds upon which a requested party may decline to provide information in response to a request from the applicant party. The expectation is that in the event of a denial, the requested party will inform the applicant party of the grounds for its decision at the earliest opportunity.[131] Article 7(1) is designed to prevent an applicant party from obtaining information that by virtue of limitations in its own domestic laws, it would itself be unable to obtain.[132] Once again, it can be seen, looking back to Article 5(5)(f), that the applicant party needs to demonstrate in its statement that its request is in conformity with its own domestic laws, the information requested would be obtainable under its own internal administrative process, and the information request conforms with the TIEA.[133]

In this article, some of the agreements repeat information requirements described under the foreseeable relevance standard in Article 5(5). For example, some of Canada's TIEAs (with Guernsey, the Isle of Man, and Jersey) permit the requested party to decline to assist where a statement that the applicant party has pursued all means available in its own territory to obtain the information, similar to that described in Article 5(5)(g) of the *Model TIEA*, is absent. Similarly, in some of Canada's TIEAs, a requested party may also decline to assist unless the applicant party

[130] *Ibid* at Art 7.

[131] See *ibid*, Commentary to Art 7 at para 71.

[132] See *ibid*, Commentary to Art 7 at para 72.

[133] See *ibid*, Commentary to Art 7 at para 76.

Table 6.10 Article 7 — Possibility of Declining a Request

	Notes					
TIEA	Art 7(1)	Art 7(2)	Art 7(3)	Art 7(4)	Art 7(5)	Art 7(6)
Canada–Anguilla	a	b	c	d	e	f
Canada–Aruba	a	b	c	d	e	f
Canada–Bahamas	a	b	c	d	e	f
Canada–Bermuda	a, g	b	c	d	e	f
Canada–Cayman Islands	a	b	c	d	e	f
Canada–Costa Rica	a	b	c	d	e	f
Canada–Dominica	a	b	c	d	e	f
Canada–Guernsey	a, h	b	c	d	e	f
Canada–Isle of Man	a, h	b	c	d	e	f
Canada–Jersey	a, h	b	c	d	e	f
Canada–Liechtenstein	a, g, i	b	c	d	e	f
Canada–Panama	a	b	c	d	e	f
Canada–San Marino	a	b	c	d	e	f
Canada–St Kitts and Nevis	a	b	c	d	e	f
Canada–St Lucia	a	b	c	d	e	f
Canada–St Vincent and the Grenadines	a	b	c	d	e	f
Canada–Turks and Caicos Islands	a	b	c	d	e	f, j
Canada–Uruguay	a	b	c	d	e	f
US–Cayman Islands	a, g, h	b	c	e	e	k

Notes:

a Article 7(1) is identical or substantially similar to the *Model TIEA*.
b Article 7(2) is identical or substantially similar to the *Model TIEA*.
c Article 7(3) is identical or substantially similar to the *Model TIEA*.
d Article 7(4) is identical or substantially similar to the *Model TIEA*.
e Article 7(5) is identical or substantially similar to the *Model TIEA*.
f Article 7(6) is identical or substantially similar to the *Model TIEA*.
g The requested party may also decline to assist where the applicant party would not be able to obtain the information in response to a valid request from the requested party under the TIEA.
h The requested party may decline to assist where the requesting party has not pursued all means available in its own territory to obtain the information except where recourse to such means would give rise to disproportionate difficulty.
i The requested party may also decline a request of the applicant party where the requirements of Article 5 are not met.
j The requested party may also decline a request for information relating to a period more than six years before the tax period under consideration unless such information is held in the territory of the requested party or in the possession or control of a person within the requested party.
k Agreement contains no provision equivalent to Article 7(6) (Non-discrimination).

would be able to honour a similar request from the requested party.[134] Canada's TIEA with Liechtenstein notes that the requested party may decline a request if the requirements of Article 5 (discussed above) are not met, which appears to represent a broader interpretation of the grounds for declining a request under Article 7. Generally, the language of Article 7(1) in Canada's TIEAs conforms with that in the *Model TIEA* and is mostly uniform, with the exceptions noted above. The language of Article 7(1) in Canada's TIEAs is also similar to that in the *US–Caymans TIEA*.

Article 7(2) is designed to recognize the difference between, on the one hand, protected intellectual property (or similar trade, business, industrial, commercial, or professional secrets) (Protected IP) and, on the other hand, information that may be treated as Protected IP under tax haven laws merely because it is held by a person identified in Article 5(4) (relating to, e.g., information held by banks or other financial institutions) or because it is ownership information.[135] In an instance dealing with the former, which is likely to occur infrequently in cases involving records on passively earned income such as interest, a document (e.g., a loan document) may contain Protected IP, and in that case the requested party may decline any portion of a request to keep that Protected IP from being revealed.[136] In an instance dealing with the latter, Article 7(2) expressly prevents the requested party from denying an information request because its domestic laws regard the information as protected in a disguised attempt to evade the new standards opposing bank secrecy. The language of Article 7(2) in each of Canada's TIEAs is generally uniform and consistent with that in the *Model TIEA*.

Article 7(3) deals with a different class of information that is protected from being disclosed under an information request and generally concerns communications made between a client and her lawyer. Under Article 7(3), the following elements are required for attorney-client (or solicitor-client) privilege to apply: the communication is a "confidential" communication (meaning that the client reasonably expected it to be kept secret), it is made between a lawyer and a client, and it is made for

---

[134] See *ibid* at Art 5(5)(f); Section Commentary on Article 5, above in this chapter.

[135] See *Model TIEA*, above note 1, Commentary to Art 7 at para 82.

[136] See *ibid*, Commentary to Art 7 at para 81.

the purpose of seeking or providing legal advice or for use in existing or contemplated legal proceedings.[137] The language of Article 7(3) in Canada's TIEAs is generally uniform regarding the attorney-client privilege and conforms with that in the *Model TIEA*. The language of Article 7(3) in Canada's TIEAs is also generally similar to that used in the *US–Caymans TIEA*.

Article 7(4) provides an extreme exception to the general obligation of a requested party to comply with an information request that otherwise meets the requirements of the TIEA. Under Article 7(4), a requested party may decline to honour a request where to provide the information would contravene a vital interest of the requested party, for example, where a tax investigation by the applicant party is driven by political or racial persecution.[138] Each of Canada's TIEAs contains a similar provision and in this regard is consistent with the *Model TIEA*.

Article 7(5) prohibits a requested party from declining to process an information request merely because the tax claim to which it relates is disputed. Each of Canada's TIEAs contains a similar provision and in this regard is consistent with the *Model TIEA*.

Article 7(6) provides an exceptional circumstance dealing with discrimination based on nationality under which the requested party may decline a request for information. Under this provision, a national of the requested party standing in the identical position as a national of the applicant party should not be subject to discriminatory substantive or procedural tax rules. Hence, this provision is not meant to apply where the tax rules differ on the basis of residence.[139] Each of Canada's TIEAs contains a similar provision and in this regard is consistent with the *Model TIEA*. Except for the paragraph dealing with discrimination against nationals in Article 7(6), the *US–Caymans TIEA* is similar to Canada's TIEAs regarding the grounds for denial of information requests.

---

[137] See *ibid*, Commentary to Art 7 at para 85. Regarding the definition and scope of the solicitor-client privilege under Canadian law, see *Solosky v Canada*, [1980] 1 SCR 821; *Canada (MNR) v Reddy*, 2006 FC 277.

[138] See *Model TIEA*, above note 1, Commentary to Art 7 at para 91.

[139] See *ibid*, Commentary to Art 7 at para 93.

3.8 Article 8: Confidentiality

Article 8 of the *Model TIEA* provides as follows:

> Any information received by a Contracting Party under this Agreement shall be treated as confidential and may be disclosed only to persons or authorities (including courts and administrative bodies) in the jurisdiction of the Contracting Party concerned with the assessment or collection of, the enforcement or prosecution in respect of, or the determination of appeals in relation to, the taxes covered by this Agreement. Such persons or authorities shall use such information only for such purposes. They may disclose the information in public court proceedings or in judicial decisions. The information may not be disclosed to any other person or entity or authority or any other jurisdiction without the express written consent of the competent authority of the requested Party (Table 6.11).[140]

Commentary on Article 8

"If governments are not confident that their taxpayer information will be shared in a fair manner with foreign governments then they may be reluctant to exchange this information, harming efficient sharing."[141] An essential theme echoed by the OECD is that governments would not engage in information exchange if they did not have certain assurances that the information would be used for the purposes agreed to under tax treaties and TIEAs and, further, that once transmitted it would continue to be treated as confidential.[142] The assurances required by these expectations are that (1) the information received by an EOI partner will be treated with the same regard to secrecy as information obtained under its domestic tax laws and that (2) the information received by an EOI

[140] *Ibid* at Art 8.

[141] Arthur J Cockfield, "Protecting Taxpayer Privacy Rights under Enhanced Cross-border Tax Information Exchange: Toward a Multilateral Taxpayer Bill of Rights" (2010) 42 *University of British Columbia Law Review* 420 at 468, advocating appropriate technology solutions and the adoption of a multilateral agreement on taxpayer rights to safeguard transferred tax information with a minimum level of legal protection, including for taxpayer privacy rights, to ensure fairness in exchanges of taxpayer information.

[142] See *Canada Peer Review Report*, above note 7 at 61.

Table 6.11 Article 8 — Confidentiality

TIEA	Notes
Canada–Anguilla	a, b
Canada–Aruba	a
Canada–Bahamas	a
Canada–Bermuda	a, b
Canada–Cayman Islands	a
Canada–Costa Rica	a
Canada–Dominica	a
Canada–Guernsey	a
Canada–Isle of Man	a
Canada–Jersey	a
Canada–Liechtenstein	a
Canada–Panama	a
Canada–San Marino	a
Canada–St Kitts and Nevis	a
Canada–St Lucia	a
Canada–St Vincent and the Grenadines	a
Canada–Turks and Caicos Islands	a, b
Canada–Uruguay	a
US–Cayman Islands	a, b

Notes:

a Article 8 is identical or substantially similar to the *Model TIEA*.

b In addition to "a," Article 9 (Safeguards) generally provides that the rights and safeguards secured to persons by the laws of the requested party (including administrative practice) remain applicable to the extent that they do not unduly prevent or delay effective EOI. This provision potentially provides another mechanism whereby a requested party could block or put up a barrier to the information exchange process under a broad legal concept.

partner will not be disclosed except to persons or authorities concerned with the administration or enforcement of the taxes covered by the agreement (including, as applicable, the determination of appeals and oversight of the aforementioned).[143] The OECD *Canada Peer Review Report* noted that Canada's TIEAs generally conform in this regard with Article 26 of the *Model Tax Treaty* and Article 8 of the *Model TIEA*.[144] The language of

[143] See *ibid.* Section 241 of the *Act*, above note 52, strictly controls the use of taxpayer information obtained for the purposes of the *Act* and is subject to a narrow list of exceptions including disclosure under a tax treaty or TIEA. It contains penalties for violations, including imprisonment for up to one year.

[144] *Canada Peer Review Report*, above note 7 at 63.

Article 8 in Canada's TIEAs is generally identical or substantially similar, and it is similar to that in the *US–Caymans TIEA* (except for the safeguard exception).

The key terms of Article 8 require that any information received under a TIEA by a contracting party must be treated as confidential. The disclosure of this information is restricted to those persons involved in the assessment, collection, or enforcement of, or the determination of appeals relating to, the taxes under the agreement.[145] Although information may be communicated to the taxpayer, the taxpayer's proxy, or a witness, the agreement does not require such disclosure to the taxpayer.[146] And although it is not considered a normal request under the agreement, the applicant party may disclose information to a third party if written consent is given by the contracting party that supplied the information.[147]

3.9 Miscellaneous Provisions

Canada's TIEAs contain additional articles on the following: costs, implementing legislation, language, other international agreements or arrangements, a mutual agreement procedure, entry into force, and termination.

With respect to costs, most of the jurisdictions that have signed a TIEA with Canada agree to sort out costs incurred in providing assistance at the competent authority level. In a few of the agreements, there is the potential to divide the costs into those to be borne by the requested party, or "ordinary" costs, and those to be borne by the applicant party, or "extraordinary" costs, with the expectation that the contracting parties sort this out in advance. The subject of costs as it relates to the broader policy objectives behind TIEAs is examined in more detail in Chapter 3, Section 6.1 and Chapter 11, Section 2, (Recommendations),where challenges like tax havens' resources and profit motives are looked at in relation to the functionality of TIEAs in combatting tax evasion.

The articles dealing with a mutual agreement procedure in Canada's TIEAs almost uniformly grant broad jurisdiction to the competent

---

[145] See *Model TIEA*, above note 1, Commentary to Art 8 at para 94.

[146] See *ibid.*

[147] See *ibid*, Commentary to Art 8 at para 97.

authorities of the contracting parties to resolve difficulties arising out of either the implementation or the interpretation of the agreement.

4 Cooperation through Tax Deharmonization versus Tax Harmonization

An overarching question in the debate on effective EOI and the use of TIEAs arises in connection with the global community's focus on achieving a victory against international tax evasion through cooperation around the implementation of a uniform set of rules and procedures. Professor Dean suggests that countries explore the merits of joining forces and cooperating to tackle international tax problems such as tax evasion through tax deharmonization.[148] Tax harmonization seeks to eliminate differences between tax systems from the perspective of the taxpayer.[149] Professor Dean observes that tax harmonization produces two key benefits: efficiency and legitimacy.[150] Like simplification, tax harmonization can potentially create efficiency by targeting the wasteful expenditures resulting from the complexities that arise with differing tax concepts and rules and that must be navigated by taxpayers operating in multijurisdictional environments.[151] Arriving at the gains of efficiency through cooperation, rather than by competition, leads to a high degree of engagement, commitment, and interaction between regimes that provides a process through which taxpayers and governments can participate in the resulting system.[152] This collaborative process of harmonization can result in an increased sense of legitimacy.[153]

---

[148] Dean, "More Cooperation," above note 37 at 127.

[149] *Ibid* at 139. As using the same language offers no assurance that tax laws will be interpreted and applied in an identical fashion, to achieve true tax harmonization, two or more nations would have to achieve a high degree of uniformity with respect to tax laws, tax rates, and the administration of those laws (*ibid*).

[150] *Ibid* at 150.

[151] *Ibid.*

[152] *Ibid* at 153.

[153] *Ibid.*

Tax deharmonization also attempts to achieve efficiency and legitimacy but without requiring that nations' tax regimes mirror one another.[154] Professor Dean uses the example of two states desiring to introduce a carbon tax. Instead of making the two regimes match one another by issuing identical laws and establishing identical agencies, the two nations could agree to distribute those functions across their boundaries.[155] As with harmonization, the resulting international cooperation would reinforce legitimacy.[156] Professor Dean acknowledges that administrative deharmonization to address offshore tax evasion through TIEAs would present high transaction costs[157] and warns that whether a bargain between two states would be worthwhile would depend largely on the balance between the costs of implementing the arrangement and the benefits that it would produce.[158] A consideration for any tax haven entering into such an arrangement would be the potential losses to its economy that would result from investors fleeing the jurisdiction due to its new commitment to investigate tax cheats.

5 Conclusion

This chapter compared Canada's TIEAs with the *Model TIEA*, each other, and the *US–Caymans TIEA*. Compared with the *Model TIEA*, Canada's TIEAs consistently reflect adherence to the essential elements of EOI specified by the OECD's international standards. There are a select number of variations from those standards, which have been noted in the commentary above, but, overall, Canada's TIEAs support the key elements necessary for effective EOI, such as mechanisms that support effective EOI, a diverse and inclusive network of treaty partners, protection of received information's confidentiality, a process that respects the rights and safeguards of the taxpayer and third parties, and timely responsiveness to requests.

---

[154] *Ibid.*

[155] *Ibid.*

[156] *Ibid* at 154.

[157] *Ibid* at 157.

[158] *Ibid* at 133.

Compared with each another, Canada's in-force TIEAs are in substance fairly uniform across the board in respect of all the key articles examined above. One of the articles in which many differences arise is Article 3, which deals with taxes covered. The differences between Canada's TIEAs regarding Article 3 are notable not so much for their legal impact on effective EOI, which is minimal, but more for the underlying economic distinctions that they call attention to. For example, many of the tax haven jurisdictions appear to lack an income or capital tax (or have income taxes with low rates) but appear to have instead a different stable of taxes like consumption taxes associated with the tourism and restaurant industry and property taxes. Therefore, many of these jurisdictions would seem to have little or no interest in requesting information from Canada regarding their taxpayers because they either levy no income taxes or apply a consumption tax that arises only on their shores. To wit, what possible or likely motivation would the Bahamian fiscal authorities have in contacting CRA regarding assistance with an investigation into a real estate stamp duty tax in the Bahamas, or the Anguillan authorities have in contacting CRA regarding an accommodation tax in Anguilla? The answer is not much. Moreover, as neither the Bahamas nor Anguilla has an income tax, what economic benefit does either of these countries derive from allocating resources to investigate investment income earned by Canadian residents for CRA?

This asymmetry in tax systems between Canada and many of its TIEA partners suggests exploring another possible form of cooperation that is different from the existing uniformity model presented by the TIEA framework. Chapter 3 investigates the problems associated with tax harmonization as represented by TIEAs and considers an alternative approach to combatting international tax evasion that is based on economic considerations that invite tax policy-makers to rethink the benefits principle.[159]

Canada has established, and is currently growing, a network of TIEAs with tax haven and other jurisdictions. As a result of this effort, the

[159] See *ibid* at 144: "The Benefits Principle assigns the right to tax active (business) income primarily to the source jurisdiction, while the right to tax passive (investment) income is assigned primarily to the residence jurisdiction," citing Reuven S Avi-Yonah, "International Taxation of Electronic Commerce" (1997) 52 *Tax Law Review* 507 at 509.

TIEAs in force will enable Canada to request taxpayer information to support its efforts to administer and enforce the tax laws of Canada and in so doing help promote tax fairness at home. Canada's proliferation of TIEAs is a direct consequence of the OECD's harmful tax competition project to advance international standards on transparency and effective EOI and to curb bank secrecy. However, it is also true that Canada's policy toward TIEAs has been motivated, and not in an insignificant way, by considerations relating to Canada's foreign affiliate system and the promotion of favourable tax and business incentives for Canada-based multinational enterprises. Based on Canada's historical record of using treaties to derive tax benefits for businesses and the connection between TIEAs and exempt surplus, it is fair to ask, has Canada really been focusing its policy efforts regarding TIEAs on combatting tax evasion, or has its attention to date been focused on other goals?

At the moment, Canadian TIEA policy appears to be on a trajectory to utilize the TIEA network solely for information by request whereas the United States and others[160] have begun to shift direction away from a pure information by request model and toward a robust automatic EOI or withholding system for dealing with low tax jurisdictions. These observations regarding tax policy and the Canadian TIEA system are further examined and evaluated in Chapter 3, Section 6.1 in looking at the effectiveness of TIEAs in helping Canada achieve stated goals of combatting international tax evasion.

[160] For a list of other countries (e.g., Germany and the United Kingdom) that have moved to an automatic EOI or withholding system, and away from a pure information by request model, in addition to current developments in this area, see Chapter 3, Section 6.1 (e.g. Germany, UK). See also Chapters 8 and 9.

7

Article 26 of the OECD *Model Tax Convention on Income and on Capital*

1 Introduction

This chapter explains Article 26 of the OECD *Model Tax Convention on Income and on Capital.*[1] Canada has over ninety double tax conventions (DTCs) in force that contain an article modelled on Article 26, and the United States has over sixty.[2] As explained in Chapter 6, both Canada and the United States generally reserve the use of DTCs for countries with more complex economies and rely on the use of tax information exchange agreements (TIEAs) for tax havens and smaller jurisdictions. Chapter 6 also explains problems with Canada's international tax policies surrounding the use of DTCs and the relationship between DTCs and the "exempt surplus" rules in the Canadian foreign affiliate tax regime.[3] Additionally, this chapter examines Article XXVII

[1] OECD, Committee on Fiscal Affairs, *Model Tax Convention on Income and on Capital* (Paris: OECD, 1992) (loose-leaf) at Art 26 [convention and commentary together: *Model Tax Treaty*].

[2] A list of Canada's DTCs in force is available online: www.fin.gc.ca/treaties-conventions/in_force-DOUBLEHYPHENeng.asp. A list of US treaties in force is available online: www.irs.gov/Businesses/International-Businesses/United-States-Income-Tax-TreatiesDOUBLEHYPHEN-A-to-Z#.Vlopa_BbY6M.gmail.

[3] See Chapter 6, Section 2.2.

D.S. Kerzner, D.W. Chodikoff, *International Tax Evasion in the Global Information Age*, DOI 10.1007/978-3-319-40421-9_7

on exchange of information (EOI) in the *Convention between Canada and the United States of America with respect to Taxes on Income and on Capital*.[4] A theme of this book is evaluating how well TIEAs and EOI work to combat tax evasion. This chapter refers to an important battle between the United States and Switzerland over the use of the EOI Article in the *Convention between the United States of America and the Swiss Confederation for the Avoidance of Double Taxation with respect to Taxes on Income*[5] to obtain information on US tax cheats with undeclared bank accounts at UBS. The challenges faced by the United States in obtaining taxpayer information on undeclared American account holders evidence important international tax policy issues regarding the efficacy of EOI as a stand-alone tool to combat tax evasion. In pursuing this information from the Swiss, the United States faced legal challenges discussed in detail in Chapter 5. Moreover, the United States faced economic, political, and historical challenges in dealing with Switzerland over EOI. These multiple challenges underscore a key policy problem in dealing with tax havens to combat tax evasion. One of the themes of this research is that these policy challenges continue to be ignored by the OECD and, more recently, by the Global Forum on Transparency and Exchange of Information for Tax Purposes and the G20 in favour of solutions that seek tax harmonization in the form of treaties and model agreements. Finally, this chapter explains the procedures used by both Canada and the United States to obtain information from and exchange information with other governments.

2 Article 26 of the *Model Tax Treaty*

2.1 Introduction

Article 26 of the *Model Tax Treaty* provides as follows:

[4] 26 September 1980 (as amended to the protocols signed on 14 June 1983, 23 March 1984, 17 March 1997, 29 July 1997, and 21 September 2007) [*Canada–US Tax Treaty*].

[5] 2 October 1996, together with a protocol to the Convention, 2 October 1996, S Treaty Doc 105–8, online: www.irs.gov/pub/irs-trty/swiss.pdf [*US–Switzerland Tax Treaty*].

1. The competent authorities of the Contracting States shall exchange such information as is foreseeably relevant for carrying out the provisions of this Convention or to the administration or enforcement of the domestic laws concerning taxes of every kind and description imposed on behalf of the Contracting States, or of their political subdivisions or local authorities, insofar as the taxation thereunder is not contrary to the Convention. The exchange of information is not restricted by Articles 1 and 2.
2. Any information received under paragraph 1 by a Contracting State shall be treated as secret in the same manner as information obtained under the domestic laws of that State and shall be disclosed only to persons or authorities (including courts and administrative bodies) concerned with the assessment or collection of, the enforcement or prosecution in respect of, the determination of appeals in relation to the taxes referred to in paragraph 1, or the oversight of the above. Such persons or authorities shall use the information only for such purposes. They may disclose the information in public court proceedings or in judicial decisions. Notwithstanding the foregoing, information received by a Contracting State may be used for other purposes when such information may be used for such other purposes under the laws of both States and the competent authority of the supplying State authorises such use.
3. In no case shall the provisions of paragraphs 1 and 2 be construed so as to impose on a Contracting State the obligation:

   a) to carry out administrative measures at variance with the laws and administrative practice of that or of the other Contracting State;
   b) to supply information which is not obtainable under the laws or in the normal course of the administration of that or of the other Contracting State;
   c) to supply information which would disclose any trade, business, industrial, commercial or professional secret or trade process, or information the disclosure of which would be contrary to public policy (ordre public).

4. If information is requested by a Contracting State in accordance with this Article, the other Contracting State shall use its information gathering measures to obtain the requested information, even though that other State may not need such information for its own tax purposes. The obligation contained in the preceding sentence is subject to the

limitations of paragraph 3 but in no case shall such limitations be construed to permit a Contracting State to decline to supply information solely because it has no domestic interest in such information.

5. In no case shall the provisions of paragraph 3 be construed to permit a Contracting State to decline to supply information solely because the information is held by a bank, other financial institution, nominee or person acting in an agency or a fiduciary capacity or because it relates to ownership interests in a person.[6]

2.2 Overview of Article 26

Article 26 is the article in the *Model Tax Treaty* that contains the rules governing EOI between the two contracting states. Through the EOI mechanism, a contracting state may acquire necessary facts from the other contracting state to enable it to properly apply the rules of the treaty and to assist it with the administration of its own tax laws.[7] Globalization has not only increased the opportunities for taxpayers to enter into cross-border transactions but also enhanced access to tax evasion and avoidance possibilities.[8] As a result of this danger, the OECD has recognized that fiscal authorities need to work in a coordinated fashion so that taxpayers incur the correct tax liability and pay that amount to the right jurisdiction. To this end, the OECD has recognized that EOI is a key part of international tax cooperation.[9]

Article 26 is part of the OECD *Model Tax Treaty*. Bilateral tax conventions are one of the main legal instruments that provide a legal basis for EOI for tax purposes to take place.[10] In addition, as discussed above, each

[6] *Model Tax Treaty*, above note 1 at Art 26.

[7] See OECD, *Update to Article 26 of the OECD Model Tax Convention and its Commentary* (Paris: OECD, 2012) Commentary to Art 26 at para 1 [*Update to Article 26*]. For further information and elaboration on the EOI rules, see OECD, *Manual on the Implementation of Exchange of Information Provisions for Tax Purposes* (Paris: OECD, 2006), online: www.oecd.org/tax/exchange-of-tax-information/36647823.pdf [*Manual on Implementation*].

[8] See OECD, *Automatic Exchange of Information: What It Is, How It Works, Benefits, What Remains to Be Done* (Paris: OECD, 2012) at 5, online: www.oecd.org/ctp/exchange-of-tax-information/automatic-exchange-of-information-report.pdf.

[9] See *ibid*. See also Section 5, below in this chapter.

[10] See *Manual on Implementation*, above note 7 at 5.

country may establish under its domestic law procedures for providing assistance to a foreign jurisdiction in the form of information exchange.[11] Article 26 permits EOI in both civil and criminal tax matters.[12] Under the *Model Tax Treaty*, each contracting party may designate a senior official (usually in the Ministry of Finance) to serve as the competent authority to bypass normal diplomatic channels and to deal directly with the other.[13]

As explained below, the parameters of Article 26 are contained in five operating paragraphs, each with its own detailed commentary.[14] Notably, Article 26(4), dealing with the obligation to exchange information in situations where the requested information is not needed by the requested state for domestic tax purposes, and Article 26(5), limiting the use of bank secrecy laws to prevent EOI, were added in 2005.[15] As observed in Chapter 6, most of Canada's DTCs have not yet been updated to include either paragraph 4 or paragraph 5.[16]

The *Agreement on Exchange of Information on Tax Matters* and Article 26 of the *Model Tax Treaty* contain the OECD's internationally agreed-upon standards on EOI.[17] In brief, these standards allow for information exchange (1) on request where the information is foreseeably relevant to the administration or assessment of the taxes of the requesting party, (2) regardless of bank secrecy or domestic interest, (3) with respect for taxpayers' rights, and (4) with adherence to strict confidentiality of the information.[18]

Unlike TIEAs, which are stand-alone bilateral agreements, Article 26 is part of a comprehensive DTC, the *Model Tax Treaty*. Another significant difference between TIEAs and Article 26 is that unlike Article 5 of the

---

[11] See *ibid.*

[12] See *ibid* at 6.

[13] See *ibid* at 8.

[14] See *Update to Article 26*, above note 7.

[15] See *ibid*, Commentary to Art 26 at para 4.

[16] See Chapter 6, Section 2.2.

[17] See OECD, *Agreement on Exchange of Information on Tax Matters* (Paris: OECD, 2002) [treaty and commentary together: *Model TIEA*]. For a discussion of the standards and the *Model TIEA*, see Chapter 6.

[18] See OECD, Global Forum on Transparency and Exchange of Information for Tax Purposes, *Information Brief* (Paris: OECD, 2013) Annex I.

Model TIEA, which provides for EOI by request, Article 26 encompasses EOI by request, by automatic exchange, and by spontaneous exchange.[19] Under the *Model Tax Treaty*, tax authorities may also consider the use of Article 25 (Mutual Agreement Procedure) for resolving disputes regarding EOI under Article 26.[20]

2.3 Article 26(1)

Article 26(1) sets forth the main rule on EOI: the competent authorities of the contracting states agree to exchange such information as is foreseeably relevant to the correct application of the provisions of the convention or to the administration or enforcement of the domestic laws concerning taxes of every kind imposed by the contracting states.[21] The foreseeable relevance standard is intended to support EOI in tax matters to the widest possible extent without allowing it to be used for fishing expeditions or for information requests that are not likely to be relevant to an inquiry into the tax affairs of a particular taxpayer.[22]

To establish that a request for information relating to a group of taxpayers is not a fishing expedition, the requesting state must provide information such as a detailed description of the group, the specific facts that have led to the request, an explanation of the relevant law, and an explanation

[19] See *Update to Article 26*, above note 7, Commentary to Art 26 at para 9.

[20] See Gracia María Luchena Mozo, "The Prevention and Resolution of Tax Conflicts within the Framework of International Exchange of Information" (2012) 52:5 *European Taxation* 226, observing that a mutual agreement procedure can provide an effective and efficient method for resolving international tax disputes but that its use depends on the will of the parties.

[21] See *Model Tax Treaty*, above note 1, Commentary to Art 26 at para 5. Where the request relates to a group of taxpayers that are not individually identified, the commentary notes that it will be more difficult to establish that the request is not some type of fishing expedition, on the presumption that the requesting state cannot point to an ongoing tax investigation of a particular taxpayer, which in most cases would prove that the request was not random or speculative (see *ibid*, Commentary to Art 26 at para 5.2). Contracting states may also use an alternative to the foreseeable relevance standard by replacing "is foreseeably relevant" with "is necessary," "is relevant," or "may be relevant" (see *ibid*, Commentary to Art 26 at para 5.3).

[22] See *ibid*. See Gilles Larin & Alexandra Diebel, "The Swiss Twist: The Exchange-of-Information Provisions of the Canada–Switzerland Protocol" (2012) 60 *Canadian Tax Journal* 1 at 31–35, for a discussion of fishing expeditions under British and Canadian caselaw and for a detailed examination of the history of the provisions dealing with EOI between Canada and Switzerland, including the new protocol signed in 2010.

supported by clear facts of why there is reason to believe that the taxpayers in the group have been non-compliant with the law.[23]

2.4 Article 26(2)

Article 26(2) concerns the privacy rights of taxpayers and acknowledges that the feasibility of reciprocity in EOI hinges on each administration's being assured that the other will regard the information received in the course of its cooperation with proper confidentiality.[24] Indeed, where the requested state has doubts that the requesting state can meet its duties regarding confidentiality, the requested state may suspend any EOI under the treaty.[25] Article 26(2) also acknowledges that the maintenance of secrecy in the receiving state is dependent on its domestic laws and calls upon the receiving state to treat information communicated under Article 26 as confidential in the same manner as it would information obtained under its domestic laws.[26]

An additional rule on EOI and secrecy is that information received by a contracting state shall be disclosed only to persons or authorities involved with the administration or enforcement of taxes.[27] Information received by a contracting state is not to be disclosed to a third country in the absence of a provision in the treaty permitting such disclosure.[28] In the 2012 update, Article 26(2) received a new last sentence that recognizes the need for and permits (subject to authorization from the competent authority of the requested state) the use of information received by a contracting state for non-tax purposes such as law enforcement (e.g., to combat corruption, money laundering, or terrorism financing).[29]

---

[23] See *Model Tax Treaty*, above note 1, Commentary to Art 26 at para 5.2.

[24] See *ibid*, Commentary to Art 26 at para 11.

[25] See *ibid.*

[26] See *ibid.*

[27] See *ibid* at Art 26(2).

[28] See *ibid*, Commentary to Art 26 at para 12.2.

[29] See *Update to Article 26*, above note 7, Commentary to Art 26 at para 12.3.

2.5 Article 26(3)

Article 26(3) enumerates limitations on the requested state's obligation to comply with an information request from the requesting state, but these are to be narrowly construed.[30] As a general premise, a contracting state is not required to exceed the limitations of its own legal system to gather information for the other contracting state.[31] Similarly, the requested state is not obligated to honour a request where it would have to carry out administrative measures that would be against the laws or practice of the requesting state — or to supply information that would be unobtainable under the administrative measures of the requesting state.[32] Where notification procedures exist in the requested state for notifying the person who provided the information, such procedures should not be applied in a manner that would frustrate, prevent, or unduly delay effective EOI.[33] Information exchange should not result in the divulging of trade secrets, although this is rarely the case in an investigation to obtain financial information.[34] Additionally, information exchange should respect aspects of lawyer-client communications that are subject to privilege under the domestic laws of the requested state and should not be contrary to public policy (or *ordre public*).[35]

2.6 Article 26(4)

Article 26(4) was added in 2005 to prevent the requested state from refusing to honour a request from the requesting state because the former does not need the information for its own domestic tax purposes.[36]

[30] See *Model Tax Treaty*, above note 1, Commentary to Art 26 at paras 16–19.

[31] See *ibid*, Commentary to Art 26 at para 14.

[32] See *ibid*, Commentary to Art 26 at para 15.

[33] See *ibid*, Commentary to Art 26 at para 14.1.

[34] See *ibid*, Commentary to Art 26 at para 19.2.

[35] See *ibid*, Commentary to Art 26 at para 19.5.

[36] See *Update to Article 26*, above note 7, Commentary to Art 26 at para 19.6.

2.7 Article 26(5)

Article 26(5) was added in 2005 to respond to limitations imposed under bank secrecy laws and to ensure that a requested state could not use the limitations in Article 26(3) to prevent EOI merely because the information is held by a bank or other financial institution.[37] Additionally, Article 26(5) contemplates that requests for information must not be declined merely because such information is held by persons acting in an agency or a fiduciary capacity or because the information relates to an ownership interest in a person (including companies, partnerships, and foundations).[38]

3 EOI Challenges: The United States versus UBS and Switzerland

A key flashpoint between the United States and Switzerland was Article 26 itself of the *US–Switzerland Tax Treaty*, which contained language significantly narrower than the internationally agreed-upon standard. At the time of the onset of the UBS bank scandal (2007–2008), the EOI parameters in both the *US–Switzerland Tax Treaty*[39] and the *Convention between Canada and Switzerland for the Avoidance of Double Taxation with respect to Taxes on Income and on Capital*[40] were significantly more restrictive than those in the internationally agreed-upon standard.[41]

The language in Article 26 of the *US–Switzerland Tax Treaty* made EOI conditional upon its being for (1) a task necessary for carrying out the provisions of the convention or (2) the prevention of tax fraud or the like.[42]

---

[37] See *ibid*, Commentary to Art 26 at paras 19.10 & 19.11.

[38] See *ibid*, Commentary to Art 26 at paras 19.12 & 19.13.

[39] *US–Switzerland Tax Treaty*, above note 5 at Art 26.

[40] 5 May 1997, Can TS 1998 No 15 (entered into force 21 April 1998) at Art 25, online: www.fin.gc.ca/treaties-conventions/switzerland-suisse-eng.asp.

[41] See *United States v UBS AG*, 09-20423 MC-GOLD (SD Fl 19 February 2009) (Amicus Brief of Government of Switzerland), petition to enforce John Doe summons at 7, citing *Bilateral Tax Treaties and Protocol: Hearing before the Committee on Foreign Relations*, 105th Cong 43–44 (1977) (statement of Kenneth J Kies, chief of staff, Joint Committee on Taxation), online: www.bj.admin.ch/dam/data/bj/wirtschaft/fallubs/amicus-brief-e.pdf.

[42] See *United States v UBS AG*, above note 41.

Generally under Swiss law, a person who, to commit tax avoidance, makes use of forged or falsified records so as to mislead tax authorities may be guilty of tax fraud.[43] Tax avoidance, by contrast, involves persons who intentionally or through negligence fail to pay all or a part of their taxes due.[44]

The United States negotiated with Switzerland a 1996 Protocol that was designed to expand the circumstances under which the Swiss authorities could exchange information to include tax fraud or fraudulent conduct in both civil and criminal situations.[45] In 2003, due to apparently rather limited EOI in practice, the United States negotiated a memorandum of understanding with Switzerland that provided descriptions of conduct constituting "tax fraud or the like" and examples of fact patterns dealing with fraud.[46] Although the language in the 1996 convention referred to a narrower scope for EOI, as necessary "for carrying out the provisions of the present Convention," in the 2003 memorandum of understanding, the United States and Switzerland agreed to memorialize additional understandings in reference to Article 26 including the understanding that ". . . Article 26 of the Convention and paragraph 10 of the Protocol will be interpreted to support the tax administration and enforcement efforts of each Contracting State to the greatest extent possible."[47]

The United States has cited a combination of factors that it says have ultimately resulted in the Swiss authorities' declining to exchange information, including lack of proof of fraud, lack of domestic interest in the information being sought, and bank secrecy laws.[48] In 2008, the United

---

[43] See Larin & Diebel, above note 22 at 12–13.

[44] See *ibid.*

[45] See United States, Congress, *Joint Committee on Taxation, Explanation of Proposed Protocol to the Income Tax Treaty between the United States and Switzerland* (Washington, DC: Joint Committee on Taxation, 2011) at 23, online: www.jct.gov/publications.html?func=startdown&id=3791 [JCT, *Proposed Swiss Protocol*]. See also *US–Switzerland Tax Treaty*, above note 5.

[46] See *US–Switzerland Tax Treaty*, above note 5; *Mutual Agreement of January 23, 2003, regarding the Administration of Article 26 (Exchange of Information) of the Swiss–U.S. Income Tax Convention of October 2, 1996*, online: www.treasury.gov/press-center/press-releases/Pages/mutual.aspx [*Mutual Agreement re Article 26*].

[47] *Mutual Agreement re Article 26*, above note 46 at para 1.

[48] See JCT, *Proposed Swiss Protocol*, above note 45 at 34. One area of concern regarding the proposed protocol signed on 23 September 2009 by the United States and Switzerland is the Swiss position on requests that do not name the taxpayer, such as in the context of the UBS case and the John Doe summons, and whether other means of identification will be admissible in the future or whether a more litigious pathway will be required (see *ibid* at 35).

States found itself confronting an epic tax evasion problem involving more than 50,000 US clients of Switzerland's UBS bank, and it was virtually no more able to obtain information on the account holders than it would have been had Article 26 of the *US–Switzerland Tax Treaty* (together with its protocol and memorandum of understanding) not existed. On the facts, the EOI mechanism during the UBS crisis did not work before the use by the United States of the threat of criminal prosecution to bust open the Swiss dam. The failure of the EOI mechanism led the United States to take unprecedented measures to secure taxpayer information in the fight against tax evasion. A more detailed description of the technical aspects of this problem is found in Chapter 5.[49]

4 Article XXVII of the *Canada–US Tax Treaty*: EOI

4.1 Introduction

Article XXVII of the *Canada–US Tax Treaty* provides as follows:

1. The competent authorities of the Contracting States shall exchange such information as may be relevant for carrying out the provisions of this Convention or of the domestic laws of the Contracting States concerning taxes to which this Convention applies insofar as the taxation thereunder is not contrary to this Convention. The exchange of information is not restricted by Article I (Personal Scope). Any information received by a Contracting State shall be treated as secret in the same manner as information obtained under the taxation laws of that State and shall be disclosed only to persons or authorities (including courts and administrative bodies) involved in the assessment or collection of, the administration and enforcement in respect of, or the determination of appeals in relation to the taxes to which this Convention applies or, notwithstanding paragraph 4, in relation to taxes imposed by a political

[49] See Chapter 5, Sections Illusions of EOI: The United States, Switzerland, and UBS and 4.4, regarding the US Department of Justice's use of criminal prosecution against UBS and the Swiss banking industry under the Swiss Bank Program.

subdivision or local authority of a Contracting State that are substantially similar to the taxes covered by this Convention under Article II (Taxes Covered). Such persons or authorities shall use the information only for such purposes. They may disclose the information in public court proceedings or in judicial decisions. The competent authorities may release to an arbitration board established pursuant to paragraph 6 of Article XXVI (Mutual Agreement Procedure) such information as is necessary for carrying out the arbitration procedure; the members of the arbitration board shall be subject to the limitations on disclosure described in this Article.

2. If information is requested by a Contracting State in accordance with this Article, the other Contracting State shall use its information gathering measures to obtain the requested information, even though that other State may not need such information for its own tax purposes. The obligation contained in the preceding sentence is subject to the limitations of paragraph 3 but in no case shall such limitations be construed to permit a Contracting State to decline to supply information because it has no domestic interest in such information.
3. In no case shall the provisions of paragraph 1 and 2 be construed so as to impose on a Contracting State the obligation:

   a) To carry out administrative measures at variance with the laws and administrative practice of that State or of the other Contracting State;
   b) To supply information which is not obtainable under the laws or in the normal course of the administration of that State or of the other Contracting State; or
   c) To supply information which would disclose any trade, business, industrial, commercial or professional secret or trade process, or information the disclosure of which would be contrary to public policy (ordre public).

4. For the purposes of this Article, this Convention shall apply, notwithstanding the provisions of Article II (Taxes Covered):

   a) To all taxes imposed by a Contracting State; and
   b) To other taxes to which any other provision of this Convention applies, but only to the extent that the information may be relevant for the purposes of the application of that provision.

5. In no case shall the provisions of paragraph 3 be construed to permit a Contracting State to decline to supply information because the information is held by a bank, other financial institution, nominee or person acting in an agency or a fiduciary capacity or because it relates to ownership interests in a person.
6. If specifically requested by the competent authority of a Contracting State, the competent authority of the other Contracting State shall provide information under this Article in the form of depositions of witnesses and authenticated copies of unedited original documents (including books, papers, statements, records, accounts, and writings).
7. The requested State shall allow representatives of the requesting State to enter the requested State to interview individuals and examine books and records with the consent of the persons subject to examination.[50]

Article XXVII of the *Canada–US Tax Treaty* is substantially similar to Article 26 of the *Model Tax Treaty*. As discussed below, Article XXVII contains additional provisions dealing with the form of information requested and providing for representatives of the requesting state to conduct examinations in the territory of the requested state. Under Article XXVII, information may be exchanged by the competent authorities upon request, routinely, and spontaneously.[51]

4.2 Articles XXVII(1) and (4): Persons and Taxes Covered

Article XXVII(1) provides that the competent authorities of the United States and Canada may exchange such information "as may be relevant" to support the implementation and administration of the treaty or their respective domestic laws.[52] This is a broader standard than that defined by the previous language, which used the wording "as is relevant." The contracting states may exchange information that relates to persons covered by the treaty under Article I (Personal Scope) as well as non-residents to

[50] *Canada–US Tax Treaty*, above note 4 at Art XXVII.

[51] See *ibid*, 1984 Technical Explanation to Art 27.

[52] See *ibid* at Art XXVII(1).

whom the treaty may not apply. The treaty applies broadly to all taxes imposed by a contracting state, which in the case of Canada include consumption taxes (sales and excise taxes such as the harmonized sales tax (HST)) in addition to income taxes.[53]

4.3 Article XXVII(1): Secrecy

In addition to the domestic provisions concerning confidentiality and taxpayer rights discussed above, the treaty incorporates language concerning confidentiality as well, similar to that in Article 26 of the *Model Tax Treaty*. Information received by a contracting state is to be accorded the same standards of confidentiality and secrecy as information obtained under the tax laws of that state.[54] Moreover, such information is to be disclosed only to persons or authorities involved in the assessment, collection, administration, or enforcement of taxes (including relevant courts and administrative bodies and those involved in the appeals process). The use of this information is restricted to the aforementioned purposes, and it may be disclosed in public court proceedings or in judicial decisions. In addition, as the treaty contains an arbitration mechanism in Article XXVI (Mutual Agreement Procedure), the competent authorities may release such information as is necessary for carrying out the arbitration procedure.

A contracting state may also provide information received from the other contracting state to a state, province, or local authority if the information relates to a tax imposed by that state, province, or local authority that is substantially similar to a national-level tax covered by Article II (Taxes Covered). However, a contracting state may not use this provision to request information on behalf of a state or local government.[55]

4.4 Articles XXVII(2) and (3): Treatment of Requests for Information

Article XXVII(2) explicitly calls upon the contracting states to use their respective regulations for accessing taxpayer information to obtain

53 See *ibid* at Art XXVII(4).

54 See *ibid* at Art XXVII(1).

55 See *ibid*, Technical Explanation, 1995 Protocol to Art 27.

information requested under this provision.[56] As with the standards in the *Model TIEA* and Article 26 of the *Model Tax Treaty*, discussed above, a contracting state is not permitted to decline a request for information from the requesting state because it has no domestic interest in such information. Article XXVII(3) contains the limitations found in Article 26 of the *Model Tax Treaty* that may excuse a contracting state from providing information under this provision.[57] Generally, a contracting state is not obligated to exchange information in circumstances where to do so would be at variance with its own laws and administrative practice, would disclose any commercial or professional secrets, or would be contrary to public policy. Additionally, a contracting state may not be called upon to provide information that is not obtainable under its laws or administrative processes, or those of the requesting state.

4.5 Article XXVII(5): Information Held by Financial Institutions

Article XXVII(5) articulates the standard against the use of bank secrecy laws to deny EOI contained in Article 26 of the *Model Tax Treaty*.[58]

4.6 Article XXVII(6): Form of Information Requested

Article XXVII(6) calls upon a requested state to provide information in the form of depositions of witnesses and authenticated copies of unedited original documents (including papers, books, and accounts) where expressly requested by the requesting state.[59] Article XXVII(6) is similar to Article 26(6) of the *United States Model Income Tax Convention*.[60]

---

[56] See *ibid* at Art XXVII(2).

[57] See *ibid* at Art XXVII(3). See also Section 2.5, above in this chapter, for discussion of the limitations in Article 26(3) of the *Model Tax Treaty*, above note 1.

[58] See *Canada–US Tax Treaty*, above note 4 at Art XXVII(5). See also Section 2.7, above in this chapter, for discussion of Article 26(5) of the *Model Tax Treaty*, above note 1.

[59] See *Canada–US Tax Treaty*, above note 4 at Art XXVII(6).

[60] (15 November 2006) at Art 26(6), online: www.treasury.gov/press-center/press-releases/Documents/hp16801.pdf.

4.7 Article XXVII(7): International Discovery

Article XXVII(7) permits the requesting state to conduct discovery proceedings and examinations of witnesses and books in the requested state with the consent of the persons subject to such proceedings.[61]

5 EOI Administrative Procedures

5.1 Canada

Canada has a long history of EOI under its tax conventions, going back almost seventy years.[62] Canada's tax treaties and TIEAs provide that the Minister of National Revenue (or an authorized representative) is the Canadian competent authority.[63] The commissioner of CRA and the assistant commissioners are delegated to exercise the powers and perform the duties of the competent authority.[64] Also the director of CRA's Competent Authority Services division is authorized to act as the competent authority and has all the powers to administer Canada's tax treaties and TIEAs.[65] In terms of organization, Canada's Exchange of Information Services section (EOI Services) is situated within the Competent Authority Services division and is physically based in CRA's headquarters in Ottawa.[66] Competent Authority Services is part of the International and Large Business Directorate of the Compliance Branch.[67] EOI Services is currently staffed by twelve full-time personnel, including one manager, ten officers, and one administrative assistant.[68]

---

[61] See *Canada–US Tax Treaty*, above note 4 at Art XXVII(7).

[62] See OECD, *Global Forum on Transparency and Exchange of Information for Tax Purposes Peer Reviews: Canada 2011 — Combined: Phase 1 + Phase 2* (Paris: OECD, 2011) at 51, online: http://dx.doi.org/10.1787/9789264110458-en [*Canada Peer Review Report*].

[63] See *ibid* at 42.

[64] See *ibid*. See also *Income Tax Act*, RSC 1985, c 1 (5th Supp), s 8(1).

[65] See *Canada Peer Review Report*, above note 62 at 42.

[66] See *ibid* at 66.

[67] See *ibid*.

[68] See *ibid*.

The principal system used to manage EOI requests is the Exchange of Information Tracking System (EITS), which records all EOI requests and tracks their progress.[69] The manager of EOI Services generally assigns each request to an experienced EOI Services officer.[70] Requests are generally acknowledged by email within three weeks, or sometimes by letter if email is not possible.[71] Requests are divided into simple and complex, based on the type of information requested and whether or not it is available in CRA or public databases.[72] An officer may also contact CRA's Knowledge and Research Centre or federal or provincial government agencies to acquire the information.[73] Generally, simple requests for which the requested information is already available in CRA or public databases are answered within thirty days.[74] Where information must be obtained outside of EOI Services, the request goes to a Tax Services Office (TSO).[75] Currently, there are forty-five TSOs located across Canada.[76] Each TSO has personnel who liaise with the EOI Services officer to obtain the information. A simple request allocated to a TSO generally has a six-month response time while a complex request is expected to be completed within a twelve-month schedule.[77]

---

[69] See *ibid.* An EOI procedure manual provides a step-by-step description of the procedures involved in the course of an EOI request and also lists relevant actions that CRA personnel must take. In addition, there is also an EOI Services reference guide that describes in great detail how Canada handles requests pursuant to automatic and spontaneous EOI mechanisms and to criminal tax matters and those that come through as a result of Canada's involvement in the Joint International Tax Shelter Information & Collaboration Network (see *ibid* at 66).

[70] See *ibid* at 43.

[71] See *ibid.*

[72] See *ibid.*

[73] See *ibid.*

[74] See *ibid* at 64.

[75] See *ibid.*

[76] See *ibid.*

[77] See *ibid.* Regarding measured response times (for substantive and complete responses), in 2009, 42 percent of the requests could be answered within 90 days, 25 percent could be answered within 180 days, and the 33 percent remaining required more than 180 days (see *ibid* at 65). Canada now notifies its partners if a request cannot be responded to within 90 days of receipt, giving a reason for the delay (see *ibid*).

5.2 The United States

As of 2011, the United States had 143 bilateral agreements, including fifty-eight tax treaties, twenty-seven TIEAs, forty-nine mutual legal assistance treaties, and two mutual legal assistance agreements, authorizing EOI under ninety tax agreements.[78] For information exchanges pursuant to tax treaties and TIEAs, the US competent authority, which is designated to interpret treaties and disclose information, is the Secretary of the Treasury.[79] For administrative reasons, the authority to exchange information with other jurisdictions is delegated to the IRS deputy commissioner (international) of the Large Business and International Division.[80] The office of the US Competent Authority comprises some twenty-four personnel who are involved with EOI on a daily basis.[81]

US tax treaties (and some TIEAs) provide for EOI on a specific request basis, an automatic or routine basis, and a spontaneous basis.[82] Spontaneous exchanges initiated by the United States are quite rare, with the United States sending about ten of these annually to its treaty partners.[83] The annual number of incoming spontaneous exchanges is approximately 300, but this number can vary widely.[84] Spontaneous exchanges received by the United States are mostly from developed countries with sophisticated tax systems.[85] The number of incoming specific information exchange requests from 2006 to 2010 was 4,815,[86] and the number of outgoing specific information exchange requests from 2006 to 2010

[78] See United States, Government Accountability Office, *Report to the Permanent Subcommittee on Investigations, Committee on Homeland Security and Governmental Affairs, U.S. Senate: Tax Administration — IRS's Information Exchanges with Other Countries Could Be Improved through Better Performance Information* (Washington, DC: Government Accountability Office, 2011) at 12, online: http://www.gao.gov/assets/590/585299.pdf [*2011 GAO Report on Information Exchange*].

[79] See *ibid* at 6.

[80] See *ibid.*

[81] See OECD, *Global Forum on Transparency and Exchange of Information for Tax Purposes Peer Reviews: United States 2011 — Combined: Phase 1 + Phase 2* (Paris: OECD, 2011) at 62, online: http://dx.doi.org/10.1787/9789264115064-en [*US Peer Review Report*].

[82] See *2011 GAO Report on Information Exchange*, above note 78 at 16–18.

[83] See *ibid* at 24.

[84] See *ibid.*

[85] See *ibid.*

[86] See *ibid* at 21 (inbound requests may involve multiple taxpayers).

was 1,022.[87] In total, between 2006 and 2010, the IRS closed out over 5,000 incoming and outgoing requests with some seventy-five treaty partners.[88] Requests for corporate records, tax return information, and third-party interviews typically composed just under 80 percent of the incoming exchanges, with requests for bank records making up 6 percent of incoming exchanges, while requests for corporate records, tax return information, and bank records composed just under 80 percent of outgoing exchanges.[89] As of 2011, the United States was engaged in automatic exchange of information (Automatic Exchange) with some twenty-five countries, sending approximately 2.5 million records annually to other countries and receiving approximately 2.1 million records annually from treaty partners.[90]

The administrative procedures dealing with specific information exchange are generally divided between those dealing with incoming requests and those dealing with outgoing requests.[91] These requests are processed by IRS tax attachés or IRS Exchange of Information and IRS Overseas Operations (together: EOI/OO).[92] The IRS has four overseas duty posts in Europe and Asia and one domestic duty post in Plantation, Florida.[93] Each foreign duty post (in Beijing, Frankfurt, London, and Paris) is headed by a tax attaché while the domestic duty post is headed by a revenue service representative. These personnel provide oversight relating to the standards on EOI contained in the various tax agreements.[94] Requests for information involving Australia, Canada, France, Japan, and New Zealand are processed through EOI/OO in Washington, DC.[95]

Incoming requests for specific information involve the following steps:[96]

---

[87] See *ibid.*

[88] See *ibid* at 22.

[89] See *ibid.*

[90] See *ibid* at 23.

[91] See *ibid* at 8: request activity is concentrated in about ten countries, which account for almost 70 percent of all requests.

[92] See *ibid.*

[93] See *ibid.*

[94] See *ibid.*

[95] See *ibid.*

[96] See *ibid*, Appendix III.

1) The request is received from a foreign competent authority by the US competent authority.[97]
2) The US competent authority evaluates the request and assigns it to the appropriate division.
3) Where feasible, the requested information is obtained by an IRS revenue agent or examiner (and possibly the Department of Justice) and sent to the US competent authority.[98]
4) The US competent authority sends a formal response to the foreign competent authority.

Outgoing requests for specific information involve the following steps:[99]

1) An IRS revenue agent or examiner identifies a need for information, which is transmitted to the US competent authority.[100]
2) The US competent authority prepares a formal request letter and sends it to the foreign competent authority.
3) The foreign competent authority receives the request, prepares a formal response, and sends it back to the US competent authority.

---

[97] Incoming requests must contain the following: specific identification of the taxpayer, an itemized list of specific information requested, a detailed narrative identifying the tax nexus of the relevance of the information sought to the taxpayer and the issues examined, and an explanation of how the request for transactions, facts, or documents pertains to a tax or a tax liability covered by a tax treaty or a TIEA (see *ibid*). More recently, a valid request for information will not always require the name of a particular taxpayer under examination (see *ibid* at 17).

[98] See *ibid*, Appendix III: information results may be incomplete, so a status update is provided at sixty-day intervals until the request is resolved.

[99] See *ibid*.

[100] The agent or examiner must prepare a memorandum justifying the request and containing the following: the name of the taxpayer in question, the requester's name and phone number and the address or fax number where the response should be sent, any background information that should not be sent to a foreign competent authority, any statutory, court, or other dates by which the information is required, and whether the request includes grand jury information (see *ibid*). An additional outgoing attachment must contain the following: the name and address of the taxpayer in question, the type of tax and tax years involved (fiscal/calendar), evidence that an investigation is being conducted, the location of the information and why the United States believes that it is there, the specific information needed, how the information is relevant to the investigation, any statutory, court, or other dates by which the information is required, and any documentation certification requirements (see *ibid*).

4) The US competent authority receives the response and sends it to the IRS revenue agent or examiner (or the Department of Justice).

With regard to the approximately 1000 cases that the United States responds to each year, it reports that it has fully responded to more than 50 percent of specific requests within 90 days, to more than 75 percent within 180 days, and to more than 91 percent within a year.[101] The IRS uses a database that is available to personnel working on EOI cases known as the Integrated Data Retrieval System (IDRS).[102] This data system maintains the federal income tax accounts of all taxpayers and their filing and payment status in the United States. Access to the system is on a need-to-know basis only.[103]

6 Miscellaneous

In addition to the primary administrative and international avenues that both Canada and the United States may pursue to obtain foreign-based taxpayer information, there are other channels through which such information may be acquired.

6.1 International Organizations

In addition to their involvement with the *Convention on Mutual Administrative Assistance in Tax Matters*[104] and The Egmont Group of Financial Intelligence Units,[105] both Canada and the United States

---

[101] See *US Peer Review Report*, above note 81 at 86.

[102] See *ibid* at 89.

[103] See *ibid*. The IRS also maintains a section on EOI in its *Internal Revenue Manual* (4.60.1) (see *ibid*).

[104] Council of Europe & OECD, *Convention on Mutual Administrative Assistance in Tax Matters*, 25 January 1988, EurTS No 127. For a discussion of the convention, see Chapter 8.

[105] The group is composed of over 151 members, or national financial intelligence units. It seeks to fight against money laundering and terrorism financing through EOI and cooperation: see The Egmont Group of Financial Intelligence Units, "About," online: http://www.egmontgroup.org/about.

participate in the Joint International Tax Shelter Information & Collaboration Network. The primary aim of the JITSIC Network is to identify and stop abusive tax avoidance transactions and arrangements.[106] Canada and the United States also promote information exchange through their treaty network as members of the Pacific Association of Tax Administrators.[107] And both Canada and the United States have entered into bilateral agreements with other jurisdictions pertaining to assistance in criminal matters.[108] The United States also exchanges information with treaty partners under the Simultaneous Examination Program and Simultaneous Criminal Investigation Program.[109]

6.2 Whistleblowers and Leaks

Both Canada and the United States have benefited from information regarding offshore accounts from insiders and whistleblowers.[110] Under the *Internal Revenue Code*, the IRS is authorized to pay rewards to whistle-

[106] See Joint International Tax Shelter Information Centre, *Memorandum of Understanding*, online: www.irs.gov/pub/irs-utl/jitsic-finalmou.pdf.

[107] For a detailed description of this organization, see Jinyan Li, Arthur Cockfield, & J Scott Wilkie, *International Taxation in Canada — Principles and Practices*, 2d ed (Markham, ON: LexisNexis, 2011) at 393.

[108] The United States has entered into approximately forty-nine mutual legal assistance treaties (MLATs): see *2011 GAO Report on Information Exchange*, above note 78 at 12. Unlike tax treaties or TIEAs, the focus of assistance under an MLAT, including on tax matters, is on the investigation, prosecution, and prevention of criminal offences, or criminal proceedings (see *ibid*).

[109] See *ibid* at 7. In circumstances where the United States and a treaty partner have common issues regarding the examination or investigation of a taxpayer, officials may meet to discuss aspects of the examination or investigation such as audit plans or information needs (see *ibid*).

[110] In February 2008, a former employee of LGT Bank in Liechtenstein provided German authorities with data on hundreds of accounts at LGT Bank, causing the bank scandal scene to erupt: see JCT, *Proposed Swiss Protocol*, above note 45 at 24. The UBS scandal unfolded in May 2008 with the leak by informant Bradley Birkenfeld: see Edvard Pettersson, "Ex–UBS Banker Sues Olenicoff for Malicious Lawsuit" *Bloomberg* (5 December 2012), online: www.bloomberg.com/news/articles/2012-12-05/exubs-banker-sues-olenicoff-for-malicious-lawsuit: Birkenfeld was a former UBS banker who had managed $20 billion of US client wealth and assisted his clients in evading IRS reporting requirements; he provided important information to the US Department of Justice and later obtained a whistleblower award of $104 million. In April 2013, a very large leak of data regarding about 120,000 offshore bank accounts, including 450 held by Canadian residents, was revealed by the International Consortium of Investigative Journalists, based in Washington, DC: see Janet McFarland & Bill Curry, "Banking: Document Leak Reveals Widespread Use of Tax Havens" *Globe and Mail* (4 April 2013), online: http://fw.to/YW5XUuW.

blowers, and the IRS maintains a Whistleblower Office.[111] CRA unveiled its own whistleblower program in 2013, the Stop International Tax Evasion Program.[112] The recent leaks also appear to have had an influence on European governments' shifting support to Automatic Exchange.[113]

6.3 Treaty Relief and Compliance Enhancement (TRACE) Program

In another separate, but related, development, the OECD has created a qualified intermediary–style withholding program, the treaty relief and compliance enhancement (TRACE) program, aimed at standardizing the procedures for claiming reduced withholding under treaties for portfolio investments.[114] As the OECD has observed, claiming such relief under the more than 3,000 tax treaties can be very resource consuming and often does not happen.[115] The program allows "authorized intermediaries" (e.g., financial institutions) to obtain reduced rates of withholding under tax treaties or domestic law on a pooled basis for their portfo-

---

[111] *Internal Revenue Code*, USC 26 (1986) of 1986, as amended, and the *Treasury Regulations* issued thereunder at Chapter 4, § 7623. For a discussion of the IRS Whistleblower Office, see Scott D Michel, Zhanna A Ziering, & Young Ran Kim "U.S. Offshore Account Enforcement Issues" (2014) 16 *Journal of Tax Practice & Procedure* 65 at 68–69.

[112] See CRA, "Informant Leads Program," online: www.cra-arc.gc.ca/leads/.

[113] See David Jolly, "Group of 20 Supports Sharing Bank Data to End International Tax Evasion" *New York Times* (20 April 2013) B6, online: http://nyti.ms/1Qsti1R: the leak by the International Consortium of Investigative Journalists caused public outrage regarding certain high-profile European political figures.

[114] See OECD, Centre for Tax Policy and Administration, "OECD Releases System to Reduce Compliance Cost and Facilitate Cross-border Investment" (Paris: OECD, 2013), online: www.oecd.org/ctp/system-to-reduce-compliance-cost-facilitate-cross-border-investment.htm ["OECD Releases System"]: the system was developed after many years of cooperation between the OECD, the European Union, governments, and businesses. In January 2013, the OECD approved the *TRACE Implementation Package for the Adoption of the Authorized Intermediary System*, which contains documents and forms that can be used by any country wishing to implement TRACE's unique system for authorized intermediaries: see OECD, "Treaty Relief and Compliance Enhancement (TRACE) — Implementation Package Approved by CFA" (Paris: OECD, 2013), online: www.oecd.org/ctp/exchange-of-tax-information/treatyreliefandcomplianceenhancement-trace.htm. For a discussion of the US qualified intermediary system, see Chapter 5, Section Background on the US Qualified Intermediary (QI) System.

[115] See "OECD Releases System," above note 114.

lio investor customers.[116] Moreover, it is hoped that through the use of Automatic Exchange protocols described in the *TRACE Implementation Package*, the source country will be able to more easily verify the entitlement of the payee to treaty benefits and that the residence country will be able to more easily verify the income reporting of the payee.[117]

7 Conclusion

The EOI article in the DTCs entered into by both Canada and the United States enables CRA and the IRS to engage fiscal authorities in treaty partner jurisdictions to use their administrative procedures to assist with examinations and audits. The IRS may use the procedures described above to request that CRA obtain information in Canada using CRA's administrative and enforcement powers, described in Chapter 4. As a result, combining the information exchange powers under Article XXVII of the *Canada–US Tax Treaty* with its own enforcement powers, described in Chapter 5, the IRS has extraordinary information-gathering powers with respect to taxpayers that it is investigating either as part of a civil audit or examination or as part of a criminal investigation. It would behoove professionals who are advising delinquent filers in Canada with US tax and reporting issues to explain to them the extraterritorial powers available to the IRS to obtain information on taxpayers in its gunsights. As detailed further in Chapter 9, the fact that an RRSP or RRIF may be excluded from being reported under the *Foreign Account Tax Compliance Act*[118] is immaterial if the IRS has the taxpayer's information, enabling it to make a treaty request under Article XXVII.

---

[116] See OECD, *TRACE Implementation Package for the Adoption of the Authorized Intermediary System* (Paris: OECD, 2013) at 4, online: www.oecd.org/ctp/exchange-of-tax-information/TRACE_Implementation_Package_Website.pdf [*TRACE Implementation Package*]. However, unlike the US qualified intermediary system, which does not require the disclosure of certain individuals to the withholding agent or to the IRS, the *TRACE Implementation Package*, *ibid* at 5, requires that an intermediary claiming benefits on a pooled basis provide to the source country tax administrators on an annual basis (rather than at the time of the payment) investor-specific information about the beneficial owners of the income.

[117] See *ibid*. The *TRACE Implementation Package*, *ibid* at 4–6, describes procedures that an authorized intermediary must follow to comply with the disclosure requirements.

[118] Enacted by Congress as part of the *Hiring Incentives to Restore Employment (HIRE) Act*, Public Law 111-147, and signed into law by the president on 18 March 2010.

Further Readings

Kerzner, David S, Vitaly Timokhov, & David W Chodikoff, eds. *The Tax Advisor's Guide to the Canada–U.S. Tax Treaty* (Toronto: Thomson Reuters Carswell, 2008) (loose-leaf).

Larin, Gilles, & Alexandra Diebel. "The Swiss Twist: The Exchange-of-Information Provisions of the Canada–Switzerland Protocol" (2012) 60 *Canadian Tax Journal* 1.

McCracken, Sara K. "Going, Going, Gone. .. Global: A Canadian Perspective on International Tax Administration Issues in the 'Exchange-of-Information Age'" (2002) 50 *Canadian Tax Journal* 1869.

Oberson, Xavier. *International Exchange of Information in Tax Matters: Towards Global Transparency*, (Cheltenham, UK: Edward Elgar, 2015)

Schenk-Geers, Tonny. *International Exchange of Information and the Protection of Taxpayers* , (Alphen aan den Rijn, NL: Kluwer Law International, 2009).

8

Automatic Exchange of Information

1 Introduction, Background, and Policy Considerations

This chapter provides important background to automatic exchange of information (Automatic Exchange) and examines key policy considerations regarding the new standard. As the OECD rules and guidance on Automatic Exchange run in the hundreds of pages, dealing with the subject at length is beyond the scope of this chapter. Instead, this chapter provides an overview of the framework for Automatic Exchange, which will not only be of importance to financial institutions, funds, and financial service providers but will also be of immense importance to lawyers, accountants, and financial planners in advising their private clients. Due to the broad scope of the rules affecting trusts, professionals advising private clients will want to understand the implications of the rules for their clients' trust structures as soon as possible.

Article 26 of the OECD *Model Tax Convention on Income and on Capital*[1] provides for three main forms of information exchange: upon

[1] OECD, Committee on Fiscal Affairs, *Model Tax Convention on Income and on Capital*, (Paris: OECD, 1992) (loose-leaf) at Art 26 [convention and commentary together: *Model Tax Treaty*].

D.S. Kerzner, D.W. Chodikoff, *International Tax Evasion in the Global Information Age*, DOI 10.1007/978-3-319-40421-9_8

request, automatic (or routine), and spontaneous. Automatic Exchange typically involves the systematic and periodic transmission of bulk taxpayer information from the source state to the residence state.[2] This information exchange generally concerns details of certain categories of income (e.g., interest, dividends, royalties, salaries, and pensions) arising in the source state and involving many individual cases.[3] The OECD describes Automatic Exchange as a process comprising the following seven steps:[4]

1) Payor or paying agent collects information from the taxpayer or self-generates it.
2) Payor or paying agent reports information to the tax authorities.
3) Tax authorities consolidate information by country of residence.
4) Information is encrypted, bundled, and sent to the tax authorities in the residence country.
5) Information is received and decrypted.
6) Residence country begins a matching process on the information received.
7) Residence country analyzes the results and takes appropriate compliance action.

In 2013, the G20 announced its commitment to seeing Automatic Exchange become the new global standard by the end of 2015.[5] In

[2] See OECD, *Manual on the Implementation of Exchange of Information Provisions for Tax Purposes* (Paris: OECD, 2006) at 3, online: www.oecd.org/tax/exchange-of-tax-information/36647823.pdf [*Manual on Implementation*]; OECD, *Automatic Exchange of Information: What It Is, How It Works, Benefits, What Remains to Be Done* (Paris: OECD, 2012) at 7, online: www.oecd.org/ctp/exchange-of-tax-information/automatic-exchange-of-information-report.pdf [*Automatic Exchange of Information*].

[3] See *Manual on Implementation*, above note 2 at 3.

[4] *Automatic Exchange of Information*, above note 2 at 9. In a survey conducted by the OECD (in which both Canada and the United States participated), all thirty-eight countries noted that they received information automatically from treaty partners, and thirty-three (87 percent) of them said that they sent information automatically to treaty partners (Denmark sent information automatically to seventy countries) (see *ibid* at 15). Five countries each reported receiving records relating to more than EUR 15 billion in a particular year, while most countries reported exchanging information relating to billions of euros (see *ibid* at 17).

[5] See G20, Communiqué, "G20 Meeting of Finance Ministers and Central Bank Governors" (20 July 2013), online: www.g20.utoronto.ca/2013/2013-0720-finance.html; Editorial, "The Group of 20 Tackles Tax Avoidance" *New York Times* (6 September 2013) A22, online: http://nyti.ms/1O0dgwK [NY Times Editorial, "G20 Tackles Tax Avoidance"].

2014, the G20 finance ministers endorsed the Common Reporting Standard for automatic exchange of tax information (CRS).[6] Just a few years earlier, in 2010, the OECD had recognized information exchange upon request as the universal standard.[7] The exchange upon request standard was largely implemented through the signing of hundreds of tax information exchange agreements (TIEAs).[8] Between 2009 and 2012 alone, more than 800 TIEAs were signed.[9] Moreover, since 2009, more than 1,500 exchange of information (EOI) relationships have been established that provide for EOI in accordance with the standards resulting from the work of the Global Forum on Transparency and Exchange of Information for Tax Purposes (Global Forum).[10] Also as a result of the work of the Global Forum, 124 peer review reports (making 818 recommendations) concerning 100 jurisdictions have been completed and published.[11] By 2013, 120 jurisdictions had committed to the OECD's international standards on transparency and EOI upon request.[12]

While the effectiveness of TIEAs is evaluated in Chapter 3, a chief complaint about TIEAs is that they require tax authorities to already have

---

[6] See OECD, *Standard for Automatic Exchange of Financial Account Information in Tax Matters* (Paris: OECD, 2014) at 10, online: http://dx.doi.org/10.1787/9789264216525-en [*Standard for Automatic Exchange*]; OECD, "Common Reporting Standard" & "Commentaries on the Common Reporting Standard" in OECD, *Standard for Automatic Exchange, ibid*, 29 (standard) and 93 (commentaries) [standard and commentaries together: CRS].

[7] See OECD, *Promoting Transparency and Exchange of Information for Tax Purposes* (Paris: OECD, 2010) at 2, online: www.oecd.org/newsroom/44431965.pdf.

[8] See *ibid.*

[9] See OECD, *Tax and Development: Draft Practical Guide on Exchange of Information for Developing Countries* (Paris: OECD, 2012) at 5, online: www.g20dwg.org/documents/pdf/view/306/.

[10] See OECD, *The Global Forum on Transparency and Exchange of Information for Tax Purposes: Information Brief* (Paris: OECD, 2013) at 4, online: http://www.oecd.org/tax/transparency/global_forum_background%20brief.pdf [*Global Forum Information Brief 2013*]. See also OECD, *Global Forum on Transparency and Exchange of Information for Tax Purposes: Progress Report to the G20 Leaders — Global Forum Update on Effectiveness and On-going Monitoring* (Paris: OECD, 2013) Executive Summary, online: http://www.oecd.org/tax/transparency/progress_report__G20.pdf [*Global Forum Update on Effectiveness*].

[11] See *Global Forum Information Brief 2013*, above note 10 at 4. See also *Global Forum Update on Effectiveness*, above note 10, Executive Summary.

[12] See OECD, *A Step Change in Tax Transparency: OECD Report for the G8 Summit* (Paris: OECD, 2013) at 5, n 2, online: www.oecd.org/ctp/exchange-of-tax-information/taxtransparency_G8report.pdf [*Step Change in Tax Transparency*].

much of the information that they are seeking.[13] Put another way, TIEAs greatly inhibit the ability of tax authorities to uncover cheating because TIEAs permit tax officials to request information only when they suspect that taxpayers are lying or concealing their wealth offshore.[14] The effectiveness of TIEAs as a means to reduce the financial flows into tax havens has also been called into question.[15] Related to the question of whether TIEAs are an effective tool in the battle against tax evasion, the Global Forum is administering its own test to validate the work that it has done for more than a decade.[16] The Global Forum has stated that the real test of whether or not it has achieved its goal lies in whether it has improved transparency and made EOI more effective in practice.[17]

The OECD has touted the Automatic Exchange process as offering many benefits, and views it as a tool to counter offshore tax evasion by increasing the voluntary compliance rate on foreign earned income going forward.[18] Some of the notable benefits that may accompany Automatic Exchange include the following:[19]

- assistance for tax authorities in identifying tax evasion involving income earned on foreign investments[20]

[13] See The Economist, "Tax Transparency: Automatic Response — The Way to Make Exchange of Tax Information Work" *Economist* (16 February 2013), online: http://econ.st/VQtEn9 [Economist, "Tax Transparency"]. International taxation deals with the tax aspects of international commerce and investment. See also Jinyan Li, Arthur Cockfield, & J Scott Wilkie, *International Taxation in Canada — Principles and Practices*, 2d ed (Markham, ON: LexisNexis, 2011) at 380: without evidence that a taxpayer is hiding income offshore, there will be no grounds for making a request, thereby complicating Canadian investigations into offshore tax evasion; Alicja Brodzka & Sebastiano Garufi, "The Era of Exchange of Information and Fiscal Transparency: The Use of Soft Law Instruments and the Enhancement of Good Governance in Tax Matters" (2012) 52:8 *IBFD European Tax Journal* 394: the international standard is inadequate to effectively tackle international tax evasion because the only form of EOI is EOI upon request, which presumes that the requesting state already knows what it is looking for.

[14] See NY Times Editorial, "G20 Tackles Tax Avoidance," above note 5.

[15] See Economist, "Tax Transparency," above note 13.

[16] See *Global Forum Update on Effectiveness*, above note 10, Executive Summary.

[17] See *ibid.*

[18] See *Automatic Exchange of Information*, above note 2 at 19–20.

[19] See *ibid.*

[20] See *ibid* at 20: Norway and Denmark reported that in certain studies Automatic Exchange had revealed rates of non-compliance of 38.7 percent and 40 percent respectively.

- assistance for tax authorities in identifying tax evasion involving principal amounts that represent undeclared income of a taxpayer, such as business income
- assistance for tax authorities in detecting the non-compliance of taxpayers with no prior history of tax evasion or tax fraud
- deterrence of taxpayers that may be contemplating tax evasion
- education of taxpayers regarding foreign reporting and increasing levels of voluntary compliance
- increased revenues
- increased fairness in a system where all taxpayers comply with their tax responsibilities

A number of international developments have helped propel Automatic Exchange to the centre of the global financial stage. Ironically, the most significant of these is the much-criticised *Foreign Account Tax Compliance Act* regime implemented by the United States.[21] Other global developments embracing Automatic Exchange are reflected in the April 2013 agreement between France, Germany, Italy, Spain, and the United Kingdom to exchange *FATCA*-type information between themselves in addition to exchanging such information with the United States.[22]

[21] Subtitle A of Title V of the *Hiring Incentives to Restore Employment Act of 2010*, Pub L No 111–147 enacted on 18 March 2010 [*FATCA*]. According to Pascal Saint-Amans, director of the Centre for Tax Policy at the OECD, with regard to Automatic Exchange, "FATCA has been a game-changer": see David Jolly, "Group of 20 Supports Sharing Bank Data to End International Tax Evasion" *New York Times* (13 April 2013) B6, online: http://nyti.ms/1Qsti1R. See also *Global Forum Information Brief 2013*, above note 10 at 5, noting that *FATCA* has been a key catalyst for Automatic Exchange. For a description of *FATCA*, see Chapter 9. See also David Jolly & Brian Knowlton, "Law to Find Tax Evaders Denounced" *New York Times* (26 December 2011) B1, online: http://nyti.ms/1I7SMjg, noting that the USD 8 billion that the US Department of the Treasury hopes to bring in over the next ten years is disproportional to the expected implementation costs for foreign institutions, and also citing a variety of critics, including Professor H David Rosenbloom, who remarks that "the FATCA story is really kind of insane" and that "Congress came in with a sledgehammer."

[22] See *Step Change in Tax Transparency*, above note 12 at 5–6. See also United Kingdom, Press Release, "New UK Multilateral Action to Combat Tax Evasion" (9 April 2013), online: www.gov.uk/government/news/new-uk-multilateral-action-to-combat-tax-evasion, describing the agreement to develop and pilot multilateral tax information exchange, under which information will be automatically exchanged between the five countries. The United Kingdom has separately agreed to Automatic Exchange with its Crown dependencies (Guernsey, the Isle of Man, and Jersey) and some of its overseas territories (Anguilla, Bermuda, the British Virgin Islands, the Cayman Islands, Gibraltar, Montserrat, and the Turks and Caicos Islands): see *Step Change in Tax Transparency*, above note 12 at 6. These jurisdictions have also agreed to join the pilot Automatic Exchange project with France, Germany, Italy, Spain, and the United Kingdom announced in April 2013 (see *ibid*).

A unique system of Automatic Exchange has also been developed and is currently being used in the European Union (the *European Union Savings Directive*).[23] The European Commission has estimated that tax fraud and tax evasion costs member states approximately one trillion euros (USD 1.3 trillion) in lost revenues annually.[24] Although Switzerland is not part of the European Union, it has been persuaded to enter into agreements with the European Union to adopt the withholding tax version (as opposed to the Automatic Exchange version) of the *EU Savings Directive*.[25] Switzerland espoused the anonymous withholding approach for its key trading partners as a means to keep Automatic Exchange from becoming the global model.[26]

---

[23] In 2003, the European Union unveiled a modified Automatic Exchange regime that began in 2005 and focused solely on interest income arising at a financial institution resident in one EU member country that was payable to a resident of another member country: European Commission, *Council Directive 2003/48/EC of 3 June 2003 on Taxation of Savings Income in the Form of Interest Payments*, [2003] OJ, L 157/38, *as amended by Council Directive 2004/66/EC of 26 April 2004*, [2004] OJ, L 168/35 and *Council Decision 2004/587/EC of 19 July 2004*, [2004] OJ, L 257/7 [*EU Savings Directive*]. The system had evolved from the competing goals of two schools — member countries seeking information exchange and member countries holding on to bank secrecy — and represented a compromise that allowed Austria, Belgium, and Luxembourg to impose a withholding tax during a transition period: see Itai Grinberg, "The Battle over Taxing Offshore Accounts" (2012) 60 *UCLA Law Review* 304 at 328. Under the *EU Savings Directive*, countries using the transitional withholding system share the revenue with the country of residence (paying 75 percent of the receipts and keeping 25 percent) (see *ibid* at 329). In jurisdictions exchanging information, the paying agent reports payments to the tax authority of the country in which it is resident, which, in turn, passes along this information to the fiscal authority of the country in which the payee is resident (see *ibid*).

[24] See Gabriele Parussini, "France's Hollande: EU Savings Directive Will Be Adopted by Year End" *Wall Street Journal* (22 May 2013). In 2011, the European Union adopted a revised mutual assistance directive to enhance EOI: European Commission, *Council Directive 2011/16/EU of 15 February 2011 on Administrative Cooperation in the Field of Taxation and Repealing Directive 77/799/EEC*, [2011] OJ, L 64/1, online: http://eur-lex.europa.eu/legal-content/en/TXT/?uri=CELEX%3A32011L0016 [EU *Parent-Subsidiary Directive*]. This directive requires member countries to automatically exchange information on additional categories of income. See also *Step Change in Tax Transparency*, above note 12 at 6: the European Union in cooperation with the OECD has created standard computerized formats for use by the tax administrations of member countries to automatically exchange information under these two directives.

[25] See Grinberg, above note 23 at 330: in return, Swiss companies have been permitted to take advantage of the zero withholding rate on dividends from European subsidiaries under the *EU Parent-Subsidiary Directive*, above note 24.

[26] See Grinberg, above note 23 at 339. For an extensive discussion of the debate on anonymous withholding versus Automatic Exchange, see *ibid* at 347–72. More recently, Switzerland entered into a new tax agreement with the United Kingdom to strengthen relations around cross-border financial services and taxation, deal with previously undeclared assets, and agree to a final withholding tax on

In another separate, but related, development, the OECD has created a qualified intermediary–style withholding program, the treaty relief and compliance enhancement (TRACE) program, aimed at standardizing the procedures for claiming reduced withholding under treaties for portfolio investments.[27] As the OECD has observed, claiming such relief under the more than 3,000 tax treaties can be very resource consuming and often does not happen.[28] The program allows "authorized intermediaries" (e.g., financial institutions) to obtain reduced rates of withholding under tax treaties or domestic law on a pooled basis for their portfolio investor customers.[29] Moreover, it is hoped that through the use of Automatic

future investment income: see Francesco Carelli, "The New Tax Agreement between Switzerland and the United Kingdom — An Analysis" (2012) 52:6 *IBFD European Taxation Journal* 301. Under the agreement, relevant UK resident individuals may opt for either a one-time penalty payment or the release of their account details to UK tax authorities (see *ibid* at 3, citing Art 5(1) of the *Agreement between the United Kingdom of Great Britain and Northern Ireland and the Swiss Confederation on Cooperation in the Area of Taxation*, 6 October 2011, UKTS 2013 No 9 (agreement, protocol, and exchange of notes entered into force 1 January 2013), online: www.gov.uk/government/uploads/system/uploads/attachment_data/file/190652/TS.9.2013.SwissDoubleTax.ProtEoN.pdf [*Switzerland–UK Agreement*]). Regarding the treatment of future income, relevant UK resident individuals have the option either to accept an anonymous final withholding tax remitted to the United Kingdom or to have the Swiss bank disclose income and capital gains derived from the assets to UK authorities (Carelli, *ibid* at 7, citing Art 19 and 22 respectively of the *Switzerland–UK Agreement, ibid*). Switzerland also signed a nearly identical agreement with Germany (Carelli, *ibid* at 1). For a discussion of the Swiss "Rubik" agreements, see Xavier Oberson, *International Exchange of Information in Tax Matters: Towards Global Transparency* (Cheltenham, UK: Edward Elgar, 2015) ch 9.

[27] See OECD, Centre for Tax Policy and Administration, "OECD Releases System to Reduce Compliance Cost and Facilitate Cross-border Investment" (Paris: OECD, 2013), online: www.oecd.org/ctp/system-to-reduce-compliance-cost-facilitate-cross-border-investment.htm ["OECD Releases System"]: the system was developed after many years of cooperation between the OECD, the European Union, governments, and businesses. In January 2013, the OECD approved the *TRACE Implementation Package for the Adoption of the Authorized Intermediary System*, which contains documents and forms that can be used by any country wishing to implement TRACE's unique system for authorized intermediaries: see OECD, "Treaty Relief and Compliance Enhancement (TRACE) — Implementation Package Approved by CFA" (Paris: OECD, 2013), online: www.oecd.org/ctp/exchange-of-tax-information/treatyreliefandcomplianceenhancement-trace.htm. For a discussion of the US qualified intermediary system, see Chapter 5, Section Background on the US Qualified Intermediary (QI) System.

[28] See "OECD Releases System," above note 27.

[29] See OECD, *TRACE Implementation Package for the Adoption of the Authorized Intermediary System* (Paris: OECD, 2013) at 4, online: www.oecd.org/ctp/exchange-of-tax-information/TRACE_Implementation_Package_Website.pdf [*TRACE Implementation Package*]. However, unlike the US qualified intermediary system, which does not require the disclosure of certain individuals to the withholding agent or to the IRS, the *TRACE Implementation Package, ibid* at 5, requires that an intermediary claiming benefits on a pooled basis provide to the source country tax

Exchange protocols described in the *TRACE Implementation Package*, the source country will be able to more easily verify the entitlement of the payee to treaty benefits and that the residence country will be able to more easily verify the income reporting of the payee.[30]

The focus of this research is not to answer the question of whether or not Automatic Exchange will be an effective tool against tax evasion. However, in as much as Automatic Exchange is being heralded by the OECD and the G20, among others, as the new saviour of tax authorities from the plague of offshore tax evasion, it is important to identify some of the concerns surrounding the implementation of this new global standard. In no particular order, these concerns are as follows:

- the difficulty or inability of putting in place the legal and practical framework to enable Automatic Exchange in all jurisdictions[31]
- the difficulty or impracticality of implementing due diligence protocols and self-certifications that contain complex legal concepts including, but not limited to, the residence of corporations, trusts, and individuals; fiscally transparent entities; and beneficial ownership[32]
- the greater challenges to the protection of taxpayer privacy interests presented by multilateral agreements, including misuse of data by corrupt administrators and rogue government employees[33]

---

administrators on an annual basis (rather than at the time of the payment) investor-specific information about the beneficial owners of the income.

[30] See *ibid.* The *TRACE Implementation Package*, *ibid* at 4–6, describes procedures that an authorized intermediary must follow to comply with the disclosure requirements.

[31] This concern is based on the apparent problems that a number of jurisdictions are having in implementing the OECD standards on transparency and EOI. In June 2012, for example, eleven jurisdictions (Botswana, Brunei, Costa Rica, Guatemala, Lebanon, Liberia, Panama, Trinidad and Tobago, the United Arab Emirates, Uruguay, and Vanuatu) were cited as being unable to move to Phase 2 of the peer review process because critical elements necessary to achieving effective EOI were not in place in their legal framework: see *Global Forum Update on Effectiveness*, above note 10 at para 10. See also Chapter 3, Section 6, and Table 3.1 therein; Arthur J Cockfield, "Protecting Taxpayer Privacy Rights under Enhanced Cross-border Tax Information Exchange: Toward a Multilateral Taxpayer Bill of Rights" (2010) 42 *University of British Columbia Law Review* 420 at 452.

[32] See discussion in Section 4.6, below in this chapter.

[33] See Cockfield, above note 31 at 441, observing that a broader community of information sharers and increased access raises the risk of improper access or usage of taxpayer information by a third-party government and that a government's ability to maintain accountability for and responsibility over transferred data may be strained as the data travels to multiple participants. See also NY Times

- the lack of taxpayer identification numbers (TINs) in the information provided under exchange[34]
- the use of sham or nominee directors and shareholders of companies in some jurisdictions[35]
- US reciprocity in providing information[36]
- the production of overwhelming quantities of data[37]
- the lack of political and economic incentives for tax haven countries that derive no benefit from Automatic Exchange

The basic steps in Automatic Exchange (described above in this section) are premised on the existence in the source country of certain fundamental legal, institutional, and administrative building blocks. Steps one and two, for example, call upon the paying agent or payor to identify the taxpayer and report the information, including payments made to the tax authorities in the source country. Steps three and four require consolidating and bundling the information according to the country of residence and ensuring secure transmission of the data with the appropriate encryption technology. Many tax haven jurisdictions that impose little

Editorial, "G20 Tackles Tax Avoidance," above note 5, noting that information may be used by villains in government who could sell personal financial data to would-be kidnappers and other unsavoury characters harbouring criminal intentions.

[34] A practical challenge for routine EOI arises where the information received by a tax authority, for example, the IRS, does not include a TIN despite recommendations from the OECD that member states provide such information. The task of "TIN perfection" or correlating the account data in the information received by the IRS with a valid TIN in its databases is time-consuming and costly: see United States, Congress, *Joint Committee on Taxation, Explanation of Proposed Protocol to the Income Tax Treaty between the United States and Switzerland* (Washington, DC: Joint Committee on Taxation, 2011) at 41, online: www.jct.gov/publications.html?func=startdown&id=3791 [JCT, *Proposed Swiss Protocol*].

[35] See James Ball, "Tax Transparency Campaigners Give Cautious Welcome to Treasury Deal" *Guardian* (2 May 2013), online: http://gu.com/p/3ftvg/stw, noting that the British Virgin Islands had more than 1 million offshore companies, that the usage of sham "nominee" directors and shareholders to mask real company owners was rife, and that such corporate secrecy could hamper the goals of automatic information sharing.

[36] The United States has come under pressure regarding its "know-your-customer" rules for financial institutions and maintenance of information on beneficial ownership. The concern is that certain policies at the federal and state levels provide foreign persons with the ability to shelter income: see JCT, *Proposed Swiss Protocol*, above note 34 at 42.

[37] See NY Times Editorial, "G20 Tackles Tax Avoidance," above note 5, observing that Automatic Exchange produces huge quantities of data and that even some European tax authorities have struggled to stay on top of the information exchanged.

or no income tax and other developing countries may simply lack these basic systems, lack the resources to build them, lack the legal or economic incentives to care, or lack a combination of the three. As a result of the asymmetry between the economic characteristics of the G20 and those of other countries, it is conceivable that the desired global reach of the new Automatic Exchange model may be unobtainable without further creative solutions that assist or lure (through a reciprocal benefits strategy) recalcitrant jurisdictions to implement Automatic Exchange. The new global standard is not intended to restrict other types or categories of Automatic Exchange, but rather sets forth a minimum standard for the information to be exchanged.[38]

2 Key Features of a Standardized Multilateral Automatic Exchange Model

2.1 Introduction

The OECD has identified certain general features required for the success of Automatic Exchange.[39] The design of the model or system must take into account the residence jurisdictions' tax compliance rather than be a by-product of source jurisdictions' domestic reporting. The model for Automatic Exchange also needs to be standardized to benefit the maximum number of residence jurisdictions and financial institutions. Furthermore, to combat global tax evasion, the model must have global buy-in to avoid merely relocating the problem to non-compliant low tax jurisdictions. The OECD has further outlined three major factors for effective Automatic Exchange: (1) a common agreement on the scope of reporting and exchange (including related due diligence procedures), (2) a legal basis for domestic reporting and EOI, and (3) common technical solutions.[40]

[38] See *Standard for Automatic Exchange*, above note 6 at 10.

[39] See *Step Change in Tax Transparency*, above note 12 at 7.

[40] See *ibid.*

2.2 Common Standard on Reporting, Due Diligence, and EOI

It is envisioned that the types of investment income in a financial information report would include interest, dividends, and similar income.[41] And to inhibit taxpayer circumvention of reporting, a comprehensive regime should not only report income earned by individuals but also have the ability to look through shell companies, trusts, or other straw person arrangements to the beneficial owner of the income, thereby revealing the owner not only of the income but also of the underlying capital.[42] Due diligence procedures are critical to ensuring the quality of the information that is being reported and exchanged.[43]

2.3 Legal and Operational Basis for EOI

The OECD plan for implementation of the new standard consists, in broad terms, of four major workstreams: (1) enacting broad framework legislation,[44] (2) selecting the legal basis for EOI,[45] (3) adopting the scope

[41] See *ibid* at 7–8.

[42] See *ibid* at 8. Straw entities, including foundations, were used by taxpayers in the UBS and LGT Bank scandals: see Chapter 5, Section 4.

[43] See *Standard for Automatic Exchange*, above note 6 at 12.

[44] See *Step Change in Transparency*, above note 12 at 9–10.

[45] Two legal platforms for Automatic Exchange are bilateral treaties incorporating Article 26 of the *Model Tax Treaty*, above note 1, and the *Convention on Mutual Administrative Assistance in Tax Matters* (together with the protocol amending the convention, CETS No 208, online: www.oecd.org/ctp/exchange-of-tax-information/ENG-Amended-Convention.pdf [*Convention on Mutual Assistance*]): see *Step Change in Transparency*, above note 12 at 11. The benefits of the *Convention on Mutual Assistance* include that it provides for all possible forms of administrative cooperation between states, it contains strict rules on confidentiality, it permits Automatic Exchange (see *Convention on Mutual Assistance*, *ibid* at Art 6), and it has a global reach, with as of June 2013 more than sixty countries, including all G20 countries, having signed it or pledged to do so (see *Step Change in Transparency*, *ibid*). The use of Automatic Exchange under the *Convention on Mutual Assistance* requires that the competent authorities of the parties (two or more) enter into a separate agreement to provide each other information automatically (see *ibid*). Alternatively, jurisdictions may rely on existing bilateral treaties, using the same competent authority agreement that would be used with the *Convention on Mutual Assistance* (see *ibid*). A further complication is that not all TIEAs provide for Automatic Exchange: see, for example, Canada's TIEAs discussed in Chapter 6.

of the reporting and due diligence requirements,[46] and (4) developing common information technology standards.[47]

A standardized multilateral Automatic Exchange model requires that the source state have appropriate domestic tax legislation to enable the scope of reporting and due diligence described above.[48] Such a model also requires a legal basis for the exchange of the information to be reported with the residence state.[49] Existing legal platforms that permit EOI include bilateral tax treaties with a provision based on Article 26 of the *Model Tax Treaty* and the *Convention on Mutual Administrative Assistance in Tax Matters*.[50] The *Convention on Mutual Assistance* provides for all possible forms of administrative cooperation between states, and one of its key advantages is its global reach.[51] Canada signed it in 2004 and the protocol thereto on 3 November 2011 and ratified the convention on 21 November 2013. It entered into force in respect of Canada on 1 March 2014.[52] Under the *Convention on Mutual*

---

[46] See *Step Change in Transparency*, above note 12 at 12.

[47] In creating a standard format for EOI, including transmission methods and encryption standards, the OECD is drawing upon work being done for *FATCA* as well as existing formats such as Standard Transmission Format (STF), which was developed by the OECD for Automatic Exchange and uses Extensible Markup Language (XML), and FISC 153, which is the standard used for the *EU Savings Directive*, above note 23: see *Step Change in Transparency*, above note 12 at 13.

[48] See *Step Change in Transparency*, above note 12 at 8.

[49] See *ibid.*

[50] See *ibid.* See also *Convention on Mutual Assistance*, above note 45. The convention was opened for signature by member states of the Council of Europe and member countries of the OECD on 25 January 1988, and it was revised in 2010 primarily to incorporate the internationally agreed-upon standards on transparency and EOI and to open it up to states that were not members of the Council of Europe or the OECD: see Council of Europe & OECD, *Revised Explanatory Report to the Convention on Mutual Administrative Assistance in Tax Matters as Amended by Protocol*, online: www.oecd.org/tax/exchange-of-tax-information/Explanatory_Report_ENG_%2015_04_2010.pdf. Under ch III (Forms of Assistance), the *Convention on Mutual Assistance* broadly provides for assistance in relation to EOI (Art 4–9), assistance in recovery of tax claims (Art 11–16), and service of documents (Art 17), and under ch IV (Provisions relating to All Forms of Assistance), it has a number of operating provisions including Art 21 on protection of persons and on limits to the obligation to provide assistance and Art 22 on secrecy. The United States ratified the *Convention on Mutual Assistance* on 30 January 1991, and Canada ratified it on 21 November 2013.

[51] See *Standard for Automatic Exchange*, above note 6 at 13.

[52] See OECD, "Jurisdictions Participating in the Convention on Mutual Administrative Assistance in Tax Matters: Status" (20 January 2016), online: www.oecd.org/ctp/exchange-of-tax-information/Status_of_convention.pdf.

Assistance, Canada agrees to exchange tax information pursuant to the OECD standard with other parties to the convention.[53] Pursuant to reservations, Canada is not obligated either to collect taxes on behalf of another country or to provide assistance in the service of related documents, but such functions may be separately negotiated as part of certain bilateral treaties.[54]

Automatic Exchange under the *Convention on Mutual Assistance* requires a separate agreement between the competent authorities of the parties, which can be entered into by two or more parties thereby allowing for a single agreement with several parties, with the benefit of actual Automatic Exchange taking place on a bilateral basis.[55] Where jurisdictions rely on a different EOI-enabling instrument, for example, a bilateral treaty, a competent authority agreement can be used to serve the same function.[56] As of February 2016, eighty jurisdictions had signed a CRS multilateral competent authority agreement under Article 6 of the *Convention on Mutual Assistance*.[57] Canada intends for its first information exchange to take place by September 2018.[58]

Some scholars believe that a multilateral treaty would be more advantageous than reliance on a bilateral framework in combatting tax and financial crimes, which frequently involve more than one jurisdiction.[59] In Canada and the United States, the legal basis for transferring taxpayer

---

[53] See Canada, Department of Finance, "Ratification of the Convention on Mutual Administrative Assistance in Tax Matters" (Ottawa: Department of Finance, 2013), online: www.fin.gc.ca/treaties-conventions/notices/maatm-aammf-eng.asp.

[54] See *ibid.*

[55] See *Step Change in Transparency*, above note 12 at 11: the competent authority agreement would activate and "operationalize" Automatic Exchange between the participants.

[56] See *ibid.*

[57] See OECD, Centre for Tax Policy and Administration, "Convention on Mutual Administrative Assistance in Tax Matters" (Paris: OECD, 2016), online: www.oecd.org/ctp/exchange-of-tax-information/conventiononmutualadministrativeassistanceintaxmatters.htm. See also OECD, "Multilateral Competent Authority Agreement on Automatic Exchange of Financial Account Information" (Paris: OECD, 2014), online: www.oecd.org/tax/automatic-exchange/international-framework-for-the-crs/multilateral-competent-authority-agreement.pdf.

[58] See OECD, "Signatories of the Multilateral Competent Authority Agreement on Automatic Exchange of Financial Account Information and Intended First Information Exchange Date" (27 January 2016), online: www.oecd.org/tax/exchange-of-tax-information/MCAA-Signatories.pdf.

[59] See Brodzka & Garufi, above note 13.

information to a foreign jurisdiction is found in both domestic and treaty law.[60] An overriding system requirement for EOI is adherence to strict confidentiality standards, including the existence in the receiving country of a legal framework and administrative capacity and processes to support those standards and to ensure that information is used only for the purposes set forth in the instrument agreed to by the parties.[61] In 2012, the OECD and the Global Forum published the *Joint OECD/Global Forum Guide on the Protection of Confidentiality of Information Exchanged for Tax Purposes*, which provides best practices related to the protection of confidentiality.[62]

2.4 Common or Compatible Technical Solutions

The OECD's primary objectives relating to information technology and EOI focus on the standardization of technical reporting formats (to achieve effectiveness and efficiency with a system that will be used by a large number of countries and financial institutions) and methods for transmission and encryption of data.[63]

[60] For Canada, see the discussion in Chapter 4. For the United States, see the discussion in Chapter 5.

[61] See *Step Change in Transparency*, above note 12 at 8. For a discussion of the confidentiality requirements under the *Agreement on Exchange of Information on Tax Matters* (Paris: OECD, 2002) [*Model TIEA*] and the *Model Tax Treaty*, above note 1, see Chapter 6, Section 3.8, and Chapter 7, Section 2.4, respectively. For a discussion of the domestic laws of Canada and the United States, see Chapter 4, Section 11, and Chapter 5, Section 2, respectively.

[62] OECD & Global Forum on Transparency and Exchange of Information for Tax Purposes, *Keeping It Safe: Joint OECD/Global Forum Guide on the Protection of Confidentiality of Information Exchanged for Tax Purposes* (OECD: Paris 2012), online: www.oecd.org/tax/transparency/final%20 Keeping%20it%20Safe%20with%20cover.pdf.

[63] See *A Step Change in Tax Transparency*, above note 12 at 9. The OECD notes that many countries already use protocols developed by the OECD for electronic EOI upon request, for example, with "point-to-point" transmission directly from one country's EOI portal to the other country's portal (see *ibid*). Within the European Union, exchanges take place through the use of a secure network (CCN) (see *ibid*).

3 The *Model Competent Authority Agreement*

The OECD *Model Competent Authority Agreement* and the CRS together constitute the common standard on reporting, due diligence, and EOI for financial account information.[64] Implementation of the standard requires translating the CRS into domestic law.[65] The signing of a competent authority agreement based on the *MCA* permits putting in place information exchange based on existing legal instruments such as the *Convention on Mutual Assistance* or double tax conventions.[66] Another basis for implementing EOI may be a multilateral competent authority agreement. Or jurisdictions may enter into a multilateral intergovernmental agreement or multiple intergovernmental agreements that would be international treaties in their own right and that would cover both the reporting obligations and the due diligence procedures, together with a more limited competent authority agreement.[67] The legal basis may also be EU legislation covering the elements of the CRS.[68]

The *MCA* provides the link between the CRS and the legal basis for EOI (e.g., the *Convention on Mutual Assistance* or a bilateral tax treaty) thereby allowing the financial account information to be exchanged.[69] The sections in the *MCA* are preceded by a number of "whereas" clauses that contain representations on the domestic reporting and due diligence rules that are the foundation of EOI pursuant to the competent authority agreement.[70] These whereas clauses also contain representations on confidentiality, safeguards, and the existence of the necessary infrastructure for

---

[64] OECD, "Model Competent Authority Agreement" & "Commentaries on the Model Competent Authority Agreement" in OECD, *Standard for Automatic Exchange*, above note 6, 21 (agreement) and 65 (commentaries) [agreement and commentaries together: *MCA*]. See *Standard for Automatic Exchange*, above note 6 at 14.

[65] See *Standard for Automatic Exchange*, above note 6 at 14.

[66] See *ibid.*

[67] See *ibid.*

[68] See *ibid.*

[69] See *ibid.*

[70] See *ibid.*

an effective EOI relationship.[71] The *MCA* contains seven sections dealing with the various provisions of the agreement: section 1 contains definitions of terms used within the agreement, section 2 covers the type of information to be exchanged, section 3 deals with the time and manner of EOI under the agreement, section 4 deals with collaboration on compliance and enforcement, section 5 covers confidentiality and data safeguards, section 6 deals with consultations and amendments, and section 7 deals with the coming into effect, suspension, and termination of the agreement.[72] The *MCA* is accompanied by separate commentaries on both the preamble and the sections in the agreement.[73] Canada signed the *MCA* in 2015.[74]

4 The Common Reporting Standard

4.1 Introduction

The CRS contains both the reporting and the due diligence standards that underpin the automatic exchange of financial account information.[75] A jurisdiction desiring to implement the CRS must have rules in place that require financial institutions to report information consistent with the scope of the reporting requirements in section I and ensure that the same institutions follow the due diligence procedures in sections II through VII. As of 2015, over ninety jurisdictions had committed to implementing Automatic Exchange.[76] The financial information to be

[71] See *ibid* at 14–15.

[72] See *MCA*, above note 64, ss 1–7.

[73] See *MCA*, above note 64.

[74] See Canada, News Release, "Canadian Government Combats International Tax Evasion by Joining Forces with International Tax Jurisdictions" (Ottawa: Canada Revenue Agency, 2015), online: http://news.gc.ca/web/article-en.do?nid=983299: as part of Canada's Economic Action Plan 2015, Ottawa also proposed an investment of CAD 25.3 million over five years in CRA to improve its offshore tax evasion risk assessment systems and business intelligence and to hire additional auditors.

[75] See *Standard for Automatic Exchange*, above note 6 at 15.

[76] See OECD, "Strengthening the International Community's Fight against Offshore Tax Evasion: Australia, Canada, Chile, Costa Rica, India, Indonesia and New Zealand Join Multilateral Agreement to Automatically Exchange Information" (Paris: OECD, 2015), online: www.oecd.org/

reported regarding reportable accounts generally includes account balance or value, interest, dividends, income from certain insurance products, sales proceeds from financial assets, and other income generated with respect to assets held in the account or payments made with respect to the account.[77] The CRS includes a requirement to look through passive entities and report on the relevant controlling persons.[78] Note that terms in capital letters and abbreviations used in the five subsections below in this chapter are generally defined in the CRS in section VIII (Defined Terms) and due to the summary format of this chapter are not defined herein.

4.2 Reporting Financial Institutions

Financial institutions covered by the CRS generally include "Depository Institutions," "Custodial Institutions," "Investment Entities," and "Specified Insurance Companies" unless they present a low risk of being used for tax evasion and are expressly excluded from reporting.[79] The CRS contains detailed rules that define the correct scope of the types of financial institutions required to collect and report the relevant information to be exchanged, which are referred to as "Reporting Financial Institutions." The four steps to identify a Reporting Financial Institution are as follows:

> "Step 1: Is it an Entity?
> Step 2: Is the Entity in the Participating Jurisdiction?
> Step 3: Is the Entity a Financial Institution?
> Step 4: Is the Entity a Non-Reporting Financial Institution?[80]"

newsroom/australia-canada-chile-costa-rica-india-indonesia-and-new-zealand-join-multilateral-agreement-to-automatically-exchange-tax-information.htm.

[77] See *Standard for Automatic Exchange*, above note 6 at 15. See also CRS, above note 6, s I.

[78] See *Standard for Automatic Exchange*, above note 6 at 15.

[79] See *ibid.* See also CRS, above note 6, s VIII(A) & (B).

[80] OECD, *Standard for Automatic Exchange of Financial Information in Tax Matters: Implementation Handbook* (Paris: OECD, 2015) at 35, online: www.oecd.org/ctp/exchange-of-tax-information/implementation-handbook-standard-for-automatic-exchange-of-financial-information-in-tax-matters.pdf [*CRS Implementation Handbook*].

A Reporting Financial Institution must be an "Entity."[81] The CRS defines Entities broadly to include legal persons and legal arrangements, such as corporations, partnerships, trusts, and foundations.[82] As a result, individuals and sole proprietorships are not Reporting Financial Institutions.[83] Additionally, the CRS targets Entities within a "Participating Jurisdiction."[84] Under the CRS, the reporting nexus of a jurisdiction includes Entities resident in the jurisdiction, their branches located in that jurisdiction, and branches of foreign Entities located in that jurisdiction.[85]

An Entity's residence is generally where the Entity is resident for tax purposes.[86] Where an Entity (other than a trust) does not have a residence for tax purposes, the Entity is regarded as resident in the jurisdiction under the laws of which it is incorporated, where it has its place of management, or where it is subject to financial supervision.[87] This may be the case because the Entity, for example, is fiscally transparent or is located in a jurisdiction that does not have an income tax.[88] For an Entity (other than a trust) resident in two or more Participating Jurisdictions, the Entity is required to report each "Financial Account" that it maintains to the fiscal authorities in the jurisdiction where it maintains that account.[89] A trust is considered to be resident for reporting purposes in the Participating Jurisdiction where one or more of its trustees are resident unless the required information is being reported elsewhere because the trust is treated as resident for tax purposes in that jurisdiction.[90]

The CRS defines Reporting Financial Institutions to include the following:[91]

---

[81] See *ibid.*

[82] See *ibid.*

[83] See *ibid.*

[84] See *ibid* at 36.

[85] See *ibid.*

[86] See *ibid* at 37.

[87] See *ibid.*

[88] See *ibid.*

[89] See *ibid.*

[90] See *ibid.*

[91] See *ibid* at 39.

1) Depository Institutions (which generally include savings banks, commercial banks, savings and loan associations, and credit unions)
2) Custodial Institutions (which generally include custodian banks, brokers, and central securities depositories)
3) Investment Entities (which generally include Entities investing, reinvesting, or trading in financial instruments, engaging in portfolio management, and investing, administering, or managing "Financial Assets")
4) Specified Insurance Companies (which generally include most life insurance companies)

"Non-reporting Financial Institutions" include the following:[92]

1) "Governmental Entities" and their pension funds
2) "International Organisations"
3) "Central Banks"
4) certain retirement funds
5) "Qualified Credit Card Issuers"
6) "Exempt Collective Investment Vehicles"
7) trustee documented trusts
8) other low-risk "Financial Institutions"

4.3 Financial Accounts to Be Reviewed

Reporting Financial Institutions are obligated to review the Financial Accounts that they maintain to identify whether any of them need to be reported to their respective fiscal authority.[93] The general rule is that a Financial Account is an account maintained by a Financial Institution, and the types of Financial Accounts that generally need to be reviewed include the following:[94]

1) "Depository Accounts" (such as chequing and savings accounts)

---

[92] See *ibid*.

[93] See *ibid* at 40.

[94] See *ibid* at 40 and 42.

2) "Custodial Accounts" (accounts for the benefit of another person, holding Financial Assets)
3) "Equity and Debt Interests" (debt and equity interests and their equivalents such as interests in partnerships or trusts)
4) "Cash Value Insurance Contracts" and "Annuity Contracts"

Generally, non-reportable accounts are the following:[95]

1) retirement and pension accounts
2) non-retirement tax-favoured accounts
3) term life "Insurance Contracts"
4) estate accounts
5) escrow accounts
6) certain Depository Accounts
7) other low-risk excluded accounts

4.4 Financial Accounts That Are Reportable Accounts

After a Reporting Financial Institution has identified the Financial Accounts that it maintains, it is obligated to review those accounts to determine whether any of them are "Reportable Accounts" as defined in the CRS.[96] Reporting Financial Institutions must ultimately report the required information relating to those accounts to their fiscal authority.[97]

A Reportable Account may be an account held either by one or more "Reportable Persons" or by a "Passive NFE" (non-financial entity) with one or more "Controlling Persons" that are Reportable Persons.[98] A two-step test is used to determine whether a Financial Account is a Reportable Account by virtue of the "Account Holder."[99] Step one examines whether

[95] See *ibid.*
[96] See *ibid* at 43.
[97] See *ibid.*
[98] See *ibid.*
[99] See *ibid* at 45.

the Account Holder is a "Reportable Jurisdiction Person."[100] A Reportable Jurisdiction Person is an individual or Entity resident in a "Reportable Jurisdiction" for tax purposes under the laws of that jurisdiction (or with its place of effective management in a "Reportable Jurisdiction" if it does not have a tax residence). A Reportable Jurisdiction is defined as a jurisdiction with which an agreement on Automatic Exchange under the CRS is in place. Each jurisdiction must publish a list of these Reportable Jurisdictions. Hence, a Financial Institution must determine whether a Financial Account that it maintains is held by a person who is resident in a jurisdiction on the published list. Under step two, unless specifically excluded a Reportable Jurisdiction Person will then be a Reportable Person.[101] Generally, if the Entity Account Holder is a Passive NFE then the Financial Institution must "look through" that Entity to identify its Controlling Persons.[102] The term "Controlling Person" generally corresponds to the term "beneficial owner" as described in the Financial Action Task Force's *International Standards on Combating Money Laundering and the Financing of Terrorism & Proliferation: The FATF Recommendations.*[103]

Regardless of whether or not a Financial Account is a Reportable Account by virtue of the Account Holder, a further inquiry must be made regarding the Controlling Persons of certain Entity Account Holders.[104] This additional test may determine whether additional information is required to be reported in relation to an already Reportable Account or whether a non-reportable account becomes a Reportable Account due to the presence of Controlling Persons.[105]

In the case of a partnership, a Controlling Person generally means, consistent with the description of "beneficial owner" in the *FATF*

---

[100] See *ibid.*

[101] See *ibid.* In general, the following persons are excluded: corporations the stock of which is regularly traded on one or more established securities markets and "Related Entities" of such corporations, Governmental Entities, International Organisations, Central Banks, and Financial Institutions (see *ibid*).

[102] See *ibid* at 47.

[103] See *ibid.* See also FATF, *International Standards on Combating Money Laundering and the Financing of Terrorism & Proliferation: The FATF Recommendations* (Paris: FATF, 2012), online: www.fatf-gafi.org/recommendations.html [*FATF Recommendations*].

[104] See *CRS Implementation Handbook*, above note 80 at 47.

[105] See *ibid.*

Recommendations, any natural person who exercises control through direct or indirect ownership of the capital or profits of the partnership or through voting rights in the partnership or who otherwise exercises control over the management of the partnership.[106]

In the case of a trust, generally, a Controlling Person is explicitly defined in the CRS to mean a settlor, a trustee, a protector (if any), a beneficiary or class of beneficiaries, and any other natural person exercising ultimate effective control over the trust.[107] Where any of the aforementioned persons is an Entity, the Reporting Financial Institution must identify the Controlling Persons of such Entity in accordance with *FATF Recommendations*.[108]

4.5 Trusts under the Common Reporting Standard

The CRS will generally apply to a trust that is either (1) a Reporting Financial Institution or (2) an "NFE" that maintains a Financial Account with a Reporting Financial Institution.[109] Generally, a trust will be a Financial Institution if it comes within the definition of "Investment Entity" in section VIII(A)(6)(b) of the CRS.[110] Generally, a trust will be found to be within this definition if it has gross income primarily attributable to investing, reinvesting, or trading in Financial Assets and is managed by another Entity that is a Financial Institution.[111] Trusts that are collective investment vehicles or similar entities established with an investment strategy of investing, reinvesting, or trading in Financial Assets may also be considered Financial Institutions.[112] A trust that is not a Financial Institution will be a non-financial entity, or NFE.[113] Trusts that are NFEs are, in turn, either "Active NFEs" or Passive NFEs, depending on their

[106] See *ibid* at 48.
[107] See *ibid.*
[108] See *ibid.*
[109] See *ibid* at 77.
[110] CRS, above note 6, s VIII(A)(6)(b). See *CRS Implementation Handbook*, above note 80 at 78.
[111] See *CRS Implementation Handbook*, above note 80 at 78–79.
[112] See *ibid* at 79.
[113] See *ibid.*

activities.[114] Generally, a five-step procedure is followed in applying the CRS to trusts, which is briefly summarized as follows:[115]

1) Determine whether the trust is a Reporting Financial Institution.
2) Identify the Financial Accounts of a trust that is a Reporting Financial Institution.
3) Identify the Reportable Accounts of a trust that is a Reporting Financial Institution.
4) Apply the due diligence rules.
5) Report the relevant information.

In the case of a trust that is an NFE and that has a Financial Account with a Reporting Financial Institution, the next step is to identify whether the account held by the trust is a Reportable Account.[116] Separate CRS rules regarding the treatment of a trust that is a Reporting Financial Institution apply but are not discussed in this chapter.[117] Generally, an account held by a trust that is a Passive NFE will be a Reportable Account if (1) the trust is a Reportable Person or if (2) the trust has one or more Controlling Persons that are Reportable Persons. The trust will be a Reportable Jurisdiction Person only if it is resident for tax purposes in a Reportable Jurisdiction and is not excluded from the definition of Reportable Person.[118] Where a trust has no residence for tax purposes, it is not considered to be a Reportable Person.[119] An account held by a trust will also be reportable if the trust has one or more Controlling Persons that are Reportable Persons such as a settlor, trustee, beneficiary, protector, or any other natural person exercising ultimate effective control over the trust.[120] Such inclusive reporting parameters dispense with the need to determine whether any of the aforementioned persons can exercise

---

[114] See *ibid.*

[115] See *ibid* at 79–82.

[116] See *ibid* at 83.

[117] See, for example, *ibid* at 79–82.

[118] See *ibid* at 83.

[119] See *ibid.*

[120] See *ibid*: the CRS draws from the *FATF Recommendations*, above note 103, on beneficial ownership.

practical control over the trust.[121] For beneficiaries identified as a class, the rules do not require that all possible members of the class be treated as Reportable Persons.[122] Whether or not a member of a class is treated as a Reportable Person will instead be determined, for example, when such person receives a distribution from the trust or intends to exercise vested rights in the trust property.[123] In addition, both mandatory and discretionary beneficiaries are generally to be included within the definition of Controlling Persons.[124] Depending on the implementing legislation adopted, discretionary beneficiaries may be reported regardless of whether a distribution is received in a given year.[125] Where a Controlling Person of a trust that is a Passive NFE is resident in the same jurisdiction as the Reporting Financial Institution, such Controlling Person will generally not be considered a Reportable Person.[126] In determining whether an account held by a trust is a Reportable Account, the Reporting Financial Institution must apply the applicable due diligence rules.[127]

Where a trust is a Reportable Person, the Reporting Financial Institution will report the account information and the financial activity for the year for that trust's account.[128] This account information will include the identifying information of each Reportable Person (e.g., name, address, residence, TIN, date of birth, and account number) and the identifying information of the Reporting Financial Institution (name and identifying number).[129] For a trust that is a Passive NFE, the Reporting Financial Institution must report the Controlling Persons of the trust including, where possible, whether a Controlling Person is a settlor, trustee,

[121] See *CRS Implementation Handbook*, above note 80 at 83. The CRS includes within the definition of Controlling Person any natural person who may exercise ultimate control of an Entity that is a settlor, trustee, beneficiary, or protector. This may impose additional due diligence requirements on Reporting Financial Institutions (see *ibid* at 84).

[122] See *ibid* at 83.

[123] See *ibid.*

[124] See *ibid* at 84.

[125] See *ibid.*

[126] See *ibid.*

[127] See *ibid.* These rules are further explained *ibid* at 84–85.

[128] See *ibid* at 85.

[129] See *ibid.*

protector, or beneficiary.[130] The reported financial information will be the account balance or the value of the account held by the trust and payments made or credited to such account.[131] The entire value of the account as well as the entire amounts paid or credited to the account will be attributed to each Controlling Person.[132]

4.6 Due Diligence Procedures

Sections II through VII of the CRS contain the due diligence procedures to be performed by Reporting Financial Institutions for the identification of Reportable Accounts.[133] Section II contains the general due diligence requirements and also deals with reliance on service providers and alternative due diligence procedures for "Preexisting Accounts."[134] Section III contains the due diligence procedures for identifying Reportable Accounts among "Preexisting Individual Accounts" and distinguishes between "Lower Value Accounts" (which do not exceed USD 1 million as of a certain date) and "High Value Accounts" (which exceed USD 1 million as of a certain date).[135] For Lower Value Accounts, the rules provide for the application of a permanent residence address test that is based on Documentary Evidence or the determination of residence on the basis of an indicia search.[136] In the case of conflicting indicia, a self-certification (and/or Documentary Evidence) will be needed, in the absence of which reporting must be done to all Reportable Jurisdictions for which indicia have been found.[137] For Higher Value Accounts, enhanced due diligence procedures apply, including a paper record search and an actual knowledge test by the relationship manager.[138]

---

[130] See *ibid.*

[131] See *ibid.*

[132] See *ibid.*

[133] See *Standard for Automatic Exchange*, above note 6 at 15.

[134] See CRS, above note 6, s II.

[135] See *ibid*, ss III and VIII(C).

[136] See *Standard for Automatic Exchange*, above note 6 at 15–16.

[137] See *ibid* at 16.

[138] See *ibid.*

Section IV of the CRS contains due diligence rules for a "New Individual Account" and provides for the collection of a self-certification and confirmation of its reasonableness.[139] The self-certification must permit the Reporting Financial Institution to determine the Account Holder's residence for tax purposes.[140] The due diligence rules acknowledge that taxpayers may have ties to multiple jurisdictions, and they refer to extremely complex tax and legal principles such as "residence," "domicile," and "dual residence."[141] According to the new rules, jurisdictions are expected to provide phone numbers, walk-in offices, and Internet channels to help the millions of taxpayers in each jurisdiction determine their residence status.[142] Given the complexity of the caselaw in Canada and the United States on interpreting the tiebreaker rules (which would include the failure of some courts in the United States to understand how the complex tiebreaker rules in a double tax convention work), the suggestion that the CRS's due diligence procedures will be correctly applied after an Internet chat with some bureaucrat or the like is deeply unsettling considering the opportunities for errors and the problems that could be caused for innocent account holders and Financial Institutions alike.[143]

Section V of the CRS contains due diligence rules for "Preexisting Entity Accounts." If applicable in a particular jurisdiction, these rules may exempt from review all Preexisting Entity Accounts with an account balance or a value not exceeding USD 250,000.[144] Otherwise, for Preexisting Entity Accounts, Financial Institutions are obligated to determine (1) whether the Entity itself is a Reportable Person, which can generally be done on the basis of available information (from anti–money laundering or know-your-customer procedures), but if not, a self-certification will be needed; and (2) whether the Entity is a Passive NFE and if so the

---

[139] See CRS, above note 6, Commentary on s IV at para 1.

[140] See *ibid*, Commentary on s IV at paras 4–6.

[141] See *ibid*. For an example of complex rules relating to residence, see the 100-page chapter on the residence rules under the tax laws of Canada and the United States in David S Kerzner, Vitaly Timokhov, & David W Chodikoff, eds, *The Tax Advisor's Guide to the Canada–U.S. Tax Treaty* (Toronto: Thomson Reuters Carswell, 2008) (loose-leaf) ch 4.

[142] See CRS, above note 6, Commentary on s IV at paras 4–6.

[143] See *ibid*.

[144] See *ibid*, Commentary on s V at para 2.

residency of Controlling Persons.[145] Review procedures for identifying Reportable Accounts among Preexisting Entity Accounts may involve, once again, considerations dealing with highly complex legal concepts, namely, the residence of a corporation or entity, the existence of a permanent establishment, whether an entity is fiscally transparent, the beneficial ownership of an entity held through holding companies, and special purpose vehicles such as trusts.[146] The rules concerning Controlling Persons found in the definitions in section VIII are astoundingly difficult. These due diligence procedures are extremely complex and require expert international legal and tax knowledge and experience that is not commonly found within the operations of most of the financial institutions and service providers that will be called upon to implement and follow these procedures in Canada, the United States, and the European Union, let alone those in tax haven jurisdictions. Again, whether an entity is passive or active under *FATCA* or under the *Internal Revenue Code* (for example) can be a confusing and difficult question for accountants. The notion that such an analysis can be straightforward is disingenuous.[147] Typically, one would find the kind of expertise necessary to deal with the complex legal concepts referenced above in the international corporate tax departments of the big four public accounting firms or in national and international law firms.

Section VI of the CRS contains procedures for identifying Reportable Accounts among "New Entity Accounts." These procedures are broadly the same as those for Preexisting Entity Accounts except that as the collection of self-certifications for New Entity Accounts is expected to be easier, the USD 250,000 threshold does not apply.[148] These procedures note that Reporting Financial Institutions are not expected to carry out an independent legal analysis of relevant tax laws to confirm the reasonableness of a self-certification.[149] Due to the complexity of these procedures and the potential absence of expertise in these tax and legal

[145] See *Standard for Automatic Exchange*, above note 6 at 16.

[146] See CRS, above note 6, Commentary on s V at paras 8–24.

[147] See *ibid.*

[148] See *Standard for Automatic Exchange*, above note 6 at 16.

[149] See CRS, above note 6, Commentary on s VI at paras 12–13.

concepts on the part of the personnel who will administer the CRS, there exist adequate grounds for concern that the regime is flawed, that errors will be made, and that opportunities will arise for tax evaders to employ tactics to hinder the intended objectives of the new standard.

Section VII of the CRS contains rules concerning special due diligence requirements, and Section IX describes the rules and administrative procedures that an implementing jurisdiction is expected to have in place to ensure effective implementation of and compliance with the CRS.[150]

5 Conclusion

The CRS's reliance on such complex international and corporate tax concepts, which permeate the due diligence rules relevant to account holders and Financial Institutions and their advisers, must call into question the credibility and the effectiveness of the OECD's system of Automatic Exchange to combat tax evasion. Once again, as with the *Model TIEA*, discussed in Chapters 3 and 6, the OECD and the Global Forum are failing to recognize the policy weaknesses in tax harmonization as opposed to tax deharmonization. In deploying Automatic Exchange, they are failing as well to recognize the lack of incentives and motivation for tax havens to participate in this new standard with the resource commitments necessary for its success. They are failing to see the big picture that tax havens simply do not have adequate infrastructure resources to implement and administer the CRS and to see that this is plainly evident from the 2013 and 2014 tax haven peer review grades, which revealed a systemic weakness in these jurisdictions' support for the standards of transparency and EOI that are central to the success of Automatic Exchange.[151] While the international cooperation surrounding Automatic Exchange and its implementation will undoubtedly assist governments in the future administration and enforcement of their tax laws and also act as a deterrent against some tax evaders, fiscal authorities seeking to gain the upper hand in defeating tax cheats should embrace Automatic Exchange as one tool in a broader arsenal

[150] See *Standard for Automatic Exchange*, above note 6 at 16.

[151] For a discussion of the tax haven peer review grades, see Chapter 3, Section 6.

of more potent weapons and policies that are described in Chapter 11. Professionals with private clients must have due regard for the CRS's application to privately held entities, including trusts, to ensure that the correct classifications are made. And for professionals advising on private trusts, it is advisable to alert clients to the potentially invasive new reporting rules applicable to settlors, trustees, protectors, and beneficiaries alike and to take care that any reporting is done correctly.

Further Readings

Cockfield, Arthur J. "Protecting Taxpayer Privacy Rights under Enhanced Cross-border Tax Information Exchange: Toward a Multilateral Taxpayer Bill of Rights" (2010) 42 *University of British Columbia Law Review* 420.

——— "The Limits of the International Tax Regime as a Commitment Projector" (2013) 33 *Virginia Tax Review* 59.

———. "The Rise of the OECD as Informal 'World Tax Organization' through National Responses to E-commerce Tax Challenges" (2006) 8 *Yale Journal of Law & Technology* 136.

Dean, Steven A. "More Cooperation, Less Uniformity: Tax Deharmonization and the Future of the International Tax Regime" (2009) 84 *Tulane Law Review* 125.

———. "Philosopher Kings and International Tax: A New Approach to Tax Havens, Tax Flight, and International Tax Cooperation" (2007) 58 *Hastings Law Journal* 911.

———. "The Incomplete Global Market for Tax Information" (2008) 49 *Boston College Law Review* 605.

Grinberg, Itai. "Beyond FATCA: An Evolutionary Moment for the International Tax System" (2012) [unpublished, archived at the Georgetown University Law Center, The Scholarly Commons, Paper 160], online: http://scholarship.law.georgetown.edu/fwps_papers/160.

———. "The Battle over Taxing Offshore Accounts" (2012) 60 *UCLA Law Review* 304.

Luchena Mozo, Gracia Ma. "The Prevention and Resolution of Tax Conflicts within the Framework of International Exchange of Information" (2012) 52:5 *IBFD European Taxation Journal* 226.

Marley, Patrick, & Susan Wooles. "Canada's Tax Information Exchange Agreements: Impact on Tax Planning" (2010) 39 *Tax Management International Journal* 606.

OECD. *Standard for Automatic Exchange of Financial Account Information in Tax Matters* (Paris: OECD, 2014).

———. *Standard for Automatic Exchange of Financial Information in Tax Matters: Implementation Handbook* (Paris: OECD, 2015).

Sawyer, Adrian. "Peer Review of Tax Information Exchange Agreements: Is It More Than Just about the Numbers?" (2011) 26 *Australian Tax Forum* 397.

Yates, Marie Thérèse et al. "The Death of Information Exchange Agreements? Part Three" (2011) 22 *Journal of International Taxation* 48.

Zagaris, Bruce. "Bilateral Agreement Alternative to FATCA Implementation Brings New Twist to International Tax Cooperation" (2012) 28 *International Enforcement Law Reporter* 113.

———. "The Procedural Aspects of U.S. Tax Policy towards Developing Countries: Too Many Sticks and No Carrots?" (2003) 35 *George Washington International Law Review* 331.

9

Foreign Account Tax Compliance Act

1 Introduction

The focus of this chapter is on providing a policy background to and an examination of the *Foreign Account Tax Compliance Act*, a unique piece of US tax legislation that has no precedent in the history of international tax law.[1] As detailed in Chapter 3, the exchange of information (EOI) upon request standard in use between 2002 and 2016 is flawed, but that is not the only weakness in the OECD's efforts to combat tax evasion. As explained in Chapter 8, the US *FATCA* initiative has been a driving force and an impetus for the G20 and OECD's launch of automatic exchange of information (Automatic Exchange). While the goal behind *FATCA*, noted below, of curbing the use of tax havens to hide income of US taxpayers residing in the United States is consistent with the principles of equity in international tax policy, discussed in Chapter 2, the same cannot be said of *FATCA*'s application to millions of individuals in Canada, the United Kingdom, and the European Union who are US nationals but not tax evaders. The new regime acts to drive these people

[1] Subtitle A of Title V of the *Hiring Incentives to Restore Employment Act of 2010*, Pub L No 111–147 enacted on 18 March 2010 [*FATCA*].

D.S. Kerzner, D.W. Chodikoff, *International Tax Evasion in the Global Information Age*, DOI 10.1007/978-3-319-40421-9_9

into the enforcement cannons of the IRS, which, as described in Chapter 10, can be financially and psychologically traumatizing. As explained in Chapter 11, refocusing American enforcement on residence rather than nationality would make the administration and enforcement of the data collected through *FATCA* more consistent with the principles of equity in international tax policy.

This chapter also provides an overview of the rules contained in the hundreds of pages of regulations and guidance relating to *FATCA*, of which any in-depth analysis is beyond the scope of this book. The overview that follows the policy discussion below explains the intergovernmental agreement (IGA) mechanism behind *FATCA* and provides a synopsis of the IGA between Canada and the United States.

2 *FATCA* and International Tax Policy

In 2010, Congress unveiled a landmark foreign-reporting weapon targeting foreign financial institutions (FFIs) that is known as *FATCA*.[2] Simply stated, *FATCA* requires FFIs to identify to the IRS accounts owned by US citizens or become subject to a 30 percent withholding on all of their US sourced investment income.[3] Notably, neither Automatic Exchange nor tax information exchange agreements (TIEAs) contain an equivalent or similar penalty feature.[4] *FATCA* is largely a congressional response to address international tax crimes and abuses of the US foreign-reporting

[2] *Ibid. FATCA* was in large measure a response to the tax evasion and Swiss bank scandals that Congress was investigating in 2008 and 2009: see Scott D Michel & H David Rosenbloom, "FATCA and Foreign Bank Accounts: Has the U.S. Overreached?" 62:9 *Tax Notes International* 709 (30 May 2011); Stafford Smiley, "Qualified Intermediaries, the EU Savings Directive, TRACE — What Does FATCA Really Add?" (2011) 38 *Journal of Corporate Taxation* 20 at 25, noting that the bank scandals involving UBS and Liechtenstein were closely watched by Senator Carl Levin, chair of the Permanent Subcommittee on Investigations of the Senate Committee on Homeland Security and Governmental Affairs, which conducted extensive hearings on tax havens and the use of FFIs by US tax evaders.

[3] See final *FATCA* regulations implementing Chapter 4, Subtitle A of the *Internal Revenue Code*, USC 26 (1986) of 1986, as amended, and the *Treasury Regulations* issued thereunder [*Code*]: *Regulations relating to Information Reporting by Foreign Financial Institutions and Withholding on Certain Payments to Foreign Financial Institutions and Other Foreign Entities*, 26 CFR Parts 1 and 301, effective 28 January 2013 [*Final FATCA Regulations*].

[4] For an examination of TIEAs and Automatic Exchange, see Chapters 3 and 8 respectively.

rules by US taxpayers and FFIs that were exposed during Congress's investigations into tax havens. Although modelled after the qualified intermediary program, *FATCA* is about reporting, not collecting withholding tax.[5] Under *FATCA*, FFIs are being deputized into the enforcement ranks of the US Department of the Treasury by being required to report to the IRS accounts owned by US persons (directly and indirectly), including extensive information relating to these accounts.

FATCA has two primary tactical objectives in fighting international tax evasion. The first is to provide to the United States additional tools supporting the enforcement of worldwide taxation on those citizens and residents who have successfully been able to illegally hide foreign income in offshore accounts.[6] The second objective is to dissuade FFIs from continuing to hide US account holders by penalizing FFIs.[7] In enacting *FATCA*, Congress is seeking to press FFIs into heavy-handedly policing a flawed US reporting system and, also, to compensate for the many shortcomings within the existing US network of information exchange protocols in tax conventions and TIEAs.[8] Moreover, the United States looks upon *FATCA* as a means of extending the scope of its domestic information-reporting regime (applicable in large part to US third-party payors) to encompass FFIs (and certain non-financial foreign entities). In doing so, the United States is striving to maintain fairness in its tax system, by inhibiting US taxpayers from using global investment opportunities to evade US tax by

---

[5] See also United States, Department of the Treasury, Press Release, "Joint Statement from the United States, France, Germany, Italy, Spain and the United Kingdom regarding an Intergovernmental Approach to Improving International Tax Compliance and Implementing FATCA" (8 February 2012), online: www.treasury.gov/press-center/press-releases/Documents/020712%20Treasury%20IRS%20FATCA%20Joint%20Statement.pdf [*Intergovernmental Joint Statement*].

[6] See Smiley, above note 2 at 25; Itai Grinberg, "The Battle over Taxing Offshore Accounts" (2012) 60 *UCLA Law Review* 304 at 334.

[7] See Smiley, above note 2 at 5; Grinberg, above note 6 at 334.

[8] See Grinberg, above note 6 at 334, noting that a purpose of *FATCA* is ensuring, by coercion, the participation of FFIs in an automatic information-reporting system. Professor Grinberg also discusses the problems posed by the unilateral reporting under *FATCA*, which benefits the United States solely, and he refers to a former US Department of the Treasury official on tax policy, Emily McMahon, commenting on such problems and offering the view that *FATCA* is a vehicle to transitioning to a multilateral system (*ibid* at 336–37). See also Chapters 4 and 5 for a discussion of the existing frameworks for international EOI between sovereigns and related current developments from the Canadian and US legal perspectives respectively.

hiding money in offshore accounts.[9] While this reasoning is applicable to US residents and citizens who live in the United States, we do not believe that it is applicable to US nationals abroad who have been absorbed by the foreign countries where they have lived and paid taxes for all or most of their lives. We believe that in this circumstance, when considering the millions of US expatriates living in Canada, the United Kingdom, and the European Union who are not tax cheats, *FATCA* poses serious questions regarding the principles of equity and fairness. One of the questions that critics have been asking is, will FFIs pay billions of dollars to comply with this new edict, or will they decide to close their operations to US clients and diversify their investments elsewhere?[10]

To obtain buy-in and support from foreign governments and FFIs, the US Department of the Treasury and the IRS have created an alternative pathway to *FATCA* implementation that will facilitate compliance under the new regime through the use of IGAs. The IGAs have been designed, in part, to address concerns that local (foreign law) rules may create impediments to implementing rules around withholding, account reporting, and account closures, in addition to assisting FFIs with reducing their compliance costs.[11] On 8 February 2012, the United States together with

---

[9] See *Regulations relating to Information Reporting by Foreign Financial Institutions and Withholding on Certain Payments to Foreign Financial Institutions and Other Foreign Entities*, 77 Fed Reg 9022 (15 February 2012). The preamble to the proposed regulations reviews the US reporting rules applicable in principle to require *US* (emphasis added) third-party payors to document their third-party payees and report certain types of payments made to those payees (e.g., Chapter 61 of Subtitle A of the *Code*, above note 3, comprising in relevant part §§ 6041–49, which require certain payors to document their third-party payees and report certain types of payments, such as interest, dividends, and gross proceeds from broker transactions). The preamble also reviews rules in Chapter 3 of Subtitle A of the *Code*, comprising §§ 1441–64, which generally require withholding agents to document their payees and to withhold and report with respect to certain US sourced payments to foreign persons. Essentially, the policy effect under *FATCA* is to impose similar reporting obligations on FFIs and certain non-financial foreign entities. This is both monumental and historic.

[10] See Smiley, above note 2 at 26; David Jolly & Brian Knowlton, "Law to Find Tax Evaders Denounced" *New York Times* (26 December 2011) B1, online: http://nyti.ms/1I7SMjg, reporting that businesses outside the United States will have to spend billions of dollars annually to comply with *FATCA*.

[11] See Jolly & Knowlton, above note 10; Bruce Zagaris, "Bilateral Agreement Alternative to FATCA Implementation Brings New Twist to International Tax Cooperation" (2012) 28 *International Enforcement Law Reporter* 113. See also *Intergovernmental Joint Statement*, above note 5; Grinberg, above note 6 at 375, remarking that *FATCA*'s requirement for reporting directly from an FFI to a foreign sovereign will violate local financial privacy and data protection laws in many jurisdictions.

France, Germany, Italy, Spain, and the United Kingdom issued a joint statement expressing the wish to intensify cooperation around combatting international tax evasion.[12] The United States stated that in return for the other countries' implementing *FATCA*, it was willing to reciprocate by collecting and exchanging (on an automatic basis) taxpayer information held in US financial institutions relating to residents of the other countries joining in the statement.[13] As of April 2016, fifty-four countries had such an IGA in effect.[14]

Some Canadian tax scholars have criticized the implementation of *FATCA* in Canada for a number of reasons.[15] Concerns have been raised that the IGA between Canada and the United States and other statutory commitments will violate international law and rights under the *Canadian Charter of Rights and Freedoms*.[16] In the recent Federal Court

---

[12] See *Intergovernmental Joint Statement*, above note 5.

[13] See *ibid*. The parties to the *Intergovernmental Joint Statement, ibid*, agreed to a framework that embraced bilateral agreements whereby each foreign partner country would agree to pursue necessary implementing legislation to require FFIs in its jurisdiction to collect and report to the authorities of the foreign partner the required information, to enable FFIs to apply necessary diligence to identify US accounts, and to transfer the information reported by the FFIs to the United States on an automatic basis. In exchange, FFIs in a foreign partner country could avoid having to enter into agreements directly with the IRS and could comply with their reporting obligations by reporting information directly to the foreign partner. FFIs in a foreign partner country would generally be regarded as participating FFIs or deemed-compliant FFIs and thereby escape withholding. They would not have to terminate the accounts of recalcitrant account holders or impose passthru payment withholding on payments to such account holders (*ibid*).

[14] See United States, Department of the Treasury, "Resource Center: Foreign Account Tax Compliance Act (FATCA)" (19 April 2016), online: www.treasury.gov/resource-center/tax-policy/treaties/Pages/FATCA.aspx.

[15] See Allison Christians & Arthur J Cockfield, "Submission to Finance Department on Implementation of FATCA in Canada: Submission on Legislative Proposals relating to the Canada–United States Enhanced Tax Information Exchange Agreement" (10 March 2014), online: http://dx.doi.org/10.2139/ssrn.2407264; Allison Christians, "Country Report: Canada" in Eleonor Kristoffersson et al, eds, *Tax Secrecy and Tax Transparency: The Relevance of Confidentiality in Tax Law, Part 1* (Frankfurt am Main: PL Academic Research, 2013) 209; Arthur J Cockfield, "Protecting Taxpayer Privacy Rights under Enhanced Cross-border Tax Information Exchange: Toward a Multilateral Taxpayer Bill of Rights" (2010) 42 *University of British Columbia Law Review* 420; Arthur J Cockfield, "FATCA and the Erosion of Canadian Taxpayer Privacy: Report to the Office of the Privacy Commissioner of Canada" (1 April 2014), online: http://ssrn.com/abstract=2433198 [Cockfield, "FATCA and Erosion"].

[16] See Cockfield, "FATCA and Erosion," above note 15. See also *Agreement between the Government of Canada and the Government of the United States of America to Improve International Tax Compliance through Enhanced Exchange of Information under the Convention between Canada and the United*

case *Hillis and Deegan v Canada (AG)*, Martineau J explained some of the essentials of the statutory terms:

> Every reporting Canadian financial institution is compelled by law to submit itself to the due diligence procedures set out in subsections 265(2) and (3) of the ITA which apply in respect of pre-existing and new individual accounts, and to designate any US reportable account (see sections 264 and 265 of the ITA). Financial institutions already have a legal responsibility to determine where an account holder resides for tax purposes. If a customer has an existing account and there is an indication that they may be a US person, or if they are opening new bank accounts, their financial institution may ask them to provide additional information or documentation to demonstrate that they are not a US person (or to self-certify that they are or are not a US person for tax purposes). Indeed, every reporting Canadian financial institution shall keep, at the institution's place of business (or at such other place as may be designated by the Minister), records that the institution obtains or creates for the purpose of complying with Part XVIII of the ITA, including self-certifications and records of documentary evidence.
>
> The reporting institutions must annually file with the Minister — that is, with the CRA — prescribed information about each reportable account maintained by the financial institution, as well as prescribed information relating to payments made to non-participating financial institutions that held accounts at the financial institution in the calendar year (for 2015 and 2016 only). The information must be reported in an information return filed for each calendar year by May 2 of the following year (section 266 of the ITA) . . . . The CRA will then annually turn the information it collects over to the IRS in bulk "on an automatic basis pursuant to the provisions of Article XXVII of the [US–Canada Tax Convention]" . . . . [17]

In *Hillis and Deegan*, the plaintiffs sought a declaration that the *Canada–United States Enhanced Tax Information Exchange Agreement Implementation Act* and Schedule 3 of the *Economic Action Plan 2014 Act, No 1* were *ultra vires* or inoperative because their provisions were unconstitutional

States of America with respect to Taxes on Income and on Capital, (5 February 2014), online: www.fin.gc.ca/treaties-conventions/pdf/FATCA-eng.pdf [*Canada–US IGA*].

[17] 2015 FC 1082 at paras 33–34 [*Hillis and Deegan*].

or infringed on the plaintiffs' *Charter* rights.[18] The plaintiffs also filed an amended statement of claim that added non-constitutional arguments, which became the focus of Martineau J's review and reasons for judgment. As stated by Martineau J, the summary trial dealt with the legality of the disclosure of US persons' personal information collected for the year 2014 by Canadian financial institutions for CRA. The information in question was scheduled to be shared by CRA with the US tax authorities on or before 30 September 2015. Hence, the plaintiffs sought a general declaration and injunction of a permanent nature that would prevent the collection of taxpayer information and its disclosure by CRA to the United States.

While the plaintiffs raised a series of arguments, the court was not convinced of the merits of any of them in terms of both the law and the evidence that was on the record before it. Justice Martineau stated:

> I agree with the defendants that the plaintiffs misread the IGA and the Canada–US Tax Treaty in a way that frustrates the intention of the parties. It is manifest that the authority to exchange automatically on an annual basis the information obtained by Canada pursuant to the terms of the IGA indeed derives from Article XXVII of the Canada–US Tax Treaty, which does not expressly prohibit such disclosure. The provisions of the IGA are clear. The IGA has force of law in Canada. Sections 266 to 269 of the ITA are compulsory. While all information exchanged is protected by the confidentiality provisions of the Canada–Tax Convention and the ITA, the exceptions created under subsection 241(4) of the ITA are applicable to the impugned provisions and the IGA.[19]

Even though Martineau J ultimately denied the declaratory and injunctive relief sought by the plaintiffs, he did acknowledge the following:

> True, a great number of Canadian taxpayers holding US reportable accounts are likely to be affected by a reporting system that in many quarters is considered unjust, costly and ineffective, considering that at the end of the day they are not likely to owe taxes to the US. In the absence of legislative

[18] *Canada–United States Enhanced Tax Information Exchange Agreement Implementation Act*, SC 2014, c 20; *Economic Action Plan 2014 Act, No 1*, SC 2014, c 20 [latter two acts together: *Implementation Act*]; *Hillis and Deegan*, above note 17 at paras 1 and 3.

[19] *Hillis and Deegan*, above note 17 at para 65.

> provisions requiring all Canadian financial institutions (provincially and federally regulated) to automatically notify their account holders about reporting to the CRA under the IGA and Part XVIII of the ITA, these taxpayers may also be taken by surprise by any consequences that flow from such disclosure. The plaintiffs may find this deplorable, but apart from a constitutional invalidation of the impugned provisions or a change of heart by Parliament or Congress, or the governments of Canada or the US, there is nothing that this Court can judicially do today to change the situation. The impugned provisions have not been held to be *ultra vires* or inoperative. Judicial courage requires that judges uphold the Rule of Law.[20]

The *Hillis and Deegan* case was the first legal challenge in Canada to international EOI under the new provisions in Part XVIII of the *Income Tax Act* and under the *Canada–US IGA*.[21] A couple of noted tax scholars have pinpointed the serious challenges to taxpayer privacy and other rights posed by these new disclosure requirements. Professors Cockfield and Christians agree that the *Implementation Act* and the *Canada–US IGA* do not enhance the reciprocal tax information exchange between Canada and the United States. They posit that these legal relations will not create a workable regime for Canada that will improve its international tax enforcement efforts on a go-forward basis. In fact, after carrying out an exhaustive study of the legal arrangements between Canada and the United States, Cockfield and Christians reach some startling findings including that the *Implementation Act* and the *Canada–US IGA* will

- unduly harm the privacy rights and interests of all Canadians;
- unduly raise compliance costs for all Canadian financial institutions and Canadian taxpayers;
- unduly raise legal exposure for Canadian financial institutions, due to ongoing potential liability for mistakenly-transferred personal financial information;
- provide potentially sensitive commercial information held by Canadian firms to the United States that, if improperly revealed, could harm firm competitiveness;

---

[20] *Ibid* at para 76.

[21] *Income Tax Act*, RSC 1985, c 1 (5th Supp) [*Act*].

- interfere with cross-border mobility of Canadian workers to the United States as these "green card holders" will be subject to costly tax compliance measures after they return to Canada;
- impede Canada's efforts to enforce its own tax laws and to cooperate on a global scale to promote the integrity of the income taxation system; and
- violate the spirit and potentially the letter of a number of Canadian laws including the *Personal Information Protection and Electronic Document Act*, the *Privacy Act*, the *Access to Banking Services Regulations*, NAFTA, and others.[22]

Although the *Canada–US IGA* is formally reciprocal, as the United States is not considered a tax haven jurisdiction for Canadian residents and as Canada has been receiving Automatic Exchange relating to interest income earned by Canadian residents for decades, the true purpose of the agreement is to drive names of non-compliant US citizens living in Canada to the IRS for enforcement action, and not to combat tax evasion by Canadians with US bank and financial accounts.[23] Moreover, the scope of the information exchange required of Canada under *FATCA*, which includes, for example, account balances, is far broader than that traditionally associated with the determination of unreported income. While it may be expected that more detailed information would be requested in the course of an audit, such broad data collection protocols purely in the context of an EOI tool offend notions and expectations of privacy and fairness.

The implementation of *FATCA* in Canada without a comprehensive solution for the enforcement and immense reporting problems facing approximately one million Americans in Canada represents a failure in international tax policy on the part of both Canada and the United States.[24] As Michael Livingston recognizes, tax policy is one aspect of a

---

[22] Christians & Cockfield, above note 15 at 1–2.

[23] See David S Kerzner, "Surviving FATCA: A Roadmap for Delinquent U.S. Filers and Their Advisors" (2014) 7 *Taxes & Wealth Management* 1, arguing that the US taxation of Canadians who have had no contact with the United States during their lifetime but received citizenship at birth or who have lived in Canada for many decades is inconsistent with concepts of equity in tax policy and that the benefits principle does not apply to these individuals, and advocating a reorientation of US tax policy with respect to this unique class of individuals within the US tax system. See also *Canada–US IGA*, above note 16.

[24] See Chapter 3, Sections 7.4 and 7.5.

broader set of political and social issues, and what scholars need to reflect more upon is an understanding of the relationship between structure and outcomes and the effectiveness (or ineffectiveness) of various historical strategies for promoting tax reform.[25] Diane Ring, commenting on international tax scholarship and echoing the vision of Livingston, calls for the exercise of practical reasoning that reflects the needs of a society and integrates analysis, facts, values, and competing goals.[26]

The motivation for *FATCA* was primarily the discovery of large-scale tax evasion by Americans living in the United States with undeclared bank accounts in Swiss and other European banks, and their apparent success at circumventing the qualified intermediary and other US reporting systems. American taxpayers living in the continental forty-eight states and Alaska and Hawaii generally do not report and pay taxes on a worldwide basis to any other country or jurisdiction. So clearly, income earned by these individuals in undeclared tax haven accounts made them tax cheats who were evading income tax and committing fraud. *FATCA* was designed to stop this. But to equate approximately one million Canadian residents who report worldwide income and pay taxes thereon to CRA with tax cheats, or to put them in the same class as the tax criminals for whom *FATCA* was created is neither just nor right. To impose *FATCA* on Canada and to drive hundreds of thousands of Canadians of US heritage into the cannons of the IRS's unfair enforcement (described in Chapter 10) is inconsistent with the goals of equity (described in Chapter 3) surrounding international tax law and EOI. Critically, as the vast majority of Americans in Canada can pay thousands of dollars each to file zero US individual tax returns (i.e., returns with no US income tax owing),

[25] Michael A Livingston, "Reinventing Tax Scholarship: Lawyers, Economists, and the Role of the Legal Academy" (1998) 83 *Cornell Law Review* 365 at 368. Livingston offers that the goal of tax scholarship should be to move beyond the normative focus of determining the "right" answer to tax problems under idealized and apolitical conditions — to encompass approaches (such as empirical studies, narrative projects, and an expanded normativity) that recognize that in the partisan nature of taxation, tax policy is one aspect of a broader set of political and social issues.

[26] Diane M Ring, "The Promise of International Tax Scholarship and Its Implications for Research Design, Theory and Methodology" (2010) 55 *Saint Louis University Law Journal* 307 at 327–28. In commenting on Livingston's conception of "empirical" work, Ring, *ibid* at 312, notes that Livingston favours the goal of gathering and analyzing relevant information in useful ways for those designing policy and that he believes a rigid adherence to highly sophisticated methodologies from the social sciences is not essential.

due to the generous exemptions and credits under the *Code*, the *FATCA* program to identify Americans in Canada and enforce the *Code* against them is illogical, especially when it drives these individuals to renounce their citizenship in record numbers.[27] Chapter 10, below, describes the injustices and illogic of applying the US foreign-reporting rules (totalling some 7,000 pages) to Canadians, and of the voluntary disclosure programs.[28] Canada failed in implementing *FATCA* by not asking about or considering the financial and social consequences of what the IRS would do with the information that it received. Canada and the United States need to develop a cross-border tax policy solution that embraces what Livingston and others (like Michael Graetz)[29] have called for: an appreciation of the unique factual, historical, social, and political circumstances of one million Americans in Canada, many of whom have lived in Canada for most, if not all, of their lives.

Under the *Canada–US IGA*, Canada agrees to adopt implementing legislation that will require certain Canadian financial institutions to identify enumerated accounts held by certain US persons and report certain information relating to those accounts to CRA, which will, in turn, annually exchange that information with the United States.[30] A serious flaw in the design of *FATCA* is that despite its implementation cost, estimated to be over $750 million in Canada[31] and over £1 billion in the United Kingdom,[32] it can be defeated with one stroke of a pen by a dishonest taxpayer who decides to lie in the self-certification process applicable to

[27] For most of the years from 2005 to 2014, making an appointment to expatriate at the Consulate General of the United States in Toronto required a couple of weeks' advance notice. As of January 2016, scheduling an appointment to expatriate requires ten months' advance notice.

[28] See Chapter 10, Section 5, discussing US voluntary disclosure programs from 2009 to 2015.

[29] See Michael J Graetz, "Taxing International Income: Inadequate Principles, Outdated Concepts, and Unsatisfactory Policies" (2001) 54 *Tax Law Review* 261 at 276–325. Professor Graetz advocates that to best articulate an international tax policy, the political as well as the economic considerations and needs of the American people should be addressed.

[30] See Canada, Department of Finance, "Explanatory Notes — Canada–United States Enhanced Tax Information Exchange Agreement" (Ottawa: Department of Finance, 2014) at clause 1, online: http://www.fin.gc.ca/drleg-apl/2014/can-us-eu-0214n-eng.pdf.

[31] See Rita Trichur, "Canada Banks Tally Their Tax-Compliance Tab" *Wall Street Journal* (27 July 2014), online: http://on.wsj.com/1teJ5K6.

[32] See Kyle Caldwell, "British Families Billed £500 — To Prevent Americans Dodging Tax" *Telegraph* (23 August 2014), online: www.telegraph.co.uk/finance/personalfinance/tax/11050777/British-families-billed-500-to-prevent-Americans-dodging-tax.html.

certain individuals and entity accounts. Without proper enforcement by the IRS Criminal Investigation division to act as a deterrent, a US expatriate taxpayer living in Canada or elsewhere can simply indicate on a Form W-8 or equivalent certification that she is not a US citizen or resident or that the controlling person of her Canadian-controlled private entity is not controlled by US citizens or residents.[33] The illogic of *FATCA* as an anti–tax evasion tool is that it relies in part on voluntary compliance by and the honesty and goodwill of individuals, in much the same way as the returns that must be filed to report secret Swiss bank accounts. If, as discussed in Chapter 1, IRS resources for audits and the Criminal Investigation division continue to dwindle, the smarter approach would be to relieve the existing system and unload the millions of long-time US expatriates by offering them a simple route to expatriation, as discussed in Chapter 11 below. IRS resources can then be reallocated to promote horizontal and vertical equity among US taxpayers who are resident in the United States, in addition to fighting the use of offshore financial centres by international crime and terrorism organizations.

3 Framework of *FATCA*

The legal rules describing the *FATCA* regime are hundreds of pages in length and extremely complex. Only a brief overview is provided in this chapter to establish a foundation for understanding their role in EOI and the serious policy problems that they are continuing to generate.[34] *FATCA*

[33] See, for example, § 7206(1) of the *Code*, above note 3, which deals with falsifying a tax return.

[34] The *Final FATCA Regulations*, above note 3, are over 500 pages long. See also, for example, additional *FATCA* guidance issued by the Department of the Treasury for financial institutions: Notice 2015-10 "Guidance on Refunds and Credits under Chapter 3, Chapter 4, and related Withholding Provisions"; Notice 2015-66 "Extensions of FATCA Transitional Rules for Gross Proceeds, Foreign Passthru Payments, Limited Branches and Limited FFIs, and Sponsored Entities; Modification to Grandfathered Obligation Rule with respect to Collateral; and Reporting of 2014 Information under a Model 1 IGA"; Notice 2014-59 "Modified Applicability Dates of Certain Provisions under Chapters 3 and 61"; Revenue Procedure 2014-47 "Application Procedures and Overview of Requirements for Withholding Foreign Partnership or Withholding Foreign Trust Status under Chapters 3 and 4; Final Withholding Foreign Partnership Agreement; Final Withholding Foreign Trust Agreement"; Revenue Procedure 2014-39 "Application Procedures and Overview of Requirements for Qualified Intermediary Status under Chapters 3, 4, and 61 and Section 3406; Final Qualified Intermediary Agreement"; Revenue Procedure 2014-38 "FFI Agreement for

comprises two separate but related pathways or tracks to compliance by FFIs. Under the first track, FFIs must individually choose to comply with the rigorous data collection, reporting, and payment protocols found in *FATCA* in a direct relationship with the IRS. Under the second track, a foreign country enters into a bilateral agreement with the United States (referred to as an IGA) under which FFIs will collect and report data to their fiscal authority, and the United States, in turn, agrees to share information on taxpayers resident in that foreign country. However, as discussed below, the IGA creates an asymmetry in reporting and exchange. The research below focuses more on the second track as this is likely the track that many OECD countries will follow, and the one that Canada has already followed.

What follows is a brief synopsis of *FATCA* and some of the key definitional components. The regulations address the following general subject matters: scope of Chapter 4 of the *Code*;[35] requirements to deduct and withhold tax on withholdable payments to certain FFIs;[36] identification of payee;[37] FFI agreement;[38] definitions applicable to *Code* section 1471;[39]

Participating FFI and Reporting Model 2 FFI"; Notice 2014-33 "Further Guidance on the Implementation of FATCA and Related Withholding Provisions"; Announcement 2014-17 "Update on Jurisdictions Treated as Having an IGA in Effect on FATCA Financial Institution Registration"; TD 9658 "Withholding of Tax on Certain U.S. Source Income Paid to Foreign Persons, Information Reporting and Backup Withholding on Payments Made to Certain U.S. Persons, and Portfolio Interest Treatment"; TD 9657 "Regulations relating to Information Reporting by Foreign Financial Institutions and Withholding on Certain Payments to Foreign Financial Institutions and Other Foreign Entities"; REG-130967-13 "Regulations relating to Information Reporting by Foreign Financial Institutions and Withholding on Certain Payments to Foreign Financial Institutions and Other Foreign Entities"; REG-134361-12 "Withholding of Tax on Certain U.S. Source Income Paid to Foreign Persons and Revision of Information Reporting and Backup Withholding Regulations"; Announcement 2014-1 "Update on FATCA Financial Institution Registration"; Notice 2013-69 "FFI Agreement for Participating FFI and Reporting Model 2 FFI"; Notice 2013-43 "Revised Timeline and Other Guidance regarding the Implementation of FATCA." The aforementioned regulations and other guidance documents are available at United States, Internal Revenue Service, "FATCA — Regulations and Other Guidance," online: www.irs.gov/Businesses/Corporations/FATCA-Regulations-and-Other-Guidance.

[35] Above note 3, reg § 1.1471-1.

[36] *Ibid*, reg § 1.1471-2.

[37] *Ibid*, reg § 1.1471-3.

[38] *Ibid*, reg § 1.1471-4.

[39] *Ibid*, reg § 1.1471-5.

payments beneficially owned by exempt beneficial owners;[40] withholding on non-financial foreign entities (NFFEs);[41] definitions applicable to *Code* section 1473;[42] liability for withheld tax and withholding agent reporting;[43] overwithholding, underwithholding, taxes paid only once, refunds, credits, and reimbursement;[44] coordination of Chapter 4 with other withholding provisions;[45] required use of magnetic media for financial institutions filing Form 1042-S or Form 8966;[46] and confidentiality of information.[47] Now Chapter 4 of the *Code* generally obligates US withholding agents to withhold a tax of 30 percent on any "withholdable payment" to (1) FFIs that do not agree to report enumerated account information to the IRS regarding US accounts and (2) certain NFFEs that do not provide information on their substantial US owners to withholding agents.[48]

Again, US withholding agents are required to withhold 30 percent of any withholdable payment to an FFI (or NFFE) that does not comply with *FATCA*'s reporting regime.[49] Although generally such withholding may be credited against any US income tax liability of the beneficial owner of the payment (or refunded according to the facts), the same does not hold true for an FFI that does not comply with the reporting requirements under *Code* section 1471(b).[50] Rather, an FFI that beneficially owns the payment subject to withholding may receive a credit or refund to the extent required under treaty.[51] Generally, a withholdable payment means any payment of interest, dividends, rents, salaries, wages, premiums, annuities, compensations, remunerations, emoluments, and other fixed or determinable

[40] *Ibid*, reg § 1.1471-6.

[41] *Ibid*, reg § 1.1472-1.

[42] *Ibid*, reg § 1.1473-1.

[43] *Ibid*, reg § 1.1474-1.

[44] *Ibid*, reg §§ 1.1474-2–1.1474-5.

[45] *Ibid*, reg § 1.1474-6.

[46] *Ibid*, reg § 301.1474-1.

[47] *Ibid*, reg § 1.1474-7.

[48] *Ibid*, §§ 1471–74 and the regulations thereunder.

[49] *Ibid*, §§ 1471(a), 1471(b), 1472(a), & 1472(b).

[50] See *Final FATCA Regulations*, above note 3, Background.

[51] See *ibid*.

annual or periodical gains, profits, and income (FDAP Income) from US sources.[52] Additionally, a withholdable payment includes any gross proceeds from the sale or other disposition of any property of a type that can produce interest or dividends from US sources.[53] The inclusion of gross proceeds from the sale or disposition of investment property in the definition of withholdable payment is notable because under the *Code* and the *United States Model Income Tax Convention*, the gains (with certain exceptions relating to effectively connected income and real property) derived by foreign persons are generally not subject to US taxation — and certainly not at the gross level.[54] This underscores that the 30 percent withholding is about sanctions, not taxing income.

Under *FATCA*, an FFI is defined as any financial institution that is a foreign entity (i.e., not a financial institution organized under the laws of the United States).[55] A financial institution is broadly defined to include any entity that (1) accepts deposits in the ordinary course of a banking business, (2) holds financial assets for the account of others as a substantial portion of its business, or (3) is engaged in the business of investing, reinvesting, or trading in securities, partnership interests, commodities, or similar interests.[56]

An FFI that wishes to avoid withholding must either enter into an agreement with the IRS regarding certain reporting obligations or be deemed to comply with the rules.[57] An FFI that enters into an FFI agreement (a participating FFI) is required to identify its US accounts and comply with certain verification and due diligence procedures.[58] A participating

---

[52] *Code*, above note 3, § 1473(1).

[53] *Ibid.*

[54] See David S Kerzner, Vitaly Timokhov, & David W Chodikoff, eds, *The Tax Advisor's Guide to the Canada–U.S. Tax Treaty* (Toronto: Thomson Reuters Carswell, 2008) (loose-leaf) ch 13. See also United States, Department of the Treasury, *United States Model Income Tax Convention* (15 November 2006) (Washington, DC: US Department of the Treasury, 2006), online: www.treasury.gov/press-center/press-releases/Documents/hp16801.pdf.

[55] *Code*, above note 3, § 1471(d)(5).

[56] *Ibid.*

[57] *Ibid*, § 1471(b). As an alternative to reporting account balances or values, and gross receipts and gross withdrawals or payments, a participating FFI may elect to report the information required under *Code*, *ibid*, §§ 6041, 6042, 6045, and 6049 as if it were a US person (*ibid*, § 1471(c)(2)).

[58] *Ibid*, § 1471(b)(1)(A) & (B).

FFI is required to report on an annual basis to the IRS the following information regarding any US account: (1) the name, address, and taxpayer identification number (TIN) of each account holder who is a specified US person; (2) the account balance or value; and (3) the gross receipts and gross withdrawals or payments from the account.[59] Where an account is held by a US owned foreign entity, the name, address, and TIN of each specified US person that is a substantial US owner of that entity must also be reported along with the other aforementioned account data.[60]

A US account is defined as any financial account held by one or more specified US persons or US owned foreign entities.[61] A financial account is any depository account, custodial account, or equity or debt interest in an FFI (other than interests that are regularly traded on a public exchange).[62] A specified US person is broadly defined to mean any US person except those entities expressly excluded from the definition.[63] A US owned foreign entity means any foreign entity that has one or more substantial US owners.[64] The regulations attempt to reduce the administrative burden associated with the identification of US accounts by basing due diligence requirements on the value and risk profile of an account and by permitting FFIs to utilize information already in their possession.[65]

[59] *Ibid*, § 1471(b)(1)(C) and (E): certain exceptions and modifications may be made to these rules from time to time by the Secretary of the Treasury.

[60] *Ibid.*

[61] *Ibid*, § 1471(d)(1).

[62] *Ibid*, § 1471(d)(2).

[63] *Ibid*, § 1473(3). The *Code, ibid*, generally excludes from the definition of US person corporate stock that is publicly traded; stock of a corporation affiliated with a publicly traded company; organizations that are exempt under § 501(a) or an individual retirement plan; the United States, any state, or district, or any agency, or instrumentality of the foregoing; banks defined in § 581; real estate investment trusts defined in § 856; regulated investment companies defined in § 851; common trust funds defined in § 584(a); and trusts that are exempt under § 664(c) or § 4947(a)(1).

[64] *Ibid*, § 1471(d)(3). Under the *Code, ibid*, § 1473(2), a substantial US owner means with respect to any corporation, any specified US person that owns, directly or indirectly, more than 10 percent of the stock of such a corporation (by vote and value); with respect to any partnership, any specified US person that owns, directly or indirectly, more than 10 percent of the profits interests or capital interests in such partnership; and in the case of a trust, any specified US person treated as an owner of any portion of such trust under Subpart E of Part I of Subchapter J of Chapter 1 and to the extent further provided by the Secretary of the Treasury any specified US person that holds, directly or indirectly, more than 10 percent of the beneficial interests of such trust.

[65] See *Final FATCA regulations*, above note 3, Background.

Generally, a 30 percent US withholding tax will apply to payments of certain US sourced income (e.g., interest, dividends, and insurance premiums) made to non-US financial institutions (FFIs) — unless the FFI establishes by registration that it is an FFI in a jurisdiction with a *Model 1 IGA* treated as in effect.[66] Reporting began in 30 September 2015 for FFIs in *Model 1 IGA* jurisdictions. The information that was to be reported with respect to 2014 included the following:

1. Account holder's name
   For passive non-financial foreign entity, the name(s) of any substantial US owners;
2. Account holder's US taxpayer identification number (TIN)
   For passive non-financial foreign entity, only the TIN(s) of any substantial US owner(s);
3. Account holder's address
   For passive non-financial foreign entity, only the address(es) of substantial US owner(s);
4. Account number;
5. Account balance or value;
6. For accounts held by recalcitrant/nonconsenting account holders: report aggregate number and balance or value.[67]

4 Model Intergovernmental Agreement

4.1 Introduction

The US Department of the Treasury first introduced its model IGA in July 2012, and later modified it in November 2012.[68] The preamble to

[66] See United States, Internal Revenue Service, "Summary of FATCA Timelines" (last updated 3 December 2015), online: www.irs.gov/Businesses/Corporations/Summary-of-FATCA-Timelines ["FATCA Timelines"]. See also United States, Department of the Treasury, *Agreement between the Government of the United States of America and the Government of* [FATCA Partner] *to Improve International Tax Compliance and to Implement FATCA* (Washington, DC: Department of the Treasury, 2012) [*Model 1 IGA*].

[67] "FATCA Timelines," above note 66.

[68] *Model 1 IGA*, above note 66. Later still, the US Department of the Treasury introduced the following model IGA: *Model 1A IGA Reciprocal, Preexisting TIEA or DTC: Agreement between the*

the *Model 1A IGA*, introduced in November 2013, recognizes that in entering into the agreement, the parties' broader goals are to improve international tax compliance, implement *FATCA* based on domestic reporting, and provide for reciprocal Automatic Exchange pursuant to their tax convention or TIEA.[69] Certainly, model IGAs do not exempt any jurisdiction from *FATCA*, but rather offer alternative frameworks for information sharing using existing bilateral income tax treaties or TIEAs.[70] The Department of the Treasury also developed a second model IGA, the *Model 2 IGA*, that is designed for a partner jurisdiction to direct its FFIs to register with and report directly to the IRS regarding US accounts.[71] This research focuses on the former model IGA as that is the preferred platform for those countries currently signing *FATCA* agreements with the United States for the benefits mentioned above. In writing about the IGAs, Professor Christians importantly observes that as "'sole executive agreements,' IGAs constitute agency rulemaking in the United States but are ratified as treaties by most 'partner jurisdictions' (a phrase that carefully avoids the usual term, 'treaty partners')."[72] Professor Christians

Government of the United States of America and the Government of [FATCA Partner] *to Improve International Tax Compliance and to Implement FATCA* (4 November 2013), online: www.treasury.gov/resource-center/tax-policy/treaties/Documents/FATCA-Reciprocal-Model-1A-Agreement-Preexisting-TIEA-or-DTC-11-4-13.pdf (for FFIs reporting to their fiscal authority). See also the *Model 1A IGA* issued on 30 November 2014: *Model 1A IGA Reciprocal, Preexisting TIEA or DTC: Agreement between the Government of the United States of America and the Government of* [FATCA Partner] *to Improve International Tax Compliance and to Implement FATCA* (30 November 2014), online: www.treasury.gov/resource-center/tax-policy/treaties/Documents/FATCA-Reciprocal-Model-1A-Agreement-Preexisting-TIEA-or-DTC-11-30-14.pdf [*Model 1A IGA*]. The Department of the Treasury also developed alternative model IGAs for indirect reporting — *Model 1B IGA Non-reciprocal, Preexisting TIEA or DTC*; *Model 1B IGA Non-reciprocal, No TIEA or DTC* — and for direct reporting to the IRS — *Model 2 IGA, Preexisting TIEA or DTC*; *Model 2 IGA, No TIEA or DTC*: see United States, Department of the Treasury, "Model Intergovernmental Agreements" (last updated 19 January 2016), online: www.treasury.gov/resource-center/tax-policy/treaties/Pages/FATCA.aspx.

[69] *Model 1A IGA*, above note 68, Preamble.

[70] See United States, Department of the Treasury, Press Release, "Treasury and IRS Issue Final Regulations to Combat Offshore Tax Evasion" (17 January 2013), online: www.treasury.gov/press-center/press-releases/Pages/tg1825.aspx.

[71] See *ibid*; United States, Department of the Treasury, *Model 2 IGA, Preexisting TIEA or DTC: Agreement between the Government of the United States of America and the Government of* [FATCA Partner] *for Cooperation to Facilitate the Implementation of FATCA* (4 November 2013), online: www.treasury.gov/resource-center/tax-policy/treaties/Documents/FATCA-Model-2-Agreement-Preexisting-TIEA-or-DTC-11-4-13.pdf [*Model 2 IGA*] (for FFIs reporting directly to the IRS).

[72] Allison Christians, "Interpretation or Override? Introducing the Hybrid Tax Agreement" (2015) 80 *Tax Notes International* 51 at 51.

admonishes this asymmetrical treatment, which creates ambiguities and inconsistencies in the law that will inevitably result in consequences.[73] The use of a protocol to incorporate the IGA into Article 26 (EOI) of a double tax convention (DTC), modelled on the *Model Tax Treaty*,[74] would have provided a stronger legal basis to argue that the terms of the EOI article applied to the IGA.

The *Model 1A IGA* is organized as follows:

Article 1:	Definitions
Article 2:	Obligations to Obtain and Exchange Information with respect to Reportable Accounts
Article 3:	Time and Manner of EOI
Article 4:	Application of *FATCA* to FATCA Partner's Financial Institutions
Article 5:	Collaboration on Compliance and Enforcement
Article 6:	Mutual Commitment to Continue to Enhance the Effectiveness of Information Exchange and Transparency
Article 7:	Consistency in the Application of *FATCA* to Partner Jurisdictions
Article 8:	Consultations and Amendments
Article 9:	Annexes
Article 10:	Term of Agreement

Highlights of select articles follow.

4.2 Article 1: Definitions

Note that terms in capital letters used in this subsection and the six subsections below in this chapter are generally defined in Article 1 of the *Model 1A IGA*. Article 1 provides critical definitions that define the boundaries

[73] *Ibid* at 52–53, observing, for example, that were a *FATCA* partner to invoke the public policy exception to exchanging information under Art 26(3) of the *Model Tax Convention on Income and on Capital* (Paris: OECD, 1992) (loose-leaf) [*Model Tax Treaty*], such a jurisdiction could find itself subject to the 30 percent withholding penalty under *FATCA* while the United States may be able to invoke the same public policy exception without facing such a sanction.

[74] *Model Tax Treaty*, above note 73.

and scope of the agreement and, in particular, those individuals, persons, and institutions affected by its regime.

The term "Financial Institution" is defined by additional technical terms to mean a "Custodial Institution," a "Depository Institution," an "Investment Entity," or a "Specified Insurance Company."[75] The term "[FATCA Partner] Financial Institution" generally refers to a Financial Institution resident in a country that is a signatory to the bilateral agreement but excludes foreign branches of such a Financial Institution.[76] The term "Reporting Financial Institution" generally refers to a Financial Institution in the "FATCA Partner" country or a Financial Institution in the United States subject to reporting (technically, the latter is referred to as a "Reporting US Financial Institution").[77] The term "Reporting [FATCA Partner] Financial Institution" means any [FATCA Partner] Financial Institution that is not a "Non-reporting [FATCA Partner] Financial Institution."[78]

Article 1 also defines the terms "Financial Account," "Depository Account," and "Custodial Account," among other financial interests. The term "Reportable Account" means a "US Reportable Account" or a "[FATCA Partner] Reportable Account" as the context requires.[79] A [FATCA Partner] Reportable Account means a Financial Account maintained by a Reporting US Financial Institution in the case of a Depository Account generally if more than $10 of interest is paid to such account in any given calendar year, or in the case of a Financial Account other than a Depository Account, the "Account Holder" is a resident of the FATCA Partner, including Entities that certify that they are resident in the FATCA Partner for tax purposes with respect to which US sourced income is generally paid or credited.[80] A Financial Account is defined in part as an account maintained by a Financial Institution.[81]

---

[75] *Model 1A IGA*, above note 68 at Arts 1(g), (h), (i), (j), & (k).

[76] *Ibid* at Art 1(l).

[77] *Ibid* at Art 1(n).

[78] *Ibid* at Art 1(o).

[79] *Ibid* at Art 1(aa).

[80] *Ibid* at Art 1(bb).

[81] *Ibid* at Art 1(s).

A US Reportable Account generally refers to a Financial Account maintained by a Reporting [FATCA Partner] Financial Institution and generally held by one or more "Specified US Persons" or by a "Non-US Entity" with one or more "Controlling Persons" that are Specified US Persons.[82] Account Holder means the person listed or identified as the holder of a Financial Account by the Financial Institution that maintains the account but generally does not include agents, custodians, nominees, or straw persons except where the person holding the account is a Financial Institution.[83] The term "US Person" generally refers to US citizens or resident individuals, partnerships or corporations organized in the United States, or certain trusts that would be considered non-foreign under the US residence rules applicable to trusts.[84] A Specified US Person refers to US Persons other than those entities listed in the definition (which are similar to the excluded entities in the *Final FATCA Regulations* definition of a specified US person, listed above).[85] The term "Entity" means a legal person or a legal arrangement such as a trust.[86]

The term "US Source Withholdable Payment" means any FDAP Income (interest, dividends, rents, salaries, wages, premiums, annuities, compensations, remunerations, and periodical gains, profits, and payments from US sources).[87]

4.3 Article 2: Obligations to Obtain and Exchange Information with respect to Reportable Accounts

Importantly, Article 2 sets forth the scope of the information to be obtained and exchanged under the agreement. The FATCA Partner generally has the obligation to obtain and exchange the following items

[82] *Ibid* at Art 1(cc).

[83] *Ibid* at Art 1(dd).

[84] *Ibid* at Art 1(ee).

[85] *Ibid* at Art 1(ff). See note 63, above in this chapter.

[86] *Model 1A IGA*, above note 68 at Art 1(gg).

[87] *Ibid* at Art 1(ii).

of information with respect to each US Reportable Account at each Financial Institution in its jurisdiction:

1) the name, address, and US TIN of each Specified US Person that is an Account Holder of the account together with the same information for each Specified US Person having the required controlling interest in a Non-US Entity[88]
2) the account number[89]
3) the name and identifying number of the Reporting [FATCA Partner] Financial Institution[90]
4) the account balance or value (including in the case of a "Cash Value Insurance Contract" or "Annuity Contract," the "Cash Value" or surrender value) as of the end of the relevant calendar year[91]
5) certain information relating to Custodial Accounts, including in part the total gross amount of interest, dividends, and other income generated with respect to assets held in the account (whether paid or credited to the account) during the calendar year and the total gross proceeds from the sale or redemption of property relating to the account[92]
6) certain information relating to Depository Accounts, including the total gross amount of interest paid or credited to the account during the calendar year[93]
7) certain information relating to an Account Holder's income for accounts generally not mentioned above[94]

The United States generally has the obligation to obtain and exchange the following items of information with respect to each FATCA Partner Reportable Account at each Reporting US Financial Institution:

---

[88] *Ibid* at Art 2(a)(1).
[89] *Ibid* at Art 2(a)(2).
[90] *Ibid* at Art 2(a)(3).
[91] *Ibid* at Art 2(a)(4).
[92] *Ibid* at Art 2(a)(5).
[93] *Ibid* at Art 2(a)(6).
[94] *Ibid* at Art 2(a)(7).

1) the name, address, and FATCA Partner TIN of any person that is a resident of the FATCA Partner and is an Account Holder of the account[95]
2) the account number[96]
3) the name and identifying number of the Reporting US Financial Institution[97]
4) the gross amount of interest paid on a Depository Account[98]
5) the gross amount of US sourced dividends paid or credited to the account[99]
6) the gross amount of other US sourced income paid or credited to the account to the extent subject to reporting under Chapter 3 of Subtitle A or Chapter 61 of Subtitle F of the *Code*[100]

4.4 Article 3: Time and Manner of EOI

Article 3 provides that generally the amount and characterization of payments are to be determined in accordance with local tax laws.[101] The required reporting of information under Article 2 is to be phased in.[102] And the information described in Article 2 is generally required to be exchanged within nine months after the end of the calendar year to which the information relates.[103] Also the Competent Authorities of the FATCA Partner and the United States shall, pursuant to the mutual agreement procedure contained in their tax treaty or TIEA, establish procedures for the Automatic Exchange described in Article 2 and prescribe rules and procedures as may be necessary to implement Article 5 (Collaboration on Compliance and Enforcement).[104]

---

[95] *Ibid* at Art 2(b)(1).

[96] *Ibid* at Art 2(b)(2).

[97] *Ibid* at Art 2(b)(3).

[98] *Ibid* at Art 2(b)(4).

[99] *Ibid* at Art 2(b)(5).

[100] *Ibid* at Art 2(b)(6).

[101] *Ibid* at Art 3(1).

[102] *Ibid* at Art 3(3)(a)(1).

[103] *Ibid* at Art 3(5).

[104] *Ibid* at Art 3(6).

4.5 Article 4: Application of *FATCA* to FATCA Partner Financial Institutions

Article 4 provides a key reward for the FATCA Partner's entering into a *Model 1A IGA* — relief from the 30 percent withholding under *FATCA* for each Reporting [FATCA Partner] Financial Institution.[105] This is achieved by treating each Reporting [FATCA Partner] Financial Institution as complying with and not subject to withholding under *Code* section 1471 provided that the FATCA Partner complies with its reporting obligations under Articles 2 and 3 and that the [FATCA Partner] Financial Institution complies with obligations further enumerated under Article 4.[106] Additionally, Article 4 suspends the application of rules under the *Final FATCA Regulations* relating to recalcitrant accounts and provides special rules relating to retirement plans.[107] Article 4 also contains provisions dealing with the identification and treatment of deemed-compliant FFIs, exempt beneficial owners, and "Related Entities" that are Nonparticipating Financial Institutions.[108]

4.6 Article 5: Collaboration on Compliance and Enforcement

Article 5 provides a process to address significant non-compliance with the obligations under the *Model 1A IGA* with respect to a Reporting Financial Institution in the other jurisdiction. Under the first step, a Competent Authority shall notify the Competent Authority of the other Party when the former has determined that there is a significant non-compliance with the obligations under the agreement with respect to a Reporting Financial Institution in the other jurisdiction.[109] In this situation, the Competent Authority of the other Party is to apply its

[105] *Ibid* at Art 4(1).

[106] *Ibid* at Arts 4(1)(a)–(e), for obligations of [FATCA Partner] Financial Institutions.

[107] *Ibid* at Arts 4(2) & (3).

[108] *Ibid* at Arts 4(4) & (5).

[109] *Ibid* at Art 5(2)(a).

domestic law (including applicable penalties) to address the significant non-compliance described in the notification.[110]

In the case of non-compliance with respect to a Reporting [FATCA Partner] Financial Institution, where enforcement actions do not resolve the non-compliance within a period of eighteen months after the first notification is given, the United States shall treat the Reporting [FATCA Partner] Financial Institution as a Nonparticipating Financial Institution.[111]

4.7 Article 6: Mutual Commitment to Continue to Enhance the Effectiveness of Information Exchange and Transparency

Under Article 6, the Parties affirm their commitment to working with other multilateral platforms, such as the OECD and the European Union, to further adapt the terms of the *Model 1A IGA* toward the goal of a common model for Automatic Exchange, including the related development of reporting and due diligence standards for financial institutions.[112]

4.8 Annex I: Due Diligence Obligations for Identifying and Reporting on US Reportable Accounts and on Payments to Certain Nonparticipating Financial Institutions

Annex I contains important due diligence rules (including key account exemptions) under the following categories: Preexisting Individual Accounts, New Individual Accounts, Preexisting Entity Accounts, New Entity Accounts, and special rules and definitions.[113]

[110] *Ibid.*

[111] *Ibid* at Art 5(2)(b). Query whether there will be any access to the arbitration provisions under the competent authority procedures if such exist, as they do, for example, in the case of the *Convention between Canada and the United States of America with respect to Taxes on Income and on Capital*, 26 September 1980 (as amended to the protocols signed on 14 June 1983, 23 March 1984, 17 March 1997, 29 July 1997, and 21 September 2007) [*Canada–US Tax Treaty*].

[112] *Model 1A IGA*, above note 68 at Art 6(3).

[113] *Ibid*, Annex I. Annex II deals with Non-reporting [FATCA Partner] Financial Institutions and products.

5 Intergovernmental Agreement with Canada

5.1 Introduction

On 5 February 2014, Canada and the United States signed an agreement creating a historic new information channel between CRA and the IRS, carrying detailed financial account information regarding US citizens and residents with accounts in Canada.[114] Canadian legislation implementing the new agreement was passed on 19 June 2014,[115] and CRA issued detailed guidance on the new Part XVIII of the *Act* in August 2015.[116] The *Canada–US IGA* is based on the *Model 1A IGA*, which is designed to provide reciprocal Automatic Exchange pursuant to the *Canada–US Tax Treaty*.[117] Professors Christians and Cockfield note that while under the *Canada–US IGA*, Canada undertakes a substantial list of new reporting and exchange requirements, the United States agrees to virtually no new reporting or EOI.[118] Under the wording of the agreement, the chief mechanism, in Article XXVII (EOI) of the *Canada–US Tax Treaty*, through which the IRS may obtain information for the enforcement and administration of the *Code* appears to remain intact, with the new IGA substantially augmenting the information-sharing process.[119] However,

[114] See *Canada–US IGA*, above note 16.

[115] *Implementation Act*, above note 18, enacting Part XVIII, ss 263–269, of the *Act*, above note 21. See also Julius Melnitzer, "Canadian Institutions Scramble in Race to Comply with FATCA" *Financial Post* (2 July 2014), online: http://natpo.st/1NIKXFG.

[116] Canada, Canada Revenue Agency, *Guidance on Enhanced Financial Accounts Information Reporting: Part XVIII of the* Income Tax Act (Ottawa: Canada Revenue Agency, 2015), online: www.cra-arc.gc.ca/tx/nnrsdnts/nhncdrprtng/gdnc-eng.pdf [*Guidance on Information Reporting*]. See also *Act*, above note 21, Part XVIII.

[117] *Canada–US Tax Treaty*, above note 111. Although the *Canada–US IGA*, above note 16, is formally reciprocal, as the United States is not considered a tax haven jurisdiction for Canadian residents and as Canada has been receiving Automatic Exchange relating to interest income earned by Canadian residents for decades, the true purpose of the agreement is to drive names of non-compliant US citizens living in Canada to the IRS for enforcement action, and not to combat tax evasion by Canadians with US bank and financial accounts: see Kerzner, above note 23.

[118] Christians & Cockfield, above note 15.

[119] *Canada–US Tax Treaty*, above note 111 at Art XXVII. The preamble to the *Canada–US IGA*, above note 16, provides in part, "Whereas, the Parties desire to conclude an agreement to improve international tax compliance and provide for the implementation of FATCA based on domestic

as noted by Professor Christians above, the failure to amend the treaty through a protocol has created legal ambiguities surrounding the use of the EOI article and the tax treaty itself.[120] A key stated aim of the IGA is to improve international tax compliance by building upon the long-standing and close relationship that Canada and the United States have in the area of mutual assistance in tax matters.[121] Another key stated aim of the IGA is to implement *FATCA*.[122] A Canadian financial institution that is compliant with Part XVIII of the *Act* and follows the procedures in the *Canada–US IGA* will not be subject to US withholding tax on US sourced income and gross proceeds (on both its own investments and those held on behalf of its customers) under *Code* section 1471.[123]

The *Canada–US IGA* is organized as follows:

Article 1:	Definitions
Article 2:	Obligations to Obtain and Exchange Information with respect to Reportable Accounts
Article 3:	Time and Manner of EOI
Article 4:	Application of *FATCA* to Canadian Financial Institutions
Article 5:	Collaboration on Compliance and Enforcement

reporting and reciprocal automatic exchange pursuant to the Convention . . . ." See also *Canada–US IGA*, *ibid* at Art 2(1): "Subject to the provisions of Article 3 of this Agreement, each Party shall obtain the information specified in paragraph 2 of this Article with respect to all Reportable Accounts and shall annually exchange this information with the other Party on an automatic basis pursuant to the provisions of Article XXVII of the Convention." The fact that Article XXVII remains intact is vital to understanding that while certain accounts maintained in Canada, for example, RRSPs, may not be subject to the reporting regime under *FATCA* or the *Canada–US IGA*, this does not mean that once the IRS has the name of a delinquent filer, it cannot request bank information on all of that person's accounts in Canada under a wide array of administrative and treaty avenues. This critical factor is often overlooked by journalists and other observers writing on *FATCA* implementation in Canada: see Kerzner, above note 23.

120 See notes 72–73 and associated text, above in this chapter.

121 See *Canada–US IGA*, above note 16, Preamble.

122 See *ibid*. See also Arthur J Cockfield, "The Limits of the International Tax Regime as a Commitment Projector" (2013) 33 *Virginia Tax Review* 59 at 98, observing that *FATCA* unduly raises transaction costs for taxpayers and non-US financial institutions, which will result in a long-term reputation cost affecting the ability of the United States to make credible commitments concerning cross-border tax matters, which will harm US economic interests, and also noting that the implementation of the regime has the unintended consequence of redistributing wealth from taxpayers impacted by the higher transaction costs to financial service and tax service providers.

123 See *Guidance on Information Reporting*, above note 116 at 7.

Article 6:	Mutual Commitment to Continue to Enhance the Effectiveness of Information Exchange and Transparency
Article 7:	Consistency in the Application of *FATCA* to Partner Jurisdictions
Article 8:	Consultations and Amendments
Article 9:	Annexes
Article 10:	Term of Agreement
Annex I:	Due Diligence Obligations for Identifying and Reporting on US Reportable Accounts and on Payments to Certain Nonparticipating Financial Institutions
Annex II:	Non-reporting Canadian Financial Institutions and Products

Highlights of select articles follow.

5.2 Article 1: Definitions

Note that terms in capital letters used in this subsection and the eight subsections below in this chapter are generally defined in Article 1 of the *Canada–US IGA*. Article 1 provides critical definitions that define the boundaries and scope of the agreement and, in particular, those individuals, persons, and institutions affected by its regime. Some preliminary observations are warranted regarding definitions and the *Canada–US IGA*. Article 4(7) of the *Canada–US IGA* provides that Canada may use and may permit Canadian financial institutions to use a definition in the relevant US *Treasury Regulations* in place of a corresponding definition in the *Canada–US IGA* provided that such use does not frustrate the purposes of the *Canada–US IGA* and is not inconsistent with Canadian legislation and CRA guidance.[124] In addition, it is important to note that there are special definitions relating to Annex I (discussed below) of the *Canada–US IGA* and the complex due diligence rules contained therein that need to be carefully considered but that are beyond the scope of this survey chapter, especially those definitions dealing with passive and active "Non-US Entities" that are not FFIs, or NFFEs.[125]

[124] See *ibid* at 12.

[125] See, for example, *Canada–US IGA*, above note 16, Annex I at VI.

Subject to the qualifications described below, the term "Financial Institution" is generally defined by additional technical terms to mean a "Custodial Institution," a "Depositary Institution," an "Investment Entity," or a "Specified Insurance Company."[126] Under the *Act*, Canada has created a definition for "listed financial institution."[127] A financial institution must be a Canadian financial institution under Part XVIII of the *Act* for it to have potential reporting obligations in Canada under that part.[128] Two conditions must be met for an entity to be a Canadian financial institution under Part XVIII: (1) the entity must be a "Canadian Financial Institution" under the *Canada–US IGA*, and (2) it must be a listed financial institution for the purposes of Part XVIII as the latter term is defined in section 263(1) of the *Act*, limiting its meaning to a specific list of entities.[129] The narrower definition of financial institution by Canada created a number of initial concerns, in particular relating to the use of trusts.[130] Canadian Financial Institution generally refers to a Financial Institution resident in Canada but excludes (1) any branch of such Financial Institution that is located outside of Canada and (2) any branch of a Financial Institution located in Canada if that Financial Institution is not resident in Canada.[131] The term "Reporting Financial Institution" refers to a "Reporting Canadian Financial Institution" or a "Reporting US Financial Institution."[132] A Reporting Canadian Financial Institution means any Canadian Financial Institution that is not a "Non-reporting Canadian Financial Institution."[133] A Non-reporting Canadian Financial Institution means any Canadian Financial Institution or other "Entity" resident in Canada that by virtue of special provisions in Annex II is treated as a Non-reporting Canadian Financial Institution or qualifies

---

[126] *Ibid* at Arts 1(g), (h), (i), (j), & (k). See also Matias Milet, "FATCA and Canadian Investment Entities" (2015) *Journal of International Taxation* 29 (Checkpoint).

[127] *Act*, above note 21, s 263(1).

[128] See *Guidance on Information Reporting*, above note 116 at 16; *Act*, above note 21, s 263(2).

[129] See *Guidance on Information Reporting*, above note 116 at 16; *Act*, above note 21, s 263(1).

[130] For an in-depth discussion of the issue, see Roy A Berg & Paul M Barba, "FATCA in Canada: The Restriction on the Class of Entities Subject to FATCA" (2014) 62:3 *Canadian Tax Journal* 587. See also Alison Bennett, "Treasury OK with Canadian Stance on Listed Financial Institutions under FATCA" *BNA Daily Tax Reporter* (7 October 2014).

[131] *Canada–US IGA*, above note 16 at Art 1(l); *Act*, above note 21, s 263(2).

[132] *Canada–US IGA*, above note 16 at Art 1(n).

[133] *Ibid* at Art 1(o); *Act*, above note 21, s 263(2).

as a deemed-compliant FFI or an exempt beneficial owner under the US *Treasury Regulations*.[134] The term "Nonparticipating Financial Institution" means a nonparticipating FFI (as that term is defined in the *Treasury Regulations*) but excludes Canadian Financial Institutions unless treated as Nonparticipating Financial Institutions under Article 5(2)(b).[135]

Article 1 also defines the terms "Financial Account," "Depository Account," "Custodial Account," and "Equity Interest," among other financial interests.[136] The term "Reportable Account" means a "US Reportable Account" or a "Canadian Reportable Account" as the context requires.[137] A US Reportable Account generally refers to an account that must be reported to the United States under the *Canada–US IGA*. More technically, the term means a Financial Account maintained by a Canadian Financial Institution and held by one or more "Specified US Persons" or by a Non-US Entity with one or more "Controlling Persons" that are Specified US Persons. An exception may apply if the account is not identified as a US Reportable Account after following the due diligence procedures in Annex I.[138] The term "Account Holder" means the person listed or identified as the holder of a Financial Account by the Financial Institution that maintains the account but generally does not include agents, custodians, nominees, or straw persons except where the person holding the account is a Financial Institution.[139] The term "US Person" generally refers to US citizens or resident individuals, partnerships or corporations organized in the United States, or certain trusts that would be considered non-foreign under the US residence rules applicable to trusts.[140] Specified US Person refers to US Persons other than those entities listed in the definition (which are similar to the excluded entities in the *Final FATCA Regulations* definition of specified US person, listed above).[141]

---

[134] *Canada–US IGA*, above note 16 at Art 1(q); *Act*, above note 21, ss 263(1) & (2).

[135] *Canada–US IGA*, above note 16 at Art 1(r).

[136] *Ibid* at Arts 1(s), (t), (u), & (v); *Act*, above note 21, ss 263(1), (2), & (3).

[137] *Canada–US IGA*, above note 16 at Art 1(aa).

[138] *Ibid* at Art 1(cc); *Act*, above note 21, s 263(1).

[139] *Canada–US IGA*, above note 16 at Art 1(dd).

[140] *Ibid* at Art 1(ee).

[141] *Ibid* at Art 1(ff). See note 63, above in this chapter. Under Art 6(4)(b) of the *Canada–US IGA*, above note 16, with respect to Reportable Accounts maintained by a Reporting Financial Institution

5.3 Article 2: Obligations to Obtain and Exchange Information with respect to Reportable Accounts

Article 2 is the key provision in the *Canada–US IGA*. It sets forth the scope of the information to be obtained and exchanged annually regarding all Reportable Accounts by each "Party" to the agreement. Canada generally has the obligation to obtain and exchange the following items of information with respect to each US Reportable Account at each Reporting Canadian Financial Institution:

1) the name, address, and US TIN of each Specified US Person that is an Account Holder of the account together with the same information for each Specified US Person having the required controlling interest in a Non-US Entity[142]
2) the account number[143]
3) the name and identifying number of the Reporting Canadian Financial Institution[144]
4) the account balance or value (including in the case of a "Cash Value Insurance Contract" or "Annuity Contract," the "Cash Value" or surrender value) as of the end of the relevant calendar year[145]
5) certain information relating to Custodial Accounts, including in part the total gross amount of interest, dividends, and other income generated with respect to assets held in the account (whether paid or credited to the account) during the calendar year and the total gross proceeds from the sale or redemption of property relating to the account[146]

---

as of 30 June 2014, Canada commits to establish by 1 January 2017, for reporting with respect to 2017 and subsequent years rules requiring Reporting Canadian Financial Institutions to obtain the US TIN of each Specified US Person.

[142] *Canada–US IGA*, above note 16 at Art 2(a)(1).

[143] *Ibid* at Art 2(a)(2).

[144] *Ibid* at Art 2(a)(3).

[145] *Ibid* at Art 2(a)(4).

[146] *Ibid* at Art 2(a)(5).

6) certain information relating to Depository Accounts, including the total gross amount of interest paid or credited to the account during the calendar year[147]
7) certain information relating to an Account Holder's income for accounts generally not mentioned above[148]

The United States generally has the obligation to obtain and exchange the following items of information with respect to each Canadian Reportable Account at each Reporting US Financial Institution:

1) the name, address, and Canadian TIN of any person that is a resident of Canada and is an Account Holder of the account[149]
2) the account number[150]
3) the name and identifying number of the Reporting US Financial Institution[151]
4) the gross amount of interest paid on a Depository Account[152]
5) the gross amount of US sourced dividends paid or credited to the account[153]
6) the gross amount of other US sourced income paid or credited to the account to the extent subject to reporting under Chapter 3 of Subtitle A or Chapter 61 of Subtitle F of the *Code*[154]

Pursuant to Article 6(4), with respect to Reportable Accounts maintained by a Reporting Financial Institution as of 30 June 2014, Canada and the United States generally agree to establish rules requiring each such institution to obtain and report US TINs and Canadian TINs respectively by 1 January 2017.[155]

---

147 *Ibid* at Art 2(a)(6).
148 *Ibid* at Art 2(a)(7).
149 *Ibid* at Art 2(b)(1).
150 *Ibid* at Art 2(b)(2).
151 *Ibid* at Art 2(b)(3).
152 *Ibid* at Art 2(b)(4).
153 *Ibid* at Art 2(b)(5).
154 *Ibid* at Art 2(b)(6).
155 *Ibid* at Art 6(4). But see *ibid* at Art 3(4), which may under certain circumstances require a Party to obtain and exchange the date of birth of a relevant person if such information is on hand.

5.4 Article 3: Time and Manner of EOI

Article 3 provides that generally the amount and characterization of payments are to be determined in accordance with local tax laws.[156] The required reporting of information under Article 2 is to be phased in. The information described in Article 2(2) is generally required to be obtained and exchanged with respect to 2014 and subsequent years except that in the case of Canada, the 2014 information to be obtained and exchanged is that relating to account name, account number, name of financial institution, and account balance.[157] In 2015, Canada is obligated to obtain and exchange generally all of the information described in Article 2(2)(a) except for the gross proceeds described in Article 2(2)(a)(5)(B),[158] but this remaining information is required to be obtained and exchanged with respect to 2016 and subsequent years.[159] The United States, on the other hand, agrees to obtain and exchange all of the information described in Article 2(2)(b) with respect to 2014 and subsequent years.[160]

The information described in Article 2 is generally required to be exchanged within nine months after the end of the calendar year to which the information relates.[161] Also, the Competent Authorities of Canada and the United States shall, pursuant to the mutual agreement procedure contained in the *Canada–US Tax Treaty*, establish procedures for the Automatic Exchange described in Article 2 and prescribe rules and procedures as may be necessary to implement Article 5 (Collaboration on Compliance and Enforcement).[162] Article 3(7) provides that all information exchanged under the IGA will be subject to the confidentiality and other protections provided under the *Canada–US Tax Treaty*.

---

[156] *Ibid* at Art 3(1).

[157] *Ibid* at Art 3(3)(a)(1).

[158] *Ibid* at Art 3(3)(a)(2).

[159] *Ibid* at Art 3(3)(a)(3). Information to be exchanged by the United States in 2014 and subsequent years is all of the data required under Art 2(2)(b) (*Ibid* at Art 3(3)(b)).

[160] *Ibid* at Art 3(3)(b).

[161] *Ibid* at Art 3(5).

[162] *Ibid* at Art 3(6).

5.5 Article 4: Application of *FATCA* to Canadian Financial Institutions

Article 4 represents the teeth behind the EOI mechanism in the *Canada–US IGA*. If avoiding pain can be called a reward, then Article 4 provides a key reward for Canada's entering into the IGA — relief from the 30 percent withholding under *FATCA* for each Reporting Canadian Financial Institution.[163] This is achieved by treating each Reporting Canadian Financial Institution as complying with and not subject to withholding under *Code* section 1471 provided that Canada complies with its reporting obligations under Articles 2 and 3 and that the Reporting Canadian Financial Institution complies with obligations further enumerated under Article 4.[164] Additionally, Article 4 suspends the application of rules under the *Final FATCA Regulations* relating to recalcitrant accounts under certain conditions and provides special rules relating to Canadian retirement plans identified in Annex II.[165] Article 4 also contains provisions dealing with the identification and treatment of deemed-compliant FFIs, exempt beneficial owners, and "Related Entities" that are Nonparticipating Financial Institutions.[166] Lastly, Article 4 contains rules relating to coordination of timing and coordination of definitions (with the US *Treasury Regulations*).[167]

5.6 Article 5: Collaboration on Compliance and Enforcement

Article 5 provides a process to address significant non-compliance with the obligations under the *Canada–US IGA* with respect to a Reporting Financial Institution in the other jurisdiction. Under the first step, a Competent Authority shall notify the Competent

[163] *Ibid* at Art 4(1).

[164] *Ibid* at Arts 4(1)(a)–(e), for obligations of Reporting Canadian Financial Institutions.

[165] *Ibid* at Arts 4(2) & (3).

[166] *Ibid* at Arts 4(4) & (5).

[167] *Ibid* at Arts 4(6) & (7).

Authority of the other Party when the former has determined that there is a significant non-compliance with the obligations under the agreement with respect to a Reporting Financial Institution in the other jurisdiction.[168] In this situation, the Competent Authority of the other Party is to apply its domestic law (including applicable penalties) to address the significant non-compliance described in the notification.[169]

In the case of non-compliance with respect to a Reporting Canadian Financial Institution, where enforcement actions do not resolve the non-compliance within a period of eighteen months after the first notification is given, the United States shall treat the Reporting Canadian Financial Institution as a Nonparticipating Financial Institution.[170] Article 5 also deals with minor and administrative errors.[171]

5.7 Article 6: Mutual Commitment to Continue to Enhance the Effectiveness of Information Exchange and Transparency

Under Article 6, the Parties affirm their commitment to working with other multilateral platforms, such as the OECD and the European Union, to further adapt the terms of the *Canada–US IGA* toward the goal of a common model for Automatic Exchange, including the related development of reporting and due diligence standards for financial institutions.[172] Article 6 also deals with Automatic Exchange reciprocity and the treatment of passthru payments and gross proceeds.[173]

---

[168] *Ibid* at Art 5(2)(a).

[169] *Ibid.*

[170] *Ibid* at Art 5(2)(b). Query whether there will be any access to the arbitration provisions under the competent authority procedures in the *Canada–US Tax Treaty*, above note 111.

[171] *Canada–US IGA*, above note 16 at Art 5(1).

[172] *Ibid* at Art 6(3).

[173] *Ibid* at Arts 6(1) & (2).

5.8 Article 7: Consistency in the Application of *FATCA* to Partner Jurisdictions

Under Article 7, Canada will be accorded the benefit of any more favourable terms under Article 4 or Annex I relating to the application of *FATCA* to Canadian Financial Institutions afforded to another Partner Jurisdiction.[174]

5.9 Annex I: Due Diligence Obligations for Identifying and Reporting on US Reportable Accounts and on Payments to Certain Nonparticipating Financial Institutions

Annex I contains the important due diligence procedures that Canada must require Reporting Canadian Financial Institutions to follow to identify US Reportable Accounts and accounts held by Nonparticipating Financial Institutions. Annex I contains due diligence rules (including, where applicable, key account exemptions and monetary thresholds) under the following categories: Preexisting Individual Accounts, New Individual Accounts, Preexisting Entity Accounts, New Entity Accounts, and special rules and definitions.[175]

5.10 Annex II: Non-reporting Canadian Financial Institutions and Products

Annex II provides information relating to Entities that are to be treated as Non-reporting Canadian Financial Institutions and hence exempt beneficial owners for the purposes of the *FATCA* withholding rules under *Code* sections 1471 and 1472.[176] Annex II also provides rules relating to Financial Institutions that are Non-reporting Canadian Financial Institutions and that are to be treated as deemed-compliant FFIs for the

[174] *Ibid* at Art 7(1).

[175] *Ibid*, Annex I. See *Act*, above note 21, s 265.

[176] *Canada–US IGA*, above note 16, Annex II at II. See *Code*, above note 3, §§ 1471 & 1472.

purposes of the *FATCA* rules under *Code* section 1471.[177] Lastly, Annex II lists accounts and products established in Canada that are to be excluded from the definition of Financial Account and hence not treated as US Reportable Accounts (e.g., RRSPs, RRIFs, RPPs, TFSAs, DPSPs, and RESPs).[178]

6 Conclusion

When *FATCA* is combined with US enforcement of its tax and reporting rules against dual nationals living and paying taxes in Canada, the United Kingdom, the European Union, and elsewhere, for the policy reasons discussed here and in Chapter 3, *FATCA* strikes a chord of inequity in respect of these taxpayers and runs counter to the principles and objectives of international tax policy and EOI, described in Chapter 2. When Canada provides information under *FATCA* on its nationals and residents with US heritage to the IRS, they can become subject to the devastating penalties of the Report of Foreign Bank and Financial Accounts (FBAR) rules, described in Chapter 10, and to the full force of US administrative enforcement powers, described in Chapter 5. The professional fees alone to represent a delinquent taxpayer before the IRS can be significant. In contrast, under Automatic Exchange, Canada will receive information on its residents who have offshore accounts in tax haven jurisdictions that impose little to no income tax. Such information exchange, by stopping tax evasion, will be consistent with the goals of international tax law. Additionally, as described in Chapter 8, in 2018 when Canada exchanges information under Automatic Exchange about income earned by residents of another jurisdiction that is also participating in Automatic Exchange where those individuals are not resident in Canada, Canada will be assisting that other jurisdiction to administer its fiscal system. Because the United States imposes worldwide taxation on individuals based on citizenship, EOI with the IRS creates the spectre of financial decimation for non-compliant Canadians and financial hardship for Canadians who,

[177] *Canada–US IGA*, above note 16, Annex II at III. See *Code*, above note 3, § 1471.

[178] *Canada–US IGA*, above note 16, Annex II at IV.

lacking the protection of their own government, yield to the intimidation of *FATCA* and file costly US tax and reporting returns. With Automatic Exchange, an individual taxpayer will, owing to the tax treaty system, generally file one return on his worldwide income, but with *FATCA*, dual nationals in Canada, the United Kingdom, and the European Union will have to file two such returns.

As explained in Chapter 8, the system of Automatic Exchange, for which *FATCA* was a key driver, remains an important tool for Canada, the United Kingdom, and the United States for combatting international tax evasion, particularly with tax havens. But both *FATCA* and Automatic Exchange pose three broad challenges in the war against international tax evasion. The first is their legal complexity, particularly relating to due diligence components. The second is the lack of economic and political incentives for tax havens to cooperate. And the third is the inadequate infrastructure relating to the standards of transparency and EOI required to implement and operate these new regimes, discussed in Chapter 3. Removing Canadians and other nationals who were born "accidental Americans" or who moved away from the United States long ago from the administrative net of the US tax and reporting system would help the United States refocus its fight against tax cheats on its residents and ramp up the fight against the use of tax havens by instruments of international crime and terrorism. If the United States will not unilaterally end taxation by nationality, Australia, Canada, New Zealand, the United Kingdom, and other European nations should work together diplomatically to pressure the US government to devise a fast and affordable mechanism to allow long-term residents of theirs to exit the orbit of the US tax system.

Further Readings

Christians, Allison, & Arthur J Cockfield. "Submission to Finance Department on Implementation of FATCA in Canada: Submission on Legislative Proposals relating to the Canada–United States Enhanced Tax Information Exchange Agreement" (10 March 2014), online: http://dx.doi.org/10.2139/ssrn.2407264.

Cockfield, Arthur J. "The Limits of the International Tax Regime as a Commitment Projector" (2013) 33 *Virginia Tax Review* 59.
Grinberg, Itai. "The Battle over Taxing Offshore Accounts" (2012) 60 *UCLA Law Review* 304.
Kerzner, David S. "Surviving FATCA: A Roadmap for Delinquent U.S. Filers and Their Advisors" (2014) 7 *Taxes & Wealth Management* 1.
Milet, Matias. "FATCA and Canadian Investment Entities" (2015) *Journal of International Taxation* 29 (Checkpoint).

10

International Collections Enforcement and Voluntary Disclosures

1 Introduction

This chapter gives an overview of the voluntary disclosure process in Canada and the United States. It also considers the US federal legal regime for the reporting of foreign bank and financial accounts under the *Bank Secrecy Act*.[1] The importance of the *BSA* cannot be understated; as described below, its penalty provisions have been a major weapon wielded by the IRS against American citizens with bank accounts outside the US. This chapter will provide important insight to professionals in the tax, accounting, and wealth management industries who have clients that are US non-filers or have undeclared offshore assets to either the IRS or CRA. This chapter will also be particularly relevant to governments and students contemplating policy changes to international tax law surrounding exchange of information, citizenship-based taxation, and the unique dilemma facing the US expatriate community in Canada, the United Kingdom, the European Union, and elsewhere.

[1] Pub L 91-508, Tit II, 84 Stat 1118, 10/26/1970, codified as amended at 12 USC 1829b, 12 USC 1951–1959, and 31 USC 5311–5314; 5316–5332 [*BSA*]. Regulations implementing Title II of the *BSA* (codified at 31 USC 5311ff) appear at 31 CFR Part 103 and, effective 1 March 2011, at 31 CFR Chapter X: see note 38, below in this chapter.

D.S. Kerzner, D.W. Chodikoff, *International Tax Evasion in the Global Information Age*, DOI 10.1007/978-3-319-40421-9_10

Congress, in passing the *BSA*, observed in 1970, "These days when the citizens of this country are crying out for tax reform and relief, it is grossly unfair to leave the secret foreign bank account open as a convenient avenue of tax evasion."[2] This chapter reviews the offshore account reporting rules under the *BSA* and their more recent enforcement by the US Department of the Treasury and the IRS. Although the *BSA* has been dormant for most of its forty-year history, it figures prominently in the US government's most recent efforts to combat tax evasion by US citizens with Swiss bank accounts and in the US government's series of offshore voluntary disclosure initiatives, which have been criticized for their lack of fairness. Recent IRS enforcement of the *BSA*'s penalty provisions strikes a chord of injustice and is motivating a new drive of expatriation by US citizens living abroad. Simply put, the draconian financial penalties for Report of Foreign Bank and Financial Accounts (FBAR) delinquencies were intended for tax evaders, and those Americans who have lived all or most of their lives in Canada, the United Kingdom, or the European Union are not tax evaders. When one is examining the international tax policy surrounding exchange of information, it is not enough to just analyze the mechanism of exchange, for example, the *Foreign Account Tax Compliance Act*.[3] One must also consider what the US government will do with the information that it receives from its treaty partners. The discussion in this chapter of US enforcement of FBAR penalties against Canadians who absolutely never heard of the FBAR and who could not have had the required willful intent described by US Supreme Court Justice Ruth Bader Ginsburg (discussed below) in the early days of US voluntary disclosure programs, in 2009 and 2011, showcases the derailment of the principle of equity in US international tax policy. Finally, this chapter provides an overview of the collections enforcement provisions in the *Convention between Canada and the United States of America with*

---

[2] Quoted in Itai Grinberg, "Beyond FATCA: An Evolutionary Moment for the International Tax System" (2012) [unpublished, archived at the Georgetown University Law Center, The Scholarly Commons, Paper 160] at 12, n 45, online: http://scholarship.law.georgetown.edu/fwps_papers/160, citing United States, HR Rep No 91-975 at 4 (1970), reprinted in 1970 USCCAN 4394 and 4397.

[3] Subtitle A of Title A of the *Hiring Incentives to Restore Employment Act of 2010*, Pub L No 111-147 enacted on 18 March 2010 [*FATCA*].

respect to Taxes on Income and on Capital[4] and gives vital guidance for lawyers and accountants with delinquent clients, whether in Canada, the United Kingdom, the European Union, or elsewhere. Professionals with clients who have undeclared foreign accounts and assets (particularly in tax haven jurisdictions) need to take great care as a result of new information exchange developments such as *FATCA* (described in Chapter 9) and the Swiss Bank Program (described in Chapter 5). The IRS may possess detailed information regarding a client's accounts, including records of the client's communications with a foreign financial institution. As discussed below, the recent introduction, in 2016, of rules regarding non-willfulness certification under the streamlined procedures for US taxpayers living abroad adds a new measure of risk for non-filers, especially those living in Canada, the United Kingdom, and the European Union.

2 Canadian Voluntary Disclosures Program

The Voluntary Disclosures Program (VDP), which is administered by CRA, is a discretionary program under the fairness provisions in the *Income Tax Act*,[5] *Excise Tax Act*,[6] *Excise Act, 2001*,[7] *Air Travellers Security Charge Act*,[8] and *Softwood Lumber Products Export Charge Act, 2006*.[9] CRA created the program to enable taxpayers to request relief from penalties and arrears interest under the various statutes that it administers. In the context of the *Act*, section 220(3.1) provides the Minister of National Revenue (Minister) with the legislative authority to waive penalties and interest with respect to federal income tax.[10] And even though some provinces have their own regime (Ontario, for example, does not

[4] September 1980 (as amended to the protocols signed on 14 June 1983, 23 March 1984, 17 March 1997, 29 July 1997, and 21 September 2007) [*Canada–US Tax Treaty*].

[5] RSC 1985, c 1 (5th Supp) [*Act*].

[6] RSC 1985, c E-15 [*ETA*].

[7] SC 2002, c 22 [*EA*].

[8] SC 2002, c 9, s 5 [*ATSCA*].

[9] SC 2006, c 13 [*SLPECA*]. The penalty and interest relief provisions are in the *Act*, above note 5, s 220(3.1); *ETA*, above note 6, ss 88 and 281.1; *EA*, above note 7, ss 173 and 255.1; *ATSCA*, above note 8, ss 30 and 55; and *SLPECA*, *ibid*, s 37.

[10] *Act*, above note 5, s 220 (3.1).

participate in the CRA program in respect of provincial income taxes), the federal Minister has the power to waive penalties and interest on behalf of the provinces in respect of provincial income taxes administered by CRA. The revenue authorities of Alberta and Quebec administer their own provincial corporate tax systems and operate their own voluntary disclosure programs separately from CRA.

The purpose of the VDP is to allow taxpayers to correct inaccurate or incomplete information or to disclose information not previously reported. If the conditions for making a valid disclosure are met, the taxpayer will be required to pay the additional amounts of tax related to the disclosure but will not be liable for penalties, and CRA can, and typically does, grant interest relief. Furthermore, CRA will not seek to prosecute the taxpayer for criminal offences relating to the previous errors or omissions.

CRA outlines in Information Circular IC00-1R4 the conditions that must be met before a disclosure will be considered valid.[11] There are four conditions. First, the disclosure must be voluntary.[12] The question that often arises here is, what is the meaning or scope of voluntary? CRA's position is that if a taxpayer is aware of or has knowledge of an audit, an investigation, or some other enforcement action that is about to be commenced by CRA or some other government authority or administration with regard to the information to be disclosed, the disclosure will not be considered voluntary. CRA also considers the disclosure to be not voluntary in a situation where there is an enforcement action relating to the information in the disclosure and where that action touches upon a person associated with or related to the taxpayer or a third party; it is necessary that this information be sufficiently related to the disclosure and the enforcement action undertaken by CRA would in all likelihood have uncovered the information that is disclosed by the taxpayer. Some challenges have been raised by taxpayers questioning the meaning or boundaries of the term "enforcement action." There is no doubt that an enforcement action includes a request, demand, or requirement

[11] Canada Revenue Agency, Information Circular IC00-1R4, "Voluntary Disclosures Program" (21 March 2014) [Information Circular IC00-1R4].

[12] See *ibid* at paras 32–34.

issued by CRA or, for that matter, any contact with CRA for any purpose relating to non-compliance. Furthermore, if an enforcement action has commenced, it does not matter whether the taxpayer is aware of the action — the disclosure will not be considered voluntary.

Whether or not a disclosure was voluntary has generated a significant amount of court review. Typically, a taxpayer can have the Minister's adverse decision reviewed by the Federal Court in a judicial review. These decisions are sometimes further appealed to the Federal Court of Appeal. One such decision was *Livaditis v Canada Revenue Agency*, where CRA denied the voluntary disclosure because enforcement action had been taken on the account before the taxpayer's disclosure.[13] The taxpayer brought an application for judicial review of the Minister's decision, and the Federal Court dismissed the application for judicial review. The taxpayer then appealed the decision to the Federal Court of Appeal.[14] In reviewing the lower court's decision, the court noted that there were few facts needed to dispose of the appeal. The applicant was the president of a real estate company whose business included the development of a residential condominium project. Before construction commenced, the applicant and four of his family members had purchased units in the project. Before completion of the project, the family members resold these units for capital gains. The taxpayer did not report the capital gain. A couple of years later, CRA issued a requirement for information to verify tax compliance by the purchasers of the units in the condominium project. At about the same time, the taxpayer received a telephone call from a representative of CRA informing him that CRA wanted to meet with him to gather information about the purchasers of units in the condominium project. After the requirement was issued and after the telephone call between the taxpayer and the CRA officer occurred, the taxpayer filed a no-name disclosure. In that disclosure, the taxpayer claimed that he was "not aware of an audit or enforcement measure being conducted on matters specifically involving the disposition" at the time of the disclosure.[15] Consequently, the taxpayer claimed that the disclosure was voluntary.

[13] 2010 FC 950.

[14] *Livaditis v Canada Revenue Agency*, 2012 FCA 55 [*Livaditis*].

[15] *Ibid* at para 9.

The Court of Appeal disposed of the taxpayer's appeal by agreeing that the telephone call from the CRA officer, alone, was sufficient reason to conclude that the disclosure had not been voluntary. Ironically, this had not been sufficient to convince the lower court. The lower court found that it was reasonable for the Minister's delegate to have found that the requirement constituted an enforcement action and that this was sufficient to determine that the disclosure had not been voluntary even though the taxpayer may not have been aware of that enforcement action.[16] Given the facts in the *Livaditis* case, the discretionary nature of the applicable statutory provision, and the consequently liberal court interpretation of the discretion, it was not surprising that the Court of Appeal agreed with CRA's determination and found that the disclosure had not been voluntary.

There are situations where taxpayers have been successful in challenging CRA on the basis that their disclosure was voluntary. In *Amour International Mines d'Or Ltée v Canada (AG)*, CRA alleged that the disclosure had not been voluntary because CRA had commenced an audit and because the information would have been discovered by CRA.[17] In this case, Greymount Associates Limited, a non-resident corporation, held shares in Orex Mines Ltd, a Canadian corporation. Greymount sold its shares in Orex. Orex owned a sizable percentage of Amour International. The sole director of Orex and Amour was Jean-Pierre Desmarais. Amour was in the process of liquidation and paid dividends to non-resident shareholders. Withholding tax (under Part XIII of the *Act*) was withheld on the dividends paid by Armour, but it failed to remit the withholding tax to CRA. CRA commenced an audit screening process before Amour initiated its voluntary disclosure indicating that it had failed to remit the Part XIII tax. CRA took the administrative position that the non-remittance of the Part XIII tax by Amour would have been discovered as a result of the audit, and therefore CRA denied the voluntary disclosure.

The taxpayer sought judicial review of the Minister's decision in the Federal Court. In reviewing the exercise of the Minister's discretion to deny the voluntary disclosure, the court applied a reasonableness standard

[16] See *ibid* at para 13.

[17] 2010 FC 1070 [*Amour International Mines*].

of review. The decision most often cited for establishing this standard is that of the Supreme Court of Canada in *New Brunswick (Board of Management) v Dunsmuir*,[18] where Bastarache and LeBel JJ stated:

> A court conducting a review for reasonableness inquires into the qualities that make a decision reasonable, referring both to the process of articulating the reasons and to outcomes. In judicial review, reasonableness is concerned mostly with the existence of justification, transparency and intelligibility within the decision making process. But it is also concerned with whether the decision falls within a range of possible, acceptable outcomes which are defensible in respect of the facts and law.[19]

After examining the evidence, the Federal Court concluded CRA's determination that the audit would have found the information disclosed had been unfounded.[20]

The second condition for a valid voluntary disclosure is that the taxpayer must provide full and accurate information for every tax year or reporting period for which information was incomplete, inaccurate, or not previously disclosed.[21] CRA regularly follows up on the information disclosed by asking for additional facts or documents to confirm or verify that information. Depending on the nature of the information disclosed, it is not uncommon for the CRA voluntary disclosure officer to ask officers in other CRA sections to review the information for the purpose of confirming its accuracy. Therefore, it is important that in making a voluntary disclosure submission, a taxpayer avoid any inconsistencies or omissions.

In *Palonek v Canada (MNR)*, the taxpayer had failed to file income tax and GST returns for eight years and, therefore, made a voluntary disclosure. During its review of the disclosure, the CRA audit section found that the taxpayer held interests in several corporations and a trust that had not been mentioned in the disclosure. The taxpayer was then asked to provide information about the corporations and trust, but the taxpayer never supplied any further information. CRA found several inconsistencies and omissions

---

[18] 2008 SCC 9 at para 47.

[19] Quoted in *Amour International Mines*, above note 17 at para 25.

[20] *Ibid* at para 27.

[21] See Information Circular IC00-1R4, above note 11 at paras 35–37.

in the taxpayer's submission, and because there was no further response from the taxpayer, CRA determined that the disclosure was incomplete. Both the Federal Court and the Federal Court of Appeal found that the ministerial determination to deny the voluntary disclosure had been reasonable.[22]

The third condition for a valid voluntary disclosure is that it must involve the application or potential application of a penalty.[23] There are various types of penalties including a late filing penalty, a failure to remit penalty, an instalment penalty, and a discretionary penalty, such as an omission penalty or a gross negligence penalty.

The fourth condition for a valid voluntary disclosure is that it must include information that is at least one year past due.[24] CRA permits a disclosure that includes information that is less than one year past due provided that it also includes information that is at least one year past due. To illustrate this situation, CRA provides the following example:

> a taxpayer had not filed tax returns for the years 2000 to 2004. On November 10, 2005, the taxpayer submitted all of the tax returns requesting they be considered under the VDP. Although the 2004 tax return is less than one year past due (filing deadline of April 30, 2005) the CRA will consider the 2004 return as part of this disclosure, provided that all other conditions have been met.[25]

As the examination of these preconditions for voluntary disclosure and some of the related cases suggests, a taxpayer should exercise great care in commencing a voluntary disclosure application. To make a voluntary disclosure, a taxpayer must send in a written submission. There is a specific CRA form — RC 199, the Voluntary Disclosures Program (VDP) Taxpayer Agreement — that should be used to commence the disclosure.[26] CRA requires the taxpayer to provide information such as the amount of tax to be paid, whether the amount reported is pretax income, the first three characters of the taxpayer's postal code, and the taxpayer's gender

---

[22] 2006 FC 494, aff'd 2007 FCA 281.

[23] See Information Circular IC00-1R4, above note 11 at para 38.

[24] See *ibid* at paras 39–42.

[25] *Ibid* at para 40.

[26] *Ibid* at para 43.

and age.[27] The taxpayer, properly advised, should prepare the disclosure with a view to explaining how she has met all four preconditions for the voluntary disclosure. Given that some of this information may involve details that are not of value to the voluntary disclosure process but could impact the taxpayer in some other fashion, it is always better to consult with a lawyer and get the protection afforded by solicitor-client privilege, and best to consult with a tax lawyer who specializes in this area of law.

CRA allows for two methods of voluntary disclosure. A taxpayer can select either the "named" disclosure method or the "no-name" disclosure method. The difference between the two is that in a no-name disclosure the taxpayer is not known to CRA. So the taxpayer's representative can have preliminary discussions with CRA before the taxpayer is fully identified to CRA. These discussions are informal and non-binding. The no-name process can lead to CRA's confirming, in an in-principle manner, that there is nothing in the disclosed information that would immediately disqualify the taxpayer from the program. The no-name process also gives the taxpayer some degree of protection if an audit is commenced. Arguably, the taxpayer can follow up with a named disclosure and claim protection from the audit by the no-name disclosure filing period. A taxpayer may decide for any number of reasons to drop a no-name disclosure application. But if the taxpayer chooses this course, he can then only apply for relief from the same issues by disclosing his name. In other words, a second submission on the same issue or issues must be in the form of a named disclosure.

The protection afforded by the VDP commences on the date of the disclosure's filing. If the no-name method has been selected, the taxpayer will be required to identify herself within ninety days of the initial application's filing.

CRA reorganized in late 2014 to enhance efficiency by centralizing the processing of voluntary disclosures in two Canadian tax centres: one in Surrey, British Columbia and one in Shawinigan, Quebec. Taxpayers residing in any province or territory outside of British Columbia and Yukon will file their voluntary disclosures with CRA's Shawinigan-Sud Tax Centre. Taxpayers residing in British Columbia or Yukon will now file their voluntary disclosures with CRA's Surrey Tax Centre.

---

[27] *Ibid* at para 44.

3 *Bank Secrecy Act*

3.1 Introduction

The *BSA* was enacted by Congress in 1970.[28] As explained more fully below, the statute obligates millions of US persons to disclose to the IRS the existence of their non-US accounts or face enormous financial penalties. The statute's provisions relating to offshore accounts had been in stasis for most of their life. But the IRS has recently begun using the statute as one of its primary weapons in the fight against international tax evasion. The application of the *BSA* particularly against the estimated one million Canadians of American heritage has come under heavy criticism for being unjust.[29]

The stated purpose of the *BSA* is to require the filing and maintenance of certain reports or records that are to be used in criminal, tax, or regulatory investigations or proceedings, or in the conduct of intelligence activities, including those directed against terrorism.[30] The information produced by the statutory scheme embodied in the *BSA* is intended to assist the government in its detection and prosecution of criminal activity and its tax code enforcement and other regulatory responsibilities.[31] Documents filed by businesses under the *BSA* requirements are heavily used by law enforcement agencies to identify and detect money laundering in the furtherance of criminal activities, terrorism, and tax evasion.[32]

---

[28] *BSA*, above note 1.

[29] See Lauren Krugel, "Attention, American Expats in Canada: The IRS Is Eyeing You" *Globe and Mail* (13 June 2014, last updated 17 June 2014), online: http://fw.to/0KsbCYC; Robert W Wood, "Canadians Attack U.S. Expat Rules, Decrying 'Accidental Americans'" *Forbes* (9 September 2014), online: www.forbes.com/sites/robertwood/2014/09/09/canadians-attack-u-s-expat-rules-decrying-accidental-americans/#5ef2b754de71.

[30] See 31 USC § 5311. See also Pub L 91-508, Tit II, 84 Stat 1118, 10/26/1970 § 202.

[31] See *United States v Simonelli*, 614 F Supp 2d 241 (D Conn 2008): the defendant failed to file an FBAR in a timely manner, and the Department of the Treasury and the IRS brought suit to collect an assessment made pursuant to 31 USC § 5321(a)(5)(2000); the defendant claimed that the FBAR penalty had been discharged at the time that he had received a general discharge in bankruptcy; holding that the FBAR penalty is a civil penalty and not a tax or a tax penalty, the court found that the FBAR penalty had not been discharged in the defendant's bankruptcy.

[32] See United States, Internal Revenue Service, "Bank Secrecy Act" (last updated 9 November 2015), online: www.irs.gov/Businesses/Small-Businesses-&-Self-Employed/Bank-Secrecy-Act [IRS, "Bank

Congress enacted the *BSA* in response to the increased use of financial institutions, particularly those located in jurisdictions with bank secrecy laws, as intermediaries by persons engaged in criminal activities.[33] The *BSA* imposes reporting requirements on financial institutions and US persons regarding specified domestic and foreign financial transactions.

Part of the *BSA* deals with foreign reporting and obligates US persons who have financial interests in or authority over bank, securities, or other financial accounts in foreign countries to report such information to the US government annually in a document known, for most years, as the Report of Foreign Bank and Financial Accounts, or FBAR.[34] The form currently in use is the FBAR, FinCEN Form 114.[35] For almost the entirety of their forty-six-year history, the FBAR provisions of the *BSA* were seldom enforced by the US government and were often unknown to taxpayers or their tax advisers.[36] But more recently, the policy of the US

Secrecy Act"]. The *BSA*, above note 1, is the first and most comprehensive federal anti–money laundering and counterterrorism financing statute in the United States: see United States, Department of the Treasury, Financial Crimes Enforcement Network, "About FinCEN: What We Do," online: www.fincen.gov/about_fincen/wwd [FinCEN, "What We Do"]. The IRS is a partner in the US National Money Laundering Strategy, and the FBAR is a report that is part of this strategy: see IRS, "Bank Secrecy Act," *ibid.*

[33] See *Ratzlaf v United States*, 510 US 135 at 138 (1994) [*Ratzlaf*], where the Court held that it was necessary to establish that the defendant had acted with knowledge that the conduct (here structuring) was unlawful to convict the defendant for willfully violating the statutory prohibition against structuring foreign currency transactions. See 31 USCA §§ 5313(a), 5322(a), and 5324(3). See also *United States v Clines*, 958 F 2d 278 (4th Cir 1992).

[34] The form had formerly been known as TD F 90-22.1: see United States, Department of the Treasury, "Report of Foreign Bank and Financial Accounts" (4 April 2014), online: www.treasury.gov/services/Pages/TD-F-90-22.1-Report-of-Foreign-Bank-and-Financial-Accounts.aspx.

[35] See United States, Department of the Treasury, Financial Crimes Enforcement Network, "File the Report of Foreign Bank and Financial Accounts (FBAR) as an Individual," online: http://bsaefiling.fincen.treas.gov/NoRegFilePDFIndividualFBAR.html.

[36] See United States, Internal Revenue Service, IR-2008-79, "IRS Reminds Taxpayers to Report Certain Foreign Bank and Financial Accounts by June 30" (17 June 2008), online: www.irs.gov/uac/IRS-Reminds-Taxpayers-to-Report-Certain-Foreign-Bank-and-Financial-Accounts-by-June-30. In 2002, it was estimated that there may be as many as 1 million US taxpayers with FBAR filing requirements and that the FBAR compliance rate was less than 20 percent: see United States, Department of the Treasury, *A Report to Congress in accordance with §361(b) of the Uniting and Strengthening America by Providing Appropriate Tools Required to Intercept and Obstruct Terrorism Act of 2001 (USA Patriot Act)* (Washington, DC: US Department of the Treasury, 2002) at 6, online: www.fincen.gov/news_room/rp/files/ReportToCongress361.PDF [*Treasury Report 2002*]. From approximately 1993 to 2002, the government considered asserting FBAR penalties in only twelve cases, and in only two of those did taxpayers receive penalties while in four they were issued warning letters (see *ibid* at 9–10). Criminal indictments were similarly few: see Michael Sardar, "What

Department of the Treasury has been to use the potentially devastating financial penalty structure of the *BSA* as a powerful weapon against US taxpayers hiding billions of dollars in unreported offshore accounts.[37]

The *BSA* authorizes the Secretary of the Treasury to issue regulations requiring banks and other financial institutions to take precautions such as the following against financial crime: establishing anti–money laundering programs and filing reports to be used in criminal, tax, and regulatory investigations, and intelligence and counterterrorism matters.[38] The Secretary of the Treasury has delegated to the director of the

Constitutes 'Willfulness' for Purposes of the FBAR Failure-to-File Penalty?" (2010) 113 *Journal of Taxation* 183. The lack of enforcement could have been due to a variety of reasons, one of which was the difficulty of obtaining admissible evidence from countries with strong bank secrecy laws and with which the United States did not have a tax treaty: see *Treasury Report 2002, ibid* at 9. Another reason stemmed from the Department of Justice's preference for charging the taxpayers with other violations relating to their illegal conduct, such as tax evasion or fraud, as these were easier to sway jurors with (see *ibid* at 9). Prosecutors also had difficulty meeting the willfulness evidentiary standard (see *ibid* at 10). In Canada, for example, until the new IRS offshore voluntary disclosure programs drew widespread media coverage, only a handful of accountants working in public accounting had been aware of the FBAR form.

[37] See statement of then IRS commissioner Doug Shulman, who remarked, "The information we gather from this action will help us detect wealthy individuals who don't pay their taxes as well as provide details about how advisors facilitate this abuse": United States, Department of Justice, News Release 08-579, "Justice Department Asks Court to Serve IRS Summons for UBS Swiss Bank Account Records" (30 June 2008), online: www.justice.gov/archive/opa/pr/2008/June/08-tax-579.html. The marked change in the direction of the US government, toward enforcement of the FBAR reporting requirements to combat criminal and civil tax violations, can be seen in government actions starting in 2008 against UBS (issuance by the district court in Florida of a John Doe summons and other relief) and key UBS executive Bradley Birkenfeld: see Sandra Brown, "IRS & the FBAR: International Focus for U.S. Tax Compliance" (20 November 2008) [unpublished] at 4–9. Birkenfeld pleaded guilty to conspiring to defraud the IRS by helping UBS clients evade US reporting laws: see United States, Department of Justice, News Release 08-850, "Banker Pleads Guilty to Helping American Real Estate Developer Evade Income Tax on $200 Million" (19 June 2008), online: www.justice.gov/archive/opa/pr/2008/June/08-tax-550.html. Additionally, the US Department of the Treasury launched a new round of offshore voluntary disclosure initiatives between 2009 and 2012 that have resulted in approximately 33,000 taxpayer filings and the collection of over $5 billion in taxes, interest, and penalties: see Janet Novack, "IRS Cuts Middle Class Expats Big (and Deserved) Penalty Break" *Forbes* (26 June 2012), online: www.forbes.com/sites/janetnovack/2012/06/26/irs-cuts-middle-class-expats-big-and-deserved-penalty-break/#28a6ea82434e.

[38] See FinCEN, "What We Do," above note 32. The regulations implementing the *BSA*, above note 1, appear at 31 CFR Part 103. On 26 October 2010, the Financial Crimes Enforcement Network (FinCEN) issued a final rule, with an effective date of 1 March 2011, reorganizing the *BSA* regulations and transferring them to a new chapter in the *Code of Federal Regulations*, from 31 CFR Part 103 to 31 CFR Chapter X — Financial Crimes Enforcement Network. This new structure is intended to organize the *BSA* regulations by industry, and it does not alter existing *BSA* regulatory obligations or impose new obligations: see United States, Federal Deposit Insurance Corporation,

Financial Crimes Enforcement Network (FinCEN) the authority to implement, administer, and enforce compliance with the *BSA* and associated regulations.[39]

3.2 Financial Crimes Enforcement Network

FinCEN, which was established in 1990, is a bureau of the US Department of the Treasury. Its mission is to support federal, state, local, and international law enforcement by analyzing the information collected under the *BSA* to combat financial crime, including money laundering.[40] FinCEN serves as the US national financial intelligence unit (FIU). It is one of more than 100 FIUs composing The Egmont Group of Financial Intelligence Units, an international organization that shares

---

Financial Institution Letter FIL-15-2011, "Bank Secrecy Act: Reorganization of FinCEN's Bank Secrecy Act Regulations" (15 March 2011), online: www.fdic.gov/news/news/financial/2011/fil11015.pdf. On 26 February 2010, FinCEN had issued a notice of proposed rulemaking addressing the FBAR rules under the *BSA* and issues such as the range of individuals and entities required to file the FBAR and the types of accounts required to be reported. Later, on 24 February 2011, FinCEN issued a final rule amending the *BSA* and implementing regulations regarding FBARs: see United States, Department of the Treasury, Financial Crimes Enforcement Network, News Release, "FinCEN Issues Final Rule on Foreign Bank and Financial Accounts Report (FBAR) Responsibilities" (24 February 2011), online: www.fincen.gov/news_room/nr/pdf/20110224.pdf; 31 CFR Part 1010, amendment to the Bank Secrecy Act Regulations — Reports of Foreign Financial Accounts, 76 Fed Reg No 37 (2011).

[39] 31 CFR § 103.56(b). While FinCEN (and the US Department of Justice) retain the general authority to enforce the law, under Treasury Directive 15-41 (1992) the Secretary of the Treasury delegated to the IRS the authority to investigate possible FBAR violations, including the review of cases by the IRS Criminal Investigation division: see United States, Department of the Treasury, *A Report to Congress in accordance with §361(b) of the Uniting and Strengthening America by Providing Appropriate Tools Required to Intercept and Obstruct Terrorism Act of 2001 (USA Patriot Act)* (Washington, DC: US Department of the Treasury, 2003) at 4, online: www.fincen.gov/news_room/rp/files/fbar3613.pdf.

[40] See United States, Department of the Treasury, Financial Crimes Enforcement Network, "Law Enforcement: Overview," online: www.fincen.gov/law_enforcement/. FinCEN's duties and responsibilities include issuing and interpreting regulations; supporting and enforcing compliance with those regulations; coordinating and analyzing data regarding compliance examination functions delegated to other federal regulators; managing the collection, processing, storage, dissemination, and protection of data filed under FinCEN's reporting rules; maintaining a government-wide access service to FinCEN's data and networks; supporting investigations and prosecutions by law enforcement; sharing information and coordinating with foreign financial intelligence unit (FIU) counterparts on anti–money laundering and counterterrorism financing efforts; and conducting analysis to support policymakers, law enforcement, regulatory and intelligence agencies, FIUs, and the financial industry: see FinCEN, "What We Do," above note 32.

information among FIUs in support of US and foreign financial crime investigations.[41] FinCEN responds to requests from other FIUs that are members of The Egmont Group and acts as the conduit for requests from domestic (federal, state, and local) law enforcement agencies to foreign FIUs for support for investigations by US law enforcement and regulatory agencies. Members of The Egmont Group exchange financial intelligence derived largely from financial industry reporting.[42] Canada is a member of The Egmont Group, whose secretariat is located in Toronto.[43] In 2003, to improve compliance with the FBAR, FinCEN delegated its enforcement to the IRS, which had greater resources.[44]

3.3 Report of Foreign Bank and Financial Accounts: The FBAR

Who Must File a FinCEN Form 114

Section 5314(a) of the *BSA* importantly provides that "the Secretary of the Treasury shall require a resident or citizen of the United States or a person in, and doing business in, the United States, to keep records, file reports, or keep records and file reports, when the resident, citizen, or person makes a transaction or maintains a relation for any person with a foreign financial agency."[45]

[41] See United States, Department of the Treasury, Financial Crimes Enforcement Network, "International Programs," online: www.fincen.gov/international/.

[42] See *ibid.*

[43] See Financial Transactions and Reports Analysis Centre of Canada, online: www.fintrac-canafe.gc.ca/fintrac-canafe/1-eng.asp, which is the Canadian national FIU member of The Egmont Group.

[44] See Brown, above note 37 at 2–3; 31 CFR Part 103, final rule (RIN 1506-AA45) (15 May 2003). The authority to enforce the provisions of 31 USC § 5314 and 31 CFR §§ 103.24 and 103.32 was redelegated from FinCEN to the commissioner of the IRS by a memorandum of understanding between FinCEN and the IRS, which is referenced in 31 CFR § 103.56(g). The authority redelegated includes that to investigate possible civil violations of these provisions, assess and collect civil FBAR penalties, employ the summons power of Subpart F of Part 103, issue administrative rulings under Subpart G of Part 103, and take any other action reasonably necessary for the enforcement of these and related provisions, including pursuit of injunctions: see 31 CFR § 103.56(g).

[45] 31 USC § 5314(a). See 31 CFR § 1010.350(a). For additional background on the FBAR, see also Hale E Sheppard, "Evolution of the FBAR: Where We Were, Where We Are, and Why It Matters"

A US person that has a financial interest in or signatory authority over one or more foreign financial accounts must file an FBAR if the aggregate value of all such foreign financial accounts exceeds $10,000 at any time during the calendar year.[46] The FinCEN Form 114 is filed annually online and for reportable years through 2015 must be received on or before 30 June of each year.[47] Generally, US citizens, individuals who are US residents for tax purposes under the *Internal Revenue Code*, and entities organized or formed in the United States must file the FBAR.[48] The definition of US person (and thereby the scope of persons required to file the FBAR) was greatly expanded with the issuance of the proposed FBAR regulations in February 2010.[49] The new regulations introduced a new class of individuals now required to file the FBAR: those considered tax residents under the *Code*. Previously, US person referred to someone who was actually living and residing in the United States and who did not plan to permanently leave his home.[50] As a result of the change, foreign

(2006) 7 *Houston Business and Tax Journal* 1; Kevin E Packman & Andrew H Weinstein, "FBAR — Foreign Bank Account Reporting Obligations: A Primer for the Practitioner" (2007) 106 *Journal of Taxation* 44.

[46] 31 CFR § 1010.350(a); United States, Department of the Treasury, Financial Crimes Enforcement Network, *BSA Electronic Filing Requirements for Report of Foreign Bank and Financial Accounts (FinCEN Form 114)* (June 2014) at 4 and 8, online: www.fincen.gov/forms/files/FBAR Line Item Filing Instructions.pdf [*FinCEN Form 114 Instructions*].

[47] 31 CFR § 1010.306(c); *FinCEN Form 114 Instructions*, above note 46 at 8. Note that certain filing exceptions may apply (see *ibid* at 6). See, generally, United States, Department of the Treasury, Financial Crimes Enforcement Network, "BSA Forms: Filing Information," online: www.fincen.gov/forms/bsa_forms/.

[48] See *FinCEN Form 114 Instructions*, above note 46 at 5–6.

[49] See note 38, above in this chapter. "Person" refers to an individual or a legal entity including but not limited to a limited liability company, corporation, partnership, trust, and estate: 31 CFR § 1010.350(a); *FinCEN Form 114 Instructions*, above note 46 at 5–6. A US person means a US citizen, US resident under the definition in § 7701(b) of the *Internal Revenue Code*, USC 26 (1986) of 1986, as amended, and the *Treasury Regulations* issued thereunder at Chapter 4 [*Code*], or entity including but not limited to a corporation, partnership, or limited liability company created or organized in the United States or under the laws of the United States and a trust or estate formed under the laws of the United States: 31 CFR § 1010.350(a); *FinCEN Form 114 Instructions*, above note 46 at 5–6.

[50] 75 Fed Reg 8844 (2010). The determination of whether an individual is a resident of the United States will now be made under the rules of the *Code*, above note 49, specifically § 7701(b) and the regulations thereunder: 31 CFR § 1010.350(a). Previously, only individuals who normally resided in the United States without any intention to move to another country were considered resident for purposes of the FBAR filing requirements: see United States, Internal Revenue Service, *Internal Revenue Manual* (Washington, DC: US Department of the Treasury, 2008) at § 4.26.16.3.1.1 — the

nationals who perhaps have never lived in the United States, or have not lived in the United States for over thirty or forty years, but who were once issued a green card (even if invalid for US immigration purposes) are now being called upon to file the FBAR or face the FBAR penalty regime. Perhaps the most overlooked financial exposure risk in this context is the invalid green card, which can carry extraordinary risk, especially under the exit tax rules in *Code* section 877A.[51]

Foreign Financial Accounts Subject to FBAR Reporting Requirements

The types of foreign financial accounts that are reportable on the FBAR form are bank accounts,[52] securities accounts,[53] and other financial accounts.[54]

Financial Interests Subject to FBAR Reporting Requirements

Generally, a US person that has a financial interest in one or more foreign financial accounts will be subject to the FBAR reporting requirements if

definition of "resident alien" found in the *Code*, above note 49, § 7701(b) is not applicable for FBAR purposes; the plain meaning of the term "resident," in this context, someone who is living in the United States and not planning to permanently leave the United States, should be used for FBAR examination purposes. Accordingly, green card holders (permanent residents) and individuals who were previously considered resident in the United States under the substantial presence test in § 7701(b) but who are not ordinarily resident in the United States are, for 2010 and afterwards, now subject to the FBAR filing requirements. Moreover, the final regulations confirm that where an individual is resident under § 7701(b) and also a resident of another country with which the United States has a tax treaty, that person may not rely on the tiebreaker rules in the residence article of the treaty to avoid the FBAR reporting requirements: 76 Fed Reg 10234 No 37 (2011).

[51] *Code*, above note 49, § 877A.

[52] 31 CFR § 1010.350(c): "bank account" includes a savings deposit, demand deposit, chequing, or other similar account held by a firm engaged in the banking business.

[53] 31 CFR § 1010.350(c): "securities account" means an account held with a firm engaged in the business of buying, selling, holding, or trading stock or other securities.

[54] 31 CFR § 1010.350(c); *FinCEN Form 114 Instructions*, above note 46 at 4: other types of financial accounts that may be reportable under the FBAR rules include accounts held by a firm that is in the business of accepting deposits as a financial agency, insurance (e.g., whole life) or annuity policies with a cash value, accounts with a firm that acts as a broker or dealer for futures or options transactions in any commodity on or subject to the rules of a commodity exchange or association, an account with a mutual fund or similar pooled fund that issues shares available to the general public that have a regular net asset value determination and regular redemptions. Exceptions are permitted for certain government-held accounts and correspondent accounts for bank-to-bank settlements.

the aggregate value of all such foreign financial accounts exceeds $10,000. A US person has a financial interest in each financial account in a foreign country of which she is the owner of record and to which she has legal title, whether the account is maintained for her own benefit or for the benefit of others.[55] A US person is also regarded as having a financial interest in each foreign account of which he is not the owner of record or to which he does not have legal title where he is regarded as the beneficial owner of that account, for example, as the principal in an agency relationship or as the donor of a power of attorney.[56]

A US person that owns directly or indirectly more than 50 percent of the prescribed interest in a corporation or partnership is also regarded as having a financial interest in a foreign account of which the corporation or partnership is the owner of record or to which the corporation or partnership is the holder of legal title.[57] Accordingly, that individual will have to report that account on her FBAR form. For US based privately held multinationals using revocable trusts and S corporations or employing multi-tiered legal structures, there exists a much greater risk of error in FBAR reporting.

A US person that owns the prescribed interest in a trust is also regarded as having a financial interest in a foreign account of which the trust is the owner of record or to which the trust is holder of legal title, and will have to report that account on his FBAR form.[58] A US person is also regarded as having a financial interest in a foreign account of which any other entity is the owner of record or to which any other entity is the holder of legal title where the US person owns directly or indirectly more than

[55] 31 CFR § 1010.350(e); *FinCEN Form 114 Instructions*, above note 46 at 5.

[56] 31 CFR § 1010.350(e); *FinCEN Form 114 Instructions*, above note 46 at 5.

[57] 31 CFR § 1010.350(e); *FinCEN Form 114 Instructions*, above note 46 at 5. With respect to corporations, a US person must own directly or indirectly more than 50 percent of the total value of shares of stock or more than 50 percent of the voting power of all shares of stock, and with respect to partnerships, a US person must own directly or indirectly an interest in more than 50 percent of the partnership's profits (e.g., distributive share of partnership income taking into account any special allocation agreement) or an interest in more than 50 percent of the partnership capital: 31 CFR § 1010.350(e); *FinCEN Form 114 Instructions*, above note 46 at 5.

[58] 31 CFR § 1010.350(e); *FinCEN Form 114 Instructions* above note 46 at 5. To be regarded as having a financial interest in a trust, a US person must be regarded as the trust grantor and have an ownership interest in the trust under the grantor trust rules in *Code*, above note 49, §§ 671–679, or a US person must have a greater than 50 percent present beneficial interest in the assets or income of the trust for the calendar year: 31 CFR § 1010.350(e); *FinCEN Form 114 Instructions*, above note 46 at 5.

50 percent of the voting power, total value of equity interest or assets, or interest in profits in the entity.[59]

Signature Authority over a Foreign Financial Account

As described above, the FBAR reporting requirements apply to a US person that has a financial interest in a foreign financial account. But the FBAR reporting requirements also apply to a US person that may not have a financial interest in a foreign financial account but rather has signatory authority over the account. A person may be found to have signatory authority over an account if she has the authority (alone or in conjunction with another individual) to control the disposition of assets held in the account by direct communication to the bank or financial institution where the account is maintained.[60] In practice, this is a huge area that practitioners often fail to address in advising clients about the FBAR. Basically, a non-US citizen spouse is not required to report bank accounts he may own on the FBAR. However, where the non-US citizen spouse or partner is the donor of a general financial power of attorney and where the US citizen spouse or partner is the donee, the US citizen with signatory authority must then report the bank accounts of the donor. This can not only be stressful for the couple, but the relevant compliance can also be very costly to administer. These kinds of problems can be avoided with careful planning.

Record-Keeping Requirements

Persons required to file the FBAR are also required to maintain bank account records for five years from 30 June of the year following the calendar year reported.[61]

---

[59] 31 CFR § 1010.350(e); *FinCEN Form 114 Instructions*, above note 46 at 5.

[60] 31 CFR § 1010.350(f); *FinCEN Form 114 Instructions*, above note 46 at 7. There are exceptions for certain prescribed officers and employees: 31 CFR § 1010.350(f).

[61] 31 CFR § 1010.420; *FinCEN Form 114 Instructions*, above note 46 at 8.

Statement of Specified Foreign Financial Assets: New Reporting for US Persons

In 2010, Congress added a new (largely redundant) foreign-reporting obligation for US citizens and residents with interests in specified foreign financial assets.[62] Generally, under this new provision, any individual who during the taxable year has an interest in any specified foreign financial asset must attach a Form 8938 to his income tax return for that year (as detailed in the form) with respect to each such asset if the aggregate value of all of his specified foreign financial assets exceeds $50,000.[63] Form 8938 carries lesser penalties than the FBAR for non-compliance, but they are still significant.[64]

4 FBAR Penalties

Generally, under the *BSA*, the IRS may assess a willful penalty or a non-willful penalty for a taxpayer's failure to file an FBAR form. The *BSA* financial penalty mechanism applicable to a willful failure to file an FBAR form is arguably one of the most powerful anti–tax evasion tools in the IRS arsenal. The IRS may assess a penalty equal to 50 percent of the highest balance of a US person's reportable account for each year of a willful failure to file for up to six years.[65] Hence, the cumulative effect of the penalty may not only wipe out the account in its entirety, but it may also decimate other assets of the taxpayer, or her estate if necessary

---

[62] See *FATCA*, above note 3, § 511, which amended the *Code*, above note 49, by adding new § 6038D.

[63] See *Code*, above note 49, § 6038D(a) and the regulations thereunder. See also United States, Department of the Treasury, Internal Revenue Service, *Instructions for Form 8938: Statement of Specified Foreign Financial Assets* (November 2015), online: www.irs.gov/pub/irs-pdf/i8938.pdf [*Form 8938 Instructions*], which detail the class of individuals to which the new reporting obligation applies, including special exemptions for certain categories of US persons living abroad who fall below certain financial-reporting thresholds.

[64] See *Form 8938 Instructions*, above note 63.

[65] 31 USC §§ 5321(a)(5)(C)(i) and (5)(D)(ii).

to satisfy the penalty.[66] In 2015, the IRS issued guidance regarding FBAR penalties in which it stated that in no event will the total penalty amount for willful failure to file exceed 100 percent of the highest aggregate balance of all unreported foreign financial accounts during the years under examination.[67]

A taxpayer facing assessment of an FBAR penalty may also face additional civil penalties that could apply under the *Code*.[68] And a taxpayer facing civil FBAR and related tax penalties under the *Code* can also be subject to criminal penalties.[69]

The *BSA* does not define willfulness for the purposes of civil or criminal penalties for failure to file an FBAR (or other infractions under the statute).[70]

---

[66] For example, a taxpayer who was discovered by the IRS with $1 million in an offshore account that had earned interest income of $50,000 a year from 2003 to 2010 could face up to $4,543,000 in tax, accuracy-related penalties, and FBAR penalties: see United States, Internal Revenue Service, "Offshore Voluntary Disclosure Program Frequently Asked Questions and Answers 2012" at Q8, online: www.irs.gov/Individuals/International-Taxpayers/Offshore-Voluntary-Disclosure-Program-Frequently-Asked-Questions-and-Answers ["2012 OVDP FAQ"]. Regarding transferee liability for the FBAR penalty, see David S Kerzner, "Advising the Delinquent U.S. Client: What Are Your Strategies? Also, IRS's New Program for Delinquent Filers" (2012) 5 *It's Personal* 14 [Kerzner, "Advising the Delinquent U.S. Client"].

[67] See United States, Department of the Treasury, "Memorandum for All LB&I, SB/SE, and TE/GE Employees: Interim Guidance for Report of Foreign Bank and Financial Accounts (FBAR) Penalties" (13 May 2015), online: www.irs.gov/pub/foia/ig/spder/SBSE-04-0515-0025[1].pdf ["Guidance for FBAR Penalties"].

[68] The IRS may impose various harsh penalties including penalties for negligence, substantial understatement, and fraud, for example, penalties for fraud under *Code*, above note 49, §§ 6651(f) and 6663 (which may apply where an underpayment of tax or a failure to file a tax return is due to fraud; the taxpayer is liable for penalties that, although calculated differently, essentially amount to 75 percent of the unpaid tax), penalties for failing to file a tax return under § 6651(a)(1) (taxpayers are generally required to file income tax returns, and if a taxpayer fails to do so, a penalty of 5 percent of the balance due plus an additional 5 percent for each month or fraction thereof that the failure continues not exceeding 25 percent may be imposed), penalties for failing to pay the amount of tax shown on the return under § 6651(a)(2) (if a taxpayer fails to pay the amount of tax shown on the return, a penalty of 0.5 percent of the amount of tax shown on the return plus an additional 0.5 percent for each month or fraction thereof that the amount remains unpaid not exceeding 25 percent may be imposed), and accuracy-related penalties for underpayments under § 6662 (a 20 or 40 percent penalty may apply depending on which component of the accuracy-related penalty is applicable). See also Scott D Michel, "Advising a Client with Secret Offshore Accounts — Current Filing and Reporting Problems" (1999) 91 *Journal of Taxation* 158.

[69] Criminal charges relating to tax returns that may apply include tax evasion (*Code*, above note 49, § 7201), filing a false return (§ 7206(1)), and failure to file an income tax return (§ 7203). Willfully failing to file an FBAR and willfully filing a false FBAR are both violations that are subject to criminal penalties under 31 USC § 5322 and are discussed below.

[70] See 31 USC § 5321(a)(5)(C)(i).

The definition of willfulness is important because it is the trigger of the IRS gun that can fire a bullet capable of decimating a taxpayer's wealth. While there have been few cases describing willfulness under the *BSA*, courts describing the willfulness standard in the context of tax law violations have consistently held that willfulness should constitute a "voluntary, intentional, violation of a known legal duty."[71] Willfulness is usually established by drawing reasonable inferences from the conduct and the facts in evidence.[72] As described below, recent judicial decisions and the conduct of the IRS in its offshore voluntary disclosure initiatives appear to deviate dangerously from this specific intent standard.

Cheek v United States raised the issue of whether a jury instruction that only an objectively reasonable misunderstanding of the law negates the statutory willfulness requirement was correct.[73] An airline pilot who had honestly believed that wages were not income contested his conviction by arguing that the district court had erred in instructing the jury that his good-faith belief that he was not violating the law had to be objectively reasonable to negate willfulness.

The US Supreme Court rejected the position taken by the district court and the court of appeals. First, the Court noted that the burden of

[71] See *Cheek v United States*, 498 US 192 [*Cheek*]; *Ratzlaf*, above note 33; *United States v Sturman*, 951 F 2d 1466 (6th Cir 1991) [*Sturman*]; *United States v Pomponio*, 429 US 10 (1976); *United States v Bishop*, 412 US 346 (1973) [*Bishop*]; Hale E Sheppard, "District Court Rules That Where There's No Will, There's a Way to Avoid FBAR Penalties" (2010) 113 *Journal of Taxation* 293 [Sheppard, "FBAR Penalties"]. In United States, Internal Revenue Service, Office of the Chief Counsel, Memorandum 200603026, "Foreign Bank and Financial Accounts Report (FBAR) Penalty, November 23, 2004" (20 January 2006), online: www.irs.gov/pub/irs-wd/0603026.pdf, the IRS favoured Blackman J's lower standard of willfulness in the dissenting opinion in *Ratzlaf*, above note 33. The willfulness standard in the CCA nevertheless provided that there is no willfulness where the account holder had no knowledge of the duty to file an FBAR.

[72] See *Ratzlaf*, above note 33 at 149; *Spies v United States*, 317 US 492 at 499–500 (1943) [*Spies*], illustrating conduct that can support the permissible inference of an "affirmative willful attempt" to evade a tax; *United States v Bank of New England, NA*, 821 F 2d 844 at 854 (1st Cir 1987) [*Bank of New England*]: willfulness "is usually established by drawing reasonable inferences from the available facts"; *Rykoff v United States*, 40 F 3d 305 at 307 (9th Cir 1994); *United States v Gormley*, 201 F 3d 290 at 294 (4th Cir 2000): "the question of willfulness is essentially a finding of fact." Under the language of the statute, the IRS has the burden of proving by a preponderance of the evidence that the taxpayer had knowledge of the requirement to file the FBAR form but intentionally chose to ignore that legal obligation: *United States v Williams*, 106 AFTR 2d 6150 (ED Va 2010) [*Williams* 2010].

[73] *Cheek*, above note 71.

proving actual knowledge of the pertinent legal duty requires negating a defendant's claim of ignorance of the law or a claim that because of a misunderstanding of the law he had a good-faith belief that he was not violating any of the provisions of the tax laws.[74] The Court observed:

> This is so because one cannot be aware that the law imposes a duty upon him and yet be ignorant of it, misunderstand the law, or believe that the duty does not exist. In the end, the issue is whether, based on all the evidence, the Government has proved that the defendant was aware of the duty at issue, which cannot be true if the jury credits a good-faith misunderstanding and belief submission, whether or not the claimed belief or misunderstanding is objectively reasonable.[75]

Second, the Court rejected Cheek's good-faith belief that the income tax laws were unconstitutional as grounds for acquittal, noting that such arguments did not arise from innocent mistakes caused by the complexity of the *Code* because they revealed full knowledge of the provisions at issue by the taxpayer, who could have reached such a conclusion only after carefully studying them.[76] However, the Court drew a distinction between Cheek's position and the line of cases that construe the wilfulness requirement in the criminal provisions of the *Code* "*to require proof of knowledge of the law*," observing that "[t]his was because in 'our complex tax system, uncertainty often arises even among taxpayers who earnestly wish to follow the law'" and that *"[i]t is not the purpose of the law to penalize frank difference of opinion or innocent errors made despite the exercise of reasonable care.*"[77]

In *Ratzlaf v United States*, the Supreme Court reviewed a question that had divided the court of appeals: "Does a defendant's purpose to circumvent a bank's reporting obligation suffice to sustain a conviction for 'wilfully violating' the anti-structuring provision?"[78] Under *BSA* section

[74] *Ibid* at 202.

[75] *Ibid.*

[76] *Ibid* at 204–5.

[77] *Ibid* at 205, citing *Bishop*, above note 71 at 360–61, quoting *Spies*, above note 72 at 496 [emphasis added].

[78] *Ratzlaf*, above note 33 at 136.

5313, banks and other financial institutions must file reports with the Department of the Treasury when they are involved in a cash transaction exceeding $10,000. Moreover, under *BSA* section 5324, it is illegal to "structure" a transaction (i.e., break up a single transaction) that is above the threshold into two or more transactions to evade a bank's reporting requirements. The defendant, Ratzlaf, admitted that he had structured cash transactions (to pay off a casino debt of over $160,000) with knowledge of and the purpose of circumventing the bank's duty to report currency transactions over $10,000.[79] Ratzlaf maintained on appeal that he could not be convicted of "willfully violating" the anti-structuring law based on his intention to circumvent the bank's reporting obligations and that the government had to prove that he had been aware of the illegality of the "structuring" in which he had engaged.[80]

Justice Ginsburg observed, for the Court, "we count it significant that § 5322(a)'s omnibus 'willfulness' requirement, when applied to other provisions in the same subchapter, consistently has been read by the Court of Appeals to require both 'knowledge of the reporting requirement' and a 'specific intent to commit the crime,' i.e., 'a purpose to disobey the law.'"[81] The Court added that decisions involving these provisions (with specific reference to section 5314 of Title 31, *United States Code*, concerning records of and reports on monetary transactions with foreign financial agencies) "describe a 'willful actor' as one who violates 'a known legal duty.'"[82] The Court found that the jury had not been properly instructed

---

[79] *Ibid* at 140.

[80] *Ibid* at 138.

[81] *Ibid* at 141, citing *Bank of New England*, above note 72: a "willful violation" of the reporting requirement in *Code*, above note 49, § 5313 for cash transactions over $10,000 requires "voluntary, intentional, and bad purpose to disobey the law"; *United States v Eisenstein*, 731 F 2d 1540 at 1543 (11th Cir 1984), quoting *United States v Granda*, 565 F 2d 922 at 926 (5th Cir 1978): a "willful violation" of the reporting requirement in *Code*, above note 49, § 5313 for cash transactions over $10,000 requires "proof of the defendant's knowledge of the reporting requirement and his specific intent to commit the crime."

[82] *Ratzlaf*, above note 33 at 141–42, citing, for example, *Sturman*, above note 71 at 1476–77, quoting *Cheek*, above note 71 at 201: a "willful violation" of the reporting requirement in *Code*, above note 49, § 5314 for foreign financial transactions requires proof of a "'voluntary, intentional violation of a known legal duty'"; *United States v Warren*, 612 F 2d 887 at 887 (5th Cir 1980): a "willful violation" of the reporting requirement in *Code*, above note 49, § 5316 for transportation of currency across international boundaries requires a defendant to "have actually known of the currency reporting requirement and have voluntarily and intentionally violated that known legal duty."

on the willfulness standard and reversed the Court of Appeals for the Ninth Circuit, remanding the case. In noting that the jury had not been properly instructed, the Court observed:

> We do not dishonor the venerable principle that ignorance of the law generally is no defense to a criminal charge. See *Cheek* v. *United States*, 498 U.S. 192, 199 (1991); *Barlow* v. *United States*, 32 U.S. (7 Pet.) 404, 410 (1833) (Story, J.). In particular contexts, however, Congress may decree otherwise. That, we hold, is what Congress has done with respect to 31 U.S.C. § 5322(a) and the provisions it controls. To convict Ratzlaf of the crime with which he was charged, violation of 31 U.S.C. §§ 5322(a) and 5324(3), the jury had to find he knew the structuring in which he engaged was unlawful.[83]

In *United States v Williams*, the Court of Appeals examined whether Williams' failure to file an FBAR in a timely manner for the tax year 2000 had been willful.[84] The court held that Williams' actions established reckless conduct that satisfied the proof requirement under *BSA* section 5314.[85] The facts in *Williams* may be briefly summarized. Williams was a tax villain. He opened two Swiss bank accounts in the name of a British corporation into which he deposited between 1993 and 2000 more than $7 million, which earned more than $800,000 in investment income. He

---

[83] *Ratzlaf*, above note 33 at 149.

[84] 110 AFTR 2d 5298 (4th Cir 2012) [*Williams* 2012], which reversed the judgment of the District Court: *Williams* 2010, above note 72. The Court of Appeals in *Williams* 2012, *ibid* at 5301, found that the district court had clearly erred in finding that willfulness had not been established.

[85] *Williams* 2012, above note 84, citing *Safeco Ins Co of America v Burr*, 551 US 47 at 57 (2007). See *BSA*, above note 1, § 5314. The court in *Williams* 2012, above note 84 at 5301, observed, "'A taxpayer who signs a tax return will not be heard to claim innocence for not having actually read the return, as he or she is charged with constructive knowledge of its contents.' *Greer* v. *Commissioner of Internal Revenue*, 595 F.3d 338, 347 (6th Cir. 2010)." The court, *ibid*, further observed, "Williams's signature is prima facie evidence that he knew the contents of the return, *United States* v. *Mohney*, 949 F.2d 1397, 1407 (6th Cir. 1991)." In reference to Schedule B (Form 1040) of individuals' tax returns, the court, *ibid*, observed, "at a minimum line 7a's directions to '[s]ee instructions for exceptions and filing requirements for Form TD F 90-22.1' put Williams on inquiry notice of the FBAR requirement." The court, *ibid*, also noted that Williams had not read line 7a of his return and had not consulted the FBAR form or its instructions and, as a result, concluded, "Williams made a 'conscious effort to avoid learning about reporting requirements,' *Sturman*, 951 F.2d at 1476." Additionally, the court, *ibid*, noted that Williams' guilty plea allocution further confirmed that his violation of § 5314 was willful.

did not report the income from those accounts to the IRS, nor did he file the required FBAR form for the accounts. For his tax year 2000 return, he completed a tax organizer for his accountant and answered no to the question whether he had "an interest in or a signature or other authority over a financial account in a foreign country." He also answered no in response to the question posed on his tax year 2000 Schedule B (Form 1040), Part III, line 7a, "At any time during 2000, did you have an interest in or a signature or other authority over a financial account in a foreign country, such as a bank account, securities account, or other financial account? See instructions for exceptions and filing requirements for Form TD F 90-22.1." Following investigations by Swiss and US authorities commenced in 2000, Williams pleaded guilty to a two-count superseding criminal information charging him with conspiracy to defraud the IRS in violation of section 371 of Title 18, *United States Code*, and criminal tax evasion in violation of section 7201 of Title 26, *United States Code*. The IRS assessed two $100,000 civil penalties against him pursuant to *BSA* section 5321(a)(5) for his failure to file an FBAR for the tax year 2000. In his allocution, Williams admitted the following: "I also knew that I had the obligation to report to the IRS and/or the Department of Treasury the existence of the Swiss accounts, but for the calendar year tax returns 1993 through 2000, I chose not to in order to assist in hiding my true income from the IRS and evade taxes thereon, until I filed my 2001 return."[86]

The court, at least in part, based its finding that Williams' actions had been reckless and therefore willful on the facts that he had signed a tax return and that he had not read the instructions on Schedule B (Form 1040) (referring him to the FBAR form) and also had not read the FBAR form or instructions. In doing so, the court has left open the door to a very broad interpretation of its holding that taxpayers who sign returns but who fail to file the FBAR form may be found to have willfully violated the requirements under *BSA* section 5314 as a result of their "conscious effort to avoid learning about reporting requirements" or "willful blindness."[87] The Court of Appeals' equation of constructive knowledge

---

[86] *Williams* 2012, above note 84 at 5301. See also *BSA*, above note 1, § 5321(a)(5).

[87] See *Williams* 2012, above note 84 at 5301, quoting *Sturman*, above note 71 at 1476. See also *BSA*, above note 1, § 5314.

with specific intent purports to substitute a strict liability offence standard for the specific intent standard required by statute. Such a broad interpretation would clearly be opposite the holdings in *Ratzlaf* and *Cheek*.[88] The decision raises the question, will Canada, the United Kingdom, and the European Union assist the United States to apply this kind of scary justice to their citizens and residents, or call for a political solution to the problems created by nationality-based taxation?

Williams was an individual who was found guilty of criminal tax evasion. Based on the facts in his case, the court had a strong motivation to find that he had willfully failed to file an FBAR form. It remains to be seen whether the IRS or another court will support the application of this constructive knowledge standard to a taxpayer who does not have a secret tax haven account and has not been engaged in such tax evasion schemes. The application of such a standard to non-filers in Canada and other foreign countries who have come forward to clean up past delinquencies and who lack any prior knowledge of the FBAR obligation would be legally wrong and morally unjust.

A person who willfully fails to report a foreign account or required account information under the *BSA* may be subject to criminal penalties in addition to the civil penalties described above.[89] In addition, such a person may also face criminal prosecution for the willful failure to report the earnings arising from the foreign account.[90]

---

[88] *Ratzlaf*, above note 33; *Cheek*, above note 71. See also Hale E Sheppard, "Third Time's the Charm: Government Finally Collects 'Willful' FBAR Penalty in Williams" (2012) 117 *Journal of Taxation* 13.

[89] 31 USC § 5321(a), 31 USC § 5322(b), or 18 USC § 1001; *FinCEN Form 114 Instructions*, above note 46 at 22. A person who willfully violates the FBAR filing requirement could face a fine of up to $250,000, imprisonment for up to five years, or both: 31 USC § 5322(a). The fine and imprisonment term increase to $500,000 and ten years if the failure to file the FBAR occurs during the violation of another law or is part of certain illegal activity: 31 USC § 5322(b).

[90] For example, for falsely answering a question on Schedule B (Form 1040), Part III, relating to foreign accounts, under the penalties of perjury (or even for omitting to answer a question), a person may be prosecuted under *Code*, above note 49, § 7206(1). Other applicable offences may arise under § 7206(1) for omission of earnings on Schedules B or D and under § 7201 for tax evasion. See *United States v Simon*, 106 AFTR 2d 6739 (ND Ind 2010) [*Simon*]: taxpayer received $1.8 million from businesses that was not reported as taxable income, did not disclose accounts on Schedule B, and was indicted for filing false income tax returns and for failure to file FBAR forms. See also Michel, above note 68 at 160.

In the absence of being able to prove a willful violation, the IRS may assert a non-willful penalty not to exceed $10,000 per violation for the failure to file an FBAR form.[91] A taxpayer will not be subject to a non-willful penalty with respect to any violation if the violation was due to reasonable cause and if the taxpayer reports the account by filing delinquent FBARs.[92] And a taxpayer who furnishes relevant information to a qualified professional and who relies in good faith on advice on a matter of tax law provided by that professional may obtain a waiver of penalties for reasonable cause for his failure to file a tax return.[93] The ability to obtain a reasonable cause waiver for filing a delinquent FBAR is a critical component in assessing a delinquent taxpayer's legal rights in the context of making a voluntary disclosure.[94] The IRS issued interim FBAR penalty guidance in 2015 applicable to willful and non-willful penalties in which it noted that in some cases, depending on the facts and circumstances, asserting non-willful penalties for each year is not warranted but that in other cases, the facts and circumstances (including the conduct of the person required to file and the aggregate balance of the unreported foreign financial accounts) may indicate that asserting separate non-willful penalties for each unreported foreign financial account for each year is

[91] 31 USC § 5321(a)(5)(A). This penalty was enacted by Congress in 2004 as part of the *American Jobs Creation Act*, Pub L 108-357, 118 Stat 1418 (2004), to address the difficulties confronting the government in asserting a civil penalty for willfulness: see Sheppard, "FBAR Penalties," above note 71 at 294. As an example of the unfairness of the voluntary disclosure programs, some agents will threaten taxpayers who seek to opt out for reasonable cause or non-willfulness by calculating what is supposed to be a one-time per year penalty of $10,000 with a $10,000 per unreported account hit per year. Hence, if Susan, a wife who recently moved from India to Indiana with her husband, had eight accounts in her former country, she could be hit with $80,000 in non-willful penalties per year instead of with the correct amount of $10,000 per year. See also United States, Internal Revenue Service, *Internal Revenue Manual* (Washington, DC: US Department of the Treasury, 2015) at § 4.26.16, online: www.irs.gov/irm/ [*IRM 2015*], for details regarding FBAR penalties.

[92] 31 USC § 5321(a)(5)(B)(ii). See also *IRM 2015*, above note 91 at § 4.26.16.

[93] *Code*, above note 49, reg § 301.6651-1(c)(1). See also *West Coast Ice Co v Commissioner of Internal Revenue*, 49 TC 345 (1968); *Boyle v United States*, 469 US 241 (1985). For a discussion of the reasonable cause exception, see Michael Saltzman & Leslie Book, *IRS Practice and Procedure* (Thomson Reuters/WG&L, 2012) (Checkpoint) at "Penalties 4.06."

[94] A taxpayer generally loses the right to request a waiver of penalties for reasonable cause when the IRS initiates an examination or audit of the taxpayer for the years in question: see Saltzman & Book, above note 93 at "Penalties 4.06."

warranted.[95] Prudence and caution are advised when counselling clients who have failed to comply with the rigorous reporting standards of the BSA, which also contains severe criminal penalties.[96] The complexities surrounding delinquent filers with foreign accounts cannot be understated and dangers can also include criminal penalties relating to unreported income on those accounts.[97]

5 US Voluntary Disclosure Initiatives

The IRS has initiated offshore voluntary disclosure programs in 2009, 2011, and 2012 with the objective of bringing taxpayers that have used undisclosed foreign accounts to avoid or evade tax into compliance with US tax and foreign reporting laws.[98] To date, the IRS has received

---

[95] See "Guidance for FBAR Penalties," above note 67, Attachment 1 at 2. In no event will the total amount of the penalties for non-willful violations exceed 50 percent of the highest aggregate balance of all unreported foreign financial accounts for the years under examination (see *ibid*, Attachment 1 at 3). A non-willful penalty will not be recommended if the examiner determines that the FBAR violations were due to reasonable cause and if the person failing to file correct and complete FBARs in a timely manner later files correct and complete FBARs (see *ibid*).

[96] A person who is found to willfully violate the FBAR filing requirements could face the following penalties: a fine of up to $250,000, imprisonment for up to five years, or both. The fine and prison sentences may be doubled under certain circumstances involving illegal activities. See above note 89.

[97] A taxpayer may face criminal prosecution for willfully failing to report his earnings arising from such an account and such evidence may be taken from information on the taxpayer's Form 1040. Criminal issues facing a taxpayer could potentially involve tax evasion and making a false statement, amongst others. See, for example, above note 90.

[98] Another objective of the offshore voluntary disclosure program is to use the information gathered from taxpayers making voluntary disclosures to further the IRS's understanding of how foreign accounts and foreign entities are promoted to US taxpayers as ways to avoid or evade tax and to develop additional strategies to inhibit promoters and facilitators from soliciting new clients: see United States, Internal Revenue Service, "Voluntary Disclosure: Questions and Answers" at Q1 & Q2, online: www.irs.gov/uac/Voluntary-Disclosure:-Questions-and-Answers ["2009 OVDP FAQ"]. The IRS initiated an offshore voluntary disclosure program in May 2009 that ran until 15 October 2009: see United States, Internal Revenue Service, "2009 Offshore Voluntary Disclosure Program," online: www.irs.gov/uac/2009-Offshore-Voluntary-Disclosure-Program. Then IRS commissioner Doug Shulman announced, "My goal has always been clear — to get taxpayers hiding assets offshore back into the system." He went on to warn, "For taxpayers who continue to hide their head in the sand, the situation will only become more dire. They should come forward now under our voluntary disclosure practice and get right with the government": United States, Internal Revenue Service, "Statement from IRS Commissioner Doug Shulman on Offshore Income" (26 March 2009), online: www.irs.gov/uac/Statement-from-IRS-Commissioner-Doug-

approximately 54,000 disclosures from the three programs and has collected over $8 billion in taxes, interest, and penalties.[99] The IRS notes that these three initiatives have enabled the agency to centralize the civil processing of voluntary disclosures and to resolve a large number of cases without examination.[100] In 2011, it was estimated that 5 to 7 million US resident taxpayers and potentially tens of millions of non-resident taxpayers were subject to the FBAR requirements, but there were only 741,000 FBARs filed that year.[101] The three voluntary disclosure programs are supplementary to a long-standing voluntary disclosure program maintained by the IRS, but taxpayers using the main program may be, and indeed have been, invited into one of the aforementioned programs.[102]

Some of the specific benefits that the IRS claims taxpayers may gain by entering a program are the following: becoming compliant with the law, avoiding substantial civil penalties, generally eliminating the risk of criminal prosecution, and being able to calculate with a reasonable degree of certainty the total cost of all penalties for coming into compliance.[103] The chief reasons that a delinquent taxpayer may have for entering a

Shulman-on-Offshore-Income. Another offshore voluntary disclosure initiative was announced on 8 February 2011 and ran until September 2011: see United States, Internal Revenue Service, "2011 Offshore Voluntary Disclosure Initiative," online: www.irs.gov/uac/2011-Offshore-Voluntary-Disclosure-Initiative. A 2012 offshore voluntary disclosure program has the same objectives as the 2009 and 2011 programs, but it does not yet have an announced termination date: see "2012 OVDP FAQ," above note 66 at Q1 & Q2, regarding the objectives of the program.

[99] See United States, Internal Revenue Service, "Hiding Money or Income Offshore Resides on the 'Dirty Dozen' List of Tax Scams for the 2016 Filing Season" IR-2016-17 *IRS Newswire* (5 February 2016) online: content.govdelivery.com/accounts/USIRS/bulletins/134bd2c.

[100] See "2012 OVDP FAQ," above note 66 at Q1.

[101] See Federal Taxes Weekly Alert Newsletter, "National Taxpayer Advocate Suggests Changes to Offshore Voluntary Disclosure Initiative" *Federal Taxes Weekly Alert Newsletter* (21 November 2012).

[102] See *IRM 2015*, above note 91 at § 9.5.11.9.

[103] See "2012 OVDP FAQ," above note 66 at Q5 & Q6, for an explanation of the potential civil and criminal penalties that a taxpayer may face if she does not come forward. For example, a taxpayer with $1 million in an offshore account that had earned interest income of $50,000 a year from 2003 to 2010 who came forward and entered the program would pay tax, interest, an accuracy penalty, and an additional penalty in lieu of the FBAR penalty of approximately $518,000 compared to the $4,543,000 that a taxpayer in the identical situation who did not come forward and who was discovered by the IRS would pay (see *ibid* at Q8). The programs also shield taxpayers from a large number of penalties that may otherwise be assessed under various foreign-reporting obligations, including those related to interests in or transactions with foreign entities such as corporations, partnerships, and trusts (see, for example, *ibid* at Q5).

program are obtaining closure on his delinquencies and having peace of mind about the future.[104] The 2009, 2011, and 2012 programs have subjected taxpayers to a penalty of 20 percent, 25 percent, and 27.5 percent respectfully of their highest aggregate account balance in any one year of the years covered by the program.[105] Reduced penalty rates ranging from 5 to 12.5 percent may also apply to certain qualifying taxpayers.[106]

These offshore voluntary disclosure programs have required that a taxpayer agree to pay an FBAR penalty in the range of 5 to 27.5 percent as part of the terms for entering the program even if the taxpayer has no prior knowledge of the duty to file an FBAR or is entitled by the facts to a waiver of all FBAR penalties based on reasonable cause. As a result, the programs have been able to impose willfulness FBAR penalties on taxpayers in the absence of showing or proving any willfulness under the *BSA*.[107]

---

[104] A taxpayer's experience in a program culminates with the IRS and the taxpayer signing a closing agreement for the years included in the program: see United States, Internal Revenue Service, Form 906, "Closing Agreement on Final Determination Covering Specific Matters," online: www.irs.gov/pub/irs-utl/form_906.pdf. The goal in the closing agreement, where possible, is to not leave prior years open for examination.

[105] For details on the penalty, see, for example, "2012 OVDP FAQ," above note 66 at Q8.

[106] Taxpayers that may qualify for a 5 percent FBAR penalty under the programs include persons who were unaware that they were US citizens and persons who lived abroad, were tax compliant in their foreign country of residence, and for each of the years in the program had less than $10,000 of US sourced income (see *ibid* at Q52). Persons who had balances in their offshore accounts of less than $75,000 in each of the program years may qualify for a 12.5 percent penalty (see *ibid* at Q53). The 2012 offshore voluntary disclosure program provides a mechanism for taxpayers to opt out of the program by irrevocable election if they disagree with the application of the offshore penalty (see *ibid* at Q51ff). Taxpayers opting out are subject to full civil examination and possible penalties, including FBAR penalties, and remain within IRS Criminal Investigation's voluntary disclosure practice requirements relating to cooperation and full disclosure (see *ibid*). From a practical perspective, the professional fees incurred in opting out, especially for retired seniors in Canada who are not willful but who do not have a letter of support for reasonable cause from their accountant can be monumental.

[107] The United States Taxpayer Advocate, Nina Olson, has been highly critical of the offshore voluntary disclosure programs. She advocates not imposing an FBAR penalty if the willfulness standard as described in *Ratzlaf*, above note 33, is not met: see Federal Taxes Weekly Alert Newsletter, above note 101. She has also remarked, "One basic problem with the OVDP [offshore voluntary disclosure program] is that it assumes all participants are tax evaders hiding money overseas, when in fact, the IRS has steered many people into the program who made honest mistakes": United States, National Taxpayer Advocate, *2011 Annual Report to Congress* (Washington, DC: US Department of the Treasury, 2011) vol 1 at 243, online: www.taxpayeradvocate.irs.gov/userfiles/file/2011-annual-report/IRS%20TAS%20ARC%202011%20VOL%201.pdf [*2011 Annual Report*], citing her memo dated 22 September 2011 to the deputy commissioner, Services and

These programs have been particularly harsh on Canadians with dual (Canadian-US) nationality (or those who have US citizenship and Canadian residency). Many dual nationals have lived in Canada for most of their lives. The vast majority of these individuals share the following characteristics: they work or are retired in Canada, they maintain bank accounts only in Canada (and not in any tax haven jurisdictions), they file tax returns reporting and pay taxes on their income, until very recently neither they nor their tax return preparers ever heard of the FBAR, and after the foreign earned income exclusion under *Code* section 911 or the foreign tax credit under *Code* section 901, they may owe little to no taxes to the United States for the years after the alternative minimum tax limitation on the availability of foreign tax credits that expired in 2004.[108] The programs' fairness has come under scrutiny and criticism from the United States Taxpayer Advocate, Nina Olson, who has called upon the IRS to, among other things, stop terrorizing the entire country of Canada.[109]

In October 2011, US Ambassador David Jacobson spoke to the Canadian Club of Ottawa in an effort to reassure worried Canadians that his government was not out to get honest grandmas who did not owe anything to the IRS.[110] The irony is that, despite what may have been the ambassador's best intentions or beliefs, in reality the IRS has thrown grandma and grandpa from the train by subjecting them to the costly professional fees related to entering a program and to its potentially eviscerating penalty structure when there would otherwise be no basis under the *BSA* for the IRS to assess and collect these FBAR penalties.[111] Many Canadian seniors have to dig into their retirement savings to fund their US compliance.

Enforcement. In her *2011 Annual Report, ibid*, Ms Olson also focuses her concern on the "2009 OVDP FAQ," above note 98 at Q35, which advises taxpayers coming into the program that "[u]nder no circumstances will a taxpayer be required to pay a penalty greater than what he would otherwise be liable for under existing statutes." She criticizes the IRS for later taking the position, in an internal memo dated 1 March 2011, that it will no longer consider whether a taxpayer would pay less under existing statutes, as undermining the IRS's reputation for fair dealing (*2011 Annual Report, ibid*, vol 1 at 258–65).

[108] See *Code*, above note 49, §§ 911 and 901.

[109] See Federal Taxes Weekly Alert Newsletter, above note 101.

[110] See The Canadian Press, "Americans in Canada Told Not to Fear IRS" *CBC News* (18 October 2011), online: http://www.cbc.ca/1.1060577.

[111] See Suzanne Steel, "Read Jim Flaherty's Letter on Americans in Canada" *Financial Post* (16 September 2011), online: http://natpo.st/1Zsirt1: then Canadian finance minister remarked that

Moreover, the penalty structure of these programs is capricious and arbitrary. A tax compliant Canadian dual national who owed under $1,800 of taxes to the US government for any single year from 2005 to 2011, who had no US sourced business or investment income during those years, and who had accounts only in Canada would be forced to forfeit approximately a third of her life savings (27.5 percent) if her father in New York died and if she was named the beneficiary of a small IRA account with $10,500 in the years covered by the program. As the beneficiary of her father's IRA at his death (something that she had had nothing to do with and may not even have known about), because her US sourced income in the year that her father died would be over the arbitrarily chosen IRS figure of $10,000, she would not be eligible for the 5 percent reduced rate and would have to pay the 27.5 percent rate even though she never heard of the FBAR. In an attempt to lure delinquent Canadian dual citizens into the system, the IRS announced a new streamlined initiative with an effective date of 1 September 2012, but it too is fraught with peril.[112] The senior citizen taxpayer who is ineligible for the 5 percent rate under the offshore voluntary disclosure program will also be ineligible under the streamlined initiative if he owes more than $1,500 in US taxes for any of the three years covered by the initiative (another arbitrary number chosen by the IRS). There are many asymmetries between the *Code* and the *Act* that could give rise to a US taxpayer's owing taxes and thereby being ineligible for the streamlined relief, not the least of which relates to investments in Canadian mutual funds or exchange traded funds, which are subject to the passive foreign investment rules. As described below, the IRS currently maintains a set

most dual citizens in Canada were unaware of their obligations to file with the IRS, paid taxes in Canada, and had no US liability but still faced the threat of prohibitive FBAR fines. It is not just the threat or application of an FBAR penalty that causes financial distress among Canadian citizens and residents caught in the crossfire of the US fiscal crisis but also the enormous burden of having to comply with the onerous and often very costly compliance and reporting rules under the *Code*, above note 49, and to navigate the many anomalies between the *Code* and the *Act*, above note 5: see, for example, David S Kerzner, "Saving Your Clients from U.S. 'Tax Cancer': Passive Foreign Investment Companies and Other Tax Troubles" (2012) 5 *It's Personal* 5.

[112] See United States, Internal Revenue Service, "New Filing Compliance Procedures for Non-resident U.S. Taxpayers" (last updated 6 July 2015), online: www.irs.gov/Individuals/International-Taxpayers/New-Filing-Compliance-Procedures-for-Non-Resident-U.S.-Taxpayers; Kerzner, "Advising the Delinquent U.S. Client," above note 66.

of different disclosure pathways for various failures to report income, pay taxes, and file information returns. In Chapter 11, we recommend that the United States study eligibility criteria for the establishment of a fund to pay restitution to earlier Canadian, UK, EU, and other participants in these programs who have been forced to pay unnecessary professional fees and FBAR penalties.

Currently, the IRS offers a number of different pathways to remedy delinquencies under the *Code* and the *BSA*. These pathways include, but are not limited to, streamlined filing compliance procedures for US taxpayers residing outside the United States,[113] streamlined filing compliance procedures for US taxpayers residing in the United States,[114] delinquent FBAR submission procedures,[115] delinquent international information return submission procedures,[116] and the 2012 (now referred to as the 2014) offshore voluntary disclosure program.[117] The juridical concept of reasonable cause noted above is very important to the general approach taken to the voluntary disclosure process, and reasonable cause may be a

---

[113] See United States, Internal Revenue Service, "Streamlined Filing Compliance Procedures" (last updated 6 August 2015), online: www.irs.gov/Individuals/International-Taxpayers/Streamlined-Filing-Compliance-Procedures ["Streamlined Foreign Offshore Procedures"].

[114] See United States, Internal Revenue Service, "U.S. Taxpayers Residing in the United States" (last updated 25 September 2015), online: www.irs.gov/Individuals/International-Taxpayers/U-S-Taxpayers-Residing-in-the-United-States ["Streamlined Domestic Offshore Procedures"].

[115] See United States, Internal Revenue Service, "Delinquent FBAR Submission Procedures" (last updated 14 May 2015), online: www.irs.gov/Individuals/International-Taxpayers/Delinquent-FBAR-Submission-Procedures: taxpayers who do not need to use either the offshore voluntary disclosure program or the streamlined filing compliance procedures to file delinquent or amended tax returns to report and pay additional tax but who have not filed a FinCEN Form 114 (previously Form TD F 90-22.1) and who are not under civil examination or criminal investigation by the IRS and have not already been contacted by the IRS about the delinquent FBAR may file under these procedures.

[116] See United States, Internal Revenue Service, "Delinquent International Information Return Submission Procedures" (last updated 25 September 2015), online: www.irs.gov/Individuals/International-Taxpayers/Delinquent-International-Information-Return-Submission-Procedures: taxpayers who do not need to use either the offshore voluntary disclosure program or the streamlined filing compliance procedures to file delinquent or amended tax returns to report and pay additional tax but who have not filed one or more required international information returns and who have reasonable cause for not filing the information returns in a timely manner, are not under civil examination or criminal investigation by the IRS, and have not already been contacted by the IRS about the delinquent information returns may file under these procedures.

[117] See United States, Internal Revenue Service, "2012 Offshore Voluntary Disclosure Program" (last updated 10 March 2016), online: www.irs.gov/uac/2012-Offshore-Voluntary-Disclosure-Program.

requirement for certain of the aforementioned pathways.[118] Accordingly, expert legal consideration of an individual's case, the doctrine of reasonable cause in the *Code*, and the jurisprudence is often indispensable to the taxpayer's representation.

The purpose of the streamlined filing compliance procedures offered by the IRS is to provide taxpayers who are able to certify that their failure to report foreign financial assets and pay all tax due in respect of those assets did not result from willful conduct on their part.[119] These streamlined filing compliance procedures are different from the original procedures first offered on 1 September 2012. Gone are the arbitrary and capricious risk assessment questionnaire and $1,500 tax threshold. The new rules also extend the streamlined procedures to US taxpayers residing in the United States.[120] Taxpayers in the domestic program are subject to a Title 26 miscellaneous offshore penalty equal to 5 percent of the highest aggregate balance or value of a taxpayer's foreign financial assets subject to the miscellaneous offshore penalty during the years in the covered tax return period and the covered FBAR period.[121] It should be noted that once a taxpayer makes a submission under either set of streamlined procedures, the taxpayer may not participate in the offshore voluntary disclosure program.[122]

Generally, eligible foreign taxpayers using the streamlined foreign offshore compliance procedures who comply with their many detailed requirements will not be subject to failure-to-file, failure-to-pay, accuracy-related, information return, or FBAR penalties.[123] While an explanation of the details of these procedures is beyond the scope of this chapter, taxpayers should be carefully advised by expert US interna-

---

[118] See sources cited at note 93, above in this chapter.

[119] See "Streamlined Foreign Offshore Procedures," above note 113.

[120] See "Streamlined Domestic Offshore Procedures," above note 114.

[121] See *ibid.*

[122] See "Streamlined Foreign Offshore Procedures," above note 113. For more details about the offshore voluntary disclosure program, including the potentially very high penalties, see United States, Internal Revenue Service, "Offshore Voluntary Disclosure Program Frequently Asked Questions and Answers 2014," online: www.irs.gov/Individuals/International-Taxpayers/Offshore-Voluntary-Disclosure-Program-Frequently-Asked-Questions-and-Answers-2012-Revised ["2014 OVDP FAQ"].

[123] See "Streamlined Foreign Offshore Procedures," above note 113.

tional tax counsel to ensure privilege and eligibility for the relief sought. In 2016, the IRS introduced a new and more onerous (or treacherous) certification form that is required from taxpayers residing outside the United States who are claiming that their filing delinquencies were non-willful.[124] Moreover, it is advantageous for taxpayers to have a detailed examination of their tax, legal, and financial affairs and their personal and business objectives as part of any voluntary disclosure considerations. This is particularly important for US expatriates living in Canada, the United Kingdom, and the European Union who may be weighing the very complex decision of expatriation. For US nationals in Canada, due regard should be paid to the exit tax under *Code* section 877A, which is a highly complex and dangerous area of the law that needs to be navigated with the utmost of care.[125] Additional cross-border issues that need to be examined often include a taxpayer's private company holdings, private trust holdings, investment holdings (especially of foreign mutual funds or flow-through investments), real estate, jointly held assets and accounts, and wills, powers, and succession planning in the two jurisdictions. Taxpayers seeking to avoid the myriad of horrors that can result from complex multijurisdictional and multidisciplinary tax puzzles need above all to select counsel with expertise in cross-border IRS tax controversy matters.

Taxpayers who are concerned that their failure to report income, pay tax, or submit required information returns was due to willful conduct and who would like assurance that they will not be subject to criminal liability or substantial monetary penalties should consider with their counsel the eligibility requirements for, procedures involved in, and penalty and professional costs of participating in the offshore voluntary disclosure program. Taxpayers coming into the program will face penalty rates between 27.5 and 50 percent, depending on factors like whether the foreign financial institution holding the account is under investigation by or cooperating with the US government.[126]

---

[124] United States, Internal Revenue Service, Form 14653, "Certification by U.S. Person Residing Outside of the United States for Streamlined Foreign Offshore Procedures" (February 2016), online: www.irs.gov/pub/irs-pdf/f14653.pdf.

[125] *Code*, above note 49, § 877A.

[126] See "2014 OVDP FAQ," above note 122 at Q7 and Q7.2.

6 Cross-border Collections Enforcement between Canada and the United States

As a legal matter, whether or not the IRS may enforce taxes and penalties under the *Code* or FBAR penalties under the *BSA* outside of the United States is a question that needs to be considered under the domestic laws of the particular jurisdiction in which such enforcement is sought together with any applicable treaties.[127] Historically, the "revenue rule" precluded a state from bringing an action in another state for the collection of fiscal claims.[128] As authors have published extensively on the subject of cross-border collections enforcement, only an overview is provided here.[129]

Article XXVI-A(1) of the *Canada–US Tax Treaty* provides that Canada and the United States agree to lend assistance to each other in the collection of all categories of taxes collected by or on behalf of the government of either state.[130] Moreover, such assistance with the collection of revenue claims is to include assistance with, in addition to taxes, interest, costs, and contributions to social security and employment insurance premiums collected by or on behalf of the government of either state.[131]

Under Article XXVI-A(2), in making an application for assistance under the article, the requesting state must be able to certify that the revenue claim has been finally determined.[132] Article XXVI-A(4) provides that where an application for the collection of a revenue claim is accepted in respect of a taxpayer by Canada, the revenue claim will be treated by

---

[127] For an in-depth examination of the legal principles surrounding cross-border collections enforcement between Canada and the United States, see David S Kerzner, Vitaly Timokhov, & David W Chodikoff, eds, *The Tax Advisor's Guide to the Canada–U.S. Tax Treaty* (Toronto: Thomson Reuters Carswell, 2008) (loose-leaf) ch 26A. See also Andrew Bonham, "FATCA and FBAR Reporting by Individuals: Enforcement Considerations from a Canadian Perspective" (2012) 60:2 *Canadian Tax Journal* 305; Vitaly S Timokhov, "Enforcing Tax Judgments across Borders: How Collection Assistance Can Overcome Limitations of the 'Revenue Rule'" (2003) 6 *Journal of International Taxation* 36.

[128] Article 15 of the Third Protocol (1995) added Article XXVI-A (Assistance in Collection) to the *Canada–US Tax Treaty*, above note 4, *ibid*, at Technical Explanation to Art 26A. Historically, states have been reluctant to enforce the revenue laws of other states: see *United States v Harden*, [1963] SCR 366.

[129] See, for example, Kerzner, Timokhov, & Chodikoff, above note 128, ch 26A.

[130] *Canada–US Tax Treaty*, above note 4 at Art XXVI-A(1).

[131] *Ibid* at Arts XXVI-A(1) and (9).

[132] *Ibid* at Art XXVI-A(2). Under *ibid*, Art XXVI-A(3), the requested state has limited discretion as to whether or not to accept the application for assistance.

Canada as an amount payable under the *Act*, and its collection will not be subject to any restriction.[133]

Under Article XXVI-A(5), there is to be no administrative or judicial review of the revenue claim, so the substantive validity of the requesting state's revenue claim cannot be challenged in an action in the requested state.[134]

For Americans living in Canada, Article XXVI-A(8) generally provides legal protection against IRS requests for assistance with revenue claims to the extent that a taxpayer can demonstrate that the revenue claim relates to a taxable period when the taxpayer was a citizen of Canada.[135] CRA has stated that it will not assist the IRS under the *Canada–US Tax Treaty* to collect non-tax-related penalties such as FBAR penalties.[136]

When an accountant, a lawyer, or a professional financial adviser is giving advice to a delinquent US filer living in Canada, it is quite common for that professional to inform her client that the IRS cannot enforce its tax claims or penalties in Canada. We hear this all the time. What these professionals do not tell their clients is that there are a number of perils that may arise as a result of their continuing delinquency. Chapter 5, on US international enforcement, describes a number of robust administrative measures that the IRS can take to enforce its audit and collections powers in the United States. Responding to even the smallest of such administrative measures, like a request for information, can be very costly in terms of professional fees. And, as described in Chapter 5, a taxpayer's failure to adequately comply with IRS demands in a timely manner may rapidly result in criminal sanctions, which may not only interfere with a taxpayer's travel plans to the United States but may also disrupt travel

[133] *Ibid* at Art XXVI-A(4).

[134] *Ibid* at Art XXVI-A(5).

[135] *Ibid* at Art XXVI-A(8): where a taxpayer became a citizen of the requested state before 9 November 1995 and is still a citizen of that state when the application for assistance is made, no assistance may be provided for taxable periods ending before 9 November 1995. See also *Chua v Canada (MNR)*, [2001] 1 FC 608 (TD), dealing with a judicial review of an IRS request for assistance.

[136] Canada, Canada Revenue Agency, "Frequently Asked Questions" (last updated 23 December 2014) at Q23, online: www.cra-arc.gc.ca/tx/nnrsdnts/nhncdrprtng/fq-eng.html. In light of the legal warfare, described in Chapter 5, that the IRS can unleash against a non-cooperative US taxpayer, CRA's statement should not provide delinquent taxpayers, their executors, or their heirs with any degree of peace of mind.

abroad if the United States places an Interpol red notice on the taxpayer. Such criminal sanctions can also have professional consequences for individuals who have corporate or fiduciary responsibilities or who are affiliated with a licensure agency. Additionally, taxpayers may be called upon to claim their rights under Article XXVI-A of the *Canada–US Tax Treaty* by attending at court with counsel to object to CRA claims made on behalf of the IRS. Furthermore, taxpayers may be forced to deal with requests for information made by CRA on behalf of the IRS under Article XXVII of the *Canada–US Tax Treaty*, dealing with exchange of information (described in Chapter 7, Section 4). A taxpayer's delinquencies may also cause problems with the administration of his estate after his death. In short, the cost of having to deal with any of the aforementioned IRS administrative legal actions may prove to be staggering for an individual and must be weighed against the cost of making a voluntary disclosure.

7 Conclusion

The legal issues facing the delinquent filer, whether they be regarding CRA, the IRS, or both, are many and complex. While it is well beyond the scope of this chapter to detail and explain all the potentially applicable rules under the *Act* and the *Code* and their administrative and judicial interpretation, a theme should by now be emerging. This theme is the imperative that a comprehensive case workup by experts in the field takes place to identify all of the material tax, legal, and compliance issues facing the delinquent client. These issues must also be given materiality by their potential civil and criminal consequences for the taxpayer. Essential in the cross-border equation is the coordination between Canadian and US counsel to ensure that integrated analytical problem solving and advice takes place. Providing single-jurisdiction advice to a client who is subject to the tax laws of two jurisdictions like Canada and the United States (or the United Kingdom and the United States) is a recipe for disaster. The appropriate investigation of a delinquent filer's facts and analysis of her tax issues will also yield an appraisal of her obligations under US tax and reporting laws. To be successful, this inquiry needs to be thorough and needs to be carried out with a solid understanding of the applicable US domestic and international tax rules. A US taxpayer must know what her tax and reporting obligations are — regardless of any perceived or actual unfairness in those rules. The US taxpayer must then be advised about her legal rights so that she may come into compliance with the law. Only political resolve can restore the principle of equity in international tax law that is currently missing between the United States and its neighbours and allies, like Canada, the United Kingdom, and the European Union. Until that time, prevention of harm is the best cure. And a holistic approach to identifying a private client's cross-border tax and legal obligations under domestic and US law is the best way to begin.

Further Readings

Chodikoff, David W, & James L Horvath, eds. *Advocacy & Taxation in Canada* (Toronto: Irwin Law, 2004).

Kerzner, David S. "Advising the Delinquent U.S. Client: What Are Your Strategies? Also, IRS's New Program for Delinquent Filers" (2012) 5 *It's Personal* 14.

Kerzner, David S, Vitaly Timokhov, & David W Chodikoff, eds. *The Tax Advisor's Guide to the Canada–U.S. Tax Treaty* (Toronto: Thomson Reuters Carswell, 2008) (loose-leaf).

Michel, Scott D. "Advising a Client with Secret Offshore Accounts — Current Filing and Reporting Problems" (1999) 91 *Journal of Taxation* 158.

Timokhov, Vitaly S. "Enforcing Tax Judgments across Borders: How Collection Assistance Can Overcome Limitations of the 'Revenue Rule'" (2003) 6 *Journal of International Taxation* 36.

11

Conclusions and Recommendations

1 Conclusions

In 1998, the OECD viewed eliminating harmful tax practices as essential to promoting healthy tax competition and, ultimately, global economic growth and development. The OECD identified the two primary contributors to these harmful tax practices as tax havens and so-called preferential tax regimes.[1] It viewed tax havens (comprising for the most part sovereign countries or fiscally sovereign territories) as possessing four key identifying features: (1) no or only nominal income taxes, (2) lack of effective exchange of information (EOI), (3) lack of transparency (relating to the legislative, legal, or administrative provisions of a jurisdiction), and (4) investment with no substantial activities.[2] The OECD established the Global Forum on Transparency and Exchange of Information for Tax Purposes (Global Forum) in 2000, which developed the *Agreement on Exchange of Information on Tax Matters*, or model tax

[1] For an in-depth examination of the OECD's war against tax evasion, see Chapter 3.
[2] See Chapter 3, Section 3.

D.S. Kerzner, D.W. Chodikoff, *International Tax Evasion in the Global Information Age*, DOI 10.1007/978-3-319-40421-9_11

information exchange agreement (TIEA), in 2002.[3] The *Model TIEA* was developed to address the issues arising from the harmful tax practices project, and in 2005 the Global Forum adopted standards on transparency relating to the availability and reliability of information. A primary objective of the *Model TIEA* was to compel tax haven jurisdictions to enact laws to override their bank secrecy laws.[4] The OECD further noted that the lack of effective EOI by tax havens denied fiscal authorities access to bank information that was critical to raising revenue and preventing tax avoidance and base erosion.

Both Canada and the United States tax their residents (and in the case of the United States, citizens) on a worldwide basis.[5] TIEAs can assist fiscal authorities to obtain foreign taxpayer information that can be used to support the administration and enforcement of their country's tax laws. In this way, it can broadly be said that TIEAs support the goals of both horizontal and vertical equity in international tax law policy.[6] To the extent that TIEAs can be a deterrent and reduce the tax motivation for taxpayers to move income-producing assets to tax havens, it can be argued that TIEAs also help advance the goal of capital export neutrality.[7] TIEAs also support the goals behind EOI that aim to facilitate the administration of tax laws of a contracting party. Although TIEAs only enable fiscal authorities to react to known or suspected cases of tax evasion, on the whole TIEAs support the general policy objectives of international taxation relating to equity and EOI.

It has been more than seventeen years since the OECD published its *Harmful Tax Competition* report as the framework for eliminating harmful tax practices. Since the OECD began its initiative against tax havens in 1998, a number of significant economic, political, and legal developments have taken place around TIEAs. At the outset of its initiative, there was ambivalence regarding tax havens in the OECD community and political controversy about the right of sovereigns to set their own

[3] See Chapter 3, Section 5; OECD, *Agreement on Exchange of Information on Tax Matters* (Paris: OECD, 2002) [*Model TIEA*].

[4] See Chapter 3, Section 4.

[5] See Chapter 2.

[6] For a discussion of the goals behind international tax policy, see Chapter 2, Section 5.

[7] See *ibid.*

tax rates. From an economic perspective, it was estimated that as of 2010 the money in offshore tax haven accounts was more than $21 trillion, and the OECD, G20, and G8 were unified in their goal to improve EOI to stop tax evasion.[8] The Global Forum membership now includes 133 jurisdictions, and never before has there been this level of international cooperation around supporting the OECD standards and combatting tax evasion. From a legal perspective, since 2005 the Global Forum has established over 1,500 EOI relationships that allow for EOI in accordance with the OECD standards.[9] Additionally, over 100 jurisdictions are participating in the Global Forum's peer review process to implement the OECD standards.[10] In light of both the dangers and the complexities posed by economic globalization, the international cooperation that has taken place around TIEAs as a result of the work of the Global Forum merits its own recognition as an important achievement in making progress to defeat tax evasion. The international cooperation and implementation of rules around EOI and transparency has also created new international norms in this field. In retrospect, the OECD, primarily through the work of the Global Forum, has made real and substantial strides in developing international consensus and cooperation on the use of TIEAs specifically and in the field of EOI to combat tax evasion more generally.

The TIEA story is a bittersweet story of success and failure. The successes in the Global Forum's work on TIEAs can be found in the strides that TIEAs have allowed the Global Forum to take toward establishing international norms on EOI and transparency (however imperfect, as noted by the 2013 and 2014 peer review ratings) and toward reaching unprecedented levels of international cooperation.[11] Both of these successes have helped to position the Global Forum to more readily take the next big leap to automatic exchange of information (Automatic Exchange). Under TIEAs, tax havens have committed to overruling domestic bank secrecy legislation to support information requests from

[8] For an overview of the problem of international tax evasion, see Chapter 1, Section 1.1.

[9] See Chapter 3, Section 7.

[10] See Chapter 3, Section 5.

[11] See Chapter 3, Section 6.

tax flight jurisdictions. However, due to a major design flaw in TIEAs known as "information upon request," the practical result has been that offshore bank accounts in tax havens with TIEAs have remained secret in the absence of an account holder's being audited by CRA or the IRS. The information upon request standard contained in the *Model TIEA* requires tax authorities to already possess much of the information that they are seeking from a tax haven jurisdiction to be able to obtain specific bank account data to audit a taxpayer. For these reasons, it can be argued that TIEAs may have supported international tax evasion by allowing undeclared bank accounts in tax havens to remain, in the absence of an audit, secret. In realizing the danger posed by continued reliance on the OECD standards contained in the *Model TIEA*, the G20 in 2013 announced its commitment to seeing that EOI take place automatically.

An important part of the evaluation of TIEAs as an effective tool for fiscal authorities to combat tax evasion with is the question, do TIEAs work better or worse than alternative tools for obtaining foreign-based taxpayer financial information? The John Doe summons and the threat of criminal prosecution have marked advantages over TIEAs because they permit the IRS to go after groups of taxpayers whose identities are not known, and unlike TIEAs, they carry teeth in the form of civil and criminal sanctions. The United States is now in effect integrating a deferred prosecution program into its EOI mechanism with Switzerland.[12] Though the final data on this new approach is still unknown, more than 100 Swiss banks are working with the US Department of Justice, and some of them are paying US attorney fees to encourage undeclared account holders to participate in the IRS voluntary disclosure program. Moreover, Swiss banks are threatening undeclared US account holders with lawsuits to recover penalties that the banks owe to the US government. Will the United States leverage EOI articles in other tax treaties with actions similar to those taken against the Swiss banks? Could or would the United States ever use criminal prosecution or a deferred prosecution program against Canada or Canadian financial institutions? There is no question that the answer to both of these questions is yes. In the global context, it is the banking and financial indus-

[12] For a discussion of the use of criminal prosecution by the United States, including the Swiss Bank Program, see Chapter 5, Section 4.

try in Canada, the European Union, and elsewhere that stands to lose the most by being re-active toward this new US assertion of its tax, reporting, and sanctions rules. Banks and financial service providers the world over will need leadership at the highest levels to adopt new strategies and policies to pro-actively manage the risks created by this new era of information exchange and extraterritorial enforcement by the United States.

A major new alternative for obtaining foreign taxpayer information is the US *Foreign Account Tax Compliance Act.*[13] *FATCA* provides the United States with three significant advantages over TIEAs: (1) detailed account information, (2) annual Automatic Exchange, and (3) teeth in the form of the *FATCA* withholding penalty on non-compliant foreign financial institutions. *FATCA* also has a number of distinct disadvantages, notably the enormous cost of its implementation and monitoring, and it raises any number of political, legal, social, and moral issues, which is certainly the case with the intergovernmental agreement between Canada and the United States, which was signed and became effective in 2014.[14] *FATCA* can be easily circumvented as it relies in good measure upon honesty in self-certification. The twin goals of (1) administering the 7,000 pages of IRS rules against millions of Americans who honestly report and pay taxes in Canada and the European Union and owe virtually no US taxes and (2) fighting the financial lifelines that fuel international terrorism and international crime are no longer compatible. New American leadership at the departments of state, justice, and the treasury and in Congress is needed to stop the madness of taxation based on citizenship.[15]

When Canada unveiled its plans for TIEAs in 2007, there were several competing policy objectives — the deductibility of interest related to foreign affiliates, the promotion of international business expansion for Canadian companies, and also the issue of non-compliant individual taxpayers

[13] Subtitle A of Title V of the *Hiring Incentives to Restore Employment Act of 2010*, Pub L No 111–147 enacted on 18 March 2010 [*FATCA*]. For an overview of *FATCA*, see Chapter 9.

[14] *Agreement between the Government of Canada and the Government of the United States of America to Improve International Tax Compliance through Enhanced Exchange of Information under the Convention between Canada and the United States of America with respect to Taxes on Income and on Capital* (5 February 2014), online: www.fin.gc.ca/treaties-conventions/pdf/FATCA-eng.pdf.

[15] For a discussion of US foreign bank account reporting for US nationals living outside the United States, see Chapter 10, Section 3.

resident in Canada.[16] Canada's growing TIEA network is an important accomplishment, but it is not up to the task of meeting Ottawa's current policy objective, which is to use TIEAs as a tool to fight tax evasion. TIEAs can assist CRA in the case of audits to administer Canada's tax laws while Canada and other countries await the implementation of the new Automatic Exchange standard. But Canada, unlike the United States and other countries, has not confronted the reality that TIEAs do not provide an effective means to combat international tax evasion. Canada has failed to adapt its policy and programs and to design and implement new strategies to increase cash hauls from tax cheats and enhance deterrence. As noted below, there are a number of pathways that Canada can explore to develop a more robust stance against tax evasion, including enhancing its TIEA network.

EOI is a highly complex subject that can best be understood by taking a multidisciplinary approach encompassing legal, economic, political, historical, and social concepts. Since 1998, the OECD and later the G8 and G20 have striven to combat tax evasion principally with a legal solution, the OECD standards as embodied in TIEAs. Although the Global Forum now includes tax haven jurisdictions, the political and economic systems and histories of these jurisdictions are very different from those of the tax flight countries. These differences have become evident in the difficulties that many of the tax haven jurisdictions are having in implementing the OECD standards, and for that matter are likely to have in implementing Automatic Exchange or *FATCA*. The trillions of dollars still held in offshore tax haven accounts serve as a sober reminder that tax evasion works and is alive and well.

The belief by the OECD, the Global Forum, and others that international tax evasion persists largely because the wrong standard (information upon request) has been used and can be defeated merely by switching to the Automatic Exchange standard is flawed. The error in this logic can be traced to the myth that our collective economies and tax systems, histories, political struggles, cultures, and priorities as peoples and as nations are one and the same, and they are not. A true partnership with tax havens, manifesting economic cooperation through tax harmonization (whether embodied in TIEAs or Automatic Exchange), will require

[16] For a discussion of Canada's tax policy and TIEAs, see Chapter 6, Section 2.2.

tax flight jurisdictions to take note of the differences and needs of the peoples and governments in tax haven jurisdictions and work together with them to design new strategies to combat international tax evasion. While progress continues in the field of EOI, that progress is likely to be slow, and its outcome is uncertain. Hence, it will be up to individual countries like Canada to seize the initiative necessary to create a new agenda, which, drawing on the successes of other countries in this field, will allow for the modification of TIEAs and the building of new tools to defeat international tax evasion. While these efforts will require Canada and other countries to allocate new resources to the recommendations proposed below, it is likely that the combined results of these efforts will generate revenues exceeding their investments.

In furtherance of the research in this book, it is desirable to consider the development of new data to increase our understanding of the complexities surrounding the use of EOI and TIEAs to combat international tax evasion. The following are proposed areas of research that if undertaken can enhance our knowledge and understanding of this field and broaden our options in addressing the problem of international tax evasion:

- research into increasing our understanding of the amounts of deposits held in tax haven jurisdictions
- research into increasing Canada's understanding of its offshore tax evasion problem by using data from its foreign-reporting forms and tax returns to build a more detailed picture of those jurisdictions where offshore deposits are more prevalent — this research can also include understanding how Canada and the United States share information relating to interest income and other portfolio investment income
- research into different approaches to sharing the costs of requests for information, including best practices approaches used by existing countries and organizations like the European Union to create greater incentives for and participation by tax havens and requested countries to bolster EOI
- research into building a group-request solution into TIEAs or the EOI mechanism in the OECD *Model Tax Convention on Income and on Capital*, to offer a benefit available with the John Doe summons[17] — what

[17] OECD, Committee on Fiscal Affairs, *Model Tax Convention on Income and on Capital* (Paris: OECD, 1992) (loose-leaf) at Art 26 [*Model Tax Treaty*].

would such a clause look like, what would the benefits be, and what would the challenges be (e.g., avoiding fishing expeditions)?
- research by Canada into the feasibility and design of tax flight treaties with tax havens (using existing TIEAs) that incorporate economic cooperation through tax deharmonization and other incentives
- research by Canada into the greater use of criminal prosecution and John Doe summonses to support EOI requests, whether under TIEAs or other treaties — what has been the outcome historically of the use of such tools, what are the challenges and likely rewards of these tools, and what might the model or prototype law or tool look like from a legal standpoint?
- research by Canadian, US, and EU tax scholars into a global solution for the approximately one million Americans living in Canada and the many millions of other Americans living outside the United States whose situation after the implementation of *FATCA* requires interim and long-term policy direction to mitigate the problems caused by historical compliance delinquencies and asymmetries between the tax systems of the United States and their home jurisdiction, and ultimately a low cost and easy expatriation
- research into the link between tax evasion and the global fine arts industry, including the estimated value of the artworks potentially involved, the role that free-ports and other tax havens play, and the registration of artworks' beneficial owners and related laws in OECD countries.

2 Recommendations

Legal scholars often prescribe new policy solutions that arise from their research, but in terms of implementation they are confronted with the challenge of governments managing an overcrowded political agenda with limited resources. The recommendations that follow are unlike other government policy ideas in that they relate directly to a country's ability to increase its revenues, and their combined impact will likely generate a return for governments like Canada's fighting international tax evasion that exceeds the investment.

2.1 Sovereignty and the Jurisdiction to Tax

Recommendation 1.1

Modernize US international tax policy by formulating a policy to transition the United States from being a jurisdiction that imposes income tax on a worldwide basis on grounds of citizenship to being a jurisdiction that imposes income tax on a worldwide basis on residence, like Canada, the United Kingdom, France, Germany, and New Zealand. This modernization should include replacing the tax rules on expatriation with rules that impose a departure tax on all individuals who sever tax residence with the United States (similar to the departure tax rules used by Canada).

Recommendation 1.2

Whether concurrently with or independently of Recommendation 1.1, above, the United States should immediately develop an international tax policy that recognizes the unique historical, political, cultural, social, and economic characteristics of US citizens who have lived in Canada for many years with the aim of creating a "cheap and cheerful" exit strategy for dual citizens and permanent residents who wish to expatriate (or abandon their "green cards") with a minimum of cost in terms of fees, time, and taxation.

2.2 Foreign Reporting

Recommendation 2.1

Canada must streamline its reporting requirements, for example, the horrifying non-resident trust rules. While the government has made great strides in improving the methods for reporting income, more work needs to be done to simplify the processes. A parliamentary committee should be established to deal specifically with foreign-reporting requirements and their simplification. Once streamlined procedures have been identified, the government should use its mandate to codify the necessary procedures and documents.

Recommendation 2.2

Canada should continue to improve Form T1135 (Foreign Income Verification Statement), to increase compliance and deterrence, by including educational information on all applicable civil and criminal penalties and a requirement to provide specific bank account information to improve voluntary taxpayer compliance and facilitate EOI requests, and by upping the rather low $2,500 penalty.

Recommendation 2.3

Evaluate the effectiveness of Canada's Voluntary Disclosures Program in attracting taxpayers with undeclared foreign assets and income compared with those of other countries (e.g., Australia, Germany, New Zealand, the United Kingdom, and the United States) to better align rules and procedures with policy goals, including around elements such as the provision of greater certainty of results by limiting the scope of years, and including the application of penalties, interest, and taxes; use of criminal prosecution; and consideration of a reasonable cause doctrine for relieving or mitigating penalties.

Recommendation 2.4

The United States should re-evaluate the US international foreign-reporting rules applicable to US citizens who have been long-term tax residents in some countries, like Canada, with the following goals in mind: first, reduce the time and cost of such reporting for taxpayers who are already burdened with their residence country's reporting; second, alleviate some of the more extreme hardships resulting from the disparities between the *Internal Revenue Code* and their residence country's tax laws (e.g., the *Income Tax Act* in Canada), particularly around retirement and education planning, home ownership, and the passive foreign investment rules; and third, incorporate a cost-benefit analysis of US international tax policy drivers taking into account the cost to administer and enforce the world's most complex tax system against taxpayers who — owing to the exemptions, deductions, and credits in the *Code* — owe little to no US taxes. Consideration should be given to using protocols to amend the *Convention between Canada and the United States of America with respect to Taxes on Income and on Capital* to accomplish some or all of these goals.[18] This recommendation should be considered either concurrently with or independently of Recommendation 1.1, above.

Recommendation 2.5

Revise the penalty provisions in the US *Bank Secrecy Act*[19] applicable to offshore undeclared accounts to (1) curb gross abuses by the IRS regarding the willfulness penalty in administering the offshore voluntary disclosure programs, (2) provide statutory guidance on what constitutes willfulness for both the IRS and the courts, and (3) create rules that clarify how the $10,000-per-violation non-willfulness penalty is to apply and create objective mitigation standards surrounding this penalty.

Recommendation 2.6

The US Department of the Treasury should establish an independent commission to provide restitution to US taxpayers (in Canada and elsewhere) who have been harmed by the inequitable terms of the 2009, 2011, and 2012 voluntary disclosure programs. The commission should determine the classes of individuals who are eligible to seek relief. These classes may realistically comprise, for example, individuals who paid an FBAR penalty (also known as the OVDI or OVDP penalty) but who can demonstrate reasonable cause, individuals who paid an FBAR penalty but who had been non-willful and had mitigating circumstances, and other appropriate groups of individuals. The commission should consider as much as possible objective standards, guidelines, and procedures to assist wronged taxpayers in seeking reimbursements of penalties and

---

[18] 26 September 1980 (as amended to the protocols signed on 14 June 1983, 23 March 1984, 17 March 1997, 29 July 1997, and 21 September 2007) [*Canada–US Tax Treaty*].

[19] Pub L 91-508, Tit II, 84 Stat 1118, 10/26/1970, codified as amended at 12 USC 1829b, 12 USC 1951–1959, and 31 USC 5311–5314; 5316–5332.

professional fees from the US government, together with interest on any awards. Imposing any willfulness FBAR penalty on Canadians who participated in the early years of the offshore voluntary disclosure programs, particularly in 2009, and 2010, when only a handful of international tax advisors globally really had ever heard of the FBAR, is a travesty of justice.

2.3 Canada's TIEAs

Recommendation 3.1

Regarding Article 1, dealing with the scope of EOI, Canada's TIEAs should refrain from using a narrower standard (e.g., "information that is relevant" in the TIEA with Bermuda) and strive to use the broadest standard possible (e.g., "foreseeably relevant") to provide the widest bridge possible for information exchange without allowing for fishing expeditions.

Recommendation 3.2

Regarding Article 7, dealing with declining a request, some of Canada's TIEAs (e.g., with Guernsey, the Isle of Man, Jersey, and Liechtenstein) provide additional grounds on which the requested party can decline a request for assistance from the requesting party that are not in the *Model TIEA*. Canada should strive to refrain from providing TIEA partners with additional grounds to hinder the EOI process.

Recommendation 3.3

Regarding Article 5, dealing with EOI upon request, some of Canada's TIEAs (e.g., with the Bahamas, Costa Rica, Guernsey, the Isle of Man, Jersey, and Liechtenstein) provide no time limits or elusive time standards instead of the recommended time standards in the *Model TIEA*, which could hinder the effectiveness of a request for information by Canada. Canada should strive to keep to the recommended time standards in the *Model TIEA*, or to those that may be superior.

Recommendation 3.4

Regarding TIEA provisions dealing with costs, most of Canada's TIEAs provide that Canada and the other party agree to sort out the costs incurred in providing assistance while in a few of the agreements there is the potential for dividing the costs borne by the requested party. Canada should develop a more favourable policy regarding the reimbursement of the requested party's costs as a minimum incentive to do the work necessary to obtain the information.

Recommendation 3.5

As part of revamping its TIEA network, Canada should draft a new template provision that will, under certain evidentiary and other circumstances (agreed to by Canada and the partner jurisdiction), permit Canada to have the partner jurisdiction perform a search for Canadian undeclared accounts at one or more particular financial institutions in the partner jurisdiction, similar in function to the US John Doe summons, described in Chapter 5.

Recommendation 3.6

Canada should delink the right to exempt surplus treatment on the repatriation of foreign earnings from the requirement that the source country enter into a double tax convention or TIEA with Canada to reduce the unnecessary proliferation of double tax conventions and TIEAs.

Recommendation 3.7

Canada should strongly consider the pursuit of an independent pathway to TIEA reform that incorporates the principles of cooperation through tax deharmonization, notwithstanding any undertakings with the OECD and Global Forum surrounding Automatic Exchange, so that Canada will not be dependent solely on the fortunes of that new standard — as it was and is on the old OECD standard — while its allies are pursuing their own innovative EOI strategies. Research for this new initiative should consider the best ways to provide economic incentives for local assistance with the historical, current, and future undeclared earnings of tax cheats. TIEA optimization should ideally include feasibility discussions with fiscal authorities from select tax haven jurisdictions, including, importantly, a cost-benefit analysis. Discussions should also include possible additional incentives that may be of particular interest to the peoples and organizations in these jurisdictions. Exploring the use of incentive rewards in return for local cooperation is an important step toward establishing a more invigorated TIEA program to combat tax evasion.

2.4 Administrative Measures and Tax Treaties

Recommendation 4.1

Members of Parliament must step to the front of the line to champion a new direction for Canada to take in the fight against international tax evasion. Very little will change unless there is the political will to implement changes and then ensure the administration of those changes. The only way that these changes will occur and become a working everyday reality is if there are parliamentary champions to encourage the implementation of these reforms. Yet, one or two parliamentary champions will likely be insufficient. What is really required is political will and consensus among many. This will require leaders but also widespread political support to make the legislative and financial commitments necessary to alter the existing legislative and fiscal landscape. As noted above, willpower and determination are the keys to winning the war against offshore tax evasion.

Recommendation 4.2

The Canadian government must increase CRA's financial resources. Over the past few years, the government has indicated in its budget measures that it will increase funding for efforts to clamp down on tax evasion, specifically that it will dedicate more resources to CRA — primarily more auditors working on audits with an international component as a way to scrutinize and ensure tax compliance. While this commitment may be genuine, at least in some form, the fact remains that CRA is woefully underfunded and, in actuality, has seen a serious reduction in the number of its employees over the past few years. Moreover, the general morale at the agency is pitiful, and employees can hardly be blamed for this state of affairs. One immediate step toward improving the performance of employees would be to establish a parliamentary committee to hold hearings for the purpose of learning from front line employees how to improve efficiencies, performance, morale, and service. In connection with this effort, there should be an immediate increase in funding and the hiring of auditors for all areas. The simple fact is that audit work is labour intensive, and there are no shortcuts for this type of work. More people are needed to effectively manage the workflow. Presently, the need for speed in reviewing a file so that one can essentially move to the next file is too great. As a result, some files are poorly reviewed, and others are settled quickly because of the pressures to move the work along. This situation results in unfairness to CRA employees and robs the Canadian public of its right to equitable administration and enforcement of the *Income Tax Act*. In addition to more money for hiring more audit personnel, CRA requires more money for technology. Better systems are needed to help review corporate and individual tax returns. And technological resources for the general monitoring and exchange of tax information can also be improved.

Recommendation 4.3

Canada should formulate a new robust policy to enforce its criminal and tax laws against appropriate foreign financial institutions to combat international tax evasion by Canadian residents. In researching the use of criminal prosecution to bolster EOI, Canada should draw upon the success of the US deferred prosecution program used against Swiss banks to bolster its EOI channels. Canada should also use all channels available through The Egmont Group of Financial Intelligence Units and under the *Canada–US Tax Treaty* to develop prosecutorial leads from information obtained by the United States.

Recommendation 4.4

Canada must increase funding for the Public Prosecution Service of Canada. Canada has failed miserably to prosecute individuals for international tax evasion, and one of the key reasons for this failure is a lack of resources. Tax prosecutions are labour intensive and costly and take a long time to bring to court, and once in the courtroom, these proceedings can take a long time to complete. It is not a quality issue. The federal prosecutors are highly intelligent and motivated. What is lacking are enough prosecutors to handle the workload. The government must hire more lawyers for the specific task of conducting tax prosecutions.

Recommendation 4.5

Canada must improve the laws dealing with tax evasion. It is time to review the existing provisions in the *Income Tax Act* and related provisions in the *Criminal Code* to determine whether amendments would be useful or needed to better serve the public's interest in securing convictions. For example, the *Act* could be amended to include specific types of tax evasion crimes. Similarly, it may serve the public's interest to incorporate specific international tax evasion crimes and penalties into the *Criminal Code*. This type of review will out of necessity involve multiple government departments and agencies such as the Department of Finance Canada, the Public Prosecution Service of Canada, and CRA.

Recommendation 4.6

Canada should attempt to fashion and use a homegrown John Doe–style summons, which, unlike a TIEA, will carry civil and criminal sanctions for refusal to comply, to fill the gap where the government has evidence of undeclared accounts at a foreign financial institution but lacks specifics regarding the account holders and account data and where under the existing EOI article the government would be unable to request help from its treaty partner.

Recommendation 4.7

Canada has too many tax treaties in force, and they have become unmanageable. Canada should as soon as possible update the EOI articles in its double tax conventions to conform to OECD standards, as the EOI articles in most of these conventions are currently non-conforming.

Recommendation 4.8

By implementing *FATCA* in 2014, Canada, in effect, expanded the information-gathering powers of the United States under Article XXVII of the *Canada–US Tax Treaty*. In so doing, Canada helped turn the IRS enforcement machinery against approximately one million Canadian residents of American heritage in a manner that is not only contrary to the purpose of the treaty (as the vast majority of these individuals are not tax evaders) but that is also inconsistent with the general principles of equity in international tax policy. Canada and other governments, like that of the United Kingdom, that have implemented *FATCA* should undertake at once to negotiate with the United States a global solution to this historical and social problem to curb any future injustices resulting from this clash of sovereigns that has been evolving for decades and that cries out for a political solution.

Recommendation 4.9

The OECD and the Global Forum should create a template to be used by tax havens to approximately quantify the deposits in their financial institutions, as held by individuals, trusts, nominee corporations, and other similar entities, and to estimate the amount of financial assets held by offshore persons. This information can be compiled annually, shared with members, and possibly be used as one indicator in the assessment of the Global Forum's work on combatting tax evasion.

Recommendation 4.10

The OECD and the Global Forum should consider undertaking research into a mechanism that could be incorporated into Automatic Exchange and would allow jurisdictions to cooperate economically by sharing income earned by account holders as an incentive for tax havens and other countries to participate in the new program. Such a mechanism could potentially have different levels of invasiveness, addressing historical tax evasion and current and future income of account holders.

Recommendation 4.11

The OECD and the Global Forum should consider amending Article 26 of the *Model Tax Treaty* to incorporate a mechanism that mimics the John Doe summons, but for double tax conventions and TIEAs. This would expedite information exchange in agreed-upon circumstances while hopefully reducing the political turbulence and unilateral stigma that may be associated with the use of the John Doe summons.

Recommendation 4.12

The OECD and the Global Forum should incorporate the broadest permissible taxpayer bill of rights into the Automatic Exchange standard.

2.5 Banking and Financial Services Industries

Recommendation 5.1

Banks and financial services firms and their professional advisers are being confronted with a tsunami of highly complex legal regimes targeting international tax evasion, crime, and terrorism. These rules are also being enforced with unprecedented vigour, determination, and coordination by the United States and international police and fiscal enforcement agencies. The scandals described in Chapter 1 evidence a grand failure of leadership on the part of the executives of banks and financial services firms. Moreover, the scandals must also be taken as evidence of the failure of the related internal departments of general counsel, risk management and anti–money laundering, taxation and compliance, and private wealth management, and the governing board of directors (as the case may be) to work together and formulate new strategies. The old ways will not suffice to prepare banks, trust companies, life insurance companies, investment advisers, funds, and others to understand how these new laws and legal regimes impact their organizations (and their products, systems, and services). Banks and financial groups with international operations must recognize that the challenges they face in the new global information age are both multijurisdictional and multidisciplinary in nature. Accordingly, it is only with a new leadership approach that seeks to open a dialogue within and among the internal organization departments named above (the key stakeholders) that a mission statement, including goals and strategies, can be arrived at. The idea that software and technology alone can hope to forestall the legal failures that will almost assuredly bring about an enforcement response costing an organization millions or billions of dollars is unrealistic. International tax and legal planning is a process. It is time for the chairs of the boards of directors of banks and financial services firms the world over to call for action to rethink and remake new approaches to ensuring successful global compliance in the new information age.

Index

Note: Page numbers with 'n' denote Footnotes.

D.S. Kerzner, D.W. Chodikoff, *International Tax Evasion in the Global Information Age*, DOI 10.1007/978-3-319-40421-9

F

G

Kolibri 360 GmbH
Ferdinand-Jühlke-Straße 7
99095 Erfurt, Deutschland
produktsicherheit@kolibri360.de